Van Alstyne's

NOTARY PUBLIC ENCYCLOPEDIA

Peter J Van Alstyne

NOTARY
LAW
INSTITUTE

Notary Law Institute
Orem, Utah

Quick Links to Alphabetical Locations:

Click on the desired letter...

Note: You may also use the "Find" menu option in Acrobat Reader to search for specific terms (Edit Menu; Find) (Windows: Ctrl + F; Mac: Cmd + F)

A

Fundamental honesty is the baseline and mandatory requirement to serve as a notary. The whole structure of 2ethical standards is derived from the paramount need for notaries to be trustworthy. The court system and the public are damaged when notaries play fast and loose with the truth.
- Committee on Professional Standards and Conduct v. Bauerle 460 N.W. 2d 452 (Iowa 1990)

Abuse of Notarial Authority
See Liability; Official Misconduct

The notary law generally characterizes the wrongful performance of the notary's official duties as "official misconduct." This is especially seen where the notary fails to comply with the notary law, fails to take reasonable care while notarizing, and fails to notarize truthfully.

There are certain aspects of the notary's performance that are improper but fail to rise up to the level of official misconduct. The courts occasionally refer to these instances as an "abuse of notarial authority." This is most notable where the notary affixes a notary seal and her signature to a document but fails to provide the necessary notarial working of the certificate. As a result, the signer believes the document has been properly notarized when it has not. If this misunderstanding results in some manner of harm or damages, the notary can be liable. Another frequent application of the term, abuse of notarial authority, appears where a notary uses their notarial commission to endorse products, services or contests.

Acknowledge

For notarial purposes, the word "acknowledge" means that the maker of a signature admits to making, and takes ownership of his signature to a document. This is done in the presence of a notary.

Acknowledged Before Me

See Acknowledgment Notarization

Acknowledgment by Attorney-in-Fact

See Acknowledgment Notarization; Authority of the Document Signer; Power of Attorney

An attorney-in-fact is a person who has been granted the power of attorney to act and sign for, and in behalf of the grantor. The power of attorney is a tricky thing, and for the notary a hazard. In a sense, the signature of the individual, made under a power of attorney can be an anathema to the notarization. The notary's core purpose is to assure the signature being notarized is genuinely that of its maker. For example, an attorney-in-fact, John Doe, would generally be authorized to sign for the principal, Ronald Reagan, in a variety of ways:

1. John Doe for Ronald Reagan;
2. Ronald Reagan by John Doe, attorney-in-fact;
3. Ronald Reagan/John Doe (by POA);
4. Ronald Reagan.

It is legally impossible, as a matter of definition, for a notary to notarize a signature purporting to belong to one person although another makes it. In some circumstances, an acknowledgment by attorney-in-fact appears as a type of disclosure statement:

Acknowledged before me this_____ day of_____by John Doe acting under power of attorney for Ronald Reagan as attorney-in-fact.

The acknowledgment by an attorney-in-fact is nothing more than a simple acknowledgment with full written disclosure concerning the authority of the signature maker to sign another person's name. The notarization for an attorney-in-fact can put a notary in a precarious position. A notary is neither required nor authorized to make a dispositive determination concerning the authority of the attorney-in-fact. The written power of attorney is not proof in and of itself. It merely represents in written form one person's intent to grant particular authority to another. The scope of this authority can be very narrow and limited in time, or it can be broad and indefinite in terms of validity. The written power of attorney can be easily abused, and easily counterfeited. An attorney-in-fact's authority can be revoked or curtailed, but the void document granting power of attorney could remain in continued unauthorized use by unscrupulous persons.

If asked to notarize for a person who is acting under a power of attorney, invoke considerable caution. If the transaction has its origins within the notary's workplace and she is personally acquainted with the persons involved, her risk of being drawn into a fraudulent ploy is substantially less than if the document signer is a complete stranger and the transaction is out of context with the nature of the notary's employment or business purposes.

It is often assumed that the notary, when accepting an attorney-in-fact's proof of authority to sign under power of attorney, is certifying the power of attorney is indeed valid and in full force and in effect; that is completely wrong. The notary is the guarantor of the probative value of the notarial certificate. Every word of the certificate must be true. A safety measure in this type of transaction may be to fully and accurately disclose within the acknowledgment certificate that John Doe acknowledged his own signature and that he was *"acting under the authority of power of attorney for and in behalf of Ronald Regan, an original notarized copy of which was presented to me by John Doe."*

Acknowledgment in an Individual Capacity

Acknowledgment notarizations have historically taken on a variety of customized characteristics. In the earliest versions of historical acknowledgments laws, acknowledgment notarizations were compartmentalized according to the nature of their use. If an individual were to have his signature notarized to his transaction, he would be said to be "acting in an individual capacity." In other words, he is acting on his own behalf and for no one else. Hence, the acknowledgment certificate would be written to reflect that fact. Often the certificate would include the clarifying wording that his signature "was made by his own free act and deed."

Acknowledgment in a Representative Capacity
See Authority of the Document Signer

A common form of acknowledgment compartmentalization is called an *acknowledgment in a representative capacity*. Here, the certificate of acknowledgment will contain clarifying wording, similar to that seen in the acknowledgment by attorney-in-fact, which discloses the signer's authority to sign a transaction on behalf of another person, business or corporation. This disclosure within the certificate of acknowledgment typically includes wording such as, *"Acknowledged before me by John Doe, Vice President of Ajax Corporation, acting in his capacity as Vice President of said corporation."*

Acknowledgments in a representative capacity often incorrectly lead notaries to assume a responsibility for verifying the signer's authority to sign the transaction, but notaries are under no legal duty to do so. Moreover, it would be profoundly unreasonable to impose on notaries such a duty. From the historical beginnings of the notarial act, the notary has been responsible for verifying the signer's identity to ensure he is not an imposter.

Although the notary is the guarantor of the truthfulness of the notarial certificate, a signer's legal authority to act on behalf of others is, as a matter of law, easily asserted but extremely difficult to prove, and authority to sign is not related to the legal issue of the signer's identity. When a person acts on behalf of another person or a company as its official, that person is acting as an agent for that person or company.

A person can be granted the authority to sign for another in writing or orally. Likewise, such authority can be revoked in writing or orally. Conceivably, a person's written or oral authority to sign for another could be revoked, but that fact could easily be withheld from the notary.

If a notary were responsible for these matters, it is likely that very few people would be willing to assume such overwhelming responsibility and risk.

It is not inappropriate, and in some instances it is encouraged, for the notary to make a reasonable effort to confirm the signer's claimed title or authority. Confirmation is a lesser burden of proof than verification. The corporate president's name may appear on the document letterhead or on a business card. Unless there is a reasonable basis to doubt the authenticity of the letterhead or business card, it may be confirmation enough.

Acknowledgment Notarization

See Certificate of Notarization; Notarial Certificate

The word "acknowledgment" has multiple uses and meanings. For the notary, this word is the name given for a type of notarization. An acknowledgment will usually be identified by the key phrase, *acknowledged before me.* When used in a notarization, this phrase declares that a document signer personally appeared before the notary, and orally took ownership or responsibility for his signature on the document.

> *"We hold that . . . when a signatory (1) appears personally before a notary for the purpose of having the notary witness and attest to his signature, (2) the signatory appears to be alert and is under no apparent duress or undue emotional influence, (3) it is clear from the overall circumstances that the signatory understands the nature of the instrument he or she is about to sign, and (4) he or she signs the instrument in the presence of the notary with the apparent intent of making the instrument effective, the signatory is effectively acknowledging to the notary that the instrument is being signed voluntarily and for the purpose contained therein."*
> *- Poole v. Hyatt, 689 A.2d 82 (Md. 1997).*

A typical acknowledgment notarization will have this appearance:

State of _____

County of _____

Acknowledged before me this _____ *day of* _____ *by*
signer is signing by authority of his employment position, such as corporate vice president, a notary cannot, as a matter of law, be responsible for certifying the signer is corporate vice president. If the

This declarative wording of the certificate asserts four material facts for which the notary is personally responsible:

1. The maker of the signature personally appeared before the notary;
2. The notary took every reasonable step to verify the signer's true identity;
3. The signer acknowledged he made the signature on the document as a willful and intentional act; and
4. The signature being acknowledged belongs to its claimed maker.

The unique quality of an acknowledgment notarization is that the signature being notarized is not being witnessed by the notary. To witness a signature, one must see the signature being made. With an acknowledgment notarization, the signature can be made on the document before it is presented to the notary for notarization. The acknowledgment certificate in no way requires the signer to sign the document in the notary's presence. That signature can be made any time before the signer appears before the notary. How long ago that signature was made is irrelevant to the acknowledgment notarization.

It is the document signer who acknowledges their signature to the notary. It is a common malapropism (error of speech) for notaries to say they "acknowledged the customer's signature."

"Acknowledgments are used where the person to whom the paper is to be presented may not otherwise know the genuineness of the signature attached or affixed thereto… an "acknowledgment" is an authentication or verification of the signature to a particular instrument and establishes merely that the instrument was duly signed and proves the identity of the person whose name appears thereon and that such person signed it.

An acknowledgment consists of two distinct parts: the oral acknowledgment by the person making it to the officer before whom

it is made that he executed the instrument; and the written certificate by the officer."
    - Independence Leasing Corp. v. Aquino 506 N.Y.S. 2d 1003 (1986).

The primary purpose for an acknowledgment notarization is to attain a reasonable level of assurance that the signature to the document is genuine; that it belongs to its alleged maker and that it was done willfully and freely. The notary is under a duty of law to ensure every word of the acknowledgment certificate is true.

"The officer who takes an acknowledgment acts in a judicial character in determining whether the person representing himself to be, or represented by someone else to be, the grantor named in the conveyance, actually is the grantor. He determines further whether the person thus adjudicated to be the grantor does actually and truly acknowledge before him that he executed the instrument."
    - Wasson v. Connor, 54 Miss. 351

This can be done easily with dispositive effect if the notary causes the document signer to sign her notary journal before she performs the notarization. The spontaneous making of a signature in the journal will prove and document four vitally important facts:

1. The signer, for whom the notary notarizes personally, appeared before her;
2. The signature in the journal will reasonably match the one on the document to be notarized;
3. The signature in the journal will ratify the notary's judgment that the signer is acting willfully and freely; and
4. The signature in the journal will effectively ratify the notary's judgment as to the signer's identity, especially if she had to ask the signer for valid ID containing his signature.

As most notarizations tend to be pre-printed, and they are most often acknowledgments, it is easy for a notary to become lost with the wording. The pre-printed certificate is very often written in legalese with twisted sentence structure and an abundance of blank spaces to be filled in by the notary. The wording is verbose and misleading. We can be sure that if we are asked to notarize with the acknowledgment, wording pre-printed on the signer's document, we have a legal duty to scrutinize it carefully for errors and thorough understanding of what it is declaring. Once it has been signed and sealed, it becomes the notary's own work product; a valid acknowledgment certificate; flaws, falsehoods, and all.

The notarial certificate must be complete and truthful before the notary may sign it.

> *"A notary betrays the public trust when he signs a certificate of acknowledgment with knowledge that the blanks will be filled in later or when he signs a completed certificate of acknowledgment but without requiring the personal appearance of the acknowledging parties. Whether the certificate blanks are empty or full is not the significant fact. The key to the statutory safeguard is the integrity of the notary in the proper discharge of notarial duties by requiring the signatories to personally appear before him and acknowledge that they did in fact execute the document.*

> *In taking acknowledgments a notary properly discharges his duty only when the persons acknowledging execution personally appear and the notary has satisfactory evidence, based either on his personal knowledge or on the oath or affirmation of a credible witness, that the acknowledging parties are who they say, they are and did what they say they did."*

>> *- Farm Bureau Finance Company, Inc. v. Carney (100 Idaho 745, 605 P.2d 509).*

> *"A careful analysis of the duties of a notary public indicates that he does not adjudicate: he witnesses and attests; he is a certifier of facts; a recorder of signatures; a keeper of a seal to facilitate and authenticate commercial transactions; and a giver of oaths."*

>> *- Transamerica Insurance Company v. Valley National Bank, 462 P.2d 814*

> *"The taking by a notary of the proof or acknowledgment of the execution of an instrument is a ministerial act and not a judicial one. A notary public in this state is not a guarantor of the absolute correctness of his certificate of acknowledgment, nor does he undertake to certify that the person acknowledging the instrument*

owns or has any interest in the land therein described, but he does undertake to certify that the person personally appearing before him is known to him to be the person described in, and who executed the instrument."
   - *Barnard v. Schuler, 100 Minn. 289, 110 N. W. 966 (1907).*

The notary is authorized to write an acknowledgment notarization in her own words, so long as it meets all of the statutory and substantive requirements of content.

"Unless a state statute specifically mandates the literal wording of an acknowledgment certificate, substantial compliance with the form provided in statute is widely accepted as valid. This is even true where the statute requires that acknowledgments 'must' be substantially in the form prescribed...It is unnecessary and unreasonable to apply technical rules of construction to certificates of acknowledgment. The states have conferred notarial authority to execute these acknowledgments on lay citizens who may be unlearned in the law."
   - *Herron v. Harbour, 75 Okla. 127,182 p. 243 (1919).*

A Little History of the Use of Acknowledgments Can Be Useful

Acknowledgment notarizations have been in use for over 460 years, and they are used in very much the same way today as they were over 80 years before the Pilgrims arrived at Plymouth Rock.

The use of acknowledgments originates back to England in 1536 when the British government enacted a law called the *Statute of Enrollments*. This new law prohibited the conveyance of land by bargain and sale unless it was memorialized (documented) by a deed that was recorded before designated officials. These officials, much like our recorders of deeds at the county level today, could not accept a deed for recording without evidence the signatures to the deed were genuine.

The Statute of Enrollments did not create the acknowledgment notarization, but acknowledgments were used by the buyer and seller to acknowledge their actions in order to furnish the required evidence to the recording officer.

The Statute of Enrollments was not enforced in the American Colonies, yet acknowledgments were used in Colonial America. Some of the colonies required by law that deeds be witnessed. The execution of acknowledgments served as a substitute equivalent to the proof witnesses could otherwise provide. In other colonies as early as 1641, recordations of deeds were also regulated by laws.

In 17th century Colonial America, transportation and communication was so poor that some colonial laws permitted the admittance of deeds for recording with a magistrate rather than with a recorder of deeds because magistrates were accessible to everyone, whereas recorders of deeds were not.

The acknowledgment notarization has evolved in law to provide three purposes: to give validity to the document, to permit the document to be introduced into evidence without requiring additional proof of proper execution, and to entitle the document to be recorded. The acknowledgment notarization is not part of the document, and it does not affect its validity.

Acknowledgments were taken in Colonial times in open court by the magistrate and entered into court proceedings. The taking of an acknowledgment was a function of the court at that time, and was therefore considered a "judicial" function. With the passage of time the taking of acknowledgments in court became increasingly tedious and an expensive use of time. It was bogged down with formalities.

Society became more and more mobile, and the frequency of real estate conveyances increased rapidly. It became expedient to confer the authority to perform acknowledgments on persons who were not of the court, namely notaries public and other local government officials. Today it is highly unusual for any official, other than a notary to take an acknowledgment.

Legal scholars occasionally discuss whether the office of the notary today is still a judicial office or now a ministerial office. Legally it matters very little, except to point out that the notary is a public officer. The notary is bound by the state laws governing the notarial act. Notaries have considerable discretion in the performance of a notarization. However, notaries have absolutely no discretion on whether to ignore or violate a state notary law.

Address Change

Every notary, in every state, has an address of record with either the state government or the county in which the notary is commissioned. This is the address by which the notary can be contacted by the government when it is time to renew the notary commission. Most states require by statute that if a notary experiences a change of address of record, she must submit notice thereof, often with a fee, to the state agency that appointed her a notary.

Address of the Notary

See Notarial Certificate; "Residing At _____." ; Venue

Many states require by statute that the notary indicate on the notarial certificate, usually below the notary's signature, the notary's county of residence, it is common for notarial certificates to have pre-printed, "Residing at:_____." Many incorrectly assume that the notary must provide her street address in this space; it would be inappropriate for the notary to do so.

In many states where the notary seal contains the notary's county of residence, it is redundant to indicate the same information below the notary's signature. Unless state statute requires that the county of residence appear both in the notary seal and in writing near the notary's signature, it is not necessary to repeat the information in the certificate.

The purpose for this information is to provide public disclosure regarding legal jurisdiction over the notary should a legal dispute arise concerning the notarization. For example, the courts in the county in which the notary resides would have jurisdiction over a dispute involving the notary. This information corresponds to the beginning of every notarial certificate wherein a statement of "venue" is required of every certificate. It will read, "State of _____ County of _____." This information is required as disclosure of the location in which the notarization is performed.

Address of the Signer
See Journal Recordation; Notary Journal Contents and Format

Administration of Oath and Affirmation
See Affirmation; Oath and Affirmation

Administrative Rules
In all states, and in federal government, state agencies are commonly granted by statute the authority to promulgate administrative rules for the purpose of interpreting and implementing the laws enacted by the legislature or Congress.

The purpose for administrative rules is to provide the details to the laws enacted in the statutes, because statutory law is not intended to delve into details of implementation. The statutes provide broad policy objectives, standards and guidelines. The state agencies are created to provide the expertise for the implementation and enforcement of the laws. The agency's expertise is relied upon for the creation and development of the rules that specify how the broader laws will be implemented.

Administrative rules have the force of law. They are created and proposed through vitally important due process of law through public notice, invitation for public review and comment, and through considerable public hearings. When adopted, the rules become codified and become part of a body of law called the administrative rules. The rules can be amended by government agency and the legislative body can override rules it finds inappropriate by legislating their repeal.

Affiant
See Affidavit; Affirmation; Oath and Affirmation

An affiant is a person who has attested to an affidavit or to any statement, written or oral. An affiant is under penalties of perjury for the content of their statements, should there be falsehood found therein.

Affidavit
See Affirmation; Deposition; Jurat Notarization; Oath and Affirmation

An affidavit is any voluntary statement in writing that is sworn to or affirmed orally by its author, before a person having legal authority to administer an oath or affirmation, such as a notary, to the individual. Affidavits are used commonly throughout the legal system and in business. Whenever a signature to an affidavit is notarized, and not all affidavits are notarized, it must be notarized by a jurat.

The difference between a deposition and affidavit has been described as follows:

> "A deposition, in its more technical and appropriate sense, is limited to the written testimony of a witness given in the course of a judicial proceeding, either at law or in equity, in response to interrogatories, oral or written, with an opportunity for cross-examination. An affidavit is a voluntary statement made ex parte, without notice to the adverse party or an opportunity to cross-examine the witness concerning the subject matter. Moreover, the giving of a deposition may be compelled, so that it is not in all instances a voluntary statement."
>
> - Jii v. Rhodes, 577 F. Supp. 1128 (S. D. Ohio 1983).

Affirmation
See Deposition; Jurat Notarization; Oath and Affirmation

An affirmation is a solemn statement or declaration made as a substitute for a sworn statement by a person whose conscience will not permit him to swear under oath. Such declarations or affirmations are permitted in all jurisdictions in the United States. They have the same force and effect in law as statements made under oath. The wording a notary may use when administering an affirmation for a jurat notarization is, "Do you affirm the statements in this document are true?" The notary is duty-bound to honor the affiant's wishes if they prefer an affirmation rather than an oath.

Affixing the Notary Seal
See Seal of the Notary Public

When a notarization is completed, the notary affixes a seal near her signature evidencing her legal authority to make the written notarial certifications she has signed. The notary seal can be affixed anytime after the notary has signed the notarial certificate. The seal should be affixed anyplace near the notary's signature so it appears clearly and legibly in its entirety.

It is considered an abuse of the notary's authority to affix her seal so it overlaps her signature, or any signature. It is also legally wrongful to affix the notary seal to anything other than the notarial certificate itself. Some notaries will affix their seal to all pages of a document to evidence they belong together, or to demonstrate that the signatures to the document have been notarized. This is likewise considered an abuse of the notary's legal authority and is wrongful conduct.

Age Limits of Document Signers Needing Notarizations

See Minors; Notarizing for Minors; Willful, Free Making of a Signature

Agent

See Agent of the State

Agent of the State

See Conflict of Interest; Fiduciary Duty of a Notary; Impartial Agent of the State; Impartiality

The notary public is in a position of public trust. As such, the notary is viewed by many as an agent of the state government by which she is commissioned. There is a vast body of law that gives definition and substance to the duties and roles of agents. It is incumbent for every notary to acquire a basic understanding of their position as an agent, and the legal principles that pertain thereto.

> *"Public office is a public agency, or trust. One, therefore, who holds a public office is an agent, or trustee, of the public. Public offices are created for the purpose of effecting the end for which government has been instituted, which is the common good, and not for the mere profit, honor or private interest of any one man, family, or class of men."*
> - *Richard B. Humphrey, The American Notary Manual (4th Ed., 1948).*

14

An agent is one who agrees with a principal to act on behalf of the principal and be subjected to the principal's control. Principals hire agents to accomplish things the principals cannot or should not personally do for themselves.

An authoritative definition of agency comes from the legal text, Restatement (Second) of Agency, Section 2(2)(1958):

> *"A servant is an agent employed by a master to perform service in his affairs whose physical conduct in the performance of the service is controlled or is subject to the right to control by the master."*

The notary's role as an agent of the state carries with it other actual or implied agent relationships with the public, the document signer for whom the notary performs, and to the notary's employer.

> *"The duty of a notary public in acting officially is not confined to the one to whom he directly renders service. His duty is to the public and those who may be affected by his act. The public has the right to rely upon the verity of a certificate, and, if one sustains injury as the proximate [result] of a willful violation of his official duty with respect to that certificate, the officer becomes liable to him."*
>
> *- Wesley Gilmer, Jr., Anderson's Manual for Notaries Public 283; (5th Ed., 1976).*

Every agent is a fiduciary for the principal. The notary is under substantial fiduciary duties when performing official acts.

All Reasonable Steps to Verify the Signer's Identity

See Credible Witness; Identity of the Signer; Personal Appearance of the Signer; Personal Knowledge; Reasonable Care; Signer Identification

Under the standards of reasonable care, a notary must take every reasonable step available to verify a signer's true identity. The phrase, "all reasonable steps" is not intended to suggest that a notary behave excessively. The operative word is "reasonable." Once a notary has made a positive determination as to the signer's true identity, no further steps need be taken. The notary may either personally know the signer, or rely upon the sworn oath of a credible witness attesting to the document signer's identity, or rely upon the signer's appropriate ID documents.

Alternatives to Notarizations Under Federal Law
See Affidavit

The federal government has enacted law pertaining to documents that are subject to federal proceedings, such as in Federal Courts, that permit them to "self-authenticate" the signatures thereto without the use of a notary and notarization. The intent of Congress is to simplify the filing of documents in federal courts. In declaring its intent, Congress stated:

> *"The purpose of this legislation is to permit the use in Federal proceedings of unsworn declarations given under penalty of perjury in lieu of affidavits sworn to before a notary public."*
>
> *- H.R. Rep. No. 94-1616, at 1 (1976).*

The legislation to which Congress refers is Section 1746 of the United States Code, which reads:

> *"Wherever, under any law of the United States or under any rule, regulation, order, or requirement made pursuant to law, any matter is required or permitted to be supported, evidenced, established, or proved by the sworn declaration, verification, certificate, statement, oath, or affidavit, in writing of the person making the same (other than a deposition, or an oath of office, or an oath required to be taken before a specified official other than a notary public), such matter may, with like force and effect, be supported , evidenced, established, or proved by the unsworn declaration, certification, verification, or statement, in writing of such person which is subscribed by him, as true under penalty of perjury, and dated in substantially the following form:*
>
> *(1) If executed without the United States:*
>
> *I declare (or certify, verify, or state) under penalty of perjury under the laws of the United States of America that the forgoing is true and correct. Executed on (date).*
>
> *(Signature).*

*(2) If executed within the United States, its territories, possessions,
or commonwealths:*

*I declare (or certify, verify, or state) under penalty of perjury that
the foregoing is true and correct. Executed on (date).*

(Signature)."

     - 28 U.S.C. 1746 (1994).

Apostille

Specifically defined, an apostille is a brief notation on the margin of a document. The term is used today in reference to a certificate of the high government official who appoints the notaries in his jurisdiction. In most states, the secretary of state issues an apostille certifying a notary is of good standing and in authority to notarize a signature to the document in question. Apostilles are commonly used in connection with documents bearing American notarizations heading overseas. Foreign governments may make demand for an apostille to accompany a notarization under the terms and provisions of treaties adopted under the Hague Conventions, post-World War II. The typical apostille issued by a secretary of state among the fifty states appears remarkably similar to that of a basic notarization itself, except the seal is the seal of the state and not a notarial seal.

Application Process

See Appointment to the Office of Notary; Commission of a Notary; Commissioning Process; Qualification for Appointment to the Office of Notary Public

Appointment to the Office of Notary Public

See Notary Bond; Oath and Affirmation; Qualification for Appointment to the Office of Notary Public

Notaries must have the authority of their state office to perform valid notarizations. This requires the notary to have met minimum qualifications of eligibility and, in most states, to file a surety bond. Until the notary receives in writing a certificate of notary commission from the state (or the official who appoints notaries), that notary has no authority to perform notarial acts.

The office of a notary is a highly esteemed public office. One cannot appoint himself or herself as a notary. It is a delegation of power and authority by the state government to the applicant. It is a formal process prescribed by state laws involving a formal written application, satisfaction of minimum requirements such as minimum age and legal residency. In many states the notary must also file a surety bond with the state and take an official oath of office before a person having the legal authority to administer such an oath, and that may be a notary. The term of office and scope of the notary's legal powers and authority are defined by state law. A notarial appointment may be denied an applicant for cause, and an appointment may be revoked for cause. Most state laws provide that the state may revoke an appointment on the grounds that the notary has violated the notarial laws of the state or has abused his legal authority.

Notaries cannot appoint themselves to become notaries. The only way to obtain the authority of the notarial office is to receive it from the body politic that is created by law to confer such authority.

The role of "authority to act" is absolutely essential to society, freedom, law and human liberties; it is the foundation of all orderliness. If people could appoint themselves to offices of authority, there would be no authority to exercise. All who claimed such self-anointed authority would be impostors. Their acts and services would be invalid, and all who relied on them to be otherwise could suffer considerable harm.

In a number of states, it is a serious criminal violation to notarize after the notary commission has expired. Such a person acts without authority, even though it was unintentional.

The authority of notaries has no ragged or vague edges. It starts on a specific date and it ends on a specific date. Any notarial acts performed before or after such dates are unlawful and invalid. It is orderly, it is reliable, and it is a good example of legal authority to act.

In most states, it is possible to serve multiple consecutive terms without interruption of authority. The subsequent term begins simultaneously as the prior term expires. This requires a bit of planning ahead on the notary's part, but it alleviates doubt as to the notary's authority in the transition period.

Attaching the Notarial Certificate

See Acknowledgment Notarization; Copy Certification; Jurat Notarization

A notarial certificate is not part of the signer's document. It is a separate document authenticating the signature appearing on the signer's document. The notarial certificate need not appear on the same page the client has signed. It is a valid procedure in every state for the notary to create a notarial certificate on a separate page and attach it to the signer's document.

From "The Notary" (September 1999)

An Attached Certificate Works Great!

It's the irony of all ironies. You are asked to notarize on a very important document but the space provided you is barely larger than a postage stamp. It is impossible to read. It usually fails to comply with the requirements of your state's notary laws. And, if you attempt to sign and seal it, you will obliterate everything. The tiny micro-certificate is impossible to use.

One obvious solution is to notarize on the backside of the document, if that side is available for use. Often times, it is not. It is increasingly common for documents to be one-side-of-the-page only because of electronic imaging, faxing, etc. That leaves you with an excellent alternative: attaching a separate notarial certificate.

An old myth has it that a notarization must appear on the same piece of paper where the customer's signature appears. The concept is illogical and without factual basis.

A notarial certificate, when signed and sealed by a notary, is literally an official document of the state government. You are an official of your

state. Every official notarial act you perform you do as an agent of your state. Your notarial certificate is not part of the signers document. It is a separate document. It is a state document created by you to authenticate the signature of a person on their document. For the notarization to share the same sheet of paper the customer signed is merely a nicety. It saves paper. It looks tidy. But, it is not required. We are lulled into assuming it is required only because it is done so commonly, and it is aesthetically appealing.

We are also lulled into assuming that this practice is done for security reasons. The notarization appearing immediately below or adjacent to the customer's signature reasonably suggests that the one pertains to the other. We assume that it is less vulnerable to abuse, misuse, and alteration this way. And, indeed it may well be.

The primary concern most notaries have with using a "loose" or attached certificate is that it can be separated from the intended document by accident or by fraudulent means. The concern is valid, if the certificate is not prepared properly. But the concern is also one-sided. A notarial certificate prepared on the document's signature page can be removed with a pair of scissors and be applied to another document with no trace of evil doing. If the notary simply identifies in writing on the attached certificate specifics about the document to which it pertains, fears over its loss or misappropriation are mitigated.

Weighed against the use of an attached notarial certificate, many notaries are convinced that signature-page notarizations are the only way a notarization can be done. Their mistaken assumption does not serve their customers and unnecessarily complicates the notarial act.

Attaching a notarial certificate to a customer's document has profound merit to it, and it may actually prove more beneficial to the transaction than forcing a large notarization into a small place on the signers document.

A major reason most people incorrectly assume the notarization is part of their document - that it verifies its legality or enforceability - is because it traditionally appears immediately adjacent to the customer's signature. By utilizing an attached notarial certificate, the message is given that it is

20

a document separate and apart from the customer's documents. The notarization is not part of the customer's transaction. It stands alone as a certificate; it is a written testimony of the notary declaring the genuineness of the customer's signature.

As in all written transactions, any additions, addenda, or appendices will be accompanied by an attribution clause, a clear and unambiguous disclosure as to what document the attachment belongs; the more specific the notice given, the better.

An attached notarial certificate should, for reasons of caution and clarity, include an attribution clause clearly seen by the reader, perhaps near the bottom of the attachment. It should inform the reader of four important facts:

 1. The statement that the certificate is an attachment to another document;
 2. The title or name of the document to which it belongs;
 3. The number of pages contained in the document; and
 4. The date of the document, or date it was signed.

There has been considerable debate on whether a separate notarial certificate must be stapled, glued or physically affixed to the signer's document. There is no firm answer as a matter of law. In fact, it has rarely been addressed by the court but in a few isolated instances. Such cases date back to the 1950's, before our modern era of electronic imaging was dreamed of. These court cases seem to suggest that the notary had the obligation to physically staple or glue the certificate to the signer's document. Their reasoning was based on the theory that the notarial certificate was the moral equivalent of a bearer bond. It was as good as cash. If it were lost or stolen, its finder could apply it anyway he wished. Finders keepers, losers' weepers. Until it found its permanent home with the document, it was invalid.

Whether this reasoning is still viable today is up for debate. A fail-safe policy, however, may be for the notary to ensure it is affixed to the signer's document. It is hard to imagine that the notary and not the customer must be the person to do the affixing. It would seem that it is enough to know to everyone's satisfaction that the certificate isn't going anywhere but with the document for which it is intended.

As notaries we are granted significant legal protections against liability for our notarial services if we exercise reasonable care. We can't prevent fraudulent or negligent use of our notarial certificates after they leave our control. It matters not whether the certificate is on the same page the customer signed or is on an attachment. What does matter is that the notarial act is recorded in our notary journals. If we are clear and specific in identifying the signer's document in our journal, it will irrefutably tie the certificate to that document regardless of subsequent events.

Your notary seal may not be used to indicate your notarization belongs to a document. An unwise and forbidden practice many follow is to affix the notary seal on every page of the document along with the notarial certificate. Even worse is the placement of the seal where two pages overlap, thus leaving half of the seal impression on one page and the other half on the other page. The courts consider this an "abuse of notarial authority."

Attestation
See Affirmation; Oath and Affirmation

Attestation of a Copy of a Document
See Conforming Copies; Copy Certification

Attesting a Signature
See Signature Verification; Witness Jurat

Most states permit, by statute or by rules of civil procedure, the authentication of a document signature by the testimony of a witness. In the event a document signature was made and must now be verified by notarization, and if the signature maker is now incompetent, deceased or inaccessible, an eyewitness can bear witness to the genuineness of the signature. This is usually done by sworn affidavit before a notary or one having the legal authority to administer an oath to the witness.

Attorney as Notary
See Conflict of Interest

It is very common for attorneys to possess notary commissions from their states in order to facilitate better and more efficient services to their clients. It is an oft-debated issue when an attorney prepares documents and advises clients on their legal affairs and the attorney consummates the document executions by notarizing the clients' signatures. As a matter of law, a notary is prohibited from coercing, encouraging, advising or giving counsel to the document signer as to whether or not the client should sign the document. This is a particularly important standard for notaries because the notarization is the law-recognized certification born of governmental authority that the document signer acted willingly and freely in signing the document. The notary cannot, with any integrity, make such a determination and then certify it, after having counseled and encouraged the signer to sign the document.

This issue lies at the heart of the debate over whether an attorney can properly perform a notarization for clients just after having given the client counsel regarding the content and purpose of the document. Moreover, the attorney has an inherent personal interest in all transactions for which he represents his clients or in which he prepares transactional documents. The attorney's collection of legal fees is dependent on the successful completion of these transactions. An attorney's notarization of client signatures in these transactions cannot possibly constitute objective disinterested notarial acts. However, unless the attorney's personal interest in the client's transaction is of a nature that disqualifies the attorney from notarizing (primarily because he is a principal party to the transaction), the attorney's notarial conflict of interest is likely benign.

Attorney General Opinions
The Attorneys General of the fifty states generally has constitutional authority to issue legal opinions on issues affecting the interest of the states. These opinions are formal and are granted in response to formal requests from officials of the state government. While an Attorney General's opinion does not have the force of law, it is, however, granted great weight in the formulation of public policies and in the courts when adjudicating a pertinent dispute. The Attorneys General also issue

informal opinions on matters requiring quick and "non-binding" legal opinion. Formal opinions are codified and published for public use, similar to state statutes, informal opinions are not.

Attorney-in-Fact

See Agent of the State; Fiduciary Duty of the Notary; Power of Attorney

An attorney-in-fact is a person who has been named in a written power of attorney as the person legally authorized by the principal to act in the principal's behalf. When acting under the power of attorney, the attorney-in-fact is authorized to sign documents on behalf of the principal and to bind the principal to the transactions in which the attorney-in-fact has entered on the principal's behalf. One who is appointed attorney-in-fact bears a sober responsibility and has a fiduciary duty to the principal to act in the principal's best interest and to do nothing injurious to the principal's interests.

Authenticity of a Signature

See Acknowledgment Notarization; Jurat Notarization; Notarization; Reasonable Care; Signature; Signature Verification

The primary purpose of notarizing a signature is to verify and document that the signature is genuine and not a forgery. The only legal way to authenticate a signature is for the maker of the signature to personally appear before the notary, for the notary to verify the signer's true identity and for the signer to prove the signature on the document is genuinely theirs. When a notary has properly authenticated a signature to a document, third parties can rely on the notarial certificate attesting to that fact. It provides the third party assurance that the document signer with whom they are transacting business is the person who signed the document.

Authority

See Notary Public; Officer; Public Ministerial Officer; Public Official

The performance or conducting of any official act requires that the person performing the act be in possession of the legal authority to perform such an act. Authority cannot be assumed or self-invoked. It must be appointed to the individual upon completion of legally prescribed requirements. A primary requisite to an orderly and secure society is the establishment of authority through a system created by law. Any society or organization that recognizes self-appointed authority claimed by individuals undermines that entity's legitimate representations concerning its own mission statement and authority to carry it out.

Notaries receive their legal authority from the state government that appoints them. The notary's authority to perform notarial acts is defined by the state statutes. It most commonly includes the execution of acknowledgment and jurat notarizations, the certification of copies of documents, and the administration of oath and affirmations.

The essential principle of authority is that it cannot be obtained by any means other than that prescribed by law and from those having the authority to confer it upon others. In all states, a person who takes upon herself the assumed authority to perform notarial acts commits a violation of state law. In most states, such conduct constitutes a criminal violation.

Authority of the Document Signer
See Attorney-in-fact; Power of Attorney; Representative Capacity of the Document Signer

It is common for notarial certificates to indicate the document signer's authority to sign on behalf of a third party, such as his company or board of directors. Unfortunately the certificate will often articulate the notary's certification of the signer's claimed authority. A notary does not have the legal authority or duty to make such factual findings and assertions within the scope of the notarial certificate.

It is one thing for a notary to certify a signer's identity was properly verified. It is quite another matter to verify the authority by which the signer purports to sign is indeed vested in the signer. The notarial acknowledgment and jurat both declare the identity of the person appearing before the notary, and whose signature is being notarized.

When the notary certifies, "Acknowledged before me by Jane Doe," she is certifying that she took all reasonable steps to verify it was Jane Doe. When the notary certifies, "Acknowledged before me by Jane Doe as Vice President of Good Service Airlines," she is still certifying she reasonably verified it was Jane Doe who appeared before her. But, should the notary also certify that Jane is Vice President of Good Service Airlines?

The certification of a notarial act does not extend to the verification of the signer's authority to sign. That is because it is a factual matter that might be proved only after extensive personal effort on the part of the notary. And even then, it may not be fail-safe.

For example, the status of our employment or our authority to act on behalf of another person can be revoked before anyone knows it. Jane Doe may think she is still corporate Vice President, but may have been terminated while she is in the notary's office. She can provide a business card, a copy of her paycheck and even corporate letterhead with her name on the top. It may indicate her position is Vice President, but it may be counterfeit or invalid because it is suddenly no longer accurate.

Notaries cannot, as a matter of law, be subjected to this enormous burden to verify a signer's authority to sign a document. It would render most notarial requests impossible to perform. Most importantly, as a matter of law, if the notary verifies a person's true identity, that person's legal authority to sign a document can be imputed by the circumstances, or be refuted subsequently by contrary facts.

The reasoning behind this is simple: A person's true identity is fixed and permanent. A person's employment title or authority to act on behalf of others is temporary. It is revocable. Once a person's identity is verified by the notary and it is subsequently alleged the signer falsely assumed legal authority he did not have, that transaction bearing the "imposter's" signature is readily voidable. And, the imposter can be criminally prosecuted. A notary cannot be liable if the signer had none of the authority he claimed to have.

Many pre-printed notarial certificates provide a place for the signer to indicate their job title or authority to sign a transaction. There isn't any harm in this. It is traditional that a document signer ought to specify their authority to sign. Just because it is embodied within the document or notarial certificate does not impute to the notary any duty to ensure the signer's authority is verified.

Perhaps if notarial employment and legal authority to act on behalf of others were as permanent and fixed as our personal identities, the rule of law would be vastly different. Only then could it be justified to require a notary to verify such facts about the signer.

The notarization is not the verification of the signer's job title or legal authority. Just because it may appear that way in a pre-printed notarization does not make it true.

The Notary, July 1999

In the business world, it is often customary, and occasionally mandatory, that people sign their names with their official title, "Bill Gates, President of Microsoft." Does this mean that the notary must verify that Bill is actually president of Microsoft if they are to notarize that signature?

Some people argue "yes," some people argue "no," and some people say "maybe." The correct answer lies in the case law. The case law says that we notarize to authenticate signatures by verifying the maker's identity, not their employment.

A notary is not required to verify a signer's job title or authority to sign a document. In every state, the notary is required to verify the signature is genuine and its maker's personal identity (not position of employment) is verified. A signature forgery can only be made under false pretenses of identity, not authority to sign.

It would be unbearably burdensome for notaries to be required to verify a signer's title, position or authority to sign a document. After all, a person's authority to sign on behalf of a company or another business partner could be revoked without notice, and it could be easily falsified.

Consider your own employment. What can you spontaneously provide a notary that proves your employment position and that you are authorized to sign on behalf of your boss or board of directors?

The higher issue is why does it matter? The answer is, it doesn't. A signer's authority to sign has nothing to do with a notarization. It is common for notarial certificates to declare, "Acknowledged before me by Bill Gates, President of Microsoft..." The title, President of Microsoft, is surplusage. It is added for clarity, or for emphasis. The signature was not acknowledged by the President of Microsoft; Bill Gates, whose job title is President of Microsoft, acknowledged it. Some certificates unfortunately declare, "Acknowledged before me by Bill Gates known to me to be the President of Microsoft..." The courts take a dim view of this wording. In fact, the notary has no legal authority to make such a claim within a notarial certificate. It is outside the scope of the notary's legal authority to make such determinations. In situations like these, the notary would do well to line out that provision of the certificate.

When you notarize for Bill Gates, it doesn't matter what he's worth or where he works. He could claim he's the King of England, but it has nothing to do with your duties as a notary.

Authorized Fees
See Fees

Authorship of Notarial Wording
See Notarial Certificate; Selecting Notarial Certificates; Unauthorized Practice of Law

B

Clearly enough if we did not have the office of notary public, we'd have to create it or something like it to take its place.
- Richard B. Humphrey

"Before Me"

See Acknowledgment Notarization; Jurat Notarization; Personal Appearance of the Signer

One of the most important defining phrases of the notarial certificate is the phrase, "before me." The document signer whose signature is to be notarized must personally appear before the notary. Notary Law requires the disclosure that the signer personally appeared before the notary in every state. The failure to recognize the presence of this wording in the certificate, and the failure to ensure the truthfulness thereof, is the leading source of legal liability for notaries and their employers in America. When a notary signs a notarial certificate containing the clear and unambiguous declaration that the signer either acknowledged his signature or signed his name under oath "before me," when in fact the signer did not appear before the notary, the notarization is false and invalid. It constitutes irrefutable proof of the notary's written falsehood and violation of law. Under the rule of law, the making of a false statement calculated to misrepresent a material fact, such as the false declaration that the document signer personally appeared before the notary when they did not, constitutes fraud.

Among the most serious of legal offenses a notary can commit is falsely certifying a fact so important as the assertion the signer personally appeared. There is no legal defense for this conduct.

Beneficial Interest
See Conflict of Interest

Bills of Exchange
See History of the Notary Public Office

Most state notary statutes make reference to a notarial service pertaining to bills of exchange. In no part of modern commercial transactions are such notarial procedures utilized. The statutory reference to this function is a vestige of generations past.

A bill of exchange was a form of letter from a person ordering another person to pay a sum of money to a third person under certain terms and conditions. Notaries were used to certify the letters, called "bills of exchange."

Blank Documents
See Completeness of the Signer's Document

Although the contents of a signer's document is irrelevant to a notarization, the statutes of a few states specify that a notary may not sign their name and affix their seal on a blank document. A significant number of people believe that this means it is unlawful for the notary to notarize a signature on a document that is blank. Others argue that because a document's contents are irrelevant to the notarization, the above referenced prohibition probably refers to the notarial certificate and not to the signer's document. It is indeed unlawful for a notary to sign and seal a blank notarial certificate.

The issue concerning the appropriateness of notarizing signatures to blank documents has several valid perspectives. It is an issue far from definitive resolution.

From "The Notary" (March 1999)

One of the oldest, common rumors

about notarial procedures is that a notary
must never notarize a blank document.

Do you ever wonder about the accuracy of folksy homilies like these? It is one thing to be conversant with the rules of thumb you hear through the grapevine; it is another to be knowledgeable about the rules of law on the same subject. The point is this: rules of thumb can be helpful, but the rules of law are the rules that govern.

It is obvious why it's foolish to sign a blank check. But it is a bit different to sign a blank document. Let's explore this further. But first, one error must be corrected. A notary notarizes signatures, not documents. It is a malapropism to say, "the document was notarized." While it is commonly expressed this way as a figure of speech, don't take it literally. The notarial certificate does not refer to the document on which it is performed. The notarial wording refers only to the signature being authenticated. As a matter of law, the contents of the signer's document are 100% irrelevant to the notarization.

Perhaps the primary reason people assume that a notary "must not notarize a blank document" is because it is assumed the notarization pertains to the contents thereof. It is further reasoned that once a document is signed and notarized, the blanks can be filled in later. It is assumed that information provided later will be attributed to the document signer and to the notary. And, it's assumed that if the subsequent provided information is false, that means double trouble for the notary.

The rule of thumb with all of its assumptions and the rule of law are in disagreement. They can't both be right.

A document bearing a signature constitutes legal evidence of the signer's willing and deliberate intent to concur with, or commit to, the contents of the document. The written signature constitutes the physical ratification of its signer.

Notarizations are performed merely to ensure that the signer was not an imposter and forger, and that he signed under his own free will and intent.

When a document is signed before it is completed, which is a common business practice in many segments of commerce and trade, the signer assumes a considerable risk. The signer is trusting that the document blanks will be filled in later with truthful and correct information. If those whom he trusts are scoundrels, he becomes the victim of fraud. Now he has a heavy burden of proof to show the document he signed contains falsehoods that he did not assent to when signing prematurely.

Exceptions to the rule that signing blank documents is foolish:

It is indeed valid in many instances to say that a person who signs a blank document is a fool. The important exception is where the signer and the document custodian (or preparer) are in a client/fiduciary relationship. Attorneys, title companies, escrow officers, trust officers, real estate agents and accountants commonly prepare incomplete documents for client signatures as a means for providing security or expediency to a transaction. If the signer cannot trust the professional on whose fiduciary duty the signer must rely, the signer is wise to refrain from signing the incomplete document prematurely and should immediately seek a more honest professional. Honesty and trustworthiness are the glue that holds society together.

Most often overlooked in discussions about notarizations on blank documents are the legal implications of the notarization itself.

Under the Uniform Recognition of Acknowledgments Act and the Model Notary Act, the definition and interpretation given to a signature notarization includes the assertion that the signer signed his name "for purposes stated within" the document.

If a document is incomplete, how can it be concluded that the purposes for signing the document are stated within the document? If you sign a contract, you are presumed to be signing for purposes of entering into the terms provided within the contract. But, document contents are not the notary's business to know and blank documents merely represent the absence of content, technically not the notary's concern.

As the document contents are not for the notary to know, it is the duty of the document signer to disclose to the notary what the document is. If he is signing a contract, the purpose of his signing is to enter into the terms of the contract, and the notary has a need to know this. What the contract says is not for the notary to know.

When a notary notarizes the person's signature to the contract, the notary is verifying that he signed for the purposes stated within his contract document. If the contract is a standard pre-printed business form that has extensive blank spaces to be filled in by the signing parties, signing the form while it is substantially incomplete may be grounds for holding the document unenforceable. The signature constitutes the signer's ratification of the document contents that, in this scenario, do not yet exist.

The dilemma boils down to this: How can a notary notarize a signature to a document that was signed for purposes stated within the document if the document is blank? Perhaps the answer lies in "how complete does a document have to be in order for it to be eligible for signing?"

How many blank spaces are too many?

The rules of law often provide society reasonable standards we can rely on for answers to questions like this. For purposes of document and signature enforceability, the legal issue is not whether the document is complete in its entirety. Rather, the issue is whether the intent of the parties to the transaction is substantially represented in writing with sufficient minimum information adhering the parties to the intended terms and objectives of the transaction. For example, a contract to purchase a parcel of land may include the property address, estimated square footage, intended sale price and intended closing date. The contract may have blank spaces to be filled in later for a legal description of the property, the tax assessment ID number, financing interest rate and terms of monthly payment. This contract, although incomplete, is eligible for a notarization because the intent of the parties is substantially provided. There is sufficient stated purpose for which the signers sign the document.

Another twist to the conflict with notarizations on incomplete documents concerns jurat notarizations. If the signer must sign the document under oath, "Carol, do you swear the statements within your document are true," to what does she attest if the document is full of blanks? Common sense dictates that it is utmost folly to notarize by jurat a signature to a document that is substantially incomplete. It is impossible to attest to a blank space within a document when the space is filled in later, Carol is under penalty of perjury for the truthfulness of the information some unseen, unknown person wrote into the blank space.

Considerable misinformation circulates among notaries about their alleged duty to scrutinize the signer's document for completeness. As a matter of law, the notary has no legal responsibility to do this, and she runs a risk of liability for invasion of privacy. The notary must walk a fine line. It is one thing to scrutinize a signer's document. It is quite another for the notary to quickly and superficially observe the document for an overall impression that the document resembles what it is represented to be, and that it appears generally complete. Scanning a document as most notaries are told to do may be overly intrusive and overbearing. Observing the document is the better standard because it is more in keeping with the principles of law that the notary is sworn to uphold.

Seeing blank spaces isn't a case for overreacting.

There is a natural tendency for some folks to take these concepts and overreact when they discover a blank on a signer document. They naturally assume because of their state's notary law that a single blank on the document prevents the signature from being notarized. A few state's notary statutes provide that the notary shall not sign a notarization where the transaction is incomplete. This provision of law is ambiguous: does it refer to blanks in the signer's document, or does it refer to blanks in the notarial certificate? The standard interpretation should be that it refers to the notarial certificate, and not to the signer's document.

If a signed notarial certificate is incomplete due to blank spaces, the notarization will likely be held invalid if those blanks pertain to required data. The standard of reasonable care imposed on every notary is to refrain from notarizing until a complete and accurate notarial certificate is provided first.

34

Never sign a blank or incomplete notarial certificate. It constitutes official misconduct on the notary's part, and can result in the notary's personal liability for damages caused thereby.

When you are asked to notarize a signature to a document, keep your attention focused on the basics. Your exercise of reasonable care and common sense on these issues will be the exercise of good judgment.

Blank Notarial Certificates

See Completeness of the Notarial Certificate; Completing the Notarial Certificate; Component Parts of the Notarial Certificate; Notarial Certificate

Most notarial certificates are preprinted on the signer's document or form. The content of the certificate is prescribed by state law. In order for the certificate to be enforceable and valid, the requisite information must be included within the certificate. If any requisite information of the certificate is missing when it is signed and sealed, the certificate is potentially invalid, and the signature is not considered notarized.

Pre-printed forms often provide for numerous blank spaces for the notary to complete. While many assume that every blank must be filled in for the certificate to be valid, the more correct principle is that all requisite information must be provided. Blank spaces pertaining to information not required by law may be left blank as they are considered surplusage and inconsequential. Unfortunately, an informed notary who understands these principles and chooses to leave an unimportant blank space empty in a notarial certificate may find the certificate rejected by one not as informed. The uninformed assumption held by many is that all blank spaces in the certificate must be completed. That, of course, is not correct.

Blind Document Signers

See Signers Who Are Blind; Physically Impaired Signer

Breach of the Notary's Duty of Care

See Duty of Care; Reasonable Care

A breach is a breaking of an obligation to perform in a certain manner or function. Every notary has a duty by law to exercise reasonable care when performing any notarial function. Failure to adhere to that standard constitutes a breach of the notary's duty of care, and the notary's personal liability therefore may ensue.

> *"Without full knowledge of his powers, obligations and limitations, a notary public can be a positive danger to the community in which he is licensed to act."*
> *- Chief Justice Charles Desmond, New York*

C

Without full knowledge of his powers, obligations, and limitations, a notary public can be a positive danger to the community in which he is licensed to act.
- Chief Justice Charles Desmond, New York

Case Law
See Civil Law Notary; Common Law

The courts lay down rules of law through their decisions and opinions. Case law is commonly recognized, but not necessarily followed, throughout the United States and is frequently cited by the courts as legal authority, granting it great weight. For the most part, only those cases that are the most representative, fundamental cases are cited as the sources of principles of law. In analyzing a legal proposition or argument, the question will be asked, "Is there any case authority" to support the argument taken?

Certificate of Notarization
See Notarial Certificate

Customarily, persons in authority make written proclamations or declarations of certain events and achievements. The authorized person signs the statement attesting to the authenticity of the facts contained within it. This signed, written statement is a certificate; a certification of the facts asserted within.

From "The Notary" (May 1999)

"Your Honor, I didn't read the notarial certificate. How can I be responsible for what it says?"

"Your honor, it is ridiculous to assume that a notary should read the certificate before signing. That would slow up everything because of all the time it wastes."

Notaries who sign a notarial certificate without first reading and examining it for truth and correctness are grossly negligent indeed. The courts take a stern and condemning attitude towards such dereliction of duty. Here are two quotations we all ought to keep firmly in mind

"The notary's complete failure to read the certificate before signing it was gross negligence and consequently a failure to faithfully perform her notarial duty as a matter of law."
- Bernd V Fong Eu, Too Cal. App. 3D 51L (1979).

"If the notary read the certificate before signing it, this omission must have been known to him; if he did not, he is equally guilty of negligence, for an officer who affixes his official signature and seal to a document (thereby giving to it the character of evidence) without examining it to find whether the facts certified are true, can scarcely be said to faithfully perform his duty according to law."
- Fogarty V. Finlay, 10 Cal. 239, 245 (1858).

The rule of thumb <u>every</u> notary must follow: With the notarial certificate, if you haven't read it, <u>don't sign it.</u> If it isn't true and correct, <u>don't sign it.</u> If you aren't willing to vouch for every word of the certificate, <u>don't sign it.</u> There is no defense in law for a false notarial certificate.

"The officer who takes an acknowledgment acts in a judicial character in determining whether the person representing himself to be, or represented by someone else to be, the grantor named in the conveyance, actually is the grantor. He determines further whether the person thus adjudged to be

the grantor does actually and truly acknowledge before him that he executed the instrument."

     - Wasson v. Connor, 54 Miss. 351.

Certified Copy of a Document By A Notary

See Conforming Copies; Copy Certification

Chain of Personal Knowledge

See Credible Witness; Personal Knowledge; Signer Identification; Unbroken Chain of Personal Knowledge

A document signer's identity can be properly and reliably verified by the attestation to a notary from a credible witness. The strongest form of signer identity is through the notary's personal knowledge of, and acquaintance with, the signer. This same level of verity can be attained vicariously through a credible witness whom the notary personally knows and who personally knows the document signer.

For this to succeed, the notary must establish a chain of personal knowledge. The chain runs from the notary, through the credible witness, and from the witness to the document signer. The chain is made of three links and all three are connected one to the other. Upon the correct application of the chain of personal knowledge, the link between the notary and the document signer is formed wherein the notary may genuinely certify the identity of the signer.

The Chain of Personal Knowledge can be validly applied only when the notary personally knows the witness and the witness personally knows the document signer. The witness must attest under oath to the notary concerning his personal knowledge and acquaintance with the document signer. Compelling case law authority indicates that the chain of personal knowledge is broken and invalid if the credible witness is not under oath when attesting to the signer's identity.

The Case of the Notary's Failure to Properly Identify His Partner's Client

Transamerica Title v. Green
(89 Cal., Rptr. 915, 11 Cal. App. 3d 693).

There were two pieces of property in San Mateo County. One parcel was owned by Joe and Mary Patrakis. The other parcel was owned by Tony and Amy Von Harten. Unbeknownst to their wives, Joe and Tony used the two properties as collateral for a bank loan. To secure the loan, deeds of trust had to be signed by the owners of the properties, as husband and wife, respectively, and their signatures notarized.

Joe and Tony went to their attorney, accompanied by two women, whom Joe and Terry claimed were their wives. The attorney introduced the four of them to a notary in the office (who happened to also be an attorney), James S. Green. Notary Green asked all four people if they had signed the deeds, to which all four replied affirmatively. Green notarized the four signatures on the deeds.

It was later discovered the 2 woman were not the wives of Joe and Tony, but were impostors who forged the signatures of Mary and Amy.

The loans on the 2 properties fell into foreclosure and lawsuits were filed, and the notary, James Green, was sued by the title insurance company for his notarial misconduct.

The California Court of Appeals held that the notary's failure to take the necessary steps to properly verify the signer's identity makes the notary fully liable for the losses suffered as a result. The Court quoted a prior case: "When the notary does not obey this statute, he should expect to be held liable; and I wish to repeat, these requirements are of great importance to the business world, and not at all too exacting."

Judgment against Notary Green for misconduct was affirmed.

Change of Notary's Address

The notary's address of record with the state by which the notary is commissioned is an important component of the notary's authority to serve. The notary must be qualified to serve under state laws, and that includes residency in the state the notary is commissioned. In some states, residents of neighboring states may obtain a notarial commission in the adjoining state if they are employed or regularly do business in the adjoining state.

Because the notary's address of record is material to the notary's qualification to serve, the address must remain current with the state agency that appoints the notary. In most states, the notary is required by law to submit notice of a change of address of record to the state within a fixed time period, usually 30 days. Such a change may, in some states, necessitate the submission of an amended notary bond ("bond rider") and the purchase of a new notary seal.

The currency of this information is also vital to the system of law in the service of process on notaries. In most states the filing of notice of address change requires payment of a filing fee.

Change of Notary's Name

A notary's change of name due to change in marital status is subject to requirements of public notification in most states. A few states grant the notary an option whereby the notary may continue to use the name that appears in the notary's seal until such time the commission expires, or proceed to submit notice to the state. In many states the notary must submit notice to the state and a fee for the name change within 30 days of the change.

The notary's name and true identity is essential to the integrity of the notary law. While a woman's name change resulting from changes to marital status does not alter her identity, it does tend to open the door to confusion in the notarial certificate. A notary in some states may sign their new name or their prior name on the notarial certificate and write the alternative name in parentheses. For example, it may read: "Jane Doe (formerly Jane Smith)." In such a situation, it is important that the notary meticulously and fully disclose the truth about her name if the signature made is not the name appearing in the notary seal.

When it comes to a notary's name change, the notary is absolutely obligated to comply with the legal requirements of the state addressing the issue. The name by which a notary serves and signs is at the core of the notarial process.

Charging Notary Fees
See Fees

Christopher Columbus' Notaries
See History of the Notary Public Office

Civil Law Notary
See Common Law

Under the historical evolution of law across the world, different nations have emerged with variations of legal systems. Of the systems of law among "western nations" that have strongly influenced the design of America's legal system two are preeminent: the civil law and the common law.

The distinction between civil law and common law is significant to legal scholars and students of the law. To notaries and the public generally, the distinctions are usually of little interest. In a nutshell, the civil law is a collection of written rules and sanctions. The common law, on the other hand, is comprised of evolving principles and rulings derived from court judgments and findings. In the common law, the advancement of principles and rules of law are built upon each other, like stacking bricks to construct a wall.

In the United States today, the laws of the fifty states are a seamless blending of common law and civil law. One state, Louisiana, prides itself as the only state that still goes by civil law in governing notarizations and the scope of the notary's authority.

Law has always co-existed with man. Humans have always banded together. Humans created rules to live by so all would know what was considered acceptable behavior within the group. Man eventually began to write down the rules so they would not be readily disputed, miscommunicated, or changed. The earliest rules of law were based on religious principles, upholding the dignity of man, the sanctity of marriage and family, and the respect for property. The Ten Commandments are among the best known of these.

Ancient dynasties were ruled by iron-fisted royalty who handed down strict laws governing how their people would live their lives. These rules were codes of behavior and conduct. The Code of Hammurabi and the Code of Justinian exemplify the collective laws controlling civil behavior.

Early civilizations are particularly noted for the sophistication and scholarly nature of many of their written codes. Codes of laws were the accepted method for enacting regulations and strictures on their societies. The ancients Greeks and Romans mastered codification of law. Each succeeding civilization thereafter built upon the history, traditions and laws of the preceding civilization. In the earliest periods of the Dark Ages, Europe, Germany, France and Spain had compiled their respective collections of laws in their Civil Codes.

In the year 1066, the Normans conquered England. The Kings of England dispatched their magistrates across the land to enforce the laws of the kings. As the magistrates traveled from town to town, they were frequently called upon to settle disputes among the locals. Often, these disputes were between powerful families of the area. As judges, the king's magistrates were not influenced by threats from litigants seeking to throw the magistrate's decision in their favor. The magistrates had the full faith and credit of the kings, along with their protection. Hence, magistrates were quite independent and effective in settling disputes.

As this system of adjudication progressed, problems with consistency and precedence began to surface. Problems with deciding which laws to apply became increasingly complicated. The rules of law they did have were brought from the European continent and were primarily unwritten and in the form of traditions. The magistrates operated in a disordered and vexing legal environment.

Whenever possible, the magistrates would base their decisions on the unwritten body of law that was most commonly understood and familiar to most of the population. This minimized dissension and perplexing questions. The widespread reliance on the commonly understood unwritten traditional laws evolved into what we call the "common law." As the magistrates handed down their decisions it became customary to record them. This then gave rise to the legal principles of consistency and precedence in the application of law to resolving disputes. The magistrates gave great weight to the recorded decisions by fellow magistrates.

The important legal doctrine called "stare decisis" came to be wherein the magistrates, and subsequently judges of the courts, would bind themselves to precedence. The adherence to precedence is a major distinguishing feature of the common law.

In the civil law, judges are not bound by precedence. The civil law judge must adhere to the written law and rely on it before it considers prior court decisions. In civil law jurisdictions, precedence is looked to for guidance in good legal reasoning, but the court relies for the most part on the written law. In the civil law systems, there is little precedence-setting by the courts. Moreover, in order for there to be comprehensive coverage of all important aspects of society's conduct under the law, the government is burdened with having to legislate more extensively than in most common law systems. The law code must provide rule of law contemplating the nearly infinite variety of legal disputes and issues that can arise. In common law systems, the codified law works hand-in-hand with the common law. Courts are authorized to create new law by casting out or ignoring written law. The common law system recognizes that neither the codified laws nor the precedence of case decisions are perfect.

The civil law is born of traditions thousands of years old, while the common law is a relative newcomer. The United States (except for Louisiana), English-Canada, and all lands of the British Commonwealth are common law jurisdictions. All of Latin America, Europe, Africa, most of Asia and Quebec are under the civil law system.

In civil law countries, notaries are high public officials empowered with broad legal authority and responsibility. In most countries, the notary is a prominent attorney attaining the notarial appointment after having distinguished himself in the profession of law. In these civil law countries, most notaries are men, whereas in the United States most notaries are women.

In this new millennium, the distinction between civil law and common law in America is so blurred that it is of little consequence, except to the notaries of Louisiana. All states codify their laws. In all states, even in Louisiana, the principle of stare decisis plays a vital role in case law. The federal courts nationwide rely on case law precedence and the written federal code of laws. We have come a very long way from the days of the Kings' magistrates.

Civil Liability
See Liability

Coercing the Document Signer
See Duress; Pressure to Notarize; Willful, Free Making of the Signature

Commission Expiration Date
See Defacto Notary Doctrine; Notarial Powers and Authority

In all states but Louisiana, notaries serve for a fixed term of years. The length of term for notaries is set by statute in each state. Most notarial commissions run for four years, some states commission notaries for five or three years. In Louisiana, notaries have a life-long commission.

A notary's commission expiration date is important because only within the authorized time frame of the commission does a notary have the authority to act. Notaries who perform notarial acts before they are commissioned or after their commission expires and is not renewed violate their state's laws. As a general rule, such notarial acts are considered void. In many states, statutes provide that such conduct will not invalidate the documents on which the unauthorized notarizations were performed.

Most states require by statute that the notary write onto their notarial certificates their commission expiration dates. Often, this appears in the notary's seal. Commonly it is written, stamped or printed below the notary's signature if it is not in the notary's seal. It is also common for pre-printed notarial certificates to provide a labeled space in which the notary is directed to write out their commission expiration date. Notaries in states where the commission expiration date is required to appear in the notary seal can ignore that pre-printed directive. Forms designers will inadvertently create redundancies from time to time. Notaries are subject to the provisions of their state's notary laws, and not to the idiosyncrasies of pre-printed forms.

There is ample merit to requiring notaries to disclose their commission expiration dates on their notarial certificates or seals. It informs the reader and all parties to the notarization that the notary was acting within their term of commission when performing officially. Disclosure of this important information eliminates uncertainties that can detrimentally affect the transaction.

Commission of a Notary

See Notarial Powers and Authority

A person cannot serve as a notary unless they have been granted the authority to serve by the state government. This grant of authority is usually called a "commission." Some areas of the country refer to it as a notary appointment. The term, commission, is the more appropriate term because of the definitional implications the term carries.

When the state government commissions a notary, the state is passing to the individual important legal powers, rights and responsibilities. The commission, by definition, also constitutes a charge to the recipient to carry out all duties with precision and care, to perform in compliance with the rules of law.

When a person is commissioned by a higher authority, it constitutes a form of directive to go forth and to carry out certain duties on behalf of that higher entity. For example, military officers are commissioned by Congress to lead and administrate on behalf of the United States. Notaries are commissioned to act on behalf of their respective states. A notary commission is a placement of trust in the individual by the state government. The commission to serve as a notary renders the notary an agent of the state government, to represent it well and to perform this state government duty with competence.

Commission Resignation
See Resigning as a Notary

Commissioning Process
See Qualifications for Appointment to the Office of Notary Public; Right to Serve as a Notary

In all fifty states, notaries are commissioned by the state government. Also, in every state, the individual must voluntarily apply for a commission. Every state requires the submission of official application forms completed by the applicant. A number of states require the notary to complete a written examination and attain a passing score. A few states even require a minimum number of classroom hours of notarial procedure training before the applicant can be considered for notarial commission.

Every person has a constitutional right to serve as a notary, if they meet minimum qualifications. Therefore, the government's review of a person's application for commission must be done with the highest standard of objectivity, fairness and impartiality. Every application must be reviewed and processed equally.

The fundamental objective in requiring people to apply to become a notary is three-fold: first, to satisfy the inherent requirement that a person be commissioned by those having legal authority to extend notarial powers to others; second, to provide orderliness to the implementation and administration of notarial services within a state; and third, to require the applicants to provide verification of their minimum qualifications to serve.

Although it is rare, the notary application process may be more rigorous than allowed by law in some states. Because the application form coming from the government directly implicates the applicant's constitutional right to serve if qualified, the government shall not require more information or qualification than the law allows on the application and its review. The notary commission application may seem to be a convenient vehicle for the state to gather up information about the applicant that is inappropriate. For example, the application should not ask how long the applicant has lived in the state, or what foreign languages the applicant speaks, reads or writes. The state is on thin ice when asking an applicant's gender and age. Most states are prohibited from commissioning people as notaries who have ever been convicted of crimes. The state may ask if the applicant has been convicted of a crime, but may not ask for details or explanation.

When an applicant receives from the government their commission certificate or written notice they are approved to be a notary, the commission vests with the applicant. From that point on, the person is in possession of all the authority and powers granted by state law to notaries.

Common Law
See Case Law; Civil Law Notary

One of the great bodies of law in America is what is called the "Common Law." The common law is a system of elementary rules and general declarations from the courts that continually expands with progress in society so it adapts itself to changes in commerce, technology, the arts and environment. It is a body of law founded largely in custom, common consent and usage. It is the application of sound reasoning to issues of law. Common law has long been recognized and acquiesced to by courts for centuries. It is even acknowledged in the words of the Seventh Amendment of the U.S. Constitution.

Common Law Notary
See Civil Law Notary

Common Sense
See Duty of Care; Reasonable Care

The most important attribute a person can bring to their commission as a notary, second only to a firm commitment to integrity, is common sense. Society cannot sustain itself if it has to look to the law for the answer to every question or problem. It is anathema to a free people to be directed in all things. Rather, it is the hallmark of an enlightened and educated society to govern itself through reliance on its values, mores and common sense.

The notary law is premised on the expectation that notaries will exercise common sense in serving the public and in solving notarial problems. The notary law is not intended to provide the answer to every problem. Notaries are expected to apply their common sense when faced with a dilemma. Common sense is one of the key elements of the standard of reasonable care. Common sense presumes the adherence to high standards of ethical conduct and to unyielding commitment to integrity.

Our individual common sense begins with us at birth and grows along with us through life's experiences. Common sense is the accumulation of life's lessons we learn. Cynics have stated, "common sense isn't very common." But conventional wisdom tells us that common sense is the set of unwritten rules we all know and are expected to follow. It is integral to the legal standard of reasonable care.

Competence to Sign
See Signer's Competence; Willful, Free Making of a Signature

When a person makes their signature on a document, that signature represents the person's intent to be bound by or to acquiesce to the terms and content of the document. Requisite to the formation of a person's intent is the condition precedent of cognition. The person must know and appreciate that which they are doing. Competence is conditioned by a person's age and maturity, educational level and mental health. Minor children, as a matter of law, are not competent to enter into binding contracts. Severely mentally ill persons are often not competent to account for their criminal deeds. The severely aged person suffering from senility may be incompetent to sign their living will.

The issue of competence is a complex and often difficult standard to define in law. Yet, competence is so crucial to so many contexts of the law. Criminal defendants must be competent to stand trial. To be found guilty of most crimes, the jury must find that the defendant intended to commit the crime and knew his conduct would produce the results that occurred.

In order for persons to enter into binding contracts, the parties to the contract have to manifest their intent to be bound by the contract terms. This, of course, is best done by signing the written contract.

For a signature to a document to be valid, the signer must know what the document is. Inherent to knowing a document's identity is the signer's possession of a modest idea of what the document is designed to accomplish. For purposes of notarizing signatures, the signer's competence to sign need not be nearly as strong as the defendant's competence to stand trial. If the requisite standards for signer competence were any higher, it would be a formidable, if not impossible, task for notaries to bear.

Ascertaining a person's depth of competence requires complex and sophisticated medical and mental health science. Even the experts will reach conflicting findings of fact. If notaries were required to apply the same level of skills and expertise of the professionals to measure signer's intent, the office of notary would no longer be occupied by the average public. Such a burden would crushingly extinguish the heart of the notarial service. That is, the notarial office would no longer be of the public in service to the community. And that would prove a tragic disservice to every American and to law and commerce.

Fortunately, the legal standard notaries must address concerning signer competency is reasonable and logical. Simply, the notary must find from observation and interaction with a document signer that they know what the document is as they proceed to sign it. Rather than expecting the notary to subject the signer to extensive examination and batteries of tests to assess competence, society in the alternative imputes to the notary a modicum of reasonableness and common sense. As a matter of public policy, the signer is presumed to possess a modicum of understanding as to the effects or consequences a document may have if the signer knows what the document is.

This standard is reasonable and is based on conventional human experience. If a person declares they will climb Mount Everest, we are entitled to assume the person is aware of the extensive equipment needed to do such things, along with the dangers and risks of such a climb. If a person declares they will rob a bank, we are entitled to assume the person understands the criminal nature of his plan and the legal consequences for his actions. If society were unable to presume the statements and actions of people were done knowingly with intent, based on our human experience with fellow beings, we as people and as a society would be utterly dysfunctional.

In assessing a signer's competence to sign a document for notarization, the notary is under the duty of law to exercise reasonable care. The notary is the commissioned officer of the state empowered to make determinations of signer competence. Excellent procedures have been articulated and proven that notaries can invoke when identifying a signer's competence to sign. These procedures fully constitute reasonable care on the notary's part.

1.   The notary should routinely converse with every person requesting a notarization. The conversation should be light and pleasant. While in conversation, the notary is able to observe if there is any indication of diminished mental capacity on the signer's part. If none is observed, the notarization can proceed.

2.   If the notary observes in the course of conversation, or is informed the signer suffers from a mental impairment, the notary should incorporate in the conversation carefully phrased probative questions about the document to be signed and notarized. Such questions must be open-ended, answerable only by phrases and complete thoughts. The notary is well served by asking the signer, "What is this document you are signing?" "Please tell me about your document. Why are you signing it?" These types of questions force the signer to articulate responses that manifest their awareness of what the document is, and their intent to sign thereto. It is failure for the notary to ask, "Are you of sound mind? Are you signing this document under your own free will and intent?" Such questions can be answered only by "yes" or "no," without any glimmer of evidence the signer is cognitive of the transaction.

3.   If the notary employs probative questioning of the signer, it is imperative the notary make a careful notation in the notary journal of such questioning. The inherent legal presumption is that if this effort of reasonable care is not recorded officially, it presumably did not take place. The document signer and person relying on the integrity of the transaction all have rights by law to expect the notary can substantiate by established procedures of

documentation that the notary properly and reasonably determined the signer was signing willingly and freely with intent.

When the notary has exercised reasonable care in determining a document signer is competent to sign for purposes of having the signature notarized, the burden of proof to establish the signer was not competent rests with the accuser. The accuser has a formidable task to overcome the legal presumption the notary conducted his assessment of the signer's competence with diligence, integrity and with due care. Should it be found the notary was mistaken in his assessment about the signer's competence, there should be no liability on the notary's part as long as the notary can provide documentation of having exercised reasonable care.

Completeness of the Notarial Certificate

See Completing the Notarial Certificate; Component Parts of the Notarial Certificate

The contents of notarial certificates are generally prescribed by law. Each required component of information is crucial to the certificate. A substantively incomplete notarial certificate is not valid. A person relying on the certificate may be harmed by his reliance on a defective, invalid certificate. The notary can be held liable for having passed off a substantively incomplete notarial certificate.

Completeness of the Signer's Document

See Blank Documents; Document Content; Signing for Purposes Stated Within the Document

It is a well-established rule of law that the notarization has no effect on a signer's document. The content of the signer's document is irrelevant to the notarization and is virtually outside the scope of the notary's rightful concern. Yet, it is often rumored that a notary should not notarize signatures on documents that are incomplete. A few states by statute provide that notarizations may be performed on completed documents only. In both circumstances, significant problems arise that cause considerable consternation among legal scholars and notaries alike.

The legal premise is firmly established that the content of the signer's document is irrelevant to the notarization. Therefore, it is not within the notary's legal purview to address the completeness of the document. Moreover, the idea of "document completeness" is a flawed concept. One cannot reasonably fix standards for when a document is complete or incomplete. The mere presence of blank spaces in a document does not in itself constitute incompleteness.

Business and legal forms are often designed to provide ample space for the user to write out all the information needed to satisfy the purpose of the form. If the form provides more space than the user needs, that does not render the form incomplete because space is left blank. On the other hand, a document may be filled with writing from top to bottom. It appears to be full and complete. However, crucial information may be omitted from the text of the document rendering it genuinely incomplete. Such a defect is invisible, never to be detected by the notary.

It is correct that in many transactions, it is imprudent for persons to sign documents that are obviously incomplete and unfinished. Once the signature is made, the signer is bound to the content of the document, some of which is to be written after the fact. It is fertile ground for fraud against the signer.

Some transactions in certain industries are routinely executed before the details are specified in the text of the document. These are judgment calls and conventions of various corners of commerce that are time-honored customs. In the context of law and potentials for legal liability, these practices may be of little concern or may constitute negligence. It is for the principal players to anguish over.

It is a slippery slope for notaries to get into the practice of addressing the completeness of signer's documents. It is beyond the scope of the notary's statutory functions and it is irrelevant to the notarial process. The concept of document completeness is ambiguous at best and potent with costly notarial intrusiveness.

Many well-informed people will declare that notaries must attend to the "completeness of the document," while intending to refer to the notarial certificate. By poorly phrasing this admonition, the hearer thinks the signer's document while the speaker thinks the notary's certificate. While the speaker is correct about the notarial certificate, it is often poorly communicated.

The notary is absolutely responsible for ensuring the notarial certificate is complete. This requires the notary to clearly understand the statutory requirements for a certificate's completeness. When the certificate is pre-printed in convoluted, verbose sentences, it is often impossible for an educated person to correctly complete the certificate. Moreover, they often provide spaces for information that has no relevance and may be left unfilled. While it is more prudent for the notary to substitute flawed certificates with their own, the notary may leave certificate spaces blank with the notation "N/A" for "not applicable."

Completing the Notarial Certificate

See Certificate of Notarization; Completeness of the Notarial Certificate; Component Parts of the Notarial Certificate

Every notarization and copy certification requires an official writing signed by the notary, and sealed where seals are required, certifying the facts contained and asserted within the certificate. State statutes define minimum information required for certificates to be valid. It is the notary's duty by law to ensure the notarial certificate is complete and true.

The notarial certificate is usually pre-printed for the notary. While the most common concern is that the certificate is poorly written and is difficult to decipher, the notary is often called upon to fill in blank spaces within the certificate. The spaces usually pertain to the date of the notarization, the name of the document signer for whom the notarization is being performed, and to the venue of the notarial act. It is most common for notaries to fill in the blanks by hand in ink.

When completing a notarial certificate, the notary should be mindful of the reader's need for legibility and clarity of information. Notarizations bear significant weight from the reliance people place on them. The notary's signature and seal to a certificate constitutes the notary's proclamation to the world that the information contained therein is true and complete. If the certificate is illegible or indecipherable, the notary and the certificate deserve rebuke. The purpose for notarizing is frustrated and the high purposes for notarizing are lost on the public.

It is human to make mistakes, especially on completing notarial certificates. For the most part, certificate errors can be corrected by the notary at any time upon its discovery. A new certificate need not be created, if the corrections can be made legibly and clearly.

Component Parts of the Notarial Certificate

See Acknowledgment Notarization; Completeness of the Notarial Certificate; Completing the Notarial Certificate; Copy Certification; Dating the Notarial Certificate; Jurat Notarization; Notarial Certificate; Notarial Seal; Official Signature; Venue

The notarial certificate is the legal instrument provided by state law that the notary is charged with creating to document and certify the truthful performance of a notarial act. Most states prescribe by statute the required information the certificate must contain. The components of notarial certificates are individually important. Collectively, they assert a series of facts that establish the verity of a person's signature to a document. In most cases, the omission of a required component of information will render the certificate incomplete, and potentially invalid.

When discussing notarial certificates, we address certificates of acknowledgments and jurats. The only certification a notary may execute is a copy certification. In all cases, these certificates must always declare the venue of the notarial act, the requisite notarial wording, the notary's signature, and the notary seal if required by state law.

The certificate venue is always required in order to establish jurisdiction in the courts should the notarization be subject to court action. Legal actions, in order to be heard, must be brought before courts of competent jurisdiction. Courts will have jurisdiction over an action if the court has jurisdiction over one of the parties to the action. The court will also have jurisdiction over an action if the transaction, event or property in dispute occurred in, or is located in, the territorial jurisdiction of the court. For this important purpose, the notarial certificate must always indicate the state and county in which the notarization is performed.

The notarial venue is widely misunderstood across America. Many notaries and their associates assume the venue statement is intended for the notary to disclose their county or city of residence. It is an unfortunate and incorrect assumption.

A number of states across the U.S. have organized themselves with jurisdictional subdivisions of cities and counties, or judicial districts or parishes. Notaries in those states and local jurisdictions are expected to accurately and truthfully disclose the location in which their notarizations are performed. For example, notaries in Alaska, where there are no counties, may declare the venue as, "State of Alaska, City of Anchorage," or "State of Alaska, Judicial District 3." Preprinted notarial certificate venues can be corrected to accurately portray the jurisdiction of the notarial act. The pre-printed certificate may provide, "State of Kansas, County of _____." The notary in Virginia may line out the name, Kansas, and write in the name, Virginia, along with the name of the local jurisdiction in which the notarization is performed.

The declarative wording of the notarial certificate must always indicate the date on which the notarization is performed, the name of the signer who personally appeared before the notary, and the declaration that the signer either acknowledged their signature to the notary, or signed their name to the document in the notary's presence after taking an oath or affirmation from the notary.

The certificate date is another often misunderstood element. Many assume the date to be written into the certificate is the date the document was signed or drafted. This is incorrect. The date to be provided in the notarial certificate is the date the signer personally appeared before the notary and acknowledged their signature or signed the document under oath before the notary.

Under no circumstance does a notarial certificate affect a document, hence there is never a justification for writing a date other than the date the signer appeared before the notary. The date of the notarial certificate is a material fact and is probative of the verity of the certificate itself. Many people assume the certificate date must match the document date, even though the document was signed before it is brought before the notary.

Suppose a document was signed January 7th and is stored in a file until August 4th, when it is brought to a notary for a notarization. As notarizations have no legal effect on the document itself, this document became effective and binding on its signer when it was signed January 7th. The notarization is performed nearly seven months later and shall be dated August 4th. While the document has been effective and binding since January, the signature has not been authenticated by a notary until August.

It is common for pre-printed notarial certificates to offer no mention of the document signer's name. As the notarial certificate is not part of the signer's document, it is derelict not to name the person whose signature is notarized. It is a material fact not to be left to conjecture. The body of the notarial certificate is nearly meaningless without the signer's name for which the asserted facts are made.

The heart of the notarial certificate is the proclamation that the signer either acknowledged their signature to the notary, or signed the document before the notary while under oath or affirmation. It is this factual assertion that sets the signer's signature apart as genuine. It is not unusual for flawed notarial certificates to erroneously state, "Subscribed and witnessed before me." This sort of statement misses the mark, and is below the standard notaries should follow.

Notarizations of signatures are performed singularly to certify the genuineness of the signatures. The facts asserted in the notarial certificate specifically establish the verity of signatures to the readers of the certificate. The document signer bears the legal burden to prove to the notary his signature on the document is genuine. The certificate therefore describes the signer's actions taken before the notary to satisfy that burden of proof. It requires nothing more than straightforward and clear wording accurately stating what the signer did. He either acknowledged his signature or took an oath or affirmation from the notary and signed the document while the notary watched. It is unfortunate when pre-printed notarial certificates are so laden with verbosity that the reader cannot reasonably decipher the material facts asserted by the certificate. It is always reasonable for the notary to decline to use such wording and substitute it with their own certificate written in clear declarative English.

Certificates of copy certification by notaries are not unlike acknowledgment and jurat certificates. The only difference is that no document signers are named or referenced. Rather, the notary declares in the first-person singular voice that a photocopy of a document is a true, correct, and complete copy of the item that was copied. It is well for the notary to indicate what the copy is made from, and perhaps who made the photocopy or reproduction. This set of asserted facts shall be signed by the notary and sealed, if required by the state law.

When a notary signs her notarial certificate and affixes a notary seal, the notary binds herself to that facts asserted within the certificate. The signature and seal constitute the notary's assertion that all facts are true and can be relied upon by any person. The notary is a public official and is required to sign the certificate in order to give the notarization full force and effect. In states where notary seals are required, the placement of the seal near the notary's signature legally "seals" the certificate as truthful and binding, bearing the full faith and backing of the state through its notary.

When correctly understood, a properly created notarial certificate is an impressive and meaningful instrument. It carries great significance on which people can reasonably rely. It sets the signer's transaction apart from the ordinary. Nearly worldwide, the notary's certificate will be recognized and honored as a bonafide governmental document created to authenticate the signature to the document. There is no defense in law for a false notarial certificate. It is incumbent for the notary to provide certificates that are simple, direct and readable. That serves everyone's best interests.

Compulsion
See Duress, Undue Influence; Willful, Free Making of a Signature

Conflict of Interest
See Disqualified Notary; Fiduciary Duty; Impartiality; Impartial Agent of the State

As a matter of law, the notary public is defined as an impartial witness to writings and agreements. The key word is "impartial." A notary has an absolute duty by law to act impartially when performing notarial duties. The issue of notarial impartiality is often debated and it consists of numerous complex sub-issues of considerable importance.

In order for there to be a conflict of interest, the notary must be in possession of at least two interests that are in conflict one with the other. By virtue of the notary's official position, the notary has a personal interest by law to perform the notarization objectively with integrity on behalf of the state. The notary's second interest must be of a nature that is personal to the notary; one that holds possibilities for the notary's personal benefit or gain. It need not be an interest that involves monetary gain. It can be an interest in becoming released from burdensome obligations, or an interest that would bring prestige or advantages to the notary. Hence, notarial conflicts of interest are struggles between objective performance of official duties and the opportunity for the notary to personally benefit from the transaction on which the notarization will be performed.

The often-quoted admonition against notarial conflicts of interest has been to strictly prohibit notaries from serving in transactions in which they have a conflict of interest. This perspective is based more on simplification than on sound legal reasoning. The former would be more reasonable if conflicts of interest were always crystal clear, identifiable and never vague. To the contrary, conflicts of interest are infinite in variety, are usually ambiguous, and rarely can two people fully agree on them. Conflicts of interest come in infinite degrees of severity and context. The potential for problems they create and the solutions for dealing with them are also countless. When attempting to articulate rules or guidelines for notaries on how to approach conflicts of interest, the poorest way is to advocate sweeping prohibitions. It ignores very helpful legal standards and obviates reality.

From the "Discussion of Notarial Conflicts of Interest" in 1 Am. Jur. 2d, Acknowledgments Section 16 at 458-59, we read:

> *"To hold that every interest renders the act ipso facto void is repugnant to sound principles of the law of evidence and in many cases must be productive of great hardship and injury. A more salutary rule declares that where there is no imputation or charge of improper conduct, bad faith, or undue advantage, the mere fact that the acknowledgment was taken before an interested officer will not vitiate the ceremony or render it void if it is otherwise free from objection or criticism. The fact of interest, however, ought to be*

regarded with suspicion and should provoke vigilance to detect the presence of unfair dealing, the slightest appearance of which the party seeking to uphold the acknowledgment should be required to clear away."

Once it is shown that a notary has a disqualifying conflict of interest in an instrument on which she notarized, and a suggestion of actual prejudice, unfair dealing, or undue advantage is raised by an adverse party, then the burden shifts to the notary or any party seeking to support the challenged document to demonstrate that no improper benefit was obtained and no harm occurred as a result of the disqualified act.

Among the states that statutorily address notarial conflicts of interest, the guidelines provided are generally helpful and reasonable. For example, these states typically prohibit notaries from notarizing on documents in which the notary's name or signature appears as a party to the transaction. Many of these states will also prohibit a notary's service if the notary will receive any financial or beneficial gain directly from the transaction. A number of states also prohibit notaries from notarizing for their family members.

In legislating these prohibitions for notaries, the states have created categories of ownership interests, or property interests, the notary's possession of which disqualifies the notary. Therein lies the better approach to conflicts of interest: notaries are expected to identify when they are disqualified from a notarial transaction.

Disqualification from notarizing typically arises when:

1. State statute prohibits service under specified circumstances;
2. The notary's name or signature appears in the document as a party to the transaction;
3. The notary will receive directly from the transaction any personal gain, benefit, right or privilege; or
4. In the event state statute prohibits it, the document signer needing a notarization is a member of the notary's family.

Conflicts of interest arguably exist to some degree in every notarization. Conflicts of interest are ubiquitous. It is in the notary's personal interest to preserve good standing with a supervisor at work by notarizing for the customers. The notary has a personal interest in maintaining friendly neighborly relations when asked to notarize for neighbors at home on weekends. These interests of the notary cannot possibly disqualify the notary from serving a document signer. However, they are personal interests nonetheless.

By focusing on disqualifications from notarizing by virtue of a property or ownership interest held by the notary we are better able to competently address the issue as it arises. Is the disqualification set by state statute, or is it up to the notary to decide? Will the notary receive a financial or beneficial gain directly from the transaction, or is the personal benefit indirect? Is the benefit or gain real and tangible, or is it speculative or a remote possibility? All of these considerations factor into the notary's decision.

Every person is endowed with his or her own sensitivity barometer. Our sensitivity to conflicting values varies from person to person. It is unreasonable to expect every notary to approach every conflict of interest the same way. Notaries are required as a matter of law to approach the subtleties of conflicts of interest, and disqualifications, with integrity and reasonable care.

By definition, a conflict of interest is the temptation to abuse one's position or authority to take personal advantage of a situation at the expense of the person being served.

> *"An officer or a person otherwise legally authorized to take acknowledgments is not qualified to act where he has a financial or beneficial interest in the proceedings or will acquire such an interest under the instrument to be acknowledged"*
> *- 1 Am. Jr. 2d Acknowledgments § 16 at 458.*

> *"Frequently it is said that this rule rests upon grounds of public policy, the purpose being to close the door to temptation to fraud. The office of notary is a 'position of public trust.'"*
> *-   Gombach v. Department of State, 692 A.2d 1127, 1132 (Pa. Commw. Ct. 1997).*

If a notary dutifully refrains from taking advantage of a situation that presents itself while notarizing, the notary has mooted the conflict of interest and moved on with integrity and diligence. The conflict of interest is short-lived. Its life span is as short as the time it takes for the notary to recognize a conflict of interest exists and to either refrain from notarizing, or to proceed to notarize with pure objectivity and integrity.

Part of the discussion on impartiality, objectivity and disqualifications has to consider the life cycle of these conditions. Is impartiality a state of mind that can be switched on and off like a light bulb? What about objectivity? Are these not attitudes and frames of mind we invoke as we perform official duties? Are they not directly connected to our personal levels of integrity and ethics? On the other hand, a notary's conflict of interest can be visible on the signer's document. If the notary proceeds to notarize with absolute objectivity, taking no advantage of the opportunity for self-dealing, that objectivity and integrity is invisible to the document reader later on. The appearance of evil is in print on the document. It could be cited as grounds for objection and rejection by third parties. In such circumstances, virtuous and high ethical conduct goes unnoticed, while circumstantial evidence can appear incriminating.

Notaries can take lessons from other public officials when faced with conflicts of interest. Judges are obligated to recuse themselves from cases. Politicians, on the other hand, are often waived from their conflicts of interest if they give timely and full public disclosure of their conflict. The city councilman may declare prior to a vote on a city road repair job, "my brother-in-law is a partner with ABC Company whose bid is before us. My vote will be strictly based on the bids and bidder qualifications."

Notaries are not afforded established means to moot their conflicts of interest by prior and full disclosure. The notary may freely add to the notarial certificate a written disclosure of their conflict and how they rose above it to perform objectively. The efficacy of this approach is untested and uncertain.

The standards judges must follow are much higher than the ones notaries are under. It is often said that a notary must never notarize for any transaction in which the notary has a personal interest, no matter how small or insignificant that interest may be. Of course, that can be a stretch from the rule of law. A notary is not under legal obligation to recuse herself from notarizing because of a conflict of interest. That obligation arises only with notarial disqualifications.

It is conventional wisdom that when a notary notarizes for a family member, the notary has a conflict of interest. Depending on the relation between notary and relative, a notary could stand to benefit ever so slightly by the well-being of family members. Successful transactions by immediate family members may affect the financial security of the family overall. On the other hand, unless the notary is a party to the relative's transaction or is banned by state statute from notarizing for this relative, the notary's personal interest in the transaction is indirect, if existent at all.

It is not unusual for a business or government entity to reject a notarization because the notary and signer are obviously related. Unless the notarization violated state law where it was performed, the rejecting party is acting out of emotion and tradition. They fail to understand the purpose in law for notarizations. We notarize signatures to establish that they are not forgeries made by imposters. The irony is that nobody knows the signer's true identity and genuineness of his signature better than a notary who is related to the signer! In reality, a notarization made for a family member can be one of the strongest forms of notarization.

When examining issues of conflicting interests for notaries, the discussion must take into balance the interests of the public and the document signers. The public has a substantial and important need for notarizations. Hence, the public has a substantial interest in the issue of notarial conflicts of interest. The public has a right to access notaries. If we overreact and apply an unreasonably stringent standard against conflicts of interest, the public interest can be harmed. Notarizations become unnecessarily difficult to come by, and transactions of all sorts bog down in a morass of well-meaning naysayers.

These two competing concepts must be balanced. While it is in the public interest to require objective, impartial notarizations, it is also in the public interest to adopt conflict of interest standards that are sensible, based on sound legal reasoning, and that are respectful of the notary's competence to make value judgments with integrity.

"The notary's disqualifying interest can result in voiding the instrument that has been notarized by him; in deciding whether to void the instrument, the court should consider whether improper benefit was obtained by the notary or any part to the instrument, as well as whether any harm flowed from the transaction; once it is shown that a notary has a disqualifying interest in the instrument which he acknowledged, and suggestion of actual prejudice, unfair dealing, or undue advantage is raised by an adverse party, the burden shifts to the notary or any party seeking to support the challenged document to demonstrate that no improper benefit was obtained and that no harm occurred as result of the disqualified act.

Where the notary has a disqualifying interest, the next question is the bearing this defect has on the validity of the instrument. We decline to follow the rule...which automatically voids a deed of trust because the trustee had acted as its notary. Such a rule can be unduly harsh, as illustrated by the facts of this case. The beneficiary of the deed of trust loses her security interest not because of any claim of wrongdoing, bad faith, or other improper conduct on her part, but solely on the basis that the notary was the trustee on the document.

If the primary purpose of the rule is to shield the parties from potential wrongdoing or fraud, then the focus of the inquiry should be shifted to this direction. Other jurisdictions have recognized the harshness of a per se rule, as evidenced by this summary from 1 Am. Jur. 2d Acknowledgments § 16 at 458-59:

To hold that every interest renders the act ipso facto void is repugnant to sound principles of the law of evidence and in many cases must be productive of great hardship and injury. A more salutary rule declares that where there is no imputation or charge of improper conduct, bad faith, or undue advantage, the mere fact that the acknowledgment was taken before an interested officer will not vitiate the ceremony or render it void if it is otherwise free from objection or criticism. The fact of interest, however, ought to be regarded with suspicion and should provoke vigilance to detect the presence of unfair dealing the slightest appearance of which the

party seeking to uphold the acknowledgment should be required to clear away."
- *Galloway v. Cinello, 188 W. Va. 266, 423 S.E. 2d 875 (1920).*

Conforming Copies
See Copy Certification

Photocopies of documents, unless altered, will always be a complete and true copy of the item copied. Copy machines do not produce fraudulent copies. Nevertheless, when photocopies are submitted for a business or legal purpose, it is common to require that the truthfulness of the copy be vouched for. This can be done formally by a notary copy certification, or by a conforming copy.

A conforming copy can be made by any person. It requires no particular authority or approval from another source. It is merely a signed written notation by an ordinary person that the photocopy is a true and complete copy. It does not require a notary seal or certificate.

In creating conforming copies with excellence, the person should place their written statement on the photocopy (front or back). It should include the date the copy was made, a statement that the copy is true and complete, and include the person's signature. If the copy is multi-paged, it is also prudent to indicate how many pages are in the copy.

Consanguinity
See Conflict of Interest; Notarizing for Relatives

This term refers to relationships between people by blood, being family members. Some states prohibit notaries by statute from notarizing for their spouse, their parents or children, or for all three groups. A few states prohibit notaries from notarizing for any person to whom they are consanguineally related. Prohibitions against notarizing for these groups are based on the premise that such acts present conflicts of interest for the notary.

Content of the Document
See Completeness of the Signer's Document; Signer's Right to Confidentiality and Privacy in Notarizations

Contest of the Notary Certificate
See Component Parts of the Notarial Certificate; Statutory Short Form Notarial Certificates

Copy Certification
See Conforming Copies

Among the several notarial acts notaries are authorized to perform in most states is the certification of photocopies. This valuable service has great value in society, law and commerce. We heavily rely on documents as evidence of certain facts or obligations made. The originals of many documents can be irreplaceable and are held in tight custody. The owner or custodian of the document does not release such originals. Only photocopies will be permitted thereof. To ensure the copy is true, correct, and complete, we rely on notaries or government officials to certify the verity of the copy.

When speaking of copy certifications, we speak of the copy and of the item that was copied. It can prove confusing and misleading to refer to the latter as the "original." Where copy certifications are specifically permitted by statute, the code usually refers to "the item that is copied" rather than the "original." The term, "copy," is likewise laden with a few incorrect assumptions. Many think that it refers only to copies made by photostatic technology (photocopiers). The term embraces any form of item or document reproduction. The photographic reproduction of a painting by camera film can technically be notary certified, as can reproductions of photographs from the same negative. Definitionally, a handmade reproduction of another item cannot be certified as a true, correct and complete copy of that item because handwork is always unique in its creation, making it a new original. It may mimic or replicate.

When a document is referred to as the original that inherently means that the document spoken of is uniquely the first one of its exact kind and that all subsequent reproductions or versions are not originals. Faulty use of the nomenclature can lead to failed communication. The most frequent defect in discussing this topic is the tendency for people to refer to the item that was copied as the original, when in fact it was not the original.

Today's newspaper, for example, was produced in tens of thousands of copies, but there may in fact not be an original. The entire content of today's paper may reside in a computer database from which multiple copies are made. A person's college transcript may also reside on the university's computer database. If the registrar prints out a complete transcript record for a student, is that printout now the original? Perhaps it does not become the original until the registrar certifies in writing and with the university seal that it is genuine. In either case, how can something be the original if it is not uniquely the first and only one of its kind?

While this discussion may seem like hair-splitting, it is pertinent to a key point: the term, "original" carries too many ambiguities for it to be the preferred term when discussing copy certifications. The better term to employ is the "item that was copied." This allows for the inclusion of certifications of photocopies made of photocopies and for copies of items for which no originals exist.

The procedure for performing a copy certification is simple. The notary is legally obligated to ensure the photocopy is true, correct, complete and unaltered. The surest means is for the notary to make the photocopy or watch it being made. Although the third option is to compare the copy with the item that was copied, it is impractical.

When convinced the copy of the item is true, correct and complete, the notary affixes certification wording to the front or back of the copy with the notary's signature and seal, if required by state law. The certificate wording shall begin with the venue of the transaction, indicating the state and county where the certification is made. The certificate goes on to declare: *I, notary's name, certify this is a true, correct, complete copy of name of the document made by name of person who made the copy."* Then the certificate is signed by the notary and the notary's seal is affixed near the signature, if required by law.

A few states require the notary to indicate in the certificate wording that the document being copied is not a recordable instrument or the original of which is not obtainable from the official custodian of the record.

Copy certifications by notaries of recordable instruments are considered nationally to be unauthorized. A number of states have codified this prohibition in their notary statutes, while most have not. There is some difficulty and confusion in the national discussion of this issue because, again, the nomenclature is sometimes misused. It is an issue between "recordable" and "recorded" documents. A document that has been filed with a court, a county recorder or recorder of deeds, with the Secretary of State, the Bureau of Vital Statistics, or with the Circuit Court is a recorded document. It will usually be stamped by the government entity with a date and the name of the entity. Some entities retain the document in its archives, while others may electronically store it and return the original to the submitting party. Each of these entities are governed under different provisions of state statute. In most cases, those statutes provide that the entity shall provide certified copies of the documents in their custody to the public upon payment of a specified fee. When issued, these copies are either computer generated, or are photocopies, and they bear the seal of the government with a signature of the official having executive jurisdiction over that entity. These certified copies, for purposes of law and business, are as valid as the original. For purposes of clarity, these can be called, "government certified copies."

When the assertion is made that a notary shall not certify a copy of a recordable instrument, the issue takes on a new dimension. A "recordable" instrument may be a document that is eligible to be recorded, or is intended to eventually be recorded, or one that has already been recorded. The phrase, "recordable instrument" may not accurately communicate what is intended.

In selecting this phrase when enacting the statute, legislatures may have intended to forbid notaries from certifying copies of documents held in custody by government entities. Arguably, it could be a legal impossibility for the state to prohibit the notary from certifying any copies of documents that are recordable. In a very real sense, nearly any document is potentially recordable. Moreover, prohibitions against copy certifications of documents not yet recorded raises questions of potential chilling effects on first amendment rights.

The issue regarding bans on notary certified copies of recorded instruments goes on. While the opinion in support of the ban is repeated so frequently that it takes on the color of law, it may in fact not be a valid doctrine.

It is not unusual to find that the statutes governing a government agency, such as vital statistics, make no restrictions on copying instruments they certify and issue. In some jurisdictions, a state-issued birth certificate will declare on the face of the document that it is unlawful to copy the document. Yet, in those jurisdictions, no such prohibition can be found in statute or administrative rule to back it up.

Another concern is that a few states enact a policy that notaries in their jurisdiction shall not perform copy certifications because it is not one of the enumerated powers granted to notaries by the statute. The genesis of this opinion has old and deep roots in the history and philosophy of law. The theory behind this policy is that if the state desires to authorize a notary to perform certain functions, those functions must be specifically named and permitted in the statutes. Hence, if it is not one of the enumerated powers, it is deemed an unauthorized function.

America's legal community does not hold this school of thought universally. Many hold the opinion that it is unreasonable to require statutes to enumerate all functions businesses, citizens and government entities are authorized to perform. Arguably, that would be impractical and unreasonable. It would require extraordinary precedence to foresee the infinite variety of activities, advances in technologies and ideas, or the abandonment of antiquated services, and then legislate for them. It could conceivably result in many thousands of more pages of statutory text, and could require the government to micro-manage our activities.

If we carry the opinion favoring "enumerated powers only" to its logical extension and conclusion it could ultimately fail under its own weight.

A number of states specifically prohibit notaries from copy certifying anything that is held in custody by a government entity. The copy certification of such a document in those states constitutes official misconduct.

A few states hold that a copy certification is a form of notarization. The more recognized definition of a notarization states that it is the act of witnessing and authenticating a signature by an authorized official. However, many state statutes provide a definition of the terms "notarizations" and "notarial acts" by listing the functions a notary is authorized to perform, including the certification of copies. A few states interpret such definitions to categorize copy certifications as notarizations. In so doing, they impute to copy certifications the same limitations and legal standards they apply to signature notarizations. The notary is obligated to be keenly informed on her state's statutory and policy rules governing copy certifications.

A few states hold that a notary may not certify a copy of a document in which the notary has a financial or beneficial interest. The majority view, however, is that copy certifications by notaries are strictly content-neutral, mooting the concern over notarial conflicts of interest when performing such acts. This view is premised on the concept that a copy certification does nothing more than certify that the copy reproduction is flawless and identical to the item that was copied.

In the absence of recent and instructive case law authority to help clarify the bright line on copy certifications and the authority of notaries to perform them, statutory law remains the most compelling framework. The policy interpretations among the states will weigh heavily, as well.

Correcting Notarial Certificates

See Completeness of the Notarial Certificate; Completing the Notarial Certificate; Component Parts of the Notarial Certificate

The notarial certificate is the document by which the notary certifies a series of facts in order to verify and attest to the veracity of a signature to a document. The notary is personally responsible for every word of the certificate, its truthfulness, accuracy and its completeness. If errors are made in the certificate and are discovered, the notary has a duty by law to correct such errors.

Procedures for correcting errors to notarial certificates are rarely specified in state statute or administrative rule. However, conventional wisdom provides that the notary has broad discretion on how to make such corrections. On one extreme, the notary may line out the entire defective certificate and replace it with a correct form. In the alternative, the notary may line out only the errors and re-write them in the margins or between the lines.

While neatness is not a standard of law, the legibility of the notarial certificate is very important. Some transactions require neatness, while others can tolerate corrections written in margins. The notary should apply common sense when deciding how to correct or replace defective notarial certificates. If a new certificate is used as a replacement for the flawed version, it is prudent to indicate at the site of the defective wording that a replacement has been used and is found either on the attached page or on the reverse side. Many notaries prefer to write their initials next to every notation and correction made. This is not required by law, but is consistent with the spirit of full and candid disclosure all notaries should embrace.

Corrections to notarial certificates can be made at any time prior to the time the terms, conditions or intent of the document vests in a third party. That is, until such time the document is filed and is accepted for public record, or becomes part of the docket file in a lawsuit, or has been acted upon by other parties, a notary can make corrections to a certificate if it is accessible. Under no circumstance may a notary make a substantive change to the certificate, as that would constitute fraud. The only justification for a notary making corrections to a certificate is where the error is such that persons relying on the certificate contents could be misled by the error. Corrections are also important where a component of the certificate that is required by law, such as a notary seal or notary signature, is omitted.

Counterfeit ID

See Identification Cards and Papers; Identity of the Signer; Signer Identification

One of the primary threats against the security of document signatures is the signer's presentation to the notary of counterfeit ID. There is a growing threat and concern over personal identification theft in the United States and worldwide. Not only is valid ID alterable to resemble the thief, it is surprisingly easy to counterfeit by skilled counterfeiters. American currency, even with the new "counterfeit resistant" designs, is the ultimate challenge for counterfeiters. For the most skilled, it is relatively easy to accomplish. Personal ID cards, on the other hand, are child's play for the experienced ID thieves.

The incidence of counterfeit ID varies in volume from region to region of the United States. However, it is a focal point for every notary to vigilantly guard against. It requires the notary to be observant, sensible, straight thinking, and informed.

Notaries are not under the duty of law to identify counterfeit ID. Rather, the notary is under the duty of reasonable care to guard against the use of counterfeit ID for obtaining a notarization. The notary is not a law enforcement officer or a trained detective. Even law enforcement can't identify much of the counterfeit ID in use across the country because it is such high quality. If the notary exercises reasonable care in scrutinizing a signer's ID, that notary will be presumed to have fulfilled her duty under law, even if the ID was a high quality counterfeit. Without this presumption in law, no reasonable person would notarize for the public they did not personally know.

When a signer presents his ID to the notary, the notary is obligated to look at the ID carefully. It must match the bearer and reasonably represent the bearer by its photo, physical description and possibly the bearer's signature. It must bear no indications of having been altered or tampered with. It should indicate the source of its issuance, and all logos or official markings should be printed clearly and crisply.

When a notary is presented with suspicious or obviously counterfeit ID, the notary must refuse to notarize and withdraw diplomatically. Depending on the circumstances, a notary may be obligated to notify law enforcement about the incident.

Credible Witness
See Signer Identification

Signer identification must be based on the most reasonably solid evidence. Second in strength to knowing the signer personally is the notary's reliance on a credible witness to attest to the notary the signer's identity.

A credible witness is a third person whom the notary must personally know, and who personally knows the document signer. The credible witness must attest to the notary under oath or affirmation as to the signer's true identity and that the signer is personally known to the witness. Credible witnesses do not attest to the signer's signature or to their document. They attest to the signer's identity only. An appropriate oath or affirmation to administer to the credible witness is, "Do you swear or affirm that this is Jane Doe and that you know her personally?"

The credible witness should be a person the notary knows personally, very well. The notary needs to be satisfied the witness has a solid reputation for integrity and that he understands the nature of the oath he is taking. The notary should also be cautious when using a credible witness who has an apparent conflict of interest in the transaction or with the document signer. A notary's failure to reasonably address the witness's apparent conflict of interest may jeopardize the notarization and render the notary liable in the event damages result from a failed transaction.

The issue of conflicts of interest among credible witnesses is most acute where the document signers are husband and wife. Employers, supervisors or clients may represent to the notary the co-signer is his wife, while in fact it is his mistress who intends to forge the wife's signature to the document. Even if the notary administered the credible witness oath to the husband, the self-obvious conflict of interest may mitigate against the notary's attempted exercise of reasonable care. In such situations, it is better for the notary to ask the co-signer for photo ID, and not rely on a credible witness in that circumstance.

When utilizing a credible witness, the notary should record the witness's name in the notary journal entry pertaining to that notarial act. Some notaries prefer to have the witness sign the journal along with the document signers. Such may be prudent, depending on the nature of the notary's work environment or nature of transactions most frequently notarized. However, it is not viewed as a requirement.

Credible Witness Liability

A credible witness can be held liable for perjury and for damages caused by a notarization where the witness falsely identified the signer. The credible witness plays an important role in the notarial process of identifying document signers. It must be undertaken with utmost integrity.

There is no limit to the liability a credible witness may be under for falsely swearing to the identity of a document signer. Moreover, the commission of perjury, a false statement made under oath, bears serious criminal sanctions under the law as well. It is utterly impossible for a credible witness to bear any risk of liability if they are truthful in their affirmation of a signer's identity.

A credible witness may be mistaken about a signer's identity. However, the witness swears to that identity. While mistaken identity is not unheard of, the witness needs to genuinely know the signer personally. It is personal knowledge of the signer, attained through interaction with the person over time, which makes it sufficient to eliminate all reasonable doubt in the witness's mind as to the signer's true identity. Under that standard, a credible witness cannot be liable if the signer is an imposter.

An example of notarial breach of the standard of care in the use of a credible witness is found in the case, City Consumer Services v. Metcalf (775 p.2d 1066). The notary was an attorney who notarized a property deed transferring a wife's ownership interest in a family home to her husband. The husband appeared in the notary's office and introduced a woman accompanying him as his wife. The husband handed the deed to the notary bearing the wife's signature and it was dated. The notary did not ask the woman if she was the individual who previously signed the deed, request that the woman present identification, or obtain an acknowledgment of her signature. Instead, the notary relied on the husband's representation that the woman was his wife. The notary then changed the date on the deed and notarized it.

The Arizona Supreme Court held in this case that the notary breached his duty of care by failing to perform his duties as prescribed by Arizona law. The court also held that the notary was liable because he wrongfully relied upon the mere introduction of the alleged woman signer by her alleged husband, whom the notary did not know personally. In no way could the attorney-notary utilize the husband as a credible witness to attest to the identity of the woman signer.

74

Crime
See Criminal Capacity

The statutes and ordinances of federal, state and local governments define certain actions as crimes. They may be actions taken by offenders that harm other people, harm property, harm themselves, or promote harm to society generally. Some crimes may constitute a person's failure or refusal to engage in a certain act. When a person violates such a provision of law, that person commits a crime. Notarizing falsely is a crime.

Criminal Capacity
Every human being is presumed to be endowed with the natural capacity to discern right from wrong. Therefore, it is presumed that unless proven otherwise, a criminal violator generally knows and appreciates that their bad acts are wrong.

Notaries are under a stronger standard than this. When becoming a notary, an oath of office is taken promising to obey the notary laws of the state. The inherent requisite in that statement is that the notary understands correct notarial procedures and is competent to discern wrongful notarial conduct from correct conduct.

Curing Defective Notarial Certificates
See Completing the Notarial Certificate; Correcting Notarial Certificates

Current ID
See Identity of the Signer

Cyber-Notary
See Digital Notarizations

D

Indeed, being able to rely on documents is the purpose of having them notarized... If business cannot depend on notaries doing [the] simple task [of properly identifying document signers and administering a proper oath to them], then there is no place for notaries in the world of commerce.
- Florida District Court of Appeal, 1996.

Dates
See Dating the Notarial Certificate

Dating the Notarial Certificate
See Component Parts of the Notarial Certificate

Among the important facts a notary certifies with a signed notarial certificate is the date the notarial act was performed. When the date of the certificate is knowingly falsified, the notarization's validity is jeopardized and the notary risks legal liability.

The certificate date is important because it evidences a material fact that is pertinent to the verity of the notarial certificate. It is not unusual for notaries to be directed to backdate or postdate a certificate so it will conform to the date of a closing on a transaction. Such conduct is illegal and constitutes fraud. It is false information intended to deceive others. Some may argue that this is a minor issue of little consequence. That position is completely untrue.

When the legal implications of a notarial certificate are correctly understood, most will insist on the truthful declaration of certificate date. They understand that a notarial certificate has no effect on a signer's document. It does not make the document legal, valid, true, or enforceable. Hence, the date of the notarial certificate never needs to match the date of the document's creation, particularly if the document signature is to be notarized by acknowledgment. If the signature to be notarized is done by jurat, the signer must sign the document under oath in the notary's presence. It may have been pre-signed, but it must be signed again, while under oath. The document will have been effective upon the original signing, but will now be notarized at a subsequent date with a jurat certificate. The jurat certificate may not match the date of the document or the date of the original signature if such a date would be a false representation.

Decisional Law
See Case Law

De facto Notary Doctrine
See Commission Expiration Date

In all probability, a significant number of notarizations are performed in the United States each year by notaries whose commissions, unbeknownst to them, have expired. If the notary performs a notarization in good faith, while unaware that her commission has expired, the common law principle of the de facto notary doctrine will probably allow the notarization to be held as valid by a court. This doctrine by law is intended to allow for fair outcomes where circumstances permit.

> *"When a notary in good faith does not know or realize that the commission has expired, and when a document signer is also unaware of that fact, there are only two possible effects on the notarization. It is either valid, or it is invalid. If the notarization were found to be invalid, the notary's mistake would be visited upon the innocent document signer. That does not seem like the right thing to do, especially since the invalid notarization might invalidate the instrument on which it appears and in turn invalidate the underlying transaction of which the instrument is a part. A notary's neglect could topple an otherwise valid transaction.*

A document signer or other consumer seeking some kind of notarial services should not have the responsibility to accurately determine the legal status of the notary's commission. The law has not imposed this duty upon the document signer or consumer even if the notary seal is imprinted with the commission expiration date (and most states either do not require notary seals to include the commission expiration dates or do not require notaries to use seals at all).

Incidentally, the de facto notary doctrine is a form of the broader de facto official doctrine, that applies to other public officers whose authority has ceased without them realizing it. Thus, if example, a county clerk's, police officer's, or judge's term in that post had terminated without the individual realizing it, and each continued to act, the law would generally find that their actions were nevertheless valid.

But, it needs to be emphasized that there is no bright line test for either the de facto official doctrine or the de facto notary doctrine. When circumstances change, the result may change. Thus, the longer the official or notary continues to act after the term has expired, the less likely the law will uphold the acts. If there were some special reason to conclude the notary or the document signer knew or should have known of the commission's expiration, the law probably would reach a different outcome. Each case will turn on its particular circumstances."

    - Law Professor Michael L. Closen, The De Facto Notary Doctrine and How to Avoid Tardy Notarizations, The Notary, May 2001 at p. 4.

Defense
See Legal Defense Against Liability

Defense Against Liability
See Legal Defense Against Liability

Deposition
A witness in a legal proceeding can issue written testimony to be submitted as evidence in the legal proceeding. The deposition is usually created in response to written or oral questioning or examination of the witness. The witness's testimony is given under oath and is recorded and

transcribed, usually by a certified court reporter. The transcription is certified to be a true, correct and complete transcription of the deposition. In most states, notaries are authorized to administer the statutory oath to the person whose deposition is being taken. In some states, notaries are authorized to record and transcribe the deposition.

Derision of the Notary Office

It is easy to belittle that which we do not understand. The majority of the public does not understand the legal function and purposes of notarizations. Many assume that a notary performs a minor technical detail of little significance. That, of course, is completely incorrect.

Because so many assume notarizations are minor details, they will assume the notary is free to "cut corners" in order to expedite a needed notarization. It is the interest of every business and professional not to inconvenience the customer or client. When a required notarization is in order, the temptation is great to disregard certain mandatory steps.

Particularly disturbing are occasions where supervisors or employers deride the notary for insisting upon complying with the statutory procedures for performing notarizations. Every notary is an official of the state government that has appointed him or her. The notary's services are governmental and are services of the private sector. Every employer and supervisor of notaries is jointly and severally liable for all wrongful notarizations performed in the workplace. Moreover, when a person in an employment position superior to the position of the notary pressures or coerces a notary to perform in violation of state law, that person is guilty of criminal conduct and is potentially liable to the notary for injuries caused by such coercion and pressure.

Derision of the notary office is unmistakable evidence of a significant lack of knowledge of the role in law notary's play. It also constitutes an unfortunate manifestation of attitude that compliance with law and integrity are available for compromise. It severely discredits the person who derides.

Destruction of the Notary Seal

In every state, as a person who terminates their notary service by resignation or by expiration of commission, the person is required either to destroy their notary seal or submit the seal to the state or county clerk for its disposal.

The notary seal represents significant legal authority. In most states the possession of a notary seal by a person who is not a notary constitutes a significant criminal violation of law. As a matter of prudence and reasonable care, the notary is obligated to destroy the seal at the end of service to prevent having the seal find its way into the hands of unscrupulous people.

Where seal destruction or reconveyance to government is required by statute but the requirement is ignored, the notary may be exposed to some risk of liability for injury caused by an imposter or forger fraudulently using the seal.

Detrimental Reliance on the Notarization
See Notarizing Falsely; False Notarizations

This phrase is primarily used in the context of contract law. It is argued that the performance of a notarial service constitutes a form of contract. When a person asks for a notarization, they ask for the performance of a service or act. Upon performing the notarization, the person making the request relies on the notarization as being legally and correctly performed. He relies on this to his detriment because he forbears any additional opportunities to have it notarized by others. He stakes his risk on the belief that the notarization is valid and will not jeopardize his business transaction.

The document signer incurs a detriment when he accepts the notary's commitment to perform the notarization. The detriment is the customer's forbearance from seeking other notaries to perform the act, and his forbearance for concerning himself with the validity of the notarization. He accepts the notarization, at his risk, as being valid and enforceable.

When a notary has notarized wrongfully, the document signer has detrimentally relied on the notary's representation that the notarization is valid. The notary now faces liability for having failed to perform competently and thoroughly as represented to the document signer.

80

Dialogue with the Document Signer

See Competence to Sign; Signer's Competence; Willful, Free Making of a Signature

The notarization of a signature inherently stipulates that the signature was made willingly and freely. A signature is willful and free if it is made without undue coercion or duress. Moreover, a signature is willful and free if the signer knows what the document is when he signs it.

It is a well-established legal principle that the notary must exercise reasonable care in the performance of every step in notarizing a signature. When it comes to ascertaining whether a signer signs willingly and freely, the notary is obligated to engage the signer in dialogue. The give and take in conversation reveals much about the person's mental acuity. While in the course of the conversation, it may be necessary for the notary to ask the signer about the document. The notary would do well to ask probative questions of the signer, such as, "What is this document you plan to sign?" This question requires the signer to assemble his thoughts and articulate or manifest an answer that is relevant to the question. Questions that can be answered "yes" or "no" are of little value, as they require little, if any, mental cognition to answer.

If a person cannot demonstrate to the notary they know what their document is, the notary should not notarize for them. A signature made to something the signer cannot identify is an invalid signature. The validity of the signature is dependent on the signer's intent to sign the document. By definition of law, there cannot be any intent to sign a document if the signer does know what the document is.

Digital Notarizations

Federal legislation enacted in 2000, along with legislation in a growing numbers of states, have given authorization for the use of electronic signatures in paperless, computer-based transactions, particularly with online systems. As America's economy increasingly becomes online dependent, it is essential for the government to establish a secure system by which contracts, conveyances, and restricted access to confidential files can be conducted electronically with the same protections that written, signed notarizations and verifications of parties' identities provide. The technology to fill this need is referred to variably as "digital notarizations and signatures" or "electronic notarizations and signatures." Electronic notaries have picked up the moniker, "cyber notaries."

Digital notarization technology derives its validity in law from the individual states and the federal government under enacted law. The technology is based on dual public and private-key cryptography. Through a sophisticated relationship between government and private entities, secure numeric codes are authorized and assigned by secured methods and are digitally entered as signatures and notarizations to transactions.

Digital notaries are notaries public. As provided by state statutes, notaries derive the additional authority to notarize digitally from the state. Following specified procedures a notary can apply to obtain digital notarization authority. It cannot be self-appointed by the notary. In order for the digital notarial service to enjoy integrity of security, it must be properly controlled and administered by the state government. Carefully crafted policies, procedures and instruction must be established in order to create the requisite level of trust people must have in the system for it to be accepted in commerce.

Digital notarizations and signatures have the potential to save businesses and consumers a great deal of time and money. Online forms that require signatures usually have to be printed, signed in ink and mailed to the recipient. With digital signatures, any form can be completed and legally signed and notarized electronically. Real estate deeds, stock transfers, and filings with court, to suggest but a few uses, are good examples of how electronic signatures and notarizations can save time and money and reduce errors.

As in most substantial transactions, proof of identity of the document signers is essential to the security of the transaction. Notaries fulfill that role by having the signer personally appear before the notary to verify signer identity. That notarial process continues under the electronic notarization. Although document signers may sign electronically by numeric code, their identity verification is done face-to-face by the notary who, in turn, digitally notarizes the digital signature of the customer.

The concept of digital notarizations and signatures faces the daunting dilemma of matching new technologies with laws on the books that are generations old. The learning curve and the growth curve will be long and plodding. Until the frequency of use of electronic signatures become statistically substantial throughout the stream of commerce and in the everyday workplace, some procedural and legal questions will need more time to develop. It is fair to speculate, however, that electronic signatures will continue to increase in frequency of use. The role of notaries in society is permanent and indispensable. Only the means for creating the notarial certificate will modernize with technological advancements. The digital notarization is merely the first prototype.

In every discussion of electronic, or digital, notarizations, the term "electronic signatures" and "digital signatures" are used loosely. Often, they are used interchangeably.

> *"Electronic signature" is a very broad term, commonly accepted by those who have looked at electronic forms of authentication to mean any electronic symbol adopted by a party with the present intention to authenticate a writing... "Digital signature," on the other hand, has come to refer to the specific technology..., in which an electronic message is transformed using an asymmetric crypto-system. This is not a merely semantic point; digital signatures provide proof of message integrity and non-repudiation by the signer which give them legal advantages over other types of electronic and traditional signatures."*
>
> *- Theodore S. Barassi, Electronic Signature Differs from Digital, 214 N.Y. L.J. 102 (1995).*

While the form and design of a digitally signed document may vary, the signature block may resemble this:

<Signed SigID=1>
Promissory Note

I, Jane Doe, promise to pay to the order of First Pacific Bank five thousand dollars and no cents ($5,000) on or before June 20, 2008, with interest at the rate of seven and a half percent (7.5%) per annum.

Jane Doe, Maker

</Signed>

```
<Signature SigID=1 PsnID-doe082>
4AB376458cc18956A29870F40188B250CD23
04B2449502DE002342B218900BA5330259C1D
30674C1623D39</Signature>
```

Similar to a handmade ink signature on a page, a person's digital signatures will never appear exactly alike.

> *"[A digital] signature is never "visibly" the same, it is only deeply mathematically the same. It responds to the same verification, even though the actual value is different. To make the signature different each time, other elements beyond the password must be thrown into the mix. One convenient way to accomplish this is to perform an algorithm using the text of the document being signed. This results in a unique, but valid, digital signature, and it also provides a way to verify that the document has not been changed after the signature was affixed. The signature itself works also as a checksum on the document. This makes a signed contract un-modifiable."*
> *- Karen Coil, "Digital Signatures: Identity in Cyberspace," 2 ALA Spectrum, Dec. 1997.*

Electronic signatures are formed through a numeric encryption procedure. The process has been described as follows:

> *"In executing an electronic or digital "signature," special software "reads" a document and "signs" it with a string of electronic numbers known only to the person signing the document. When the document is received, corresponding software "reads" the signature and verifies its authenticity. More technically, a data file is reduced into a unique number or sequence of bits representing that file, using a mathematical algorithm. When the original file is modified, a unique number is generated and encrypted, using an individual's private key. The result (the electronic signature) is sent with the document. Generating the electronic signature may be accomplished by clicking on an on-screen icon or executing a simple command - the software performs the encryption process."*
> *- Richard Raysman & Peter Brown, Electronic Signatures, NY.L.J. Oct. 30, 1995.*

The commercial and legal communities have taken a keen interest in the advent of electronic signatures. The American Bar Association (ABA) promulgated electronic signature guidelines constituting helpful instruction to the state governments and to industries seeking to enable the use of this new technology.

The ABA stipulated that digital signatures "should indicate who signed a document, message, or record, and should be difficult for another person to produce without authorization." The ABA also asserts that the signature should identify what is signed, making it impracticable to falsify or alter either the signed matter or the signature without detection.

The guidelines also provide useful instruction that helps ensure that electronic signatures parallel the legal value of handmade signatures on paper. They are as follows:

> "*SIGNER AUTHENTICATION: If a public and private key pair is associated with an identified signer, the digital signature attributes the message to the signer. The digital signature cannot be forged, unless the signer loses control of the private key...*
>
> *MESSAGE AUTHENTICATION: The digital signature also identifies the signed message, typically with far greater certainty and precision than paper signatures. Verification reveals any tampering, since the comparison... shows whether the message is the same as when signed.*
>
> *AFFIRMATIVE ACT: Creating a digital signature requires the signor to use the signer's private key. This act can perform the "ceremonial" function of alerting the signer to the fact that the signer is consummating a transaction with legal consequences.*
>
> *EFFICIENCY: The processes of creating and verifying a digital signature provide a high level of assurance that the digital signature is genuinely the signer's... the creation and verification processes are capable of complete automation [and compared] to paper methods such as checking specimen signature cards... digital signatures yield a high degree of assurance.*"

Will electronic and digitalized transactions and signatures lead to a paperless society? It is unlikely that will happen. While paper transactions are vulnerable to corruption, and handmade signatures can be uncertain, paper will remain the common medium for transactions. The new technology may never be a practical means of doing business by private individual, or for certain businesses and government agencies. Paper is easier. It is easier to acquire, easier to save, easier to access, easier to research, easier to protect and easier to copy. It is easier because it requires no additional electronic and telecommunication equipment. Paper and electronic transactions will both have highly beneficial roles throughout the future.

Digital Notary
See Digital Notarizations

Direct Interest
See Conflict of Interest; Disqualified Notary

In any circumstance a notary receives from the signer's transaction a direct, immediate financial or beneficial gain, that notary has a direct interest in the transaction. In every state, such an interest is an automatic disqualifier of the notary from performing the notarial service. While direct interests are readily identifiable for notaries, the issue becomes more complex when the notary's interest or benefit is indirect and not immediate. Many argue that a notary should refrain from notarizing in any transaction in which the notary has some interest or gain, no matter how remote or insignificant that interest or gain may be.

The theory in law is that a notary is to be a disinterest third party who invokes her governmental authority to perform a notarial procedure impartially and objectively. The standards of impartiality are rarely black and white in their daily application. They are varying and changing shades of gray. Their standards commonly overlap creating some anxiety for the notary. While it is prudent to refrain from the notarization when in doubt about impartiality, that may be a bit excessive. Instead, the notary might carefully analyze the interest she has in the transaction. When we weigh these issues against the public's need for a competent notarization, we often find that we can notarize with full objectivity and integrity even where the notary has a negligible, indirect interest in the transaction.

Disabled Notaries

In no state shall a person who is physically disabled be denied a notarial commission if they otherwise qualify for such an honor. Such a denial would violate federal law. However, many states provide by statute that a notary must be able to read and write the English language.

The issue some argue is whether or not the requirement that the notary read and writes English exclusively means that the notary must be literate in English. There is some concern that such requirements might be applied, rather, to persons who are legally blind or mute. These issues have not seen their day in court, and may never do so. However, arguments that notaries must not be blind or mute may have poor legal footing to stand on.

It is commonly known that the blind and mute have extraordinary means for competently communicating and for providing themselves with requisite environmental cognition. Likewise, there are numerous instances where a blind notary may competently identify a document signer and notarize for him.

Persons who have lost the use of their hands and arms likewise may not be considered ineligible for a notary commission because of their impairment. Their ability to write in any language is commonly accommodated by creative and often physically demanding means. But for extraordinary circumstances, concern over a notary's physical impairments has little place in the arena of notary commissions.

From "The Notary" (July 1998)

Are the Disabled Prohibited from Serving as Notaries?
Americans with Disabilities Have Rights

Many states require their notaries to be able to "read and write" in the English language. Once in a while, the question comes up: may a legally blind person serve as a notary if they are fluent in the English language?

This simple question has some interesting hidden implications. For example, does the statutory requirement to read and write in English pertain to literacy in the English language? Or, on the other hand, does the requirement mean that the notary must be in possession of their eyesight and in possession of the full use of their hands in order to read and write in English?

The way the question is answered can make a very big legal difference in the lives of millions of people.

There are a number of professions a person cannot possibly hold if they are physically impaired in certain ways. Airline pilots must possess minimum strength of eyesight. A licensed dentist must have use of her hands to perform dental procedures. But, must a notary be in possession of her eyesight also? Must a notary be able to write on a piece of paper?

Many states have statutorily made English the official notarial language. In these English-only states, the hot political debate often continues about making English the overall official language of the state. Yet, under their noses their notary laws are English-only laws.

It is not unreasonable to require notarizations to be written in English. After all, a notarization is a simple government document created by a notary who is legally an official of the state that appointed her. The notarial certificate is created by legal authority of the state to authenticate the person's signature on a document. When written in English, the notarization, along with the document to which it belongs, will be admissible for filing in a government agency or in court. Notwithstanding the political rhetoric over making English the official language of a state, all transactions of government are performed in English. In many circumstances, they are additionally translated into another language to assist groups of individuals for special reasons. The same can be done for notarial certificates executed in English. Yet, the English version controls.

A notarial certificate has profound legal weight. It declares important facts about the authenticity of a signature. A notary who is not competent in the English language could not possibly write nor sign a pre-printed certificate they did not read or understand. It is axiomatic that a notary must understand the English language to the same extent that a symphony orchestra must be able to read music.

It is not quite so clear that a notary must not be legally blind nor physically unable to write. Musicians can be legally blind and deaf yet perform brilliantly.

Federal Law Prohibits Discrimination Against the Disabled; Even Notaries

One of the most important new laws of the past twenty years, affecting every U.S. resident, is the Americans with Disabilities Act. One of the key premises of this federal law is the outlawing of discrimination against persons with disabilities. It is illegal to discriminate against a person because of a physical or health-related disability. The unanswered and unsettling question is whether it is discriminatory for a state to refuse to commission a person as a notary because they are legally blind or because they have lost the use of their hands for purposes of writing.

It becomes even more entangled if a state government revokes a notary's commission because the notary has lost her eyesight or physical capacity to write while in the course of her notary commission. Does a person in either circumstance have legal protection here under the ADA? It is the kind of issue legal scholars enjoy debating.

The office of the notary public is an office of the people. It is probably the most democratic office of government where any qualified human being can serve. (One does not even have to be a U. S. citizen or registered voter to serve as a notary because those requirements are unconstitutional.) People who are physically impaired are intellectually as qualified as a person who is marginally competent in English. The only barrier erected is based on physical capabilities, not intellect.

No state has enacted a law prohibiting people who are judged mentally incompetent from serving as notaries. Yet, the mentally incompetent may possess their eyesight and ability to write by hand.

Notaries are "Witnesses." Is Eyesight Necessary?

Perhaps the fundamental issue regarding physical disabilities and notaries lies within the definition of the notarial act. The word, notary, in its historic definitional derivatives, means "witness" and "scribe." The word, witness, is legally defined as a person who "has knowledge of a fact or occurrence sufficient to testify in respect to it." The word, scribe, refers to a person who records in writing statements or records of what transpired.

A notary is a witness, on behalf of the state government that appointed her, to specific facts or events that reasonably prove the authenticity of a signature on a document. In an acknowledgment notarization, the notary certifies, "acknowledged before me this 4th day of July, 1998, by John Doe." As a witness to that declaration, the notary certifies she has knowledge that it was John Doe who personally appeared before her and that the signature, which John Doe acknowledged to the notary, in fact, belongs to John Doe.

In today's world of remarkable technological advances enabling the legally blind to function in the written form, there is little doubt a notarial certificate can be prepared and journalized by a blind person. There is also little doubt that a legally blind notary could competently identify a document signer they know personally or identify the signer through a credible witness known personally to the notary. Arguably, a legally blind notary could not reasonably rely on a signer's identification documents to verify their true identity.

For the most part, a blind notary is able to verify a signer's identity through personal knowledge or through a credible witness. She is also able to make a written journal entry about the transaction and write a notarial certificate and affix her notary seal thereto. But, how can a legally blind notary possess knowledge that the signature on a document actually belongs to the person appearing before her? Knowledge is not based on assumption or "safe guesses." Knowledge is based on actually

90

seeing, hearing, or feeling an event or fact. On this tricky legal issue within the notarial act hinges the question of whether a legally blind person can notarize a signature.

Notaries who are physically impaired with the loss of their hands surely must not be denied their notarial commissions. There are numerous means for producing written notarial certificates and for signing them. If beautiful oil paintings can he painted by holding brushes in the artist's toes or teeth, then the blind can write notarial certificates as well.

When we think of the notary public, we often think narrowly. We envision notarizations of signatures only. A notary can also administer oaths and, in most states, certify copies of documents. Because no signer and signature must be identified for these transactions, one's eyesight is less requisite.

Clear and Reasonable Thinking Is Needed

As in most aspects of law, there are very few black and white answers. When it comes to denying a notarial commission because of physical disability, it is unanswered on whether it violates the Americans with Disabilities Act.

Perhaps each state should take steps to ensure their statutory qualifications for service as a notary are not discriminatory.

Good state notary law will clearly define and outline how a notarization must be performed. If a person cannot possible perform the specific notarial act in conformance with the requisite steps outlined in the law, then that notary must refrain from performing that specific act.

Disinterested
See Conflict of Interest; Impartial Agent of the State

Notaries are expected to serve as disinterest third parties in the performance of their official duties. This means that the notary does not stand to gain any benefit, advantage, privilege or right from the signer's document. This standard is a reasonable expectation to which notaries are held. It establishes clear and safe standards by which conflicts of interest may be avoided; however, the problem most notaries face is that they have a small interest in every notarization they perform.

While notarizing on the job, the notary's interest is in her preservation of employment and a positive performance evaluation from her supervisor. This inherently requires the notary to provide customers her notarial services cheerfully, efficiently and competently. While notarizing for a neighbor at home on weekends poses a personal interest for the notary in maintaining good neighborly relations. When discussing the notary's need to be disinterested, it is essential to recognize that the key issue is the notary's interest in the signer's document, and not necessarily in the notary's interest in peripheral matters.

Disposal of the Notary Seal
See Destruction of the Notary Seal

Disqualification; Disqualified from Notarizing
See Disqualified Notary

Disqualified Notary
See Conflict of Interest

While discussions tend to focus on conflicts of interest for notaries, the higher legal standard notaries should address on a sustained basis is notarial disqualification. A notary is barred by law from performing a notarial act if that notary is disqualified from performing in that instance. A disqualification amounts to a momentary suspension of the notary's legal authority to perform a notarization for the transaction in question.

Notaries are disqualified from notarizing outside of their statutorily defined jurisdiction, being their state's borders in most cases. In most states, a notary is disqualified from notarizing if they are a signer to, or are named in, the document to be notarized. A notary who is a party to the signer's transaction is always disqualified from notarizing on that transaction.

In most cases, disqualifications are based in a substantial conflict of interest. Such conflicts of interest are called "disqualifying interests." Not all conflicts of interest, however, disqualify the notary. There is a temptation to proclaim all conflicts of interest grounds for disqualifying notaries. The presumption may be that if a notary has a conflict of interest, the notary must withdraw from the transaction. That presumption is not supported by case law or statutory law.

Upon entering into any notarial service, the notary must first address the potential for disqualification in that transaction. The notary's honest; good-faith assessment of the signer's request will almost always result in a prudent and defendable decision on whether or not the notary is disqualified from notarizing.

Document

See Document Content

Document Content

See Blank Documents; Completeness of the Signer's Document; Identification of the Signer's Document

The public often assumes that the notary notarizes documents. To the contrary, notaries notarize signatures on documents. The notarization has no effect on the signer's document. The document the signer signs is merely a written expression of information or data intended for a specific use for the purpose for which the document is written.

> *"The notary does not attest to any of the facts contained within the document, but merely verifies that the signer is who he or she purports to be."*
> - *Butler v. Encyclopedia Britannica, Inc., 41 F.3d 285 (1994).*

It is impossible for the notary to notarize a signature unless the signature pertains to a document. The person's signature constitutes proof of the person's intent to be bound by, concur with, or assent to, the terms and content of the document. The notarization is done to certify the person signed the document willingly and freely for the purposes provided within the document.

When a person requests a notarization of his signature to a contract, for example, the person has disclosed the purpose for which he signed the document is to enter into the contract. The content of the contract is irrelevant to the notarization. Moreover, it is an established rule that a notary has no authority to read the document or to be concerned with its content. Unless the notary knows, or has reason to know, the document contains provisions that are criminal or fraudulent in nature, the notary is duty-bound to disregard the document's content. Some notaries hold the belief they are required to read the signer's document to ensure all names are spelled correctly and that lines and spaces are filled in. In no way is this authorized conduct of the notary. To the contrary, it is an abuse of the notary's powers.

> *"The notary is not required to give inspection for legal flaws and the guaranty of validity of every document which he notarizes when he is hired only in his capacity as a notary and not as a drafter or guarantor of the validity of such documents."*
> - Dale v. Corriere, 537 So.2d 346.

The notary is legally obligated to know what the signer's document is, and to record that information in the notary's journal. This can be done casually by asking the signer, by looking for an identifying headline across the top of the first page, or by recognizing the document form because of familiarity with the form. The notary ought to record in the notary journal the date of the signer's document as further verification of the notary's effort to accurately identify the document.

The document date, of course, has no relevance to the date of the notarization. The document becomes legally enforceable when the party signs the document. The document date never needs to match the notarial certificate date. When a notary "post-dates" or "back-dates" a notarial certificate to match the date of the document, that notary makes a fraudulent representation of a material fact within the certificate, for which there is no legal defense.

It is common for notaries to be concerned with the legality or validity of the signer's document. Notaries observe substantial flaws and defects in the signer's document and might feel obligated to refuse to notarize on the basis alone. Likewise, some feel obligated to instruct the signer to correct

94

the errors. Flaws and defects in the signer's documents are outside the scope of the notary's responsibilities.

> *"The notary's duty as regards to the execution of the will was simply to take the acknowledgment by the testator that he was the person who executed the document and to so certify; having done so the notary performed her duty under law and her failure to volunteer information as to the legal effect of the manner of its attestation, i.e., that the acknowledgment of his signature, as believed by testator, would not result in creating a valid will, was not actionable; the notary was not liable, either on theory or in breach of contract or negligence, to the individual who would have taken the will, which was not acknowledged by two witnesses.*

> *The defendant's duty as a notary public was simply to take the acknowledgment by the signer that he was the person who executed the document in question and to so certify. Having done so she performed her duty under the law. The failure to volunteer information as to the legal effect of the manner of its attestation is not actionable for the reason that she not only had no duty in this respect, but for her to have done so would have been an illegal act."*
> - *Vanderhoof v. Prudential Savings and Loan, 120 Cal. Rptr. 207 (1975).*

Document Date
See Document Content

Document Signer
See Signature

The only thing a notary is legally authorized to notarize is a document signer's signature. A notary shall not notarize a document and shall not notarize a signature without a document to which it pertains. The document signer is at the heart of the notarial process. The signer must personally appear before the notary and be positively identified by the notary. The document signer should sign the notary's journal to give evidence of his personal appearance before the notary and that the document signature in fact belongs to him.

Documents in a Foreign Language

See Document Content; Foreign Languages

The content of a document is irrelevant to the notarization. A notary has no legal authority to probe the document's contents. Therefore, if the document is written in a foreign language the notary does not understand, it matters not. The notarial certificate, according to case law, must be written and executed in English. That official certificate can subsequently be translated to the language of the document for the convenience of the reader.

The notary is legally obligated to identify what the document is. This requires the notary to either ask the document signer what his document is, or have an independent translator inform the notary what it is.

The notary should record in the notary journal what the document is, how it was identified, and in what language the document was written. If a translator was used, the journal should record the translator's name as well.

Due Process of Law in Sanctioning a Notary Public
See Government Regulation of Notaries; Revocation of a Notarial Commission

Every notary in every state is subject to the statutory authority of the state to sanction a notary for misconduct, or for criminal conduct. Most notaries apply for their notarial commissions as a requisite of their employment. If a notary's commission is sanctioned or revoked, it could adversely affect the security of her employment.

Under constitutional law, government must implement procedural due process when applying sanctions against its citizens and licensees. This means that the accused notary must be given proper and reasonable notice of that which she stands accused, and be granted reasonable opportunity to examine the evidence supporting the accusation. The accused is legally entitled to an impartial hearing in which evidence and a defense can be presented to refute the accusations. Should the decision hold against the notary, the notary has a legal right to appeal the decision.

Some states have statutory authority to levy fines against notaries for alleged misconduct. Rules of due process apply there too. A fine cannot be issued without first following the steps outlined above to ensure the notary's due process rights are protected.

A popular saying from mid-nineteenth century America underlies the fundamental purpose for due process rights of citizens so wisely created by America's founding fathers: "It unfortunately becomes some men that when conferred a little authority they proceed to exercise unrighteous dominion over others." Our precious due process rights are indispensable and must be meticulously observed in all actions against notaries and citizens by government administrators.

Duress
See Undue Influence; Willful, Free Making of the Signature

A person who is overwhelmed by force or fear to the extent they are unable to exercise or freely express their will is under duress. Actions, commitments, contracts, and representations made under duress are most often held invalid because the person was unable to formulate the requisite intent to act willfully with freely. The person under duress is in fact carrying out vicariously the will and intent of the oppressor. In no way may such conduct be binding upon the duressed. A notary may not notarize a signature of a person that the notary knows was made under duress.

Duty of Care
See Reasonableness

Every person, every profession, and every task performer is under a legal duty of care to act reasonably with caution and prudence. We universally share a legal obligation to refrain from behavior or activities that would foreseeably harm others or the property of others. This legal obligation is generally referred to as the "duty of reasonable care."

> *"A notary public owes to his clients a duty to act honestly, skillfully, and with reasonable diligence. This duty imposed on a notary public requires the notary to ascertain the identity of the person whose signature they attest. Therefore, this duty cannot be fulfilled unless*

the transaction is done by or before the notary. For these reasons the duty of the notary public requires that he not willfully and intentionally certify that a person has acknowledged the execution of a conveyance when the person did not acknowledge the execution before the notary. When a notary does such, this would constitute constructive fraud. The grantor's mere presence is not sufficient to constitute a valid notarization. In order to be effective there must be an actual signing or acknowledgment of a signature in the presence of the notary."
    - First Bank of Childersburg v. Florey, 676 So.2d 324 (1996).

In the case decision of St. Louis V. Priest, 152 S.W.2d 109 (Mo. 1941), the court held that the *"negligence on the part of an officer consists only in a failure to use that degree of care which an ordinary reasonable and prudent man would exercise under the same or similar circumstance and conditions."*

Notaries are under extensive duties of reasonable care in every step of every notarial function. The notary's duty of care is rooted in integrity, common sense, good judgment and prudent thinking. A finding that an accused notary has fulfilled her duty of care in performing her legal functions will usually acquit that notary of any accusation of wrongdoing.

E

We add that the private employer of a notary public might be liable for the notary's breach of duty if the employer participated in that breach, as for example if the employer should ask or encourage the notary to act without appropriate inquiry.
- New Jersey Supreme Court, 1967.

Electronic Notarizations
See Digital Notarizations

Electronic Signatures
See Digital Notarizations

Embosser Seal
See Seal of the Notary Public

For many generations the notary seal has been in the style of an embosser that, when affixed to paper, creates a raised image on the page. Difficult to counterfeit and impressive in its appearance, embosser seals have been a venerated symbol of notarizations worldwide for many generations.

The notary's embosser seal consists of a handgrip clamp that contains embosser plates in the top and bottom disks that squeeze together to form the raised circular image on the page. In the past few decades, the widespread adoption of photographic media to archive documents has cast the embosser seal into a status of declining use. The crimped image, unless darkened by some means, is not photographically reproducible.

Most documents that are required by state or federal law to be notarized are documents that are likely to be filed with a court or government entity. In almost every instance, such documents are archived by electronic or photographic means, such as CD, microfilm, or computer scanner. Embossed notary seals on such documents appear omitted from the archived record.

Increasingly, states are recognizing ink stamp notary seals as valid substitutes for the embosser seal. The ink stamp seal archives clearly by electronic and photographic means. Moreover, the stamp gives the notary greater flexibility in its placement on the page. The embosser limits its seal placement to the margins of the page, often with insufficient space without obscuring document text or signatures.

As old traditions and habits die hard, there is a strong and lingering preference among many communities for the embosser seal. Notaries in states permitting ink stamp seals are accustomed to hearing signers complain that "the document hasn't been notarized" because it lacks the raised, crimped seal image. In most countries, the notary seal remains the embosser. Their acceptance of ink stamp notary seals from various states of the U.S. is commonly reluctant or summarily denied. Use of the ink stamp seal is one of the leading reasons officials of other nations require an apostille to certify a notary is authorized by the state. In the opinion of millions overseas, an American ink stamp notary seal constitutes a phony notarization. Notaries frequently engaged in international transactions will commonly affix an embossed seal adjacent their required ink stamp seal to mollify those who love old world ways. The embossed seal constitutes a "surplusage." It is not a valid seal, but it does not detract from the verity of the notarial certificate.

Employer and Notary Relations
See Employer's Legal Duty to the Notary; Employer Liability for Notarizations

The notary is a public official performing a function of state government. Although the notary's fees and tools to become a notary are frequently paid for by the employer, the employer has no legal jurisdiction over the notary's services. The relationship between the employer and the notary is commonly awkward and occasionally marred by conflict.

"Among all the professional groups that regularly use the services of notaries, attorneys are most often the bullies, the intimidators, the arrogant so-and-so's who say, 'I know the law and you don't, so just do it.' Well, they usually don't know notarial law, or they think the rules are trivial. It almost seems that their familiarity with the law has bred contempt for it."

> *- Charles N. Faerber, "Being There: The Importance of Physical Presence to the Notary," 31 Marshall Law Review 761.*

The employer and the notary mutually share a duty to create a work environment that is open to communication. The employer must attain a clear understanding of the notary's duties and legal standards or performance. The notary should identify how notarizations in the workplace can be performed with expedience and competence, and ensure that all requirements of law are satisfied.

From "The Notary" (March 1999)

Employer & Notary Relations

Notaries are in a pickle. We are appointed by our state governments to perform government services. We usually become notaries at the request of our employers to have the luxury of having a notary available at the workplace. The old cliché "you can't serve two masters," becomes really sticky for notaries.

As a matter of law, the notary is a public official performing official state government services. As a matter of law, it is irrelevant whether the fees and supplies to become a notary were paid for by you or by your employer. It is your name on the notary commission, and it is your signature to your notarial certificates that you guarantee to be true and correct.

The conflict comes from the understandable assumption employer's make that they have dominion over your notarial services. It is a well-established legal principle that employers do not have any jurisdiction or authority over your notarial commission. Yet, under the law, your employer has a legal duty to ensure that you notarize properly in full compliance with the law because if you notarize falsely or recklessly while on the job, you and your employer can both be liable for damages caused. That puts your employer in a pickle of his own.

There is a simple and fail-safe solution to all of this. Employers of notaries have a duty to provide, and notaries have a right to expect, three things:

1. Clearly written policies and guidelines regarding notarizations to be performed while on the job.
2. Proper and adequate on-going training of all employees on these policies and guidelines;
3. Adequate supervision of all employees to ensure the policies and guidelines are complied with.

The courts hold that employers might avoid legal liability for the wrongful or negligent conduct of their employees if they can prove their employees are properly trained and supervised concerning clear guidelines and policies. An employee, who is beneficiary of adequate policies and guidelines, proper training and proper supervision from management may "be on her own" if she notarizes negligently in violation of company policies, training and supervision.

The key is for employers to understand and respect the notary's legal responsibilities. Likewise, the notary needs to understand and respect the position the employer is in. The employer's highest commitment is to quality service for customers. His values and objectives easily conflict with the laws and standards for correct notarial services. The single most effective mitigation against this conflict is to foster clear and open communication between the employer and the notary. Exemplary employers will actively strive to promote and maintain a work environment that is honest, fair, and full of integrity and mutual respect.

Employers often do not realize that when they pressure a notary into violating state notary law, they are violating the state notary law themselves! An employer or supervisor must never pressure a subordinate into committing violations of law, lest they become subject to prosecution themselves.

The hallmark of a wise, competent employer and supervisor is his commitment to learn all he can about the duties of the notary and then create a workplace environment where integrity and attention to correct procedure is encouraged and expected. An informal survey of notaries in various states indicates that only half of their employers expect and mandate correct notarial services. In almost every circumstance, where this is not the employer's policy, this improper attitude results from the employer's complete lack of awareness of the law and procedures for notarizations. The more employers know and understand about notarizations, the more valuable you and your employer become to the public you serve.

The value of informed notaries and their employers cannot be overstated. It is the foundation to excellent employer/notary relations.

Employer's Legal Duty to the Notary
See Employer and Notary Relations; Employer Liability for Notarizations; Respondeat Superior

When an employee becomes a notary, that employee takes on a new responsibility that is not subordinate to the employer's direction. The notary is subordinate to the state government that appoints her. The employer is legally obligated to ensure the notary is properly trained in all notarial responsibilities and to ensure they are faithfully followed.

The employer owes the notary a duty to be trained in notary law and procedures in order for the employer to effectively and correctly supervise the notary in her notarial services. When the employer and the notary share common understanding about the rules and procedures for notarizing, the work environment becomes more hospitable to correct notarial services. In fact, the employer and the notary foster a high standard of ethical conduct and competence in notarial services and in all services of the workplace.

Employers have an absolute duty by law not to request, require or coerce a notary into violating any provision of notary law or the notary's legal standard or reasonable care. This duty extends to the employer's obligation to instruct and prohibit all employees from asking staff notaries to violate state law or to breach the standard of reasonable care. As a matter of law, employers are considered to be in the best position to properly supervise and train employees on their duties and on any applicable requirements of law. Arguably, notaries are entitled to insist on being properly trained in their duties and being permitted to perform their duties unimpaired by wrongful pressure, derision or coercion from employers and coworkers.

From "The Notary" (November 1996)

It's *Your* Notary Commission, *Not Your Employer's*

Maybe your employer instructed you to become a notary. Perhaps they paid all of the fees and expenses for you to file the application, to buy a bond, to purchase a notary seal, and even to purchase a notary journal. Guess what your employer probably thinks about your being a notary? If they are like most employers, they assume they <u>own</u> your notary commission. They do not.

Your state government appointed you to a public office created by state law to perform a government function. There is no such thing as a "notary private." You are a Notary <u>Public.</u> When you "put on your notary hat" you assume a governmental role that belongs to the state, not to your employer.

Because it is common for employers to believe they own their notary's commission, it is also common for employers to instruct their notaries to wrongfully perform notarial acts. They don't mean any harm by it. Such requests are usually made out of urgency or expediency. They don't fully understand the importance and duty under law to which a notary is subject. When an employer or supervisor requests a notary to perform a notarial act, that employer or supervisor must subordinate their request to the decision-making of the notary. In a very real sense, the notary is the final judge in notarial matters in the workplace.

Notaries who leave their employment often find they are required by their employer to leave their notary bond, their notary seal and their notary journal prior to their final departure. Employers mistakenly believe these items belong to them because they paid for them. Moreover, some erroneously believe that this will best protect them from wrongful notarizations performed after the notary has left their employ.

The notary's commission runs with the notary, not with the notary's employment. Legal counsel could inform employers that under proper procedures, employees can be required to reimburse employers for tools provided them at company expense, such as notary seals and notary journals. Under no circumstance should a notary yield possession of their notary journal to an employer. A few states have even made it an illegal act for an employer to require a departing employee/notary to hand their notary journal over to the employer upon departure. In every circumstance, it is an extremely unwise practice.

It is a well-established principle of law that an employer may not prohibit an employee/notary from performing notarial services at home or away from the office on personal time. A notary's appointment runs 24 hours a day. It is not conditioned or based on the notary's employment, or the approval of the notary's employer. When a notary provides notarial services outside of and away from the workplace, the notary's employer has no share in any liability for that notary's misconduct, if there is any.

The only means by which an employer can be held jointly liable for a wrongful notarization is when the notarial act has a connection in some way to the business of the employer. This principle of law is called _respondeat superior._ It is not relevant whether the employer paid for the notary's expenses and tools, or whether the notary became one at her own initiative and expense. Thus it is absolutely imperative that employers take reasonable care to ensure their employee/notaries are exercising reasonable care when performing their notarial services.

Having notaries on staff in the workplace can be a wonderful convenience and benefit. Once the legal relationship between employee/notaries and their employers is understood, everyone benefits. Notaries are good for business.

From "The Notary" (September 1999)

The Absolute Best Cure for Notarial Fraud in the Workplace is to Take Five Preventative Steps:

1.   Cause management to adopt clear policies and guidelines governing notarizations in the workplace. The policies should include clear statements on what is prohibited and what is permitted. It should include proscribed ways to "say no" to a customer without offending them.

2.   Adopt standardized notarial certificates to be used by on-staff notaries. Uniformity and standardization is effective in minimizing confusion and mistakes.

3.   Adopt standardized notary journals with the mandate that every notarization be journalized and that the signer signs the journal.

4.   Mandate that every employer subordinate their notarization needs to the judgment of the notary, that no person may pressure a notary into a breach of the adopted standards, and that no person may unduly criticize or ridicule a notary for the decision she makes about a notarial request.

5.   Require every notary and all personnel at the workplace to receive training on correct notarial principles and on the policies governing notarial services. Notarizations are rooted in the most rudimentary principles of integrity. They require absolute truth and commitment to high ethical conduct. There is no room for shading the truth or for cutting corners. Taking a notarization over the telephone can never be justified Like a Texas court once said, "a singing artist performing live can't stay home and just perform for the audience over the phone." Personal appearance before a notary means personal appearance.

Employer Liability for Notarizations

See Employer and Notary Relations; Employer's Legal Duty to the Notary; Quiet Acquiescence; Respondeat Superior

One of the foundation principles in common law is the employer's liability for the wrongful or negligent conduct of their employees. This principle is often referred to in law as the doctrine of *respondeat superior* meaning, "let the superior respond, that is, let the principal or master be answerable for the acts of his agent or servant." This common law principle is anciently rooted in the law of agency founded on the principle that a duty rests on every person, in the management of his own affairs, whether by himself or by his agents, or servants, to conduct them as not to injure another person. If another person is injured as a result thereof, the person must answer for the damage.

Until the late seventeenth century, an employer was not liable for wrongful acts committed by employees unless they committed the acts under the employer's direct command or subsequent assent. However, since 1699, the modern doctrine of *respondeat superior* has developed. That is, an employer is vicariously liable for his employee's wrongful acts committed within the scope of their employment. This theory of vicarious liability did not result as a rule of logic, but rather as a rule of public policy, and is sustained by the courts.

In the employer's supervision over notarizations performed in the workplace, *respondeat superior* imposes on the employer liability for damages caused by wrongful notarizations created under their supervision. While the employer has no legal authority to control or restrict the notary's performance of notary services, the employer is responsible to ensure they are performed correctly. The notarization is a state government function and not a function of the employer's business. This unique fit of a governmental function within a workplace does not exculpate the employer of potential liability if the government function is performed wrongfully.

Employers are under a common law duty to properly hire, supervise and train their employees. The reasoning behind this is that the actions of his employees may impute liability to the employer. In other words, the wrongful acts of the employee, while done in the scope of her employment, subject her employer to liability for the acts. Notaries and their employers are not exempt from these common law rules.

The key test of whether a notary's misconduct imputes liability to the employer is whether or not the notary was acting within the scope of her employment. Scope of employment is clearly defined:

The Restatement (Second) of Agency § 228 (1958) definition of "scope of employment" provides in part:

> 1) *Conduct of a servant is within the scope of employment if, but only if:*
>   a) *it is of the kind he is employed to perform;*
>   b) *it occurs substantially within authorized time and space limits;*
>   c) *it is actuated, at least in part, by a purpose to serve the master, and*
>   d) *force is intentionally used by the servant against another, the use of force is not unexpectable by the master.*

The principle of "scope of employment" is further explained in the law text, "The Law of Torts," by Prosser and Keaton, Section 70 at 502 (5th Ed. 1984):

> *"The scope of employment refers to those acts which are so closely connected with what the servant is employed to do, and so fairly and reasonably incidental to it, that they may be regarded as methods, even though quite improper ones, of carrying out the objectives of the employment.*
>
> *As in the case of the existence of the relation itself, many factors enter into the question: the time, place and purpose of the act, and its similarity to what is authorized; whether it is one commonly done by such servants; the extent of departure from normal methods; the previous relations between the parties; whether the master had reason to expect that such an act would be done; and many other considerations... [I]n general the servant's conduct is within the scope of his employment if it is of the kind which he is employed to perform, occurs substantially within the authorized limits of time*

and space, and is actuated, at least in part, by a purpose to serve the master."

Without question, if a notary is instructed to engage in notarial misconduct by her employer, that employer cannot escape liability and cannot use as a defense that the transaction of wrongful conduct was outside the scope of the notary's employment.

"We add that the private employer of a notary public might be liable for the notary's breach of duty if the employer participated in that breach, as for example if the employer should ask or encourage the notary to act without appropriate inquiry.

While the results reached in Commercial Union could be reconciled with the general law on the subject of employers of public officials...we are of the opinion that the quasi-official designation given to notaries public does not, in and of itself, shield their employers from liability for their negligent acts. In our opinion this issue must be decided under the rules pertaining to agency in general. The test applicable here is: Whether the employee was acting within the scope of her employment at the time the alleged negligent act took place."

- Transamerica Insurance v. Valley National Bank 462 P.2d 814.

According to the Restatement (Second) of Agency, Section 219 (2)(a)(d) (1959):

"A master will be subject to liability of his servant's actions outside the scope of his employment if: (1) the master intended the conduct or consequences; (2) the master was negligent or reckless; (3) the conduct violated a non-delegable duty of the master; or (4) the servant purported to act on behalf of the master and the third party relied upon the apparent authority of the servant."

From "The Notary" (November 1997)

Telling Your Boss No:
Make It a Teaching Moment
Without Embarrassing Anyone

When Richard A. instructed Laura R. to notarize two signatures on several real estate documents, she had a bad feeling about it. She had only worked for Richard for the past six months and was familiar with his casual ways. He liked to do things fast and easy, including his business deals. Richard's style of business was "Don't sweat the small stuff. Away with the bureaucracy!"

Laura looked at the documents Richard handed her and saw they contained acknowledgment wording for her to sign and seal as a notary. The words, "acknowledged before me by . . ." sent chills down her spine. This statement she was being directed to sign as a notary was not true. She had never met nor seen the signers, and they most definitely were not before her personally. She knew she had to tell her boss "no," but she feared he would become furious with her. She needed her job most desperately and could not afford to lose it.

Laura gave her boss a concerned look and meekly questioned whether it wouldn't be better if the signers appeared before her personally. Richard had no time for this. He accused Laura of being difficult and overly concerned with petty details. He demanded she notarize the signatures that moment. Laura quietly complied.

Laura should have followed her instincts. She unknowingly notarized signatures her boss, Richard, had forged on fraudulent real estate conveyances. When Richard was caught, Laura's world caved in on her. She was charged with criminal fraud along with her employer. After several thousand dollars in lawyer fees, the criminal charges against her were finally dropped. However, her life would never again be the same.

110

Is this case real? Yes. (The names have been changed for obvious reasons.)

How do you tell your employer or supervisor "no?" This is probably the primary occupational hazard notaries face. Your employer paid all of the fees and expenses for you to become a notary, and, therefore, they think they "own and control" your notarial commission. However, you are appointed by the state as an official of the state. It comes as a shock to some employers to learn they should not control the notarial powers and duties of their employee-notaries. There is a fine line between being a subordinate and being a notary within the workplace.

Wise and prudent employers will seek to learn the notaries' duties and ensure the notaries employed in their organization do their jobs in total compliance with the law. So, how do you tell employers and supervisors "no" when they ask you to notarize wrongfully?

One of the most valuable skills any person can acquire is the ability to tell someone "no" in such a manner that the individual is neither offended nor severely disappointed. It is the mark of a great leader who can tell a person "no" and still make that person glad he asked. It can be done!

It is a matter of how we say it, not what we say. Calmness, self-assurance, respectfulness, and genuine warmth are the essential traits of diplomacy a notary should seek to develop. You can acquire calmness and self-assurance by becoming increasingly knowledgeable about the laws and procedures for proper notarizations. Your knowledge that you are protecting your employer and yourself from potential legal problems by refusing to notarize incorrectly will give you added determination to assert your position.

No employer enjoys having employees refuse to carry out directives or instructions. Moreover, they really dislike being made to look foolish! If you show respect and friendliness when explaining why you cannot notarize wrongfully, you will minimize the employer's embarrassment and possible scorn.

Most importantly, when you tell a person you cannot notarize as requested, take the time to explain to them why you can't. Keep your explanation simple and brief. Phrase it in such a way that it sounds positive, and not as if the employer just asked you to commit a terrible crime. In Laura's case at the beginning of this discussion, she could have calmly explained to Richard that the state notary law requires the signers to personally appear before her. The discussion between them could have run something, like this:

Laura: Richard, I really want to be as helpful and productive as I can be. I really love my job. But, being a notary is something apart from my regular job responsibilities. My notary commission comes from the state government and the law is very clear that I cannot notarize anybody's signature unless they first appear before me. Is there any way I can arrange for these signers to meet with me, even if I drop by where they work or live?"

Richard: Come on Laura, don't make such a big deal out of this. I need these notarized now and I can't wait. It's such a trivial matter. Just do it, please!

Laura: Richard, it is not up to me. It would be illegal for me to do this. Please understand that if I do my notarizations properly, then you and your client's are legally protected. The notary law is designed to protect everybody involved if the notarization is done truthfully and correctly. If I notarize these signatures I will be doing so falsely and both you and I could get into a ton of legal trouble over it. Look at the notarial wording. See what it says? "Personally appeared before me." This clearly states the signers have to appear before me. There is no other way. Let me give them a call and arrange to notarize this the right way. It will prove to your clients you really know every tiny detail of your business and that you have utmost integrity. So, Richard, how about it?

If this little dialogue had been real and Richard had been smart, he would have listened and asked Laura to arrange for the signers to see her personally before notarizing. But in the real-life case, Richard used his authority as employer to intimidate Laura into notarizing falsely. In the end, Richard went to prison.

Laura went on to other employment and was later permitted by the state to renew her notary commission.

Employer's Quiet Acquiescence
See Employer's Legal Duty to the Notary; Quiet Acquiescence

Endorsement of the Notary Applicant
See Commissioning Process; Qualification for Appointment to the Office of Notary Public

A number of states require persons applying to become notaries to obtain the signatures of one or more persons who endorse the applicant as a person of good character. Often, the endorser vouches for the applicant's qualifications to serve as a notary.

There appears to be no record of any endorser ever having been held liable for their endorsement when the applicant either falsified their application or abused their notarial office. For the most part, the use of endorsements on notary applications is a formality that gives the state government a degree of assurance that the applicant, absent a background check, is suitable for commissioning as a notary.

There have been instances where the state requires the endorsers to either be U.S. citizens or registered voters. Such requirements are unconstitutional, as they violate the Equal Protection clause of the 14th Amendment.

Equal Protection
See Fourteenth Amendment to the United States Constitution; Government Regulation of Notaries

The Fourteenth Amendment of the United States Constitution provides every person a guarantee that no person, or class of people, shall be denied the same protection of the laws which are enjoyed by other persons or classes of people in similar circumstances. This all-important constitutional protection has significant application to notaries public. For example, a state cannot refuse to grant a notary commission to a person because of their race, religion, gender, political persuasion or national origin.

The United States Supreme Court has applied the 14th Amendment to prohibit states from requiring their notaries be registered voters or U.S. citizens. In the late 1990's, the 14th Amendment was invoked to prohibit a state from denying a notary application because the applicant crossed out references to God in his written notarial oath of office.

Under the Equal Protection clause of the Constitution, every person has a right to serve as a notary if they meet minimum qualifications of residency in the state, legal age, fluency in English, minimum knowledge of notarial procedures, and absence of a criminal record. It can be truly said that the office of notary public is a pure democratic office, as it is an office of the people without favoritism or prejudice.

Errors and Omissions Insurance
See Notary Bond

This commercial product, commonly referred to as "Notary E & O Insurance," is available for notaries to purchase anywhere in the United States. In no state is notary E & O Insurance required to be purchased by the notary.

Errors and Omissions insurance generally indemnifies the insured notary against payouts on the surety bond, against court judgments, and against out-of-court settlements made on the notary's behalf. Often, this very-limited type of insurance will pay the notary's legal fees as well.

Not all E & O insurance policies are alike. They vary according to what the customer selects for coverage, and according to the terms and conditions set forth by the individual insurance underwriter. It is not uncommon to find these policies excluding any coverage for damages caused by the notary's violation of state law or commission of fraud. Unfortunately, the majority of cases holding notaries financially liable for damages arise out of the notary's statutory violation or signing a false notarial certificate.

Arguably, the most secure form of insurance for notaries is to be properly trained in the notarial law and process, and to notarize with utmost accuracy and integrity. Notary E & O insurance is not to be dismissed out of hand. For many, it is essential protection. The obvious caveat is to shop around and read very carefully the terms and conditions of the insurance before buying it. Be sure to know what items are insured, and on what grounds may the insurance company refuse to indemnify the notary. While it is surprisingly affordable insurance, it is not for everyone.

Executed Document

In legal parlance, an executed document (also called an "instrument") is one that has been signed. In its modem usage, it seems to suggest that everything that needs to be done to the document has been done. It has been "signed, sealed and delivered."

Again in legal parlance, the term, instrument, will be used to distinguish a document that is formal and is created for legal purposes to accomplish a substantive end result. All instruments, for purposes of notarizations, are documents. But, not all documents are instruments.

Executed Instrument

See Executed Document

F

A notary betrays the public trust when he signs a certificate of acknowledgment when notarizing any signature without having the signer personally appear before him and without properly identifying the signer.
- *Farm Bureau Finance v. Carney, 100 Idaho 745, 605 P.2d 509 (1990).*

False Certification
See False Notarization

False Notarial Dogma
See Notary Training

It is unfortunate, but understandable, that many notaries of America learn their notarial duties from other notaries. Traditions and notarial folklore pass from generation to generation of notaries. Rules of thumb and procedures that are not found in the law are passed down through the years. Perhaps, they made sense generations ago, but make little sense today.

The saying goes that "a rumor repeated often enough takes on the appearance of fact." The same goes for notarial dogma. While notarial dogma may be well intended, it can often disserve the public and the notary. Moreover, it can occasionally cause the notary to violate state notary law.

A good example of false notarial dogma is the idea that if the signer's document consists of multiple pages, "fraud can be prevented" by affixing the notarial seal across the seam between two overlapping pages. Case law authority indicates that the notary's seal is to appear clearly and entirely adjacent the notary's signature. The placement of the notary seal anywhere other than in a notarial certificate adjacent the notary's signature constitutes an abuse of the notary's legal authority.

Notaries have an absolute duty to learn the notary laws of their respective states and obey them faithfully. This requires the notary to discern false dogma from the rule of law, especially where the dogma contradicts the rule of law.

False Notarization
See Notarizing Falsely

A false notarization is any notarization that contains statements of material fact that are false. False notarizations are the natural result of the act of notarizing falsely.

A notary notarizes falsely when the maker of the signature to be notarized has not personally appeared before the notary, where the notary has failed to make the requisite effort to verify the signer's identity, and where the notary fails to place the signer under oath when notarizing by jurat. There is no defense in law for notarizing falsely. Moreover, the false making of a notarization is documented by the notarial certificate containing false statements of fact. It is wrongful conduct, which cannot be obfuscated or disregarded as minor.

Courts have held notaries liable for their false notarizations since the earliest periods of our history. They have held the notary liable for:

> *"'Gross and culpable negligence' for not 'faithfully' performing his official duties."*
> - *Bernd v. Fong Eu, 161 Cal. Rptr. 58 Cal. App. Ct. (1979).*

In 1858, a notary was sued for failing to complete a notarial certificate before signing it. An incomplete certificate can share the same probative effect as a false certificate. The court ruled:

> *"If the notary read the certificate before signing it, this omission must have been known to him; if he did not, he is equally guilty of negligence; for an officer who affixes his official signature and seal*

to a document (thereby giving to it the character of evidence) without examining it to find whether the facts certified are true, can scarcely be said to faithfully perform his duty according to law."
  - Fogarty v. Finlay, 10 Cal. 239, 245 (1858).

Even now, there is little tolerance for notarial negligence in the execution of a notarial certificate.

"Even if [the notary] did not know that the signatures on the contract were forgeries, he knew that by authenticating the document, as notary, he was telling the world that the parties had appeared before him and affixed their signatures in his presence. Thus, he committed fraud in that he purposely let third parties rely on a document purporting to be genuine but actually without validity as an authentic act. The proof of validity he supplied was misleading to all who relied on the contract."
  - Summers Bros. Inc. v. Brewer, 420 So. 2d 197 (La. 1982).

The legal precedence and case law authority establishing notary liability for false notarizations is overwhelming. A few examples may help illustrate the strength this principle of law enjoys.

- In Willow Highlands Co. v. United States Fidelity & Guar. Co., 73 A.2d 422 (Pa. 1950), the court held the notary liable for negligently certifying that the property owners had personally appeared before him and acknowledged a mortgage where the property owners had in fact neither appeared before the notary nor had knowledge of the transaction.
- The court in Lewis v. Agric. Ins. Co., 82 Cal. Rptr. 509 (Cal. Ct. App. 1969) found that notary's act of "falsely certifying purported signatures of [an] individual who had never appeared before her to subscribe or acknowledge subscription to any of the instruments in question constituted 'official misconduct or neglect' of the notary."
- In Immerman v. Ostertag, 199 A.2d 869 (N.J. Super. Ct. Law Div. 1964), the court concluded that the notary displayed a "high degree of negligence" in certifying an acknowledgment without determining whether the individuals purporting to have made the statements even knew of the nature or the contents of what they were signing.

118

False Representation
See False Notarization; Falsehood; Fraud

Falsehood
See Fraud

A willful act or declaration that is contrary to truth constitutes a falsehood. In notary law, there is no legal defense for any falsehood found in a notarial certificate. Every word of the certificate must be true. The notary statutes of many states provide that the notary's signing and sealing of a notarial certificate containing any falsehoods constitutes a criminal violation of law.

Familial Notarizations
See Notarizing for Relatives

Fees Charged by Notaries
All notaries in all states are authorized by law to charge fees for their notarial services. In the majority of states the fees notaries are authorized to charge are set by statute. A number of states permit the notaries to charge fees in any amount.

In all states, the charging of fees for services is totally optional. Whether a notary charges a fee for notarial service or not has no effect on the validity of the notarization or on the notary's potential for legal liability. Fee charging is independent from the notarial act.

It is estimated that less than 25% of all notaries charge a fee for their notarizations. This is based primarily on the fact that most notaries are such as part of their employment. Most notaries perform their services as part of their regular job assignments and view the notarization as a service to the customer. It is a commendable attitude. Serving as a notary is indeed a valuable and appreciated public service.

Another reason many notaries do not charge a fee is because the fee amount authorized by their state's notary laws are nominally low. In fact, many view the authorized amount to be so low that the fee is trivial and embarrassing to charge.

The range of authorized notary fees in America is profoundly diverse. It is as low as a dollar or less. In many states, the fee averages between $3 and $5 per notarization, and runs as high as $10 per notarization in some of the country's largest states. A good number of states permit their notaries to charge whatever the market will bear. It is not unusual to find notaries in some of those states to charge $20 or more per signature notarized.

In the states where the authorized fee is particularly low, many notaries will feel justified in charging fees far in excess of the authorized amount. Not only is that practice a violation of state law, in some states it is a criminal violation of law. Notaries who charge more than the authorized amount are usually doing so at the direction of their employer. In such cases, the employer, along with the notary, are subject to legal action for violation of law.

It is not unusual for a notary to decline charging a fee when the customer insists on paying the notary anyway. Customers are occasionally known to leave the notary a generous "tip" rather than the payment of a fee. A tip is not a fee payment. It is a gift from the customer served to the service provider. As long as the notary does not solicit the tip, it is not a fee and should therefore not be subject to the statutory limits placed on notary fees.

Across the United States, notarizations are viewed with less respect than they deserve. Their importance is vastly misunderstood and they are generally taken for granted. If a notary provides a notarization free of charge, a silent message is sent to the client that the notarization is indeed perfunctory and of little value. On the other hand, if the notary was authorized to charge five or ten dollars for a notarization, the client would naturally associate a higher value to the notarization just performed.

The public tends to associate value of goods and services with the price they pay for them. We are inclined to better appreciate an item if we pay good money for it. But if it comes to us for free, we are inclined to view it as insignificant and of little value. If we notarize free of charge, signers often value the notarization as a mere technical detail of little value. Signers who pay a substantial fee for the notarization will likely consider the notarization as something more than a small detail.

When notaries are asked to travel a distance to notarize for a person, a number of states allow the notary to charge a reasonable travel fee (an amount often suggested by the United State Internal Revenue Service, such as 58 cents per mile traveled round-trip).

Notaries often face problems with their employers about charging notary fees. Employers commonly prohibit charging fees. They might prohibit notaries from notarizing for fees after work hours at home, and they commonly require notaries to charge fees from non-customers and to notarize for free for customers. There is scarce case law authority that helps clear the air on some of these issues.

According to a few sources, employers have the authority to prohibit notaries on their payroll from charging fees for their notarizations while on the job. However, if the employer permits or requires the notary to charge fees for on-the-job notarizations, the fee revenues rightfully belong to the notary and are not to be treated as part of the notary's employment compensation package. The basic reasoning given is that employers have a right to prohibit their employees from "moonlighting" while on the job. Yet, it is the notary's name on the commission and the notarial service is provided by that notary whose signature and seal bears her name. It is irrelevant whether the employer paid all of the fees for the employee to become a notary, including the notary bond and seal. The notarial act is an act of state government and not of the employer.

Notary commissions are not connected to the notary's employment. The notary commission runs 24 hours per day, seven days a week. Employers are unauthorized to prohibit their employees from notarizing after hours away from the work place. Such notarizations do not expose the employer to any risk of legal liability, even if they paid all of the employee's expenses to become a notary. Employers who wrongfully prohibit their employees from notarizing after hours are vulnerable to legal action in court.

In the industry of financial institutions, such as banks and credit unions, it is not unusual to find company policies requiring notaries to notarize free of charge for customers and to charge fees from non-customers. This conduct is likewise wrongful and potentially subject to legal action by the state government and by the public. Employers do not own, nor have legal jurisdiction of, the notarial service. It is a governmental service controlled by the state government. Employers enjoy the convenience of having notaries in-house to serve customers. But, the notarial service as a matter of law is legally accessible by all persons, customer or non- customer, on an equal basis. Policies that grant notary services free of charge to one group of people and then charge a fee of another group of people are wrongful. It is the employer's wrongful intervention and control over a government service, over which the employer has no authority to restrict. Taken to its extremes, such arbitrary delineations and classifications of people may infringe on certain protected civil liberties. Such infringements could be actionable and very costly to defend against.

Notary fees are taxable income. Notaries may report their notarial services as a business venture in certain circumstances and thereby deducting their costs to become a notary and their expenses for notary tools and education.

Felony Crime
See Crime

A crime is labeled a felony by statute according to the severity of the punishment against the guilty party. Generally, a felony crime will be punishable by considerable fines and/or time served in prison.

Female Signer
See Feme Covert

Feme Covert
A great number of states have in their notary statutes a provision instructing the notary that the acknowledgment of a married woman could be taken as if she were sole. This is based on archaic laws that have long since been held unconstitutional.

Under early Colonial American law, through the mid-19th Century, women were under the English doctrine of "feme covert." They had no access to public office nor the right to vote. A woman who was married, was "sub-potestate viri," or "under the power of a husband." The laws governing property rights were oppressive and detailed, as they applied to married women. One scholar characterized such laws as "barbaric laws of chattel - slavery days."

An important study of feme covert laws in early America described them as follows:

> *"Under the common law, a married woman (feme covert) could not own property, either real or personal. All property a woman brought to marriage became her husband's. He could spend her money, sell her stocks or slaves, and appropriate her clothing and jewelry. He gained managerial rights to her land houses, and tenements... He also controlled the rents and profits from all real estates."*
>
> - *Marilynn Salmon, Women and Property in South Carolina: The Evidence from Marriage Settlements, 1730 - 1830, 39 Wm. & Mary Qtly. 655-685 (1982).*

The treatment of married women in the procedure by having their signatures notarized was demeaning. From *The Notaries Manual of 1892,* by Benjamin F. Rex, we read the instructions to male notaries on how to handle this belittling procedure:

> *"1. He should require the husband to leave the room, if he has accompanied his wife. The object of this is to withdraw her from his personal influence; and during the examination he should not be allowed to come either within sight or hearing of her.*
>
> *2. He should ask if the signature to the instrument is hers. If she answers in the affirmative, he should proceed to the next procedure.*
>
> *3. Read and explain the instrument to her... An officer does not comply with the law if he simply asks the woman if she know the contents of the deed and understands it, and accepts her answer in the affirmative as final. She may believe that she knows its contents when she does not.*

The object of the law is to afford her a distinct and official source of information, apart from her husband, or what he or anyone else may have told her.

4. She should be asked if the instrument is her act and deed... It is best to explain to her that she can retract if she wishes to."

Today, the doctrine of feme covert is moot. It has long since been overturned and cast off as archaic and unconstitutional.

From "The Notary" (November 1996)

"Feme Covert:" *An Anachronism that Lingers*

"An acknowledgment of a married woman may he made in the same form as if she were unmarried."

It's hard to believe, but many states still have this law on their books! Isn't this unconstitutional? Hasn't America long left this kind of discrimination behind? By law, yes. But cleaning up statutes requires legislation, and that sometimes takes a lot of pushing. So, old vestiges of past eras linger.

This odd provision of law is the result of an old legal concept called "feme covert." Items like these are holdovers from America's 19th Century. In those times, law and society were extremely sexist. Under the law, a married woman was presumed to be under the physical and intellectual domination of her husband, a feme covert. This presumption in law was designed to protect the interests and rights of women at that time.

In those days a notary was required to question the women privately about the transaction she was signing to ensure that the woman was signing free of coercion or duress. In the 1920s women won the right to vote. Women's rights to equal treatment began to unfold. Notary statutes were amended requiring notaries to notarize for women on an equal basis as they do for men. Thus, the revised statutes included the new warning that a woman's signature can be notarized in the same form as if she were unmarried.

This odd provision of state notary law is a mere relic of a past era in history.

Fiduciary Duty of the Notary
See Agent of the State

Notaries have a fiduciary duty to many people when performing their notarial services.

> *"Notaries owe a duty to anyone who employs them officially for the performance of a notarial service."*
> *- Ky-Aetna Cas. & Sur. V. Commonwealth, 25 S.W. 2d 51, 233 Ky. 142 (1930).*

Very few people in our society are free from a fiduciary duty to others, in one form or another. A fiduciary duty is a duty of trust. We trust others to perform tasks or services for us in a manner that will not harm our interests. The notary's fiduciary duty requires the highest quality of integrity, fairness, fidelity and care for others. The notary's fiduciary duty is a duty of trust.

Notaries hold positions of public trust. Every government official holds a position of public trust; some more than others. When we talk of positions of high public trust we usually have in mind our city mayors, county sheriffs, Governors, members of Congress and the President of the United States.

We expect that they will perform their duties with fidelity and in compliance with the law. Most of all, we expect they will place the best interest of the public far above and ahead of their own interest.

By definition, public officials have a fiduciary duty to their constituencies; to the people they represent and serve. They are obligated to look out for the best interests of the public and make every effort to protect and benefit those interests. Notaries are public officials and are charged with the same fiduciary duties to the public they serve, proportionate to the scope of service they provide and contextually pertinent to the services they are authorized to perform.

> *"[T]he fiduciary's obligations to the dependent party include a duty of loyalty and a duty to exercise reasonable skill and care."*
> - Restatement (Second) of Trusts § 170, 174 (1959).

Married couples owe fiduciary duties to each other not to put the family budget in ruins over excessive consumer purchases. The marital relationship is founded on trust, fidelity and loyalty.

The world "fiduciary" and the word "trust" are semantic sister words. They are both anciently rooted in the Latin word, *"fides,"* meaning faith, trust, and confidence. In ancient times it was said, *"fides est obligatio conscientiae alicujus ad intentionem alterius"* meaning a trust is an obligation of conscience of one person to the wishes of another. In ancient Roman law, the rule *"fides servanda"* applied wherein good faith was to be observed by all. In business transactions among Roman merchants a promise, or fiducia, was made between parties to ensure the parties would fulfill their obligations to the other.

Hence the modern word - fiduciary - sprang from the principles of trust, loyalty and good faith.

Judge Benjamin Cardozo wrote the most famous passage describing fiduciary duties:

> *"Many forms of conduct permissible in a workaday world for those acting at arm's length are forbidden to those bound by fiduciary ties. Not honesty alone but the punctilio of an honor most sensitive is the standard of behavior. There has developed a tradition about this standard that is unbending and inveterate. Uncompromising rigidity has been the attitude of courts of equity."*
> - Meinhard v. Salmon, 164 N.E. 545 (N.Y. 1928).

Notaries are in fiduciary relationships with the public they serve, with the state governments that appointed them, and to their employers when notarizing on the job. A fiduciary relationship is one that also provides confidentiality between persons, such as lawyers and clients or doctors and patients.

Fiduciary relationships are not necessarily formal. Parents are fiduciarily responsible to their children, landlords to their tenants, husbands to their wives, wives to their husbands, and schoolteachers to their students.

The fiduciary relationship as a matter of law requires utmost good faith between the parties in every aspect of their undertakings. Between the parties there is often opportunity to take unfair advantage as a result of the trust that has been reposed in the fiduciary.

By honoring our fiduciary duties to others we manifest some of the highest attributes of human goodness; that of integrity, fairness, concern for the interests of others, and loyalty.

It is a well-established, and long observed, principle of law that a notary is under fiduciary duty to perform her services with utmost care, truthfulness, objectivity, and competence. This duty co-exists with the relationship the notary has to her document signer, to the state that appointed her, and to her employer while notarizing on the job.

The fiduciary duty does not ebb or flow according to the nature of the transaction being notarized. Nor does it accelerate or more boldly manifest itself either because the notary personally knows the document signer or is unfamiliar with him. The notary's fiduciary duty is constant, unchanging and immutable.

It is easy to understand one's fiduciary duties as a notary. Observance of these duties is merely a matter of awareness and a commitment to truth in notarizing.

A notarization is nothing more than a written verification that a person's signature is genuine. They are asking because another person has either instructed them to have it notarized, or the notarization is printed on the signer's document as a requirement. The signer has come to the notary with every justifiable expectation that she will perform the notarization competently so that the needed notarization will be viewed as valid and enforceable. The document signer is relying on the notary, along with the third party receiving the completed document, to perform correctly. Others place considerable trust in the notary. It is the notary's fiduciary duty to perform the notarization with honesty, fairness and to the best of her ability.

The notarial certificate a notary writes, completes, signs and seals is a government document. It is created by the notary, a public official of the state, on behalf of the state to authenticate the signature of a person appearing on their transaction that may be private in nature. The notarial certificate is a statement of facts to which the notary attests. The notary has a fiduciary duty to ensure each declared fact within the certificate is true.

In most states, minor technical errors in a notarial certificate are not considered fatal to the notarial certificate. For the most part, the document signature is still considered validly notarized as a matter of substantial compliance with the rules of the notary law. However, in no state is the falsehood of a material fact within a notarial certificate considered minor.

The notary has a fiduciary duty to ensure each declared fact within the certificate is true. These facts are:
1. The document signer personally appeared before the notary;
2. The notary took every reasonable step to verify the signer's true identity; The signature being notarized genuinely belongs to the person for whom the notary is acting;
3. In the case where the notary is notarizing by jurat, the signer has made his signature under oath in the notary's presence; and
4. All other collateral facts such as the date of notarization, the venue where the notarization was performed, and the notary's lawful authority to perform are attested to as well.

There is a purpose to every notarization performed. Third persons are relying on the notarization to mitigate against some degree of risk that the document signature may be fraudulent. The stakes can be high. Material falsehoods within the notarization certificate, and the false making of a notarization, could directly cause substantial financial harm. It is the notary's fiduciary duty to refrain from such conduct.

Notaries in the workplace expose their employers to risks of liability for wrongful notarizations performed within the scope of their employment. The notary has a fiduciary duty to the employer not to abuse notarial authority by performing falsely or recklessly. The employee/notary is under a duty to the employer to conduct herself at all times with the interests of her employer foremost, with the subordination of her personal interests as evidence of her loyalty to the interests of the employer. Taking unfair advantage of one's position of trust in one's employment violates the fiduciary duty just as much as performing an official duty with reckless abandon for the standards of reasonable care and integrity.

Notaries who fail to understand their notarial fiduciary duties and perform them wrongfully not only harm the interests of their signers, their employers and the interests of third parties relying thereon, but they also injure society as a whole. Abusers of the notarial authority diminish the public's respect and esteem for notarizations. They cheapen the value and credibility of notarial acts. In so doing, the interests of the state that appointed the notary are injured.

The notary's fiduciary duty to the state government is synonymous with the notary's fiduciary duty to the public at large. The office of notary public is an office of public trust. The notary laws are enacted to provide society a substantive means by which written transactions can be rendered reasonably secure from signature fraud. The state government is vested with the constitutional authority to legislate for and regulate its citizens to provide for health, safety and welfare of society. For commerce and law to thrive there must be orderliness and there must be an environment in which law is respected and obeyed. The notary public is an important player in that system of orderliness and respect for law. The state has an interest in this system and it becomes the notary's fiduciary duty not to impede or harm that interest.

Between the notary and the state government, the most damaging and costly fiduciary breach is arguably the attempted rationalization to justify false notarial certificates. Rationalizers assuage themselves by thinking the notarizations don't mean anything and that it is merely a small detail.

When a person knows a statement is false and makes the statement with the intent to pass it off as valid or true, it constitutes a lie. It escapes comprehension how a false notarial certificate can be written, signed and sealed without the notary recognizing that it is false. The certificate says what it says. It means what it says. When enough notaries notarize falsely frequently enough, the interests of the state and the public are severely harmed. Credibility and confidence in the notarial process are diminished, if not lost, indefinitely.

Thomas Jefferson wisely observed, *"He who permits himself to tell a lie once finds it much easier to do it a second and third time, till at length it becomes habitual; he tells lies without attending to it, and truths without the world's believing him."*

To those who don't understand the meaning and implications of a notary's multifaceted fiduciary duty, the concept probably sounds legalistic and dry. To the contrary, notarial fiduciary duties are the heart and vibrancy of the notarial process. It exacts the highest qualities of human virtues and serves to help cultivate such virtues in the workplace and in other people. A society that embraces these principles sets itself apart from those found in the ash heaps of failed societies in modern and ancient times.

Financial Interest
See Conflict of Interest; Disqualified Notary

A notary will have a financial interest in a transaction to be notarized if the notary will receive from that transaction any money or financial gain from the transaction. Depending on the notary's state laws, a financial interest may or may not automatically disqualify the notary from notarizing thereon.

Notaries, as a matter of common law, are required to be impartial in the notarial services they perform. Having a financial interest of any amount in the transaction is generally viewed as grounds for the notary to withdraw from the transaction.

Some people overstate the issues raised by notarial financial interests. For example, charging a fee for the notarization does not constitute a financial interest in the transaction. For the financial interest to pose a problem it must be, for example, a share in the proceeds from the sale of a property or commodity. The transaction might result in a promised share of stock to the notary or a right to use a resort condominium one month per year.

If we carry the argument too far, it can be said that every notarization performed while at work includes a financial or beneficial interest on the notary's part. It is in the notary's interest to stay employed, which requires the notary to serve the customer with accuracy and courtesy.

The recognized rule of law, and it is written in many state notary laws, is that the notary is disqualified from notarizing if the notary has a direct financial interest in the transaction. The operative word, direct, enables the notary to exercise careful discretion and analysis on what types of interests disqualify the notary. It is important for the notary to establish well-conceived policies and standards to define when a financial interest is direct and when it should disqualify the notary.

Fingerprints and Thumbprints in the Notary Journal

See Journal Recordation; Notary Journal; Notary Journal as Evidence; Notary Journal Contents and Format

"The Notary's Duty to Meticulously Maintain a Notary Journal."

By Peter J. Van Alstyne; 30 John Marshall Law Review 794-798 (1998).

There has been considerable interest in the California model for requiring notaries to obtain the thumbprints of document signers in the notary journal. Fingerprinting document signers is characterized by proponents as another means for notaries to protect against notarizing for imposters, and thereby minimizing the perpetration of certain types of fraud. California is the only state so far to have enacted such procedures by statute or administrative rule.

Taking document signer thumbprints in notary journals began in Southern California in 1992 as a pilot program in an effort to combat significantly

high rates of real estate fraud in the Los Angeles area. The three-year pilot program began January 1, 1993 wherein the notary was required to obtain the right thumbprint of any person attempting to notarize a deed, quitclaim deed or deed of trust involving real property located in Los Angeles County. The legislation enacting the pilot program also provided for the Los Angeles County Recorder to notify property owners of deed recordations and assessor identification numbers on the deed as a condition precedent to its filing with the Los Angeles County Recorder.

The Los Angeles County pilot program was initiated after a twenty-year gradual increase in real estate fraud starting in the 1970s. Southern California experienced unprecedented increases in property values and homeowners found themselves with high accumulations of equity in their properties. By 1990, this newfound wealth became a target for fraud. Between July 1990 and November 1992, approximately $131 million dollars were stolen from homeowners in Los Angeles County by con artists.

The nature of real estate fraud involved the forging of property owner signatures on blank deeds, having them notarized by careless or unscrupulous notaries, and filing them for recordation with the Los Angeles County Recorder. Upon recordation, the perpetrator, or "new owner," applied for mortgage financing secured by the forged quitclaim deed and a new deed of trust. The perpetrator then fled with the funds. This scheme succeeded primarily with mortgage brokers who, likewise were careless or unscrupulous, failed to obtain proper appraisals for title insurance and failed to conform to conventional due diligence procedures. Other scams involved perpetrators posing as door-to-door salesmen promoting home improvement products and services. Unbeknownst to the homeowner, among the purchase agreements the buyer signed, were lien contracts on the home. Suddenly, the homeowners found themselves owing large sums to finance companies under threat of foreclosure on their homes.

California lawmakers turned to the notary journal as the first line of defense against these types of property fraud. The theory behind requiring a thumbprint in a notary journal is that a thumbprint constitutes the "ultimate identifier" of a person, be it on a murder weapon, the steering wheel of a stolen car, or in a notary's journal. Therefore, the thumbprint in the notary journal, proponents argue, is inherently the most effective deterrent to fraudulent real estate transactions.

Proponents cite several compelling reasons for requiring thumbprints in journals. The first reason is that it may be an effective deterrent to criminal fraud, as no impostor or forger would engage the services of a notary if they must leave their incriminating thumbprint in the journal. Second, the thumbprint effectively protects the notary from allegations of carelessness or failure to properly verify the signer's identity prior to notarizing the transaction. Third, the requirement protects the public from fraud and gives clear notice of the importance of the notarial act upon the transaction they are about to sign.

Proponents of mandatory thumb printing in notary journals deemed the three-year test a success. Claims were made that the incidence of real estate fraud dropped.

> "As for the property-owner notification part of the Los Angeles County program, in one 10-month period, more than 3,400 real-property owners were notified of deed filings they had not authorized and 372,571 notices of deed recordings were mailed out. Proponents also cited numerous written endorsements from law enforcement and consumer affairs investigators, and from prosecutors claiming their forgery caseloads 'significantly diminished since the thumbprint requirement has been in effect'" (A Journal Thumbprint: The Ultimate ID., Nat'l Notary Mag, May 1996 at 9, 11).

In 1992, California became the first and only state to enact statewide mandatory thumb printing requirements in notary journals for notarizations when certain real estate transactions are involved. The new law is imposed on any notarizations of quitclaim deeds, warranty deeds and deeds of trusts. The law exempts notarizations of signers to deeds of reconveyance and trustee's deeds that result from a decree of foreclosure or a nonjudicial foreclosure. Enactment of statewide mandatory thumb printing by notaries passed overwhelmingly in the California legislature.

Mandatory thumb printing by notaries, although popular among law enforcement and consumer protection groups, has not been universally *popular with other segments of the population. Some groups object to the requirement on the grounds that it unduly interferes with the signer's right of privacy. Others question whether the requirement is overkill and warranted by the data under the three-year test program. This particular question cannot be easily dismissed.*

The Los Angeles County three-year test program involved three procedural tests: mandatory thumb printing, Recorder's office disclosure to property owners of deed filings, and compulsory disclosure of assessor identity on the deed. In the literature and reports written on this important experiment, there is an absence of empirical data detailing the incidence of fraud for the period of time leading up to the implementation of the test. There is also an absence of empirical data detailing the levels of fraud during and after the three-year test was conducted. Instead, there is only the often-repeated conclusion that "journal thumb printing is a four-month-old, permanent success story in California, where it is dramatically reducing the incidence of forged real estate deeds," as quoted by the National Notary Magazine in its May, 1996 issue.

The imposition of mandatory thumb printing is a radical new public policy with far reaching legal and public policy ramifications. Advocates of mandatory thumb printing in notary journals urge its nation-wide adoption, however, before another state adopts mandatory thumb printing, there must be better documentation of the efficacy of journal thumb printing with respect to the reduction of real estate fraud in Southern California. Advocates need to substantiate their stance by factually demonstrating that the rest of the nation currently suffers from a comparable rate of real estate fraud and that mandatory thumb printing is the only effective and least intrusive way to solve the problem. Advocates claim the reduction in Los Angeles County's real estate fraud was the direct result of mandatory journal thumb printing. However, thumb printing was only one of three procedures tested. It is reasonable to suspect that the other two procedures also produced positive results. For example, over 3,400 property owners in a ten- month period were given notice of unauthorized deed filings affecting their properties; a clear indication mandatory reporting of deed filings had a very substantial beneficial effect.

There is another reason to doubt the advocate's justification of mandatory thumb printing. Advocates rarely discuss other factors that could have contributed to the reductions in property fraud in Los Angeles County. Relationships between cause and effect are rarely simple. They are usually the result of complex interactive forces sometimes working together for a common goal, and often times not. For example, if there were measurable reductions in the incidence of real estate fraud during the three-year test period, it could have risen out of better or more aggressive prosecution of fraud or because of heightened consumer awareness. A reduction in the incidence of fraud could have occurred because the County Recorder's Office was more prepared to identify potential problems, the real estate and mortgage brokerage industries were alerted to such transactions, and notaries were more prudent in providing notarial services and journal-keeping.

Unless careful collection of data was kept and competently analyzed, it cannot be assumed that most of these factors did not play a critical role in the success journal thumb printing seems to claim for itself. If the claims of a successful three-year test are factually justified, then the test in its entirety is to be lauded because no single aspect of its three parts is documented to have outperformed the others.

Should a notary have the document signer place a thumbprint in her notary journal? The old cliché, "necessity is the mother of invention," is also true in the reverse. Inventors often have to create a need for their inventions. With so much publicity accorded to the new California thumb printing laws, it is particularly timely to carefully consider the ramifications of such a practice. It seems as if the enthusiasm over thumb printing is luring the traditional role of the notary towards new and possibly inappropriate directions.

Advocates of ink thumb printing in notary journals make important and clear arguments by identifying a number of benefits the practice can produce.

However, the practice of thumb printing tends to negate the established and tested legal purpose of the notary. It suggests that notarial procedures prescribed by law and followed by millions of notaries nationally are inadequate. Moreover, such advocacy suggests a misunderstanding or *underestimation of the statutory and common law principles that govern notarial services.*

The core purpose of the notarial act is to authenticate signatures of persons appearing before the notary. The heart of that act is the notary's legal duty to take all reasonable steps to verify the signer's identity. The notary may do so through personal knowledge of the signer's identity or by reliance on the oath of a credible witness personally known to the notary. The notary, by common law, and by statutory law in most states, may rely on certain forms of identification cards to verify the signer's identity. Once signer identity is confirmed, the prudent notary should obtain the document signer's signature in the notary journal, along with other key information.

It could be argued that journal thumb printing should be discretionary, rather than mandatory. However, thumb printing in the journal under any circumstances raises important questions. Advocates of thumb printing assert that it will screen out imposters and forgers and thereby protect the notary and the public. The argument goes to the heart of the notary's duty to exercise reasonable care in verifying the signer's identity. If there is any doubt about the true identity of a signer, a reasonable and prudent notary should summarily withdraw and refrain from performing the notarization anyway. Requiring a notary to obtain the signer's ink thumbprint in addition to the signer's signature and all of the other vital information in a notary journal is illogical and unreasonable. It is overkill.

Under centuries of well-established rules of evidence and procedures, a notary's personal knowledge of the identity of a document signer is irrefutable. As a form of evidence, the value of a signer's ink thumbprint in the notary's journal will be inferior to the evidentiary value of the notary's personal knowledge, or the personal knowledge of a credible witness, when it comes to documenting signer identification in the journal. Proper reliance on a signer's ID card is not superseded or enhanced by a thumbprint in the notary journal. The common law standard by which a notary's conduct is judged is the standard of reasonable care. Mandating journal thumb printing is inharmonious with this venerated historical standard.

Reportedly, the most vocal support group for mandatory journal thumb printing is law enforcement. This is due largely to the computerized, state-of-the-art Automated Fingerprint Identification Systems (AFIS) that can now match crime scene fingerprints in a matter of minutes with files of millions of such prints. To law enforcement officials, the journal thumbprint constitutes invaluable evidence in solving and prosecuting fraud by forgery and imposter.

The benefits to law enforcement notwithstanding, thrusting the notary into a law enforcement role is inappropriate. The assumption that journal thumb printing will eliminate problems with document fraud and signer identification is not justified. Advocates have not made their case. It appears to be advocacy based on fear of fraud and "what ifs." More than a century ago, Charles Dickens commented that Americans have a uniquely skeptical attitude about the direction in which society is headed. Dickens wrote that in America the "one great blemish in the popular mind... and the prolific parent of an innumerable brood of evils, is Universal Distrust. Yet the American citizen plumes himself upon this spirit, even when he is sufficiently dispassionate to perceive the ruin it works."

If there is in fact a growing problem with signature fraud slipping past American notaries, it is not notary law that has failed. The appropriate policy response is to better train notaries on correct notarial procedures. Compelling notaries to take a more aggressive stance against signature fraud by implementing questionable new procedures is not an appropriate response. If the notary performs the notarial act correctly, taking a signer's thumbprint in the notary journal cannot be considered a useful requirement.

Foreign Languages
See Document Content; Documents in a Foreign Language

The content of a signer's document is completely outside the scope of the notary's responsibilities. What the document says has no bearing on the notary or the notarization. However, when a document is written in a foreign language, many notaries become concerned.

It is irrelevant whether the document is written in English or another language. The notarization has no effect on the document. It does not render the document true, valid or legally enforceable. Such concerns belong to the document signer and not the notary.

The notarial certificate must be written in English, according to age-old case law. A properly completed notarial certificate can be subsequently translated into another language for the convenience of the parties receiving the document. The notarial certificate is an official document of the state government the notary creates on behalf of the state to authenticate the signer's signature.

The notary may elect to include within the notarial certificate the title of the document for which the notarization is performed. For example, the notary could indicate, *"Acknowledged before me by Iracema Jantu, known personally to me to be the signer of the foregoing request for extension of a student visa."*

Another common problem notaries face is document signers who do not speak or understand English. It is impossible for a notary to perform a notarization without communicating with the document signer. The notary must verify the signer's identity and determine the signer is signing willingly and freely. The notary must know what the document is to ensure the signer knows what it is.

The notary has the option to rely on an independent, impartial translator to close the communication gap between the notary and the non-English speaking signer. The essential concern the notary must resolve is documentation proving the notary handled the situation with solid judgment and reasonable care. It may prove useful for the notary to cause the translator to sign a sworn affidavit the translation was performed truthfully and to the best of the translator's knowledge and belief. The signature to the affidavit can also be notarized by jurat. The notary can cause the affidavit to attach to the notarial certificate. The notary's journal should fully document the entire transaction, including documentation of the translator's notarized affidavit.

If for any reason the notary has reason to be concerned over the translation or the parties involved, the notary should consider withdrawing from the transaction. In the ideal world, the translator would be a person the notary personally knows and trusts. Because the ideal circumstance is extremely rare, the notary is duty-bound to exercise extraordinary care when dealing with foreign language translators.

Foreign Notary Officials
See Notarial Acts by Federal Authorities and Military Offices; Notaries in Foreign Countries

Forged Signature
See Imposters; Signature; Signature Verification; Signer Identification

One of the foremost objectives in notarizing document signatures is to verify the signatures are not forgeries - that they are genuinely those of the persons who claimed to have made them.

The act of forging, or making a forgery, is the crime of making or altering something with the intent to deceive. Well over one century ago, the esteemed English law scholar, Lord Cook, said of the crime of forgery, *"To forge is metaphorically taken from the smith who beateth upon his anvil, and forgeth what fashion or shape he will; the Latin word 'to forge' is the offense called `crimen falsi' and it is done in the name of another."*

To make a forgery is to fabricate, by false imitation, a false document in similitude of another document. The words "forge," "forger" and "forgery" all involve fraudulent deceit. The intent to deceive another is requisite for the act to constitute fraud by forgery. Documents and signatures to documents can be forged.

The crime of forgery is almost always a felony, the prosecution and conviction of which can result in extensive prison sentences and fines. This includes the signing of another person's signature with intent to deceive, the creation of a phony document with the intent to deceive, and the creation of an object with the intent to deceive. We are all too familiar with these sorts of crimes, as they tend to be prevalent in the news media. Forging monetary currency, signatures of others and valuable consumer products such as Levi Strauss jeans are accomplished often without detection by very skilled artisans. In the arena of legal documents, signatures to title deeds, wills and powers of attorney are too often forged, much to the pain and anguish of others. It is for this reason that notarizations are instituted by government to mitigate against the incidence of signature forgeries.

Forged signatures are made by imposters. Therefore, every document signer must personally appear before the notary to prove their true identity and to prove the signature belongs to them, and that it was made willingly and freely. A signature made under duress, force or coercion is not valid. In fact, it is made to deceive others into believing it was made willingly and freely. Hence, the signature was made falsely even though it belongs to its maker. A falsely made signature intended to deceive others constitutes the crime of forgery.

The term, counterfeit, is closely associated with the crime of forgery. It, too, constitutes the making of a false image or representation with the intent to deceive. In contemporary law, the term, counterfeit, is used primarily in the making of false money or false brand name products.

Our signatures are our personal ink marks to documents evidencing our intentions to be bound by the terms of the documents or by the assertions and representations the documents make. Our signatures to transactions are serious business because other persons are relying on the validity of the signature, even to their detriment. They will take risks or commit to transactions based on the verity of the document's signature.

A person's signature has always represented profound significance, influence and value in every society and system of law. A signature to a transaction signifies the signer has read, understood, agreed to and committed himself to the contents, terms or obligations set forth in the instrument. The signature unmistakably and unambiguously represents the maker's deliberateness. It is tangible evidence of the signer's intent. When another makes a person's signature fraudulently, it constitutes a most serious criminal act.

140

property, without due process of law; nor deny any person within its jurisdiction the equal protection of the laws."

The notary statutes of many states retain archaic vestiges of generations past that require notaries to be registered voters and/or United States citizens. Such requirements have been held squarely unconstitutional as they violate the equal protection clause of the 14th Amendment, and it discriminates against non-citizens on the basis of alienage.

Historically, most states required applicants to be citizens of the United States and residents of the state and/or county in which appointment is sought. The U.S. Supreme Court struck down the requirement that notaries be U.S. Citizens in 1984. In Bernal v. Fainter (467 U.S. 216) a Mexican native and longtime resident of Texas applied to become a Texas notary. Texas denied his application solely because he was not a United States Citizen as required by Texas statute. In reversing the Court of Appeals the U.S. Supreme Court used a strict scrutiny test since the constitutional question was one of alienage. Since there was no relation "to the achievement of any valid state interest" the statutory limitation was declared an unconstitutional restriction under the Equal Protection clause of the Fourteenth Amendment.

Any statute or administrative rule restricting the office of notary public to citizens of the United States cannot stand, unless it advances a compelling state interest by the least restrictive means available. To the extent that a state determines that the notary must be competent in the English language and in the customs of the country in order to qualify for notarial appointment, the equal protection clause requires the state to do so in a manner that is confined to that specific objective.

States have authority to impose citizenship requirements on high state positions, which are at the heart of representative government, its formulation and execution of policy. The position of notary public is ministerial in nature. It does not involve discretionary decision-making or execution of policy. Imposing citizenship requirements on notaries is not supported by or related in any way to the achievement of a valid state objective.

A few states require notary applicants to be registered voters within the county in which they reside as a condition to appointment. A requirement of voter registration as a condition to notarial appointment is clearly an unconstitutional infringement on the applicant's equal protection rights. Voter registration requires U.S. Citizenship, and has no relevance to the office and functions of the notary public. It affects every business and government agency that has notaries on their payroll. In order to become a notary in such states one must waive precious constitutional rights.

A voter registration requirement to be a notary effectively means that a person cannot be employed, and an employer should not hire her, for any job that requires her to be a notary unless she is a registered voter. The vast majority of notaries are notaries because it's required for their employment. Notaries are found in nearly every workplace. For most, the notary appointment is as requisite to employment as a valid driver's license is to a traveling salesman.

Employers are prohibited from requiring their employees be registered to vote. A person's choice to register is a protected privacy under the U.S. Constitution. The voter registration rolls themselves are public records, and every American has the inalienable right to refuse to be listed thereon, albeit good citizenship includes voting at every public election.

In a 1973 Connecticut case, the U.S. Supreme Court took up the question of required U.S. Citizenship as a condition for admission to the Connecticut Bar. The Court held the requirement invalid and set forth a standard for review of citizenship requirements. The state needs to justify its classification (U.S. Citizenship) by showing some rational relationship between the interest sought to be protected and the limiting classification. A U.S. Citizenship requirement is arguably defensible for state government positions that are elective or are important nonelective executive, legislative and judicial positions. The requirement may also stand for positions that participate directly in the formulation, execution or review of broad public policy that goes to the heart of representative government.

Attorneys general of many states have issued formal opinions concurring with the principles set forth by the Bernal case and its progeny of subsequent reaffirmations by courts across the country.

U.S. Citizenship is a requisite to voter registration. The Attorney General of North Carolina, in formal opinion, explained it clearly by stating that a *"state's requirement that notaries be registered voters violates the Equal Protection Clause of the Fourteenth Amendment. Citizenship is a prerequisite to voter eligibility."* (54 N.C. Op. Atty. Gen. 7).

It also violates First and Fifth Amendment rights. A person's choice not to register to vote is also a free speech issue. A person's choice not to register to vote can be based on a political view, perhaps as a form of protest or repudiation with one's government or the electoral process.

Fraud
See False Notarization; Notarizing Falsely

A person commits fraud when he makes representations he knows to be false and does so with the intent to deceive others to induce them to act in reliance on the false representations.

Fraud is comprised of four elements:

1. *Misrepresentation of a material fact;*
2. *Made willfully to deceive, or recklessly without knowledge;*
3. *Which was justifiably relied upon by the plaintiff under the circumstances; and*
4. *Which caused damage as a proximate consequence.*

   - Ramsay Health Care, Inc. v. Follmer, 560 So. 2d 746 (Ala. 1990).

The Restatement (Second) of Torts provides further definition to when a misrepresentation of a fact constitutes fraud:

§ 526 Conditions Under Which Misrepresentation Is Fraudulent (Scienter) A misrepresentation is fraudulent if the maker

1. *Knows or believes that the matter is not as he represents it to be,*
2. *Does not have the confidence in the accuracy of his representation that he states or implies, or*

3. *Knows that he does not have the basis for his representation that he states or implies.*

When a notary signs and seals a notarial certificate that contains false representations of material facts, that notary commits fraud. The notarial certificate asserts a series of facts, which are required by law, that induce its readers to believe the signature being notarized has been properly authenticated as asserted. If the signer has not appeared before the signer and be properly identified, or did not sign under oath as asserted in a jurat, the notarization is materially false. But, the reader does not know that. They are entitled to reasonably believe the notarization is true and valid. They are entitled to believe the signature to the document is genuine and binds the signer to the terms and content of the document.

When fraud enters into a transaction, it is said to "permeate and taint it throughout."

The notary's signature and seal constitute the notary's attestation the contents of the certificate are true. When they are not, the falsehoods in the certificate are prima facie proof of the notary's commission of fraud. The notary cannot raise a defense that there was no intent to deceive. The notary cannot raise a defense by saying she didn't know or understand what the certificate said that she signed and sealed. The certificate means what it says, and when it is signed it is binding upon the notary. Hence, the notary is strictly liable for the truthfulness of the notarial certificate.

From the Restatement (Second) of Torts, we find the well-established legal principles that assign liability to purveyors of fraud.

§ 525. Liability for Fraudulent Misrepresentation

One who fraudulently makes a misrepresentation of fact, opinion, intention or law for the purpose of inducing another to act or to refrain from action in reliance upon it, is subject to liability to the other in deceit for pecuniary loss caused to him by his justifiable reliance upon the misrepresentation.

148

§ 531 General Rule

One who makes a fraudulent misrepresentation is subject to liability to the persons or class of persons whom he intends or has reason to expect to act or to refrain from action in reliance upon the misrepresentation, for pecuniary loss suffered by them through their justifiable reliance in the type of transaction in which he intends or has reason to expect their conduct to be influenced.

§ 532 Misrepresentation Incorporated in Document or Other Thing

One who embodies a fraudulent misrepresentation in an article of commerce, a muniment of title, a negotiable instrument or a similar commercial document, is subject to liability for pecuniary loss caused to another who deals with them or with a third person regarding the article or document in justifiable reliance upon the truth of the representation.

Notarial certificates clearly fall under this section of the Restatement.

As a matter of public policy, law and society cannot tolerate a defense that false notarizations are not intended to deceive. This applies to nearly all legal documents bearing signatures that are intended to induce others to act thereon. If the courts and the law permitted the defense of "no intention to deceive" in connection to signed false statements, there would be little reason to place any trust in written statements or notarizations to begin with. The distinction between truth and falsehood would become blurred because the latter can be promulgated with impunity. The notary would only have to declare, "I didn't intend to deceive anyone even though I knew the facts were not true." The commission of fraud can wreak havoc on society and its orderliness. Permitted to go unchecked, rampant fraud can completely undermine and eventually destroy society. Fraud is a serious crime for good reason.

Full Faith and Credit Clause

Under Section One of the Fourth Article of the United State Constitution, we find a provision called the "Full Faith and Credit Clause." Section One states, "Full Faith and Credit shall be given in each State to the public Acts, Records, and Judicial Proceedings of every other state."

Under this clause, all legal acts originating in any state of the Union shall be enforceable and binding equally in all states. This constitutional provision is absolutely crucial to the survival of the Union of the fifty states. Without it, our nation would be little more than a loosely assembled confederation of independent states.

Under the full faith and credit clause every legal notarization performed in any state shall be honored and enforceable in all fifty states. It is unfortunately all too common for businesses or government agencies to refuse a notarization performed in another state because the notarization does not conform to the local state's notary law.

For example, notaries in Virginia are not required to affix a notary seal to the notarial certificate. The document is sent to another state for filing or other business purposes and that state requires all notarizations to bear a notary seal. The recipient has no authority or cause for rejecting the Virginia notarization without a seal because of the 4th Article of the Constitution. If the notarization is legal in the state under whose authority it is created, then it shall be enforceable in all states.

It is not unheard of for the recipient to reject the notarization from another state because it does not conform to the requirements of the recipient state and significant financial damages result because of the delay (for which there was no legitimate reason). It behooves all persons to investigate the legitimacy or completeness of a notarial certificate before it is rejected out of hand. Wrongfully rejecting an otherwise valid notarization from another state could arguably result in a legal cause of action in court.

G

Good laws lead to the making of better ones; bad ones bring about worse.
- *Jean Jacques Rousseau (1762).*

General Custom in Notarizations

In law, the customs of a community, state or nation can be taken into account by the courts for context when defining a new principle of law pertaining to matters before the courts. General custom cannot take on the color of law without the holding of the court. Moreover, if the general custom violates provisions of statutory law, the court cannot overrule the statute, unless its provisions are unconstitutional or unlawful.

Defendants in notary law cases often attempt to raise general custom of the community as a defense for their wrongful conduct. For example, in a metropolitan area, it may be common for lawyers to have client signatures notarized without having the client appear personally before the notary. That may be the custom of the legal community, but it violates state notary law. Such a defense has no validity.

The common refrain, "but everybody does it that way," is relevant if it helps the court understand that a particular act or procedure is lawful, but is not relevant if the action is unconventional or deviant from routine or the norm.

Giving Legal Advice as a Notary
See Unauthorized Practice of Law; Practice of Law

Gold Seals
See Seal of the Notary Public

In no state are notaries required to use a gold foil embossed notary seal. Although they are highly decorative and impressive, they are from generations long past.

Until a few decades ago, notaries commonly embossed their notary seals to gold foil circles glued to the signer's document. This technique did not add to the security or verity of a notarization.

Government Regulation of Notaries
See Equal Protection; Notary Statutes

Notaries serve at the pleasure of the state government. The notary's power and authority to act derives from the state. Administration of the notary law and the process of commissioning notaries are governed by state law. The state statutes and administrative rules define what shall be done. Commonly, small details for implementing the notary law are not defined by statute and are left to the discretion of the state agency that commissions the notary. A few states enact administrative rules in order to define the small details. Unless administrative rules are adopted in accordance with correct procedures of law, it is not uncommon for the notary clerk and the state agency to fend for themselves by handing down ad hoc "rules" and policy interpretations. It is not uncommon for such policies or rules not to conform to rule of law.

It is also not uncommon for well-meaning people to emphasize "form over substance." From 17th Century French comes the word, "Martinet," referring to the military rank of General. Today, a martinet refers to individuals who zealously look for conformance to format and appearance, and sharply discipline or condemn deviations from their self-created standards. There are notarial martinets in society. They are those who, for example, reject notarizations on documents because the wrong color ink was used or because corrections to writing were not initialed, although not required by law.

It is the legal duty of every notary, government official, and professional to attain a competent knowledge and understanding of the notary law.

Lack of knowledge or understanding is a vacuum of information that is too quickly and easily filled by false and misleading "information." It is particularly troubling when notaries phone the government for guidance on a notarial problem and are given incorrect answers, often based on unwritten ad hoc "rules and policies."

The notary statutes of the fifty states vary in thoroughness, detail, currency and antiquity. When amending the notary law, state officials are often disadvantaged. The legal principles and theories behind the notary law are not commonly understood. Hence, changes to the law might be made without realizing the legal ramifications of their changes. Like a bull running loose in a China shop, undisciplined legislative initiatives in the notary law can be harmful. For every amendment to law, there should be an assessment of the practical and legal ramifications that might result. The benefits to the public must be weighed against the financial and societal costs. There is little room for zealous legislative corrections or reform in notary law.

In his book <u>The Death of Common Sense,</u> Philip K. Howard wrote that *"modern law tells us our duty is only to comply, not accomplish. We should stop looking to law to provide the final answer."*

Howard goes on to explain his concept in these words: *"principles allow us to think. Responsibility requires the attributes we used to value most: effort and courage and leadership."*

Governmental Act
See Agent of the State; Ministerial Officer; Notary Public

The office of notary public is created and administered by government. There is no such thing as a private notary. The notary serves under the authority of the state government, empowered by the state to exercise certain legal powers. No person can invoke these powers on their own. The notary is an agent of the state government. Every function the notary performs is a governmental act.

In every notarial act, the notary binds the state to that act. The full faith and backing of the state stands behind the notarization. It is literally a state government function the notary performs. It is irrelevant whether the notary's employer paid all of the notary fees for the employee to become a notary. Employers have no jurisdiction or authority over the notary's commission or services performed. They are governmental acts.

Gross Neglect
See Liability

A notary is guilty of gross neglect when the seriousness or frequency of the neglect becomes so serious that it is harmful to the public interest.

Gross Negligence
See Liability

A notary's conduct that constitutes gross negligence is conduct that is absent of any reasonable care to perform official duties without causing harm to any party. This type of conduct is not inadvertent. It is conduct that is reckless and wanton. It is where the notary disregards the consequences of their reckless conduct and evinces the suggestion that the notary possessed some degree of intent to cause such harm to others.

Arguably, a notary could be liable for gross negligence by notarizing a signature known to be made by a person other than its asserted maker. For example, the notary's employer asks that the notary notarize his spouse's signature, although she cannot come down to the office to appear before the notary, as required by law.

Gross negligence often arises when the notary, for reasons of expediency or friendliness, fails to verify the signer's identity as required by law. Perhaps the signer has no valid ID, but the notary relies on the signer's business card instead. Or, the signer's ID card is obviously counterfeit or fraudulently altered, but the notary accepts it anyway. In these examples, the notary's failure to fulfill the most basic of notarial duties is wanton and reckless. The notary disregards the possible consequences of the misconduct to the extent that it appears to be intentional.

154

Guarantor of the Probative Value Accorded the Notarial Certificate
See Completing the Notarial Certificate

The notary is personally responsible for the material facts asserted within the notarial certificate she signs. As a matter of law, the notary is the guarantor of the probative value accorded the notarial certificate. In other words, notarial certificates assert a series of facts that establish the verity of a signature. The certificate is probative of the signature's genuineness. Great faith and reliance is placed in notarizations, and the notary bears the burden for ensuring every word thereof is factually true.

H

"[T]he time has come for a revival of soul and practice. The notary must be restored to the position of respect which his office merits."
- *John H. Wigmore (1928).*

Hearsay Evidence
See Notary Journal; Notary Journal as Evidence

The rules of evidence treat hearsay as any statement made by a person who is not a party to a transaction, has no interest in the transaction, and the statement is not made under oath. For example, the witness might say in court, "John said he saw the red car speeding before it crashed."

This sample statement is not admissible in court because its truth cannot be verified. Only John can prove the truth of his statement if he is under oath and is subject to cross-examination and corroborating evidence.

The rules of evidence provide exemptions to the ban on hearsay evidence. Of particular benefit to notaries is the "business record exemption to the hearsay rule." This exemption pertains to the notary's notary journal. Under this rule, everything recorded in a notary's journal is deemed probative of the truthfulness of the notarization being recorded, and therefore shall be deemed factually true. Part of the reasoning behind this rule of exemption is that regularly maintained business records are unlikely to be falsified, lest the record-keeper fatally jeopardize his business interests. Such records are deemed accurate because they protect the record-keeper's interests.

Hiis Testibus Clause
See Witness Signatures

Pronounced, "hi-is test-ibus clause," is an ancient legal phrase referencing the format on documents that require witnesses to sign in witness of the principal's signature. It is often expressed as, "signed, sealed and delivered in the presence of..," or, "signed and sealed in the presence of..."

The notary, of course, is not responsible for the hiis testibus clause. For the most part, such a clause is of little use in contemporary business and law.

His Mark
See Signature; Signature Made by a Mark; Signers Who are Blind; Willful, Free Making of a Signature

State laws will occasionally require documents to be executed with the signature or mark of the grantor or principal. The phrase, "his mark," is a vestige of bygone eras where large pockets of population were illiterate and could not write their names. In lieu of a signature, the person could make a distinctive mark signifying his intent to enter into and be bound by the document he is signing by a mark. Marks were often the letter "X" or an ink thumbprint.

History of the Notary Public Office
The office of the notary public has been esteemed and venerated down through the centuries. In the time of the ancient Roman Empire, approximately during the time of Cicero in the First Century B.C., common people were almost universally uneducated and illiterate. The ability to read or write was the source of tremendous power and influence. The Roman government created the office of notaries, to be filled by one who could read and write. It became the duty of these highly respected and trusted officials to write and safeguard documents of agreements, contracts and wills. When entering into an agreement or transaction, signers who could not write their names used clay or metal engraved disks representing their "mark" or insignia. It involved the ceremonial melting of wax onto the document and impressing the engraved image of the signer into the wax.

It is thought that the world's first known notary was a Roman scribe named Marcus Tullius Tiro. As secretary to Marcus Tullius Cicero, Tiro invented a form of shorthand notes, called "notae," from which the word "notarius" derives.

As the centuries evolved, it became most prestigious to own a "signet ring" bearing the engraving of the family coat of arms. It was indeed the status symbol of nobility and clergy.

The importance of the notary's authority became ever more realized throughout the Roman Empire and it even continued after the Empire's demise. The office of notary was viewed as so important, Charlemange ordered every bishop, abbot and count to have a notary.

Across the world, civil law notaries number relatively few because the requirements to become a notary are stringent. This is especially so in Latin America, and countries such as Japan and France where there are less than 550 notaries and 7,500 notaries respectively.

The English notary, on the other hand, evolved into a unique form of officer. Notaries in England first appeared in the thirteenth century. For several hundred years the importance of the English notary expanded into document preparation in the ecclesiastical courts and secular courts. The Roman Pope granted English notaries their legal authority prior to 1279 and thereafter, the authority to appoint notaries was extended to the Archbishop of Canterbury. This authority firmly vested in 1533 when the English Church seceded from the Roman Church.

Prior to the Reformation period, there were four categories of English notaries: general notaries, district notaries, ecclesiastical notaries, and scrivener notaries. Their substantive functions declined steadily after the Reformation and much of them were taken over by solicitors as the volume of work for notaries had declined so significantly. In the 1880's there arose a resistance movement against the total control of notarial functions by solicitors. Ultimately the decline in the number of notaries continued leaving a very few number of notaries throughout English history. By the end of the 1920's there were fewer than 500 notaries in all of England and Wales.

The first notary to step foot in the Americas was a Spanish member of the crew accompanying Christopher Columbus to San Salvador in 1492. Not until the populating of the American colonies is there any known notary serving in the Americas.

The early American colonists were quick to discover that their commercial documents were acceptable only upon the completion of the European format of document and signature authentication by a notary. Most of the colonial notaries were appointed under the authority of the Archbishop of Canterbury, while others were appointed by local authority. The American colonists copied the English notarial system to authenticate documents used in international commerce. Each colony quickly established rules for appointing people to serve as notaries whose signatures and seals would affix to documents to assure its acceptance throughout the world. The colonies' growing trade with Europe drove the need and demand for more notaries because trading partners needed reliable bills of exchange witnessed by knowledgeable, responsible persons with no interest in the dealings.

The first colonial notary to be commissioned was in the Province of New Haven in 1639. Appointments soon followed in the Massachusetts Bay Colony in 1644, in Virginia in 1662, and in New York in 1664. The practice of appointing notaries expanded steadily thereafter. These colonial notaries were men of high trustworthiness, of substance and literacy.

Early American notary history is not without its notary scoundrels. The first notary to be appointed in the colonies was Thomas Fugill of New Haven. He was stripped of his notarial office for fraud.

The office of notary in Colonial America was important to society and commerce because there were so few notaries. They kept extensive records of the documents they prepared, in keeping with the long tradition of the English notaries of the ecclesiastical courts. As commerce and population increased in the colonies, the functions of notaries began to transfer to officials of the courts and those in the legal profession, whose numbers were growing as well. Similar to the decline of notaries in England, the notaries of colonial America also declined in number.

There are few notaries in early American history. They were appointed by the President of the United States or by the governors of the states, often limiting the number of notaries to just one notary for a county or city. In the nineteenth century, the states developed and enacted their own notary laws and procedures for appointing and empowering notaries. As the nation's population grew, so did the number of state appointed notaries. All the while, the powers of the notary slowly diminished in substantive ways, especially in the area of bank and marine protests, the standard procedure of the time in trade and law to resolve discrepancies in shipments and bills of laden.

The legal community began to assume more and more of the functions of the 19th Century notary, including the official record keeping of public documents. Until that time, the notary was the official keeper of public and official documents. The government office of recorders replaced that function.

Today, the notary public office is primarily ministerial and clerical, allowing for little discretion or room for judgment calls. However, in the 350 years since the appointment of America's first notaries, the growth in the volume of documents needing notarizations has exploded, thus creating a nearly insatiable demand for notaries across America. As the Wall Street Journal wrote on June 15, 1993, "Notaries witness the signatures on all that paper that keeps the nation ticking."

History of the Notary Seal
See Seal of the Notary Public

Although the office of notary public spans over two millennia of history, the use of some form of seal or emblem of the notary's authority to authenticate the documents did not evolve until the later part of the twelfth century. Around 1167, Pope Alexander extended to notarized documents a "Decretal Meminimus" that elevated all notarized documents to the status of official documents, with the full probative value that was previously reserved only to official documents.

While the status of the notarial act rose substantially in prestige and importance, the laws of twelfth century France restricted the role of the notary to the courts. Under French law, a notarial document was not considered authentic until the seal of the court in the jurisdiction where the notary was of record was affixed to the document.

In the late seventeenth century, King Louis XIV dissolved the restriction on notaries as court functionaries. The King eliminated the need for the seal of the court to affix to all documents to establish authenticity. Rather, the King granted to each notary a seal of their authority that they were to affix to all notarizations. These were, of course, wax and seals. Their popularity caught on and spread quickly across all of Europe.

The historical use of notary seals in England is quite different from that on the continent. Under old English common law practices, documents were not required to be authenticated by a notary with a seal. However, if they were, it was more for effect than for substance. The use of private seals was commonplace to merely add solemnity to transactions. However, prior to the twelfth century, the use of a seal was reserved only unto the king and his representatives. The commonality of the private seal eventually gave rise to a problem: to distinguish documents that were official under the authority of the crown, from those that were not.

At the end of the thirteenth century, the crown supported reforms to the church and granted only representatives of the Church of England the authority to use an authentic seal.

By the fourteenth century, the use of notaries and their official seals became commonplace throughout Europe. The pattern of their services and procedures became the template by which much of our contemporary notary law is formatted today.

Holographic Will
See Testamentary Documents

This is a form of last will and testament that is recognized in most states and is entirely handwritten in a person's own hand, dated, and signed. The validity of a holographic will owes its origin to the fact that the successful counterfeit of another person's handwriting is extremely difficult. The holographic will must be made in the testator's own hand in order for the presumed protection against forgery to apply.

I

"A notary public who certifies to the identity of the person executing an instrument of his own knowledge, without taking the precautions required by statute, is liable to one relying on the acknowledgment for loss caused by the fact that such person is not the one he represents himself to be."
- Anderson v. Aronsohn, 181 Cal. 294 (1923).

Identification Cards and Papers
See Identity of the Signer; Signer Identification

Identification of the Signer's Document

As a matter of law, when a person signs their name to a document, he signs for purposes stated in the document. The signature represents the signer's acquiescence to the content and terms of that document.

When a notary notarizes a signature, the notary certifies the signature is genuine and was made for the purposes stated within the document. If a signer is signing a contract and needs it notarized, he is signing for the purpose of entering the contract. The notarization is inextricably connected to the assertion the signature is intended to manifest the signer's intent to enter that contract. Therefore, the notary is legally obligated to identify the document being signed and notarized.

The notary's duty to identify the signer's document does not imply the notary must know the contents of the document. In fact, the notary has no authority or need to know what a document contains. A notary's uninvited intrusion into the contents of the signer's document raises legal issues of invasion of privacy.

162

The notary has a duty to use reasonable care to identify what the document is. It can be done by asking the signer, or by merely glancing at the front page for a headline or title. By recording in the notary journal what the document is the notary establishes irrefutable proof that reasonable efforts were made to identify the document bearing the notarized signature.

News Item:

In 1993, a young man walked into the lobby of a downtown bank in Salt Lake City, Utah. He wanted his handwritten document to be notarized. He covered the letter with a blank page so the notary could not see the document. The notary made no effort to identify what the document was and proceeded to notarize his signature.

A few days later, the notary and her employer learned that she had notarized the young man's suicide letter to his parents. The parents, in turn, assumed the notary had to have known it was a suicide letter and therefore was liable for failing to refuse to notarize and for failing to notify proper officials of a seriously disturbed young man.

Although legal action was never brought in this matter, the notary could have protected herself and her employers by taking reasonable steps to identify what the young man's document was. She could have achieved this by merely asking him, or by asking to see it without reading it. Had the young man replied that he wanted his signature on a letter to be notarized, this would have been sufficient for recordation in the notary journal and to satisfy the notary's duty to exercise reasonable care.

Identity Fraud
See Identity of the Signer; Signer Identification

Identity of the Signer
See Signer Identification

From "The Notary's Duty of Care of Identifying Document Signers"

By Peter J Van Alstyne, 32 J. Marshall L. Rev. 1003-1031.

Constat de persona, or proof as to the person, is surprisingly fragile. The ultimate, irrefutable identity of a person is rooted in but a few cherished sources. A person's identity requires some sort of incorruptible "base line." Moreover, one of the most cherished of American civil liberties is the person's right to keep his identity private.

Our identity baseline is the continuous personal acquaintance our parents and immediate family members have had with us since our births. Furthermore, our baseline lies in the scientifically identified uniqueness of our fingerprints and, moreover, our DNA. We are positively identifiable by the personal knowledge of our parents from the moment of birth and by the uniqueness of our genetic codes. Anything else is inferior. Our families' life-long personal knowledge of our identity and our unreplicatable DNA is relatively error-proof and most likely immune to corruption.

While many consider the birth certificate to be a wholly reliable determinator of our existence and true identity and, therefore, a valid identity baseline, it is rife with weakness. The only thing a birth certificate certifies is that an individual of particular gender, weight, height and race was born to the two parents identified. As a sheet of paper, it does not certify its bearer as the person described.

From the point of birth through adulthood, our verifications of birth are public record through birth certificates. However, our birth certificates hardly prove identity. They are but a piece of paper, the written contents of which are not absolute in their accuracy. Humans provide the information. Humans complete the forms. Humans make mistakes. And birth certificates are not immune from falsification or alteration.

Birth certificates are relatively easy to obtain, even under false pretenses. Remarkably, they are heavily relied upon for the issuance of U.S. passports and driver's licenses in most states. An impostor's acquisition of a valid birth certificate of a person of similar age, race and gender as themselves can be the catalyst to an undetected life under one or many aliases.

Our individual constat de persona is something to which most of us rarely give much thought. We are a free society, unaccustomed to having to produce identification papers at a moment's notice. Those who have resided or traveled in totalitarian countries recognize how one's very life may hinge on the immediate presentation of their identification documents to authorities in those countries. In that environment, it is the government regime that determines and ratifies one's identity.

According to the U.S. Department of State 1990 Human Rights Report, "Union of Soviet Socialist Republics" (Feb. 1, 1991), a visit across town without one's government issued ID could result in imprisonment. (One of the most notable characteristics pre-1989 life in the Soviet Union and its satellite states was the citizen's tightly restricted freedom of mobility. The Author resided in Brazil for two years in 1970 and 1971. One's continuous possession of government issued ID to every citizen and alien resident was the key to freedom of travel anywhere within the nation of Brazil.)

Although an infant may be named by his parents, his recognized identity must be ratified by the government through the issuance of official identification papers that he must bear throughout his life.

The American system of individual identification is a stark contrast to those described above. No free American is required to bear ID, and there is no central source for uniform identification. The identification we as Americans obtain is typically procured voluntarily in connection with some higher objective. Americans generally do not set out to obtain ID in the belief they ought to have it. Rather, we obtain our ID because it comes to us, for example, when our primary goal is something else; in the firm of a driver's license to be legally able to drive, as student ID for a matriculated college student or as military ID for a new recruit. Perhaps our most commonly used ID is our driver's license; however, it is obtained not for identification purposes but for the privilege to drive.

Employment or school IDs are issued for security reasons or for receiving special benefits reserved only, for authorized persons.

Our identification documents are very much ancillary to other pursuits in life. Yet, so much depends on them. For business and government to mitigate against exposure to risk that individuals may be impostors, heavy reliance is placed on the identification card the individual presents. While a driver's license certifies that the bearer of the card is licensed to drive, it provides little or no assurance that the person featured thereon is who he claims to be. We take it on the reasonable expectation that somehow the driver's license was issued by the government only after a reasonable screening of the applicant's true identity. And, even a state's licensing process is often superficial because it depends almost entirely on the applicant's presentation of a birth certificate purportedly belonging to the applicant.

As discussed earlier, there is no irrefutable means to connect a birth certificate to the person it purports to represent. We can only accept it on reasonable good faith. Hence, in America we have no fail-safe system of personal identification in written form of any kind. This is abhorrent to many totalitarian regimes; which is why they have promulgated their own centralized system of national identification. An individual is who the regime says he is by virtue of his government issued ID. This keeps society orderly and less threatening to the regime. Identifying document signers for notarizations in this environment would present little challenge.

Notaries Are Required by Law to Meet Their Duty of Care in Identifying Document Signers

America's notaries face formidable challenges in identifying document signers because of our open society. Every person is free to document his or her identity in any manner he or she wishes, or even not at all. Yet, at one time or another, nearly every person has need of a notarization. Fortunately, there are procedures and standards of care a notary may invoke to ensure protection from risk of personal liability in notarizing for the public, with its sundry methods of identification.

166

The bedrock of American notary law is the principle in tort of reasonable care. Reasonable care is the standard by which notaries and their official conduct are judged it is borne out of the necessity to provide ordinary people, untrained in the law or sciences, a means of protection against liability for the public services they provide to their communities as notaries. The standards of reasonable care serve as parameters by which a notary can gauge whether her official notarial conduct is protected. A notary is expected to act reasonably, as would any reasonable and prudent person in like circumstances, in the performance of every notarial procedure. The notary is liable to all persons who suffer injury as the proximate result of the notary's breach of her duty of care.

The notary's responsibility to reasonably verify the identity of every person for whom she notarizes is profound. It is the cornerstone of the notarial act by which a notarized signature is reasonably verified not to be a forgery. A notary who takes this duty lightly does so at her very grave peril.

The notary performs this function of signer identification as a fiduciary of the public. The notary is expected to perform with integrity and diligence. It is not enough to simply follow what other notaries customarily do, especially if the business and notarial habits of others are negligent.

> *"We believe that the manifest intent of the legislature in requiring a notary public to execute a certificate of acknowledgment is to provide protection against the recording of false instruments. The sine qua non of this statutory requirement is the involvement of the notary, a public officer, in a position of public trust... If the notary conspires with a forger, or fails to require the personal appearance of the acknowledger, or is negligent in ascertaining the identity of the acknowledger, the statutory scheme is frustrated... In taking acknowledgments a notary properly discharges his duty only when the persons acknowledging execution personally appear and the notary has satisfactory evidence, based either on his personal knowledge or on the oath or affirmation of a credible witness, that the acknowledgers are who they say they are, and did what they said they did."*
> *- Farm Bureau Fin. Co., Inc. v. Carney, 605 P.2d 509, 514 (Idaho 1980).*

Conformity with the customs of the workplace or community does not equate with the standard of reasonable care. In fact, if material questions arise over the notary's proper verification of a signer's identity, the burden of proof by a preponderance of the evidence shifts to the notary to establish that reasonable care was exercised.er

> *"[I]f it is established that a notarized signature is forged, the burden of persuasion shifts to the notary to prove by a preponderance of the evidence that he exercised reasonable care in ascertaining the identity of the person. [J]ustification for shifting the burden of persuasion is the probability that the notary was negligent... and the strong public policy of ensuring the accuracy of notarial certifications."*
> *- Meyers v. Meyers, 503 P.2d 59, 62-63 (1972).*

The Uniform Acknowledgment Act and the Uniform Law on Notary Acts clearly indicate that document signers must personally appear before the notary. This is for the express purpose of enabling the notary to verify the signer's identity and that the signature to be notarized is genuinely that of its maker. However, only the Uniform Law on Notary Acts adequately prescribes standards for signer identification. Section 2 of the Uniform Law on Notary Acts provides:

> *[I]n taking an acknowledgment, the notarial officer must determine, either from personal knowledge or from satisfactory evidence, that the person appearing before the officer and making the acknowledgment is the person whose true signature is on the instrument.*

> *In taking a verification upon oath or affirmation, the notarial officer must determine, either from personal knowledge or from satisfactory evidence, that the person appearing before the officer and making the verification is the person whose true signature is on the statement verified...*

> *A notarial officer has satisfactory evidence that a person is the person whose true signature is on a document if that person (i) is personally known to the notarial officer; (ii) is identified upon the oath or affirmation of a credible witness personally known to the*

168

notarial officer or (iii) is identified on the basis of identification documents.

The Model Notary Act, promulgated by the National Notary Association in 1984, applies a more stringent standard for signer identification. The Model Act clearly and forcefully emphasizes the unmistakable requisite for signer identification in its definitions of Acknowledgment and Jurat. It states that "a notary certifies that a signer, whose identity is personally known to the notary or proven on the basis of satisfactory evidence..." is personally before the notary.

The Model Act further tightens the scope of discretion a notary may exercise in her assessment of the signer's identity. The Model Act defines personal knowledge of identity and satisfactory evidence of identity as follows:

"[P]ersonal knowledge of identity means familiarity with an individual resulting from interactions with that individual over a period of time sufficient to eliminate every reasonable doubt that the individual has the identity claimed." (Model Notary Act Section 1-105 (10)).

"Satisfactory evidence of identity means identification of an individual based on: (i) at least 2 current documents, one issued by a federal or state government with the individual's photograph, signature, and physical description, and the other by an institution, business entity, or federal or state government with at least the individual's signature; or (ii) the oath or affirmation of a credible person who is personally known to the notary and who personally knows the individual." (Model Notary Act Section 1-105(11)).

The Notary Public Code of Professional Responsibility, also promulgated by the National Notary Association, asserts the imperative for thorough signer identification. "The notary shall carefully identify each signer through either personal knowledge, at least one reliable identification document bearing a photograph, or the sworn word of a credible witness."

(The identification a notary should require under the Model Notary Act is contradicted by the standard provided by the Notary Public Code of Professional Responsibility. The Model Act requires two current forms of ID, while the Code of Responsibility refers to only one.)

Many legal scholars lament the fact that most states provide little statutory clarity on the standards and procedures a notary should use to verify the signer's identity. The long-standing standard for a notary's verification of a signer's identity has been by the notary's personal acquaintance with the signer, or by satisfactory evidence.

The Notary's Personal Knowledge of Identity

A notary's personal knowledge of a signer's true identity constitutes the strongest form of signer identification. In the notarial certificate, this form of signer identification is often phrased "personally known to me to be the person whose name is subscribed" thereto. One individual's claim to personally know another defies refutation. It is premised on a substantial level of acquaintance "derived from association with the [person] in relation to other people, and establishes [his] identity with at least reasonable certainty." (Black's Law Dictionary).

Personal knowledge of another's identity cannot be based on the representations of other people. Moreover, identity cannot be based on assumption or conjecture. Identity must be based upon a chain of circumstances surrounding the person that, in its totality, would lead one to believe the person is who he claims to be. Within that chain of circumstances, some affirmative evidence of the person's identity must manifest itself

> *"The phrase 'personally acquainted with' in... a certificate means knowledge independent and complete in itself, and existing without other information and it imports more than a slight or superficial knowledge."*
> *- Anderson v. Aronsohn, 184 P. 12, 15-16 (Cal. 1919).*

A number of states have laudably enacted concepts from the Model Notary Act that provide within their notary codes definition to the element of

170

personal knowledge. The notary code of Oregon provides, for example, that "personally known means familiarity with a person resulting from interactions with that person over a period of time sufficient to eliminate every reasonable doubt that the person has the identity claimed." Every detail within the framework of personal knowledge calls for the notary's subjective assessment of the facts and circumstances. Appropriately so, a notary's determination of personal knowledge is rooted in the exercise of reasonable care.

If a notary is personally acquainted with an individual over a substantial period of time and has interacted substantively with that person, the notary's common sense and instinct might lead her to reasonably believe the person is who he claims to be. This would occur naturally out of the absence of anything contradicting the person's representations as to who he is.

Human history has never been without its impostors and aliases. In contemporary society, no American community is immune from having within its midst residents living under aliases for purposes of evading detection by law enforcement or for bizarre psychological deficiencies. The notary may know this person on a personal basis sufficient to qualify as adequate identity verification for notarial purposes. The fact that the notary's acquaintance is with the person's alias is inconsequential. The notary's reliance on her experience with, and observation of, the person reasonably confirm for the notary that the person is whom he claims to be, his alias notwithstanding.

Satisfactory Evidence of Identity

Both The Uniform Law on Notary Acts and the Model Notary Act refer to the notary's reliance on satisfactory evidence to identify signers. The Model Act goes further by defining the term "satisfactory evidence" in the context of notarial services. Only a dozen states have followed suit in their statutes.

Satisfactory evidence is a user-friendly legal term because it is simple and rather self-explanatory. Satisfactory evidence is sometimes called "sufficient evidence," that "amount of proof which ordinarily satisfies an unprejudiced mind." In relying on satisfactory evidence, the correct question for the notary is not whether it is possible that the document signer is an impostor, but whether there is sufficient probability the signer is who he claims to be. This important standard is not unlike the legal axiom that an accused person is presumed innocent until proven guilty. Although the document signer bears the burden of proof as to his true identity, there should never be a presumption of attempted false identity on the signer's part unless the notary reveals such falsity through the signer's presentation of satisfactory evidence.

The term "satisfactory evidence" often applies to two methods of signer identification: the use of a "credible witness" or an "identifying witness," and to the use of identification cards or papers. The phrase "credible witness" has a number of applications within the arena of the laws of evidence.

Credible or Identifying Witnesses

Credible, or identifying, witnesses are vital to the successful performance of notarizations for millions of people at any given moment. Identifying witnesses constitute satisfactory evidence of a person's identity before a notary and are often the only means by which a signer may be identified for a notarization. Vast portions of the American population are without identification cards or documents, as they either have no need for any, or they are momentarily sans ID.

Credible witnesses are utilized to attest to the notary the true identity of the document's signer. As articulated in the notary statutes of several states, the notary identifies the person "upon the oath or affirmation of a credible witness personally known to the notarial officer." In some instances, the state codes specify that the witness must also know the document signer.

In every use of an identifying witness by a notary, there must be the fulfillment of three requisites, which will constitute an "unbroken chain of personal knowledge":

1. The notary must personally know the identifying witness;
2. The identifying witness must personally know the document signer; and

172

3. *The identifying witness must attest under oath to the notary as to the witness' personal acquaintance with the document signer.*

A notary is entitled to detrimentally rely on the affirmation of someone she knows personally regarding the identity of a complete stranger. The notary's personal knowledge of identity runs to the credible witness. In turn, the witness' personal knowledge runs to the document signer for whom the notarization is being performed. The notary's reliance on the words of the identifying witness is secured by the administration of an oath or affirmation to the witness.

A notary can administer an oath or affirmation to an identifying witness with simple phrasing such as, "do you swear or affirm that this is Jane Doe and that you know her personally?" Notaries are rarely, if ever, trained on the laws and procedures for oaths and affirmations. They are prone to shy away from having to administer oaths and affirmations, as many may regard it as pretentious or "overkill." A prudent notary and employer of notaries will discuss the procedures for administrations of oaths with colleagues and clients, and thereby ameliorate some of this discomfort of the responsibility.

The use of a credible witness to identify document signers is not without inherent risks to the notary. The use of the witness is a substitution for requesting the document signer to produce valid identification. The actual identity of the signer is just as easily obfuscated by a derelict credible witness as it is by counterfeit identification. However, if the notary performs her role correctly in using an identifying witness, the notary is relieved of liability upon the showing that the notary exercised reasonable care throughout the transaction.

The notary's reasonable care in using a credible witness to identify a signer's identity requires utmost objectivity on the notary's part. The notary must personally know the identifying witness to the same degree, if not higher, as if the notary were notarizing for the witness on the basis of personal knowledge. The notary's acquaintance with the witness is the premise by which she determines a signer is who he claims to be. This is quite different from notarizing for the individual a notary knows personally. The bar for measuring personal knowledge of the credible witness's identity is by necessity higher.

Unlike the notarization for a person the notary knows personally, an identifying witness must be known to the notary as having a reputation for integrity. The witness must manifest no inclinations towards deceit, and must be known as one who esteems integrity and manifests it by his example. The witness must be cognizant of his sober responsibility under penalties of perjury for attesting to the identity of another person. And, the witness should be impartial and free of any interest in the transaction.

The Notary Public Code of Professional Responsibility (National Notary Association) provides, "[t]he notary shall disqualify any person from serving as an identifying witness if that individual is named in or affected by the document signed by the principals." Perhaps one of the most vexing problems a notary faces in identifying document signers is the disqualification of the credible witness. Inasmuch as the identifying witness must be a person the notary knows well, the social awkwardness of having to disqualify that person can be daunting. The witness may very likely be the notary's employer or supervisor, leaving the notary with a perception of having to play a subservient role. The notary feels pressured into abusing the use of a credible witness for reasons of expediency or fraud.

Any responsible discussion on disqualifying conflicts of interest in the context of notarial services must consider a balanced overview. The primary objective for notarizing a signature is to mitigate against the risk that the document's signature is not genuine. The heart of that process is the reasonable verification of the signer's true identity. This may be through the attestation of a person the notary personally knows and believes to be credible. The fact the identifying witness is a party to the transaction does not, in and of itself, denigrate the veracity of the witness' affirmation of the signer's identity. To the contrary, a witness who also happens to be a party to the transaction may truthfully and credibly verify the signer's identity. The objective is still fulfilled.

The issue argued by many is whether persons who have an interest in, or are parties to, transactions should be disqualified from serving as credible or identifying witnesses. While this is advocated in the Notary Public Code of Professional Responsibility, the premise on which it is based may be inadequate.

174

The employment of credible witnesses by notaries to identify document signers is superior to the notary's reliance on the signer's ID documents. One's personal knowledge of the identity of another is the oldest and most venerated form of identification. It is irrefutable and enjoys profound evidentiary weight. The entire concept of the credible or identifying witness is founded upon the high trust our system of law places in one's personal knowledge.

A notary's employer or supervisor is generally affected by the execution of documents within his workplace and, according to the *Notary Public Code of Professional Responsibility*, is disqualified from attesting to the identities of his employee's clients. A cosigner personally known to the notary is disqualified from attesting to the other signer's identity under this standard as well. These disqualifications ironically leave the notary with no other choice but to rely on the inferior form of identity verification: ID cards and papers. The bar for disqualifying witnesses is set so low that the imagined problems this standard seeks to prevent could flourish by compelling notaries to rely on the weakest form of signer identification. In other words, the cure may be worse than the illness.

The primary evil in using interested persons as credible witnesses is that their conflict of interest creates a temptation to abuse their position and benefit themselves in some way. Conflicts of interest are ubiquitous in every facet of modern life, business, law and government. Very often the mandatory disqualification of the interested party accomplishes little good, and may even cause a degree of harm to the public or client. Therefore, the higher standard invoked among many professions and governmental bodies is to require full and timely disclosure of one's conflict of interest. The degrees of interest one may have can vary widely, thus necessitating the disqualification of the person in severe cases. In other instances, the mere candid disclosure of the person's interest serves notice to other parties relying on the transaction that they may wish to withdraw from the situation.

There is a more reasoned approach to credible witnesses who have an interest in the transaction. Notary statutes could require that the notarial certificate disclose the notary's reliance on the witness, even though the witness attests to the signer's identity as an interested party. By this *approach, material information is disclosed from which reasonable minds may draw informed decisions.*

It is ironic that while the whole premise of the valid use of credible identifying witnesses is the chain of personal knowledge between the notary, the witness and the document signer, several state statutes permit the use of two credible witnesses who are not personally known to the notary. The two unknown witnesses attest to the identity of a signer also unknown to the notary. The merit behind this approach is that it provides an alternative means for a signer to have a signature notarized, although he knows no notaries and possesses no ID.

The Florida notary code (Fla. Stat. Ann. § 117.05(5), for example, permits this manner of dual credible witnesses under limited circumstances. The witnesses must sign sworn affidavits that are notarized by the notary, the text of which fully discloses the nature of the parties' relationships and how the notary identified the two witnesses.

Identification Cards and Documents

Identification documents serve as perhaps the most commonly used means for identifying document signers. The most commonly used form of ID seems to be the driver's licenses. It is universally viewed as the most reliable form of ID because the state government issues it. It contains a photograph and other pertinent information about the bearer. The assumption is that the states invoke substantial procedures to verify the license applicant's true identity as a condition precedent to its issuance. The states and their citizens have a lot at stake over this process. So, if it is good enough for the state, then it is supposedly good enough for a notarization.

There is no limit to the variety of identification cards in use across America. They originate everywhere: public schools, employment sites, the military, licenses to drive and memberships to clubs and co-ops. ID cards can even be purchased from retailers. There is no such thing as an "official ID." This characteristic of our society is a testimony in action to our individual liberties: the freedom to associate, the freedom to express ourselves and the freedom to live anonymously. There is no central source

176

of identification cards, and there is no uniformity to their style, content or construction.

ID cards are easy to make for legitimate purposes and are easy to counterfeit for fraudulent purposes. But it must be clear in any discussion of this type that there is no need for centralized, uniform identification cards for the residents of this nation. However, the technology for such centralization is readily available. ID cards with microchips of data, often called "smart cards," could be the only ID a person would ever need regardless of employment, university matriculation or licensure to drive a car or to practice dentistry.

The problem with ID cards for notarial purposes is complex. There is no clearly articulated universal standard for classifying an ID as valid, adequate, reliable or credible. Moreover, the strength and reliability of a person's ID usually depends on the purpose for which it is designed. In applying for a U.S. passport, the standard for valid identification of the applicant is manifestly higher than it is for admission of a teenager into an "R" rated movie. A notary's standard for acceptable signer ID will be considerably different than that of an employee's ID to pass into a secured area of his high-tech company.

There has been occasional public discussion over the perceived need for uniform ID, perhaps issued by the federal government. It is an appealingly simple solution for achieving uniformity, dependability and credibility, and for mitigating against the vast volumes of counterfeit ID circulating within American society. Needless to say, such discussion is the "political third rail," whereby any politician in advocacy thereof will suffer quick political death. More importantly, the idea of centralized federal ID, even on a volunteer basis, raises serious constitutional and public policy questions. The very concept abrogates our openness as a society and emasculates the human soul's divine right to freedom. No serious thinker could take the idea seriously. Sadly, however, there are those posing as advocates for the public's wellbeing who support a voluntary system of federally issued ID. Their reasoning appears to be based on unsound principles and analysis.

The appropriate standard by which a notary should examine a signer's ID card is unchanged from over the generations. The standard of reasonable care, regardless of changes to notary statutes, always applies. Although the known volumes of counterfeit ID that circulates in our country is alarming, there is a tendency for some to assume that the notary may be incapable of adequately screening signer ID in such an environment. Critics argue that the likelihood is too great that a signer's ID may look authentic, but really be counterfeit.

Therefore, the reasoning goes, the notary's scope of discretion in accepting and examining a signer's ID must be restricted in order to save the notary and the public from signature fraud.

It is a curious argument that notaries should not be permitted to decide what types of ID they will accept. The argument is even more peculiar where a person's valid ID comprises the important legal standard of "satisfactory evidence" on which the system of law and notaries has relied successfully for centuries.

The notary statutes of a number of states impose stringent limitation on what constitutes satisfactory evidence in the form of identification cards or papers. Of particular concern are the requirements in many states that a signer's ID be "current," and be issued from a state or federal government entity.

The Model Notary Act advocates,
> *" 'Satisfactory evidence of identity' means identification of an individual based on: (i) at least 2 current documents, one issued by a federal or state government with the individual's photograph, signature, and physical description, and the other by an institution, business entity, or federal or state government with at least the individual's signature..."*
> *- Model Notary Act § 1-105(11) (1984).*

Many states require that a signer's ID be "valid," without defining what constitutes "validity." That is left to the notary's sense of reasonable care and to the context in which the signer produces ID to the notary. Many have speculated that "valid" means "current." Others have added to that by asserting that valid also means "official." Neither speculation is very helpful to the notary or to the public in general.

The experience in a number of states exemplifies the problems created by unduly restricting the types of ID a notary may accept from a document signer. While it may appear reasonable to require that the ID be current, it is not necessarily logical. This means, for example, that a signer's state-issued driver's license that was current yesterday was valid for the notary to verify the signer's identity yesterday. But today, the driver's license is expired and is no longer a valid basis for the signer to identify himself to the notary. The owner of the driver's license hasn't expired in bodily terms; only his privilege to drive has.

Millions of Americans are not licensed to drive and they possess no government issued ID. Unduly restrictive statutory provisions such as those mentioned exclude millions from obtaining a notarization of their signatures, unless they personally know the notary or are accompanied by a credible witness the notary personally knows. The unfortunate obstacles these strictures create are exacerbated by states that require the signer to produce two forms of ID cards.

Unless a notary is free to accept any form of ID that reasonably verifies the signer's identity, major population groups are unduly impeded in their personal and business transactions. The elderly and the youth of America are particularly vulnerable under these restrictions. Such impedance is literally self-defeating. Moreover, they contravene the very purpose of providing ready access to notarial services in America.

Notaries are very hard-pressed to strictly comply with the statutory requirements for current ID, especially when it requires two forms. Most notarizations occur within the workplace as a service to the customer. Strict adherence to these strictures often causes the notary to appear overbearing and unreasonable to the client and to the notary's employer. Too frequently, the notary finds little logical justification for strict compliance with the statute and begins a practice of cutting corners and shading the truth when it comes to identifying the document signer.

It is often the sad consequence of poorly conceived or unreasonable legislation that it is soon disregarded by notaries and document signers, and the majority become scofflaws.

Overbearing Identification Requirements May Be Self-defeating

The fundamental purpose for notarizing signatures is to render a higher degree of security to transactions between people. If the notary laws of the various states erect too high a barrier between the public and the services of notaries, the public will either take their business elsewhere, or avoid notarizations wherever possible. However, this is a troubling prospect because so many transactions are required by law to be notarized, such as real estate conveyances and estate documents. It can hardly be said that overly restrictive identification standards are justified by the anticipated benefits they provide. To the contrary, remedies such as these are most often quite worse than the problems they were meant to prevent.

One of the more frequently discussed issues in notary literature in recent years concerns America's growing problem with counterfeit and false identification cards and documents. The problem is real, but it overshadows other issues notaries face routinely when attempting to identify document signers.

Notaries struggle with having to notarize for people they do not know, who have no identification or any acquaintances that can serve as credible witnesses. Presently, notaries in this situation have no alternative but to refuse to notarize for the individual. It is even more frustrating when the signer has identification in forms that do not conform to the statutory requirements.

Suggestions for Reasonable Standards

The notary statutes of all fifty states should be amended to provide the notary with additional tools and better-defined standards for signer identification. This would be particularly beneficial to document signers who are patients in hospitals and other long-term health care facilities, to the elderly and the youth, to incarcerated people, and to those who have had recent name changes due to changes in marital status.

Any statutory amendment addressing these situations should foremost contemplate the infinite variety of circumstances notaries face. A notary's exercise of reasonable care is society's optimal protection against signature fraud in every circumstance.

The states should be encouraged to amend their notary statutes to:

180

1. *Provide language and definitional parameters that require the notary to exercise reasonable care in verifying a signer's identity.*

2. *Authorize the notary to verify a signer's identity by reasonable means other than ID cards or identifying witnesses. This authority would apply only in situations where other information would reasonably corroborate the signer's identity, and where refusal to notarize based on the signer's lack of valid ID cards or inability to produce a qualified identifying witness would serve undue hardship on the document signer. A provision of this kind would enable notaries to verify identities of hospital and nursing home patients through patient ID wristbands or medical records. The elderly could be identified by medical prescription labels, utility bills or by senior citizen center records. Students in public schools could be identified by school enrollment records, while prison and jail inmates could be identified by inmate records or by the inmate's stamped name on his prison uniform. People who have recently changed their names through marriage or divorce could be spared from having to prove to the notary their recent change of marital status.*

3. *Grant the notary broad discretion in examining and accepting signer identification cards and documents. Define the optimal standard a notary should seek, including a photograph of the signer, a signature of the signer, and some description of the signer and some indication of the ID's source of origin. The notary should be required to reasonably examine the ID for indications that it is credible.*

4. *Require the notary to fully disclose within the notarial certificates of acknowledgment and jurats how the signer was identified, be it by personal knowledge, by identifying witness (the name of whom is disclosed and accompanied by the witness' signature), or by identifying documents (the specifics of which are fully disclosed).*

Notarial services and procedures are not exacting in nature or quality. They require considerable common sense and attention to the fundamentals. Most importantly, they require the notary to pass judgment on a number of issues. The most subjective issue is the verification of the signer's identity.

Conclusion

A person's true identity cannot be dispositively proven in written form. Even the attestation of a person's identity by an identifying witness is vulnerable to deceit and fraud. The truest shield of protection against signature fraud is the notary public that faithfully exercises genuine reasonable care with skill and prudence. Attempts to pave over this time-honored standard with overbearing legislation disserves the public for whom such efforts were intended to protect.

The notary's exercise of reasonable care in verifying a signer's identity is the optimal assurance of signature authenticity. It always has been, and it most likely always will be.

Ignorance of the Law
See False Notarial Dogma; Legal Defense against Liability; Notary Training; Quiet Acquiescence

Ignorance of the notary law is not an excuse, or a defense, for violation of notarial law and procedure. Every fortunate occupant of the United States has a duty by law to take the initiative to learn the basic fundamentals of law in order to successfully function within society.

Many complain that the states do not provide new applicants to become notaries any training on their legal duties. This is not the role or mission of government. It is the individual's duty to attain such training.

In all states, the applicant to become a notary takes an oath of office in one form or another. Such oaths all invoke the applicant's promise to obey the notary law (which inherently implies the applicant has learned what the notary law requires).

Some states specifically provide within the oath the applicant's attestation that they have actually read and understand the state's notary laws. Falsely attesting to such a statement constitutes perjury in most of those states.

Notaries are not expected to be legal experts on all aspects of the notary law.

They are, however, required to be fully familiar with the basic rules and procedures most commonly used. The underlying principle of notary law is integrity: absolute truth. Every word of the notarial certificate the notary signs and seals must be true. This is an easy standard for every literate person to meet every time a notarization is performed. Most legal causes of action against notaries involve a falsehood within the notarial certificate, for which there is no excuse or defense.

Absolute truthfulness in notarizations, as a standard of law, supersedes the procedural rules and laws on notarizing. The latter without the former is meaningless.

Illegible Notary Seal
See Seal of the Notary Public

When required by state statute to affix a notary seal to each notarial certificate, the seal represents the notary's legal authority to make the certifications asserted in the certificate. The seal declares key information regarding the notary's authority. It will usually declare the name of the notary, the title, "notary public," and the name of the state by which the notary is commissioned. Often, the seal indicates the county in which the notary resides and the date of commission expiration.

When the notary's seal is illegible for any reason, the intended purpose for affixing the seal is frustrated. An illegible seal does not inherently invalidate the notarial act. The question of acceptability is generally up to the party receiving the document. They might reject it for lack of seal legibility, or accept it notwithstanding the flawed seal. A flawed, illegible impression of a seal can be corrected readily. The notary need only affix the seal again in clear, blank space adjacent the flawed seal image.

The embossed notary seal is inherently difficult to decipher, as its raised image is hardly distinguishable from the color of the page on which it appears. It is common for notaries to discolor the raised portion of the embossed seal so it is legible and reproducible by photographic means, such as telefax or digital scanner.

Ink stamp notary seals are becoming increasingly preferred nationally. If the notary's seal leaves a smeared or otherwise illegible impression, it too can be reaffixed adjacent the defective seal image. Notaries should keep in mind the purpose for a notary seal and judge for themselves whether or not the image they affixed substantially fulfills that purpose. The image affixed should substantially comply with the requirements of law, which might not be defeated by partial illegibility. If the key required information is indecipherable by an average person, then the notary should reaffix the seal. A smudged seal boarder or the smudging of the words "state of," "public," or "My Commission," are the least likely to be cause for concern.

The notary should strive to legibly display by the seal the notary's full name by which the commission was issued, the word, "Notary," the name of the notary's state, and the notary's date of commission expiration.

Illegible Signatures and Writings
See His Mark; Signature

A signature is not necessarily the written name of the person making it. A signature is the handmade inscription to a document signifying the maker's intent to commit to the contents of the document.

Notaries are not judges of penmanship. Rather, notaries judge the signer's verification of identity and ownership of the signature, regardless of how scribbled it may be.

Many people and cultures place great importance on the elegance of the signature: the more ornate and artistic, the better. It represents the maker's personality and flair. It has little to do with the alphabet. Rather, it is like the cowboy's branding iron: unique and identifiable.

Notaries should be mindful, however, that regardless of the legibility of the signature, it must be irrefutably established that the signature in fact belongs to the signer appearing before the notary. The surest evidence of the signer's ownership of a signature is to require them to sign the notary journal. If there is a reasonable degree of similarity between the signature on the document with the one made in the journal, by the rules of evidence that is sufficient.

184

Millions of Americans are physically incapacitated and unable to sign their names in the manner they did while young or healthy. By no means does this suggest they are now unqualified to sign a document for notarization. To the contrary, they are entitled to sign anything if they are doing so willingly and freely. The signature is merely the written evidence of the signer's intent to be bound by the document contents. If the elderly, incapacitated signer's intent to be bound is reasonably verified, the feeble signer may scribble a "loop-dee-loop" on the document and in the notary's journal.

As a matter of common sense and professionalism, an illegible signature ought to be accompanied by the signer's printed name. Law does not require this for a few states, but it can be profoundly helpful to person's relying on the transaction down the road. In the notary journal, this rule of thumb has extra merit.

Impartial
See Impartiality

Impartial Agent of the State
See Agent; Conflict of Interest; Impartiality

Notaries serve on behalf of the state government that has commissioned them. The notary is the state government's agent authorized to perform notarial services on behalf of the state.

The rule of law regarding agents provides that an agent is a substitute or representative of the principal party or entity from which the agent derives his authority. For an agency relationship to exist there must be a principal that delegates authority to an agent to act on his behalf. The agent has the authority to bind his principal to the transactions he enters into, and the agent's actions must be of a nature that induces other parties to rely on the agent's actions. This legal definition of agency perfectly describes the relationship of the notary to the state government that commissions her.

Notarizations are state government functions the state has delegated to others. Notaries represent the state government, from whom their authority is derived. The notarial powers of the state are delegated to qualified private persons who volunteer to serve as notaries on behalf of the state. The notary binds the state to the notarial acts officially performed.

As agents of the state, the notary is to serve impartially, without bias or self- dealing. Such conduct is otherwise unlawful and an egregious abuse of the important powers conferred upon the notary. It is not unlike a court judge issuing case decisions that benefit the judge in personal ways. In order for notarizations to retain their credibility and venerated reliability, the notarial process must be free of any shadows of suspicion. In order for the legal objectives of notarizations to be realized, notaries must be purely impartial agents of their state governments.

Impartiality
See Conflict of Interest; Disqualified Notary

Notaries, as a matter of law, are to be impartial to the transactions upon which they notarize signatures, and to be impartial to the notarizations themselves. Impartiality means that the notary is completely indifferent to the transaction and to the parties to the transaction.

Impersonation of a Notary
See Fraud; Imposters

In all states it is a criminal violation of law to impersonate a notary public. In some states, it is treated as a felony crime and the notarizations they falsely perform are fraudulent.

Many states place no restrictions on the acquisition of a notary seal. It is presumed that people generally recognize that one must be commissioned prior to obtaining such a device. However, some people suppose they can become notaries by simply purchasing a notary seal. They have not proven their legal qualifications and they have not been granted the legal authority to perform the functions of a notary.

One is not a notary unless granted the legal authority by the government of the state in which the person resides. A notarization made without the authority of law is not a notarization. It is a fraudulent act.

186

The principles of authority and power to perform certain actions are as old as humanity. Without its unmitigated recognition and adherence, all of society and law would dissolve into chaos. A United States Ambassador to any nation must be in possession of the authority and power to represent and act on behalf of the United States government. Such positions cannot be self-appointed, and such authority cannot be self-granted.

Imposters under the cloak of authority to perform important acts, when let loose and unchecked, are potentially dangerous to the institutions that provide us stability and orderliness. In the arena of notary law, there can be no tolerance for the impersonation of a notary.

Impossible to Notarize
See False Notarization; Fraud

The notary law establishes a series of circumstances where it is legally impossible to perform the notarization. When the term, impossible, is applied to a function of law, it provides that the specified action is incapable of being performed in any manner that would render it legally valid or binding. It is impossible to perform in any lawful manner.

1. It is legally impossible to notarize a signature where the maker of the signature does not personally appear before the notary.
2. It is legally impossible to notarize a signature of a person whose identity the notary has not verified.
3. It is legally impossible to notarize a signature where the written certification thereof contains a material falsehood of any kind.
4. It is legally impossible for the notary to notarize a signature the notary knows, or has reason to believe, is not the signature of its claimed owner.
5. It is legally impossible to notarize a signature by executing an incomplete notarial certificate, the contents of which are specified by statute.
6. It is legally impossible to perform any notarial act without having possession of the legal authority granted by the state to perform such acts.

When a notary engages in a legal impossibility, the notary acts falsely and in violation of law. The notarial act is inherently void and the survival of the document on which it appears may be jeopardized. The notary is personally liable for all damages resulting from such unlawful conduct.

Imposters
See Forger; Fraud; Identify of the Signer; Signer Identification

From "The Notary's Duty to Care for Identifying Document Signers"

By Peter J. Van Alstyne, 32 J. Marshall Law Review 1003-1005.

Since the dawn of human history, one's true identity has been integral to any degree of societal orderliness. Humans have always interacted with one another for personal interests and for the good of the community. Knowing with whom we interact assures a degree of security and safety. Sadly, Earth's earliest inhabitants had to learn quickly that not all people could be trusted. Knowing whom to deal with and whom to avoid has always been a prerequisite for self- preservation.

As ancient rudimentary systems of trade, commerce, and law evolved, ancient societies faced, growing risks in dealing with unfamiliar people. On whom could they rely? How could one be certain a stranger was not an impostor, but was who he represented himself to be? The notaries of ancient Rome, for example, were very limited in the exercise of their authority. There were no identity cards in ancient Rome, so the notary either had to personally know the signer or use witnesses who would attest to the signer's identity.

Unless the parties knew each other personally, there was justified concern over the individual's true identity. Even then, scoundrels could pull off clever disguises.

Perhaps the earliest recorded perpetration of fraud by an impostor is recorded in the Book of Genesis of the Old Testament. The 27th chapter of Genesis speaks of the ancient prophet Isaac intending to confer upon his eldest son, Esau, a blessing or endowment. The elderly Isaac was blind. He asked Esau to hunt for venison, his favorite meat, for the important celebratory meal in preparation of the conveyance of the blessing. Rebekah, Isaac's wife, overheard this and conspired with the couple's other son, Jacob, to defraud Esau (Jacob's twin brother) and Isaac and thereby cause the blessing to be conveyed to Jacob under false pretenses.

Rebekah instructed Jacob to "go now to the flock, and fetch me from thence two good kids of the goats; and I will make them savory meat for thy father, such as he loveth: And thou shalt bring it to thy father, that he may eat, and that he may bless thee before his death." Jacob was concerned that his blind elderly father would recognize him and not convey Esau's blessing to him. "And Jacob said to Rebekah his mother, Behold, Esau my brother is a hairy man, and I am a smooth man: My father peradventure will feel me, and I shall seem to him as a deceiver; and I shall bring a curse upon me, and not a blessing." The mother-son perpetrators conspired to conceal Jacob's true identity from his father by dressing Jacob in Esau's cloak and by covering Jacob's arms and hands with goat skins.

The fraudulent scheme worked as intended. Jacob went to his father saying, "m[y] father...here am I." Isaac asked, "who art thou my son?" Jacob replied, "I am Esau thy firstborn: I have done according as thou badest me..."

Isaac said to Jacob, "[c]ome near, I pray thee, that I may feel thee, my son, whether thou be my very son Esau or not." Jacob approached his father so he could feel his hands and arms. Isaac declared, "[t]he voice is Jacob's voice, but the hands are the hands of Esau." Isaac "discerned him not, because his hands were hairy, as his brother Esau's hands." Isaac beckoned Jacob to come near him so he could kiss him. Isaac smelled the cloak of Esau that Jacob wore. Confirmation of Esau's identity by his blind elderly father was complete. On reliance on Jacob's charlatanic performance, Isaac unknowingly bestowed the all-important blessing upon Jacob instead of Esau.

Throughout the ages, it has been necessary for people to protect their transactions from charlatans. In more recent generations, society has relied on identification documents in disparate circumstances, ranging from admittance to foreign nations, to cashing a bank draft. Where warranted by circumstances, officials of high public trust authenticated certain promises and agreements. The stakes were too high to risk admitting impostors claiming privity to certain transactions. Hence, the venerated and historic office of the notary public has long served this vital need.

> *"Then men learned to write, and it was found that cold letters remain after the fragile structures of memory have jailed. So transfers began to be made in writing. But it would inevitably happen that A or B or C would sign a paper and thereafter say he did not sign it; and that D, E, or F would learn to forge another's name. So that, notwithstanding it had been at first thought that a written transfer would forever settle all disputes, it was found that a writing was only helpful, not always conclusive. So someone hit upon the idea of having the signature witnessed. From this it was but another step to having as such witness an officer under bond. The notary was that officer..."*
>
> *- Richard B. Humphrey, American Notary Manual*
> *11-12 (4th ed. 1948).*

A person who takes on the name, title, or authority of another person or nonexistent person for the purpose of deceiving others is an imposter. One of the primary purposes for having signatures notarized is to ensure the signature is not made by an imposter posing as the person whose signature is asserted to be genuine.

Imposters may possess high quality counterfeit ID cards or papers, and are cunning and skilled signature forgers. Imposters may also fraudulently abuse the credible witness process by having a co-conspirator serve as the credible witness to falsely attest to the identity of the imposter. In either situation, so long as the notary correctly and faithfully follows correct

190

notarial procedures taking all reasonable steps to verify the signer's identity, documenting in the notary journal how the signer was identified, the notary is not liable if it is later found the signer was an imposter.

If notaries were legally responsible for foiling all imposters seeking notarizations, few, if anyone, would serve as a notary. Law enforcement at the federal and local levels struggle with the proliferation of expert counterfeit ID created by master ID fraud artisans. The notary is required only to exercise the level of caution and common sense required by law to deter attempts at forging signatures for notarizations.

Prudent, effective notaries may unwittingly notarize a forged signature made by an imposter, after having followed correct notarial procedures to the utmost. It is a fact of life in our contemporary society, in which the well-informed notary plays an invaluable role.

Occasionally people will live under an alias, or an "also known as." It is not unheard of where a reputable citizen residing in a notary's community for years is known as John Doe. However, unknown to all, John has a dark past. He is wanted by the FBI for exploding a science lab during the Viet Nam war protests decades earlier. His real name is Mike Smith. His signature as John Doe has been notarized multiple times, and he carries state issued ID bearing the name and photo of John Doe. All notarizations performed under this scenario of facts would be considered valid because no reasonable, prudent notary would have detected John's false identity.

In America's correctional facilities, many inmates are serving their second, third, or higher, convictions and sentences. It is common for repeat offenders to adopt new identities by which they are arrested, charged, convicted and incarcerated. The prison officials know the inmate under a different name from a prior term in prison. Nevertheless, the notary in the correctional institution, when notarizing for such persons, is expected to utilize the inmate's current name of record in the criminal justice program by which he is currently incarcerated. It is not inappropriate for the notary to note on the notarial certificate and the notary journal that the signer is "also known as _____."

Incapacitated Document Signers
See His Mark; Signature Made by a Mark

Incomplete Documents
See Blank Documents; Completeness of the Signer's Document

Incomplete Notarial Certificates
See Completeness of the Notarial Certificate; Completing the Notarial Certificate

Inculcation of the Essence of the Notarial Act
See Short Form Notarial Certificate

Ink Color
See Seal of the Notary Public; Signature

Most states do not specify in their notary laws the color of ink a notary must use for the ink stamp seal. No state has legislated the color of ink a notary must use to make her official notarial signature on a certificate of notarization.

Where the states have regulated the seal stamp ink color, the statutes specify the color black. However, it is not intended to be a guide for notaries elsewhere in selecting an ink stamp seal color. Under law, any photographically reproducible ink color is lawful, unless otherwise specified by statute.

Any law restricting the color of ink a person or notary must use to make a signature would be "pushing the envelope" on reasonableness and sustainability. Prudent people will sign their names with an ink color that is legible, and is capable of photographic reproduction. The spectrum of ink colors a notary may use to make signatures offers considerable possibilities for individuality and expression.

Ink Thumbprints of Document Signers
See Fingerprints and Thumbprints in the Notary Journal

Instrument
See Document Content

The formal term used to identify a legal document is to call it an "instrument." The term denotes the legal qualities of the document, that it is created and signed for the purpose to convey rights, ownership, or some other change of legal standing. The term, instrument, also suggests the utility of the document, that it is actually a tool to accomplish a specified end.

The notarial certificate is officially an instrument. It is a document intended to guarantee that the signatures to another instrument have been reasonably and thoroughly authenticated, that those relying on the other instrument may allay their concerns regarding the legitimacy of the signatures.

Instrument Content
See Document Content

Integrity of the Notary
See Duty of Care; Notary's Role in Society

The immutable requisite for a notary public is to possess and exercise integrity at all times. This is eloquently articulated by the courts.

> *"Fundamental honesty is the baseline and mandatory requirement to serve as a notary. The whole structure of ethical standards is derived from the paramount need for notaries to be trustworthy. The court system and the public are damaged when notaries play fast and loose with the truth. The damage occurs without regard to whether misleading conduct is motivated by the client's interests or the notary's own."*
> - Conduct v. Bauerle, 460 N. 2d 452 (Iowa 1990).

> *"When the notary does not obey this statute, he should expect to be held liable; and, I wish to repeat, these requirements are of great importance to the business world, and not at all too exacting.*

> *Such strict interpretation is necessary because the purpose of the certificate of acknowledgment is to establish the identity of such person and the genuineness of the signature attached to the*

instrument, and the certificate is prima facie evidence of the truth of the facts stated therein.

When a notary public assumes his office, he is required to perform his duties with honesty, integrity, diligence, and skill."
- Transamerica Title vs. Green, 2 Cal. App. 3d 693 (California 1970).

Interpreting the Notary Law
See Statutory Law; Statutory Authority of the Notary; Statutory Definitions in State Notary Laws; Statutory Procedures Statutory Provisions Every Notary Should Know

Interstate Reciprocity of Notaries
See Multiple Notary Commissions

Interstate Recognition of Notarizations
See Full Faith and Credit Clause

J

When the notary does not obey this statute, he should expect to be held liable; and, I wish to repeat, these requirements are of great importance to the business world, and not at all too exacting.

Such strict interpretation is necessary because the purpose of the certificate of acknowledgment is to establish the identity of such person and the genuineness of the signature attached to the instrument, and the certificate is prima facie evidence of the truth of the facts stated therein.

When a notary public assumes his office, he is required to perform his duties with honesty, integrity, diligence, and skill.
- Transamerica Title vs. **Green** *2 Cal. App. 3d 693.*

Jointly Liable
See Employer Liability for Notarizations; Respondeat Superior; Severally Liable

Employers of notaries who wrongfully or negligently perform notarizations while in the course of their employment are "jointly liable" with their notaries for the damages caused by their conduct. Employers are under duty of law to ensure the notaries in their employ perform in compliance with state law and exercise reasonable care and diligence. Under the legal rule of respondeat superior, employers are liable for the negligence of their employees. Therefore, the notary and the employer jointly share in the potential liabilities for negligent and wrongful notarial conduct.

The phrase most commonly invoked to describe this structure of shared liability is, *"the notary and the notary's employer are jointly and severally liable."* By this principle, the plaintiff suing to recover damages resulting from notarial misconduct can sue the notary and the employer jointly, or the plaintiff can bring action against each party separately. The plaintiff can also sever the notary from the complaint and go after the notary's employer only, as the employer usually has "deeper pockets" than the notary.

Joint and several liability is an important legal concept necessary, as a matter of public policy, to provide some means of remedy for persons harmed by the wrongful conduct of people who have a legal duty not to cause such harm. Employers of such persons share the duty of their employees not to permit such harmful conduct from occurring in the first place. By causing both employers and their employees to share liability, both feel the pressure to ensure no harmful conduct takes place. Employers are in the best position to ensure their employees are properly trained in the notary law and procedures, and are best positioned to ensure employees are properly supervised to ensure notarizations are performed according to law.

When the employee/notary is found to have been negligent or in violation of law, the law imputes to the notary's employers a presumed breach of their legal duty of care. As a result, both parties face liability.

Journal Recordation
See Notary Journal; Notary Journal Contents and Format; Notary's Duty to Maintain Journal Records

Notary journals are nothing new. They have been around for centuries. The purposes for keeping a notary journal are important and obvious.

What is routinely recorded in a notary's journal is not readily refutable.

A notary journal is a complete, accurate record of every notarization the notary performs. It constitutes a valuable form of legal evidence proving how the notary performed the service noted in the record. The notary journal provides the notary and the document signer indispensable forms of legal protection:

1. It directs the notary into notarizing properly and error-free in each notarization;
2. The journal refreshes the notary's memory when asked to explain a past notarization, even if it occurred many years earlier;
3. Faithful journalizing establishes one's reputation and credibility as a competent and accurate notary; the kind of person others want to do business with;
4. The people for whom we notarize have a right to expect that the notarization will be held valid years from now and that it can withstand tough scrutiny while under suspicion. The journal entry refutes accusations of misconduct; and
5. Journal keeping teaches the public the importance of a notarization, which it is not to be trifled with. Notarizations mean what they say and bear significant legal weight.

Under federal and state rules of evidence, the contents of a notary's journal are automatically deemed factual. The journal entry constitutes the notary's own "personal knowledge" of the facts recorded therein. Under these rules of evidence, a notary's journal is valuable evidence as a "business record exemption to the hearsay rule." In other words, what's written is fact. If it's in the journal, it happened. If it's not in the journal, presumably it didn't happen. That alone is sufficient reason why every notary in America should journalize every notarization performed.

"Under the business records exception to the hearsay rule, documentary records of a business concerning acts, events, or conditions may be introduced as evidence so long as foundational evidence demonstrates that the record was prepared by an employee of the business who had a duty to report the information, the person providing the information contained in the record had personal knowledge of the event or transaction reported, the record was prepared at or near the time of the event or transaction, and it was a regular practice or custom of the business in question to prepare and retain the type of record (Rules of Evid., Rule 803(6))."
  - McCormick v. Mirrored Image, Inc., 7 Ohio App. 3d. 232, 454 N.E.2d 1363 (1982).

The standard by which a record, such as a notary journal, may be treated as a business record is simple.

"Business records defined as any writing or article... kept or maintained by an enterprise for the purpose of evidencing or reflecting its condition or activity. Business records... [are] generally regarded as reliable since any risk or insincerity will be minimized because the business will want accurate records to rely on."

- The People v. DeLuca,178 A. D. 2nd. 426, 577 N.Y.S.2d 293 (1991).

Perhaps one's state's notary laws do not require notaries to keep a notary journal. Journalizing every notarization is mandated as a standard of reasonable care. The lack thereof is arguably a form of negligence. It is wrongful to think it is discretionary.

Record keeping is an implied duty in almost every walk of life. It is rooted in ancient human history.

Businesses who fail to keep accurate records of their transactions are doomed to financial ruin, and if sued, they are doomed to be presumed negligent and derelict in their business responsibilities. Taxpayers who fail to keep thorough and accurate financial records are looked upon by the IRS with distrust during a tough tax audit. Notaries who perform an essential notarial function of law without making a complete record thereof are less likely viewed as dutiful, diligent and credible.

Not any "journal" will do. The key is in understanding simple concepts of evidence in the role of law and notarizations. Not all notary journals conform to these essential principles. They may read, "Notary Journal," on the cover but miss the most important component parts on the inside. They may be designed to look like an accountant's ledger journal, but in practice are cumbersome to use. They may give the notary a sense of security and protection, but they are in fact superficial and inadequate.

The notary journal is the notary's best friend. If used properly, it won't permit serious mistakes. It prevents notaries from committing notarial misconduct or from notarizing falsely. The journal will steer the notary in the right direction every time. It will enable the notary to solve notarial problems and to correctly decide how to proceed.

The notary journal documents every fact asserted by the notarization.

Under the rules of evidence, what is written in a journal is automatically deemed factually true.

A notarization may declare:

> *State of Illinois*
> *County of Cook*

Acknowledged before me by Sally Brown this 15th day of November, 2002.

This overly simplified notarization acknowledgment asserts these material facts:

1. The venue: this notarization took place in Cook County, Illinois;
2. The signer acknowledging her signature was Sally Brown;
3. The signature being acknowledged was in fact made by Sally Brown;
4. Sally Brown personally appeared before the notary, to acknowledge her signature; and
5. The date this transaction occurred was November 15, 2002.

The purpose of this notarization for Ms. Brown is to authenticate her signature as genuine. The notary is declaring it was Sally Brown who appeared before her.

The journal entry proves the notary took all reasonable steps in verifying the signer was Sally Brown and not an imposter. How can the notary prove she did not notarize a signature to a document that was merely mailed to her? How can the notary prove the signature was not a good forgery?

The facts asserted in a signature notarization are material and must be documented as truth. That is the purpose for maintaining the notary journal. What is recorded in the journal becomes very important. If the journal requests insufficient information, or the wrong information, the journal actually jeopardizes the notary's legal safety. And, the notary is lulled into the belief by the notary journal that she is fully protected against accusations of wrongdoing, when in fact, she is not.

What she records and how she records matters greatly.

The singular most important bit of information to record in the journal is the signature of the person for whom a notarization is made. This signature should be made while the notary watches and before she notarizes. It will prove the signer personally appeared before her. It should match the signature of the document to be notarized. It should match the signature of the customer on the ID card she relied on to verify his identity.

Focus on the points of evidence. The notary journal should compel the notary to record the following information for every notarization performed:

1. The signature of the customer being served. (As illustrated in the model below, the journal should permit one to use a single journal entry for multiple signers to the same document to sign in the entry space. This saves time and avoids overkill);
2. The date and time of the notarial act;
3. The date of the customer's document (if undated, so indicate);
4. The type of notarial act performed;
5. The type of document on which the notary notarized. (One need not write a lengthy title of the transaction. If one journal entry for the same signer to multiple documents is used, one may refer to the documents by a generic label, such as "closing documents" or "lien releases");
6. The signer's address (residential or business);
7. The manner in which the notary verified the signer's identity. (The signer is known personally, what ID card is relied on, or the name of the credible witness relied upon); and
8. Any additional notations about the transaction that are helpful.

Sample Notary Journal entry space. This format is considered the most thorough and user-friendly notary recordation book in the United States. It was created and is published by the Notary Law Institute, Orem, Utah (Notarylaw.com).

295- Notary Journal Entry

Person whose signature is notarized signs here: _____

Date_____Time_____AM/PM Charge$_____ Date of document_____

Type of Notary Act _____Type of document: _____

Signer's address: _____

The manner in which the signer was identified: _____

Special Comments:_____

From "The Notary" (May 1997)

Your Notary Journal is More Than a Ledger; It's Your Legal Protection

Three undeniable truths can be said about keeping a notary journal:

1. *It helps prevent the notary from making serious mistakes;*

2. *It proves the notary performed properly and truthfully; and*

3. *It protects the document signer's legal interests.*

In other words, the benefits and legal security provided by the simple act of journal keeping are so compelling; it is foolish not to journalize every notarial act performed.

Notary journals have been around and in use across the country for decades. They are often referred to as "notary records," or "notary logs," or as "notary ledgers." The preferred term is "notary journals."

Most states do not require their use by notaries. In fact, the vast majority of notaries do not journalize their notarizations. In states where journal keeping is required by law, surveys indicate that a substantial percentage of notaries do not comply with that law.

If the benefits from journalizing notarizations are so tremendous, then why do so few notaries bother to do so? We can only speculate on answers. Perhaps it is due mostly to an unawareness of the idea of a journal. For some, it may be an avoidance of "extra steps to worry about." And it is not uncommon for employers of notaries to prohibit journal keeping because it "inconveniences customers." These are weak excuses.

When the purpose of a notary journal and its extensive legal benefits are understood, it is reasonable to conclude that every notary must keep a notary journal, even if it is not required by state law. Under the common law rule of reasonable care in every state, every notary is required to exercise reasonable care when performing notarial duties. The keeping of a notary journal in a proper manner is "proof positive" the notary is more than a competent notary. It proves the notary is extensively knowledgeable about the duties and procedures of the notarial office and fulfills them with utmost accuracy and professionalism. It protects the notary from accusations of wrongdoing, and it protects the document signer from risks of having his transaction challenged over a questionable notarization.

Your notarizations are functions of law. They are very much "legal documents" with profound legal weight. As notaries we are part of the system of law. We are subject to the rules of procedures and rules of evidence the courts must follow.

Rules of evidence give a very special status to notary journals. Under these rules, which the courts must follow, notary journals are admissible into evidence without any extrinsic evidence of their genuineness or authenticity. In other words, what you record in your notary journal will be presumed by the courts to be truthful This protection against accusations of wrongdoing is so remarkable, it makes no sense for an informed notary not to journalize every notarial act. Not to do so is quite foolish. In fact, it is arguably negligence on the part of the notary.

The courts consider the notary to be the "guarantor of the probative force accorded the notarial certificate." This means that the courts hold the notary personally responsible for the truthfulness of every word of the notarization performed. The notary journal irrefutably documents the probative force accorded the notary's certificate. As a notary you and your notary journal should be inseparable.

Not all notary journals are designed nor created equal. Many are little more than a superficial notation that a notarization occurred. In order to fully benefit from the extensive legal protections journals provide, certain information must be recorded for each notarial act. If the journal is focused on the simple principles of the notary law, and is designed correctly, your journal entry should take less than 45 seconds to complete. There is no excuse for a notary journal to be inconvenient or a burden.

Your journal must allow you to quickly record seven simple items of information:

1. The document signer's signature.

This documents that the signer for whom the notarization is performed appeared personally before the notary. It also establishes that the signer's ID card presented the notary was reasonably reliable because the signatures match. The journal signature will match the signature on the instrument to be notarized. The journal signature arguably demonstrates a substantial degree of signer intent and mental capacity to execute the instrument on which the notarization will be performed.

2. The signer's printed or typed name.
3. The date and time of the notarial act.
4. The date, if any, of the instrument.
5. What notarial service was performed on the document?

Terms 2 through 5 give specificity and details of the notarial act that is being recorded. The credibility of the journal entry and of the notary is enhanced by the detail of documentation recorded.

    6.   A statement on how the notary verified the signer's identity.

This documents exactly what means of signer identity verification was employed by the notary in this transaction. The more detail recorded, the better. For instance, recordation of an ID number and source of issuance, or a credible witness' name and signature as well is essential. This journal entry may irrefutably establish that the notary indeed took all reasonable care to verify a signer's identity.

Most notary journals are designed in the format of a financial ledger or "spread sheet" where every journal entry line runs across two pages 14 inches long, for a total of 28 inches. This spreadsheet format may work well for accounting purposes, but it is very poor for notarial recordations.

A user-friendly notary journal with self-containing recording boxes is a far better way to journalize a notarization. All the required information in a simplified design can be completed in seconds without confusion or mistakes.

Notary journals are permanent records and therefore must be permanently bound volumes. A journal made from a spiral or loose-leaf notebook will not suffice. Their contents are easily lost or tampered with. Some notaries will photocopy their notarizations and store them in a file. This too will not suffice.

The key value of a notary journal is to prove you notarize properly and accurately every time you notarize. Never permit another notary to record their notarizations in your journal. It is your personal record and no one else's. Keep it safe, keep it pure, and keep it tamper-proof.

Complete your journal record before you perform a notarial service. When you are asked to notarize a signature, your immediate and automatic response should be to have the customer sign your journal first, after which, you will complete the required information. It only takes a moment.

204

Most people have never heard of nor seen a notary journal. It is not unusual to encounter some resistance from employers or colleagues when a notary begins to insist on journalizing every notarization. It even happens in states where journals are required by law.

When you keep a notary journal you demonstrate a significantly high level of expertise as a notary. You prove your competence. Inherently, you have a responsibility to educate and diplomatically persuade others that your effort to journalize every notarization protects not only you, but it also protects them.

In performing notarial services, with all of their important legal implications, it is crystal clear that keeping a notary journal is compulsory as a matter of common sense. Arguably, a notary's failure to keep a journal is a form of negligence.

It matters little whether or not your state's notary laws require a notary journal. Your obligation to keep one already exists.

Journalized Notarization
See Journal Recordation; Notary's Duty to Maintain Journal Records

Judicial Officer
See Ministerial Officer

Jurat Notarization
See Affidavit; Affirmation; Oath and Affirmation

Jurats are distinctive in procedure and effect. A jurat is a statement that a document is subscribed and sworn to, or affirmed, before a notary public without further articulation that it is the free act or deed of the person making it.

A jurat is traditionally defined as a certificate "of the officer or person before whom the writing was sworn to. In common use, the term is employed to designate a certificate of a competent administering officer that the writing was sworn to by the person who signed it. It is the clause written at the foot of an affidavit, stating when, where, and before whom such an affidavit was sworn."

A notarial jurat certificate is best known by the wording, *"Subscribed and sworn before me this _____ day of_____, by John Doe."*

The jurat notarization is a written certificate guaranteeing that the signer to a document signed his name under oath, attesting to the contents of the document, in the presence of the notary. The notary certifies that the signer attested to the truthfulness of the document contents under penalty of perjury. Any person may reasonably rely on the facts asserted in the signer's document as truthful, based on the signer's oath thereto.

> *"If business cannot depend on notaries doing this simple task [of properly identifying document signers and administering a proper oath to them], then there is no place for notaries in the world of commerce."*
> *- Florida District Court of Appeal, 1996.*

In order for a jurat notarization to be performed accurately, the document signer inherently must read and understand the document contents prior to the notarization. A person cannot attest to written statements they have not read, lest they do so at their own peril. If a notary knows or has reason to believe the signer has not read the document, the notary cannot effectively place the signer under oath as to the contents thereof.

Any document can be attested to under oath and signed in front of a notary, although in many transactions it would be overkill. However, as long as the jurat procedure is done truthfully, it legally matters not whether the transaction required a jurat notarization or not.

Jurat notarizations are required for transactions where the signer must attest to the content of the document, such as all affidavits and pleadings in court. They are used when notarizations are needed on insurance claims, employment applications, loan applications, and so forth.

Jurat notarizations place the document signer under a higher legal obligation for the truthfulness of his document contents. The jurat subjects the signer to potential criminal liability to third persons entering into such transactions because the threat of a perjury conviction hangs over the signer's head should falsehoods in the document subsequently be found. Jurats prove the signer is willing to stand up for the document contents under the penalty of perjury.

Jurat notarizations do not prove a document is true, legal, valid or enforceable. They do not prove the document signer is truthful in his assertions made in his document. They do not prove that he swears honestly to their truthfulness. Jurats are not affidavits.

The jurat does not prove the signer understood the contents of the document, nor the legal ramifications of the provisions thereof. Jurats do not make the document more reliable or less risky. Jurats are not guarantees as to the safety, factualness or truthfulness of a signer's document.

Jurisdiction
See Authority; Venue

The term, "jurisdiction," is derived from the Latin "jus dicere," meaning "the right to speak." In contemporary law, "jurisdiction" has multiple applications. Overall, it applies to the authority of a court or public official to officiate in a matter. A court, for example, must have competent jurisdiction to hear a case. A police officer must be within proper jurisdiction to exercise police powers. A notary must be within the jurisdiction of the state that authorizes her to perform notarial services.

Unlike the past, all notaries in all states today enjoy statewide jurisdiction in their state of residence that has appointed them. But for only a handful of states, a notary has no authority to perform notarial acts outside their state boundaries.

Every notarial certificate in all states must declare the venue, or location, where the notarial act was performed. The venue statement must verify the notary was within her jurisdiction while performing the service certified by the notarial certificate. Any notarial act performed outside of the notary's authorized jurisdiction is inherently invalid, and constitutes an actionable violation of law.

A careful analysis of the duties of a notary public indicates that he does not adjudicate; he witnesses and attests; he is a certifier of facts; a recorder of signatures; a keeper of a seal to facilitate and authenticate commercial transactions; and a giver of oaths.
- *Transamerica Insurance Company v. Valley National Bank, 462 P.2d 814.*

Keeper of the Great Seal
See Secretary of State

Occasionally one will see reference to the "keeper of the great seal." The phrase is old English in origin and is sometimes applied to the list of duties of a state's Secretary of State or Lieutenant Governor. They often possess the ceremonial responsibility to guard against the unauthorized use of the "great seal" of their respective states. It does not refer to notary seals and has nothing to do with the role or functions of notaries.

Historically, the keeper of the great seal was the chancellor or lord keeper, who was the custodian of the king's great seal, and who enjoyed great importance and power in the kingdom.

Kissing the Book
See Oath and Affirmation

Historically, in the taking of an oath in a tribunal or court setting, the person taking the oath sealed their promise to be truthful by kissing a Bible. Such action is completely unsuitable in contemporary American law, but does continue in other nations. In such places, it is often done under the administration of a notary.

Know
See Knowledge

Know What the Document Is
See Identification of the Signer's Document

Knowingly
See Knowledge

Knowledge
See Personal Knowledge

Under the rule of law, knowing a fact can be actual knowledge or presumed knowledge. A person knows something because they have a certainty in their perception of the truth of the matter. As people we know things personally as result of our interaction or involvement with things, people, events or ideas. Our beliefs, when taken to a moral certainty, constitute knowledge. It is indubitable. As opposed to a reasonable belief, knowledge is incontrovertible.

The verb, "to know" is, as a matter of law, almost synonymous with "reasonable belief." This is because reasonable belief falls very little short, if at all, of the requisites of knowledge. If a reasonable person has reason to believe a fact is true, it is presumed that person has knowledge it is true.

A notary cannot use as a defense that she didn't know an asserted fact was false when she had a duty to discover whether the asserted facts were true or false. The notary has a legal duty to know the truthfulness of all facts asserted within the notarial certificate. By law, the notary either knows or should have known the truthfulness or falsehood of such facts. Hence, there is no defense for signing a notarial certificate that misrepresents material facts.

The material contents of notarial certificates that are required by statute put the notary on notice that such contents must be verified before the certificate is signed and sealed. As a matter of law, a person who has actual notice of information is presumed to have knowledge of that information.

It is clear from several perspectives of law that a notary is utterly defenseless when certifying material falsehoods in notarial certificates. The notary's signature and seal to a certificate constitutes that notary's certification that she actually knew, or should have known, the truthfulness or falsity of the asserted facts, and that she had actual notice thereof.

It is unfortunate that some notaries will have knowledge aforethought regarding the falsity of their certificates. Knowledge aforethought constitutes "thought beforehand, or premeditated." In such cases, the false notarization is intentional. It is calculated to deceive its readers as to the truth of the matters asserted.

There is a fine line between the reckless false notarization and the premeditated false notarization. The former is arguably extreme negligence, and the latter is intentional misrepresentation or fraud. The resulting harm is usually the same, but the scope of liability varies.

The fine line between the reckless and the premeditated is compromised by the fact that notaries are presumed by law to have read, understood and concurred with the truth of the facts asserted in the notarial certificate. For whatever reason a notary might sign a false notarial certificate, that notary places herself in legal peril of being found to have acted with knowledge aforethought.

Knowledge Aforethought
See Knowledge

L

[T]he veil of "public officialdom" behind which the notary may seek to conceal his misdeeds is far too thin to afford protection.
- J. Michael Gottschalk, 48 Neb. L. Rev. 503 (1969).

Lawful
See Legal

Legal

The terms "legal," "legal document," and "legality" are part of our ordinary vernacular. They are used loosely with little thought to what they actually mean. Strictly applied, the terms, "legal" and "legality" refer to compliance with the rule of law or statute.

Generally, "legal" looks to the letter of the law, and "lawful" looks to the spirit of the law. "Legal" is appropriate to describe conformance to the rules of law, that all requirements are met. "Lawful" addresses compliance with ethical standards as framed by law; that the action substantively complies with the intent of the law.

Notaries will commonly refer to their signers' documents as "legal documents." The term of art is handy and convenient, but it is technically misapplied. Notaries are not in a position to know or assess the legality of a document. That is for the document's author or signer to decide. At the very most, notaries should take notice whether the signer's document is "lawful."

If a notary notarizes a signature on a document the notary knew, or should have known through the exercise of reasonable care, is unlawful, that notary bears liability. If the notary is informed or discovers the document to bear her notarization is unlawful because it involves criminality, fraud or dishonesty, that notary is duty-bound by law to refuse to notarize thereon.

If the notary knows, or has reason to know, the signer's document fails to conform to the standards of legality, such as a defective contract or deed, the notary is not liable as a notary for failing to refuse to notarize or inform the signer thereof. However, the notary may be liable for such silence as an employee of the company where the notarization is performed. For example, a notary in the loan department of a bank may be liable as a bank employee for failing to inform the signer that the loan agreement fails to conform to statutes or federal banking regulations.

Legal Defense against Liability
See Ignorance of the Law; Liability; Strict Liability for Official Misconduct by Notaries

Notaries are under the legal duty to exercise reasonable care when performing notarial services. That means the notary strictly obeys the rules of the notary statutes, properly verifies the signer's identity, thoroughly documents the notarial act in a notary journal, and carefully scrutinizes the notarial wording to ensure every word thereof is true. The breach of any of these duties can result in the charge of liability.

The notary cannot use as a valid defense that she was coerced or misled into the wrongful conduct. There may be shared liability with an employer, colleague or document signer who pressured the notary to breach her legal duties. Codefendants can be sued jointly with the notary, or severally. The notary can cross-claim against such parties and sue them for having pressured or falsely induced the notary into the misconduct.

The notary's primary legal defense against liability is to prove that none of the duties of care were breached. This means that the notary might concede that the notarized signature was proven to be a forgery, but such a fact would be utterly undiscoverable by any reasonable person in the notary's position having exercised all reasonable care to perform the notarization.

The notary is not, as a matter of law, the guarantor the signature to be notarized is not a forgery. To the contrary, the notary certifies that she has faithfully followed all of the requirements of law that people may rely upon to presume the signature is genuine. No notarial certificate declares a guarantee the signature is not a forgery. Rather the notary's certificate declares all required steps were taken to reasonably verify the genuineness of the signature.

The notary's surest defense is to comply with every requirement of the notary law. The notarial wording of the certificate is an automatic self-administered truth test. Every word thereof must be true. If they are, then the notary enjoys automatic protection against liability.

Legal Document
See Legal

Legal Effect of a Notarization
See Purpose for Notarizations; Probative Value of the Notarial Certificate

Legal Jurisdiction Over the Notary
See Equal Protection; Government Regulation of Notaries; Venue

Legalese
See Certificate of Notarization; Completing the Notarial Certificate; Component Parts of the Notarial Certificate

From "The Notary" (November 1996)

Res est misera ubi jus est vagum et incertum!

This Latin phrase means, "It is a sorry affair when the law is vague and uncertain."

It is also a sorry affair when a notarization certificate is vague and uncertain because of the way it is written. This isn't the notary's doing. It is the product of decades of tradition within the legal community. It is commonly called "legalese" and it creates confusion.

Legalese commonly found in notarial certificates includes phrases like "subscribed to the within instrument" and "witnessed hereto, who being duly sworn, deposes and says," and so forth. Average citizens don't understand it, and most law-trained professionals struggle with it as well. But we as notaries have to work with it.

Or do we?

If you are asked to notarize a signature using a certificate that is smothered in legalese, don't give in. You must not sign and seal any notarial certificate you do not fully understand and endorse as true and correct. Either have the author of the document explain and define the terms of the certificate, or use your own notarial certificate that is written in plain English.

Guidelines for notarial wording of a certificate are provided by state law. State statutes provide us the required elements of information that must be included within a notarial certificate. How to phrase and construct a notarial certificate is up to the notary, so long as all required elements are included. This is called "substantial compliance." Most notary statutes require that notarial certificates "must be substantially in the following form..." This grants the notary considerable latitude to use simple English to write notarial certificates.

Notaries are not the only ones who are getting fed up with legalese. State bar associations across the country are urging their member attorneys to draft their law filings and documents in simple English. A number of states now require by law that all legal documents and consumer contracts be written in understandable English. It is said that lawyers are reluctant to give up their law lingo because it creates a mystique and sense of

214

importance. Remember, this is a tradition that dates back centuries and won't change quickly.

Every one of us can make an impact. Do not be shy in rejecting documents that do not make sense, especially if the document is prepared for you as a client. As a notary, be prepared for the likelihood that a notarial certificate will not be understandable. Have your own certificates ready to use, ones that you and your customer will easily understand

People have much more respect for you and your notarial service when they can understand the certificate you have completed, signed and sealed.

Legality
See Legal

Liability

Notaries are responsible for the damages they cause by their wrongful notarial conduct. Such responsibility is referred to in law as "liability." Notaries are liable to the persons harmed by the notary's breach of notarial duties and standards of performance.

In order for a notary to be held liable, the injured party must bring a cause of action against the notary in a court of law. The court must enter a finding of liability and order a judgment against the notary. Until such point, the notary is only accused of liability.

The notary's liability is established by the court when certain findings are made under 58 Am. Jur. 2d, Notaries Public Section 23, the requisite tests are defined:

"In order to recover for the act or default of a notary in the performance of his duties as such the burden is upon the plaintiff to show first that the notary did not faithfully perform the duties of his office, and, secondly, that the plaintiff was injured and damaged as a result of such failure, and that such failure was the proximate cause of the loss and injury which he sustained."

In matters concerning the notary's wrongful conduct, the courts have almost always taken a stern position. The courts hold the notary responsible for proving she performed with reasonable care, even though the notarized signature is not legitimate.

> *"If it is established that notarized signature is forged, burden of persuasion shifts to notary to prove by preponderance of evidence that he exercised reasonable care in ascertaining identity of person; justification for shifting burden of persuasion is probability that notary was negligent and strong public policy of ensuring accuracy of notarial certifications."*
> *- Meyers v. Meyers, 81 Wash. 2d 533, 503 P.2d 59 (1972).*

If the court finds the notary was in fact negligent and breached the required level of care in performing official duties, liability shall impute to the notary.

> *"The court gave the following instruction in its oral charge to the jury:*
>
> *I charge you ladies and gentlemen that where a notary public is called on to perform an act authorized by law, and he does so carelessly and fraudulently, the notary is liable for any loss resulting from the fraudulent conduct."*
> *- First Bank of Childersburg v. Florey 676 So. 2d 324 (Ala. Civ. App. 1996).*

When a notary is found liable for the damages caused by her negligence or misconduct, she can be ordered to compensate the persons harmed thereby. The court can assess actual damages and punitive damages. Actual damages will be measured according to the actual financial loss, or its financial equivalent of loss, that the court finds to be the result of the notary's misconduct.

The court can also assess punitive damages for the purpose of setting an example for others to learn by. Courts do not often apply punitive damages, except in egregious circumstances.

A court judgment awarding financial damages serves an important public purpose. When we engage in wrongful conduct, and it is foreseeable our conduct could harm others, our knowledge that we could be financially liable for such harm should induce us to withdraw and behave with prudence. Financial liability serves as a preventative against negligence, misconduct and breach of the duty of care.

Plaintiffs who allege the notary is liable for wrongful conduct must conduct a self-examination. If they knew or had reason to believe the notarial certificate was defective, or false in any way, and they failed to act on such knowledge, the plaintiff severely diminishes the notary's share of liability. Such persons acquiesce to the fatal flaws of the certificate, knowing the notarization is untrue, and thereby assume the risk that injury might result. Their failure to require a correction to the notarization, or failure to reject it, could be an effective mitigating defense for the notary.

From "The Notary" (November 1996)

Notary Laws Protect Notaries

On a cold, rainy afternoon, two cars were driving down a twisting, winding road. Car #1 exceeded the speed limit as if the road were a thrilling public racecourse. Car #2 drove below the speed limit on account of the slick road surface, slowing at sharp turns and avoiding dangerous puddles of water. Unfortunately, both cars skidded out of control and crashed into guardrails. In a court of law, which one of these drivers would be found liable for negligent driving? The obvious answer is driver # 1, who drove like Mario Andretti on a sunny day. Driver #2 exercised reasonable care, and thus his accident is genuinely an "accident" which could have happened to anyone.

This little example illustrates the legal principle of "reasonable care" and "negligence." When notaries fail to exercise reasonable care, they are negligent. Negligent behavior by anyone can cause harm and injury to another person or to their property. Notaries are liable for their negligence when they fail to exercise reasonable care when notarizing.

The legal standard of "reasonable care" is the notary's shield of protection in American courts of law.

The notary's standard of reasonable care is defined is the degree of care, attentiveness and caution that would be exercised by an ordinary, prudent person acting in the same position as the notary. Thus, reasonable care is measured by common sense, by wisdom borne out of experience, and by rational thinking. There are no black and white rules because reasonable care will vary case by case. Each of us are different, thus each of us will exercise a slightly different approach to reasonable care.

Reasonable care is the notary's shield of protection because all a notary must prove is that she did everything a reasonable and prudent person would do in a similar circumstance. When it comes to performing notarial services, the notary's burden of proof is surprisingly easy.

The basic principles of law pertaining to notary liability are widely misunderstood. As a result, there is considerable anxiety and paranoia among some notaries. Misconceptions lead to incorrect notarial practices and procedures, which in turn lead to incorrect teachings and directives to notaries. We end up severely restricted in our ability to function as notaries as the law intended because of misconceptions about the role of law in our performance of our notarial duties.

There is much talk about the increase of fraud in the United States. There is an unfortunate perception that the increase in fraud poses a challenge, and even a threat, to notaries. The misguided idea is that notaries are increasingly susceptible to liability because of the increased risk of exposure to criminals seeking notarizations. On the surface, this may sound logical. But, when considered more thoroughly on principles of law, there is no basis for such fears. If the notary exercises reasonable care in performance of her duties, that notary cannot be held liable if anything goes wrong.

Another unfortunate misconception is that by complying with a certain set of notary rules of procedures, a notary will never be sued. That is also untrue. Even the meticulous exercise of reasonable care is not a guarantee

218

a notary will not be sued. Lawsuits can be filed by anyone against anyone. American litigiousness casts a cold shadow on our society.

To illustrate how cold that shadow can be, consider the multitude of lawsuits in the aftermath of the tragic fire at the MGM Grand Hotel in Las Vegas many years ago. The fire was arson-set. Many people were either killed or injured because of deficient fire safety features in the hotel. The many lawsuits filed against the hotel owners were also filed against the many hundreds of building contractors and subcontractors who worked on the construction of the hotel years earlier. Wrongful death lawsuits were even filed against the subcontractor who painted the lines in the parking lots surrounding the perimeter of the hotel! Most of the suits were frivolous and were thrown out.

A notary can be found liable for a wrongful notarization only where the notary conducted the notarial act in a negligent manner. The plaintiff suing the notary will have the burden of proof to prove the notary committed an "official misconduct." An official misconduct constitutes a substantial breach of the standard of reasonable care. Official misconduct consists of a notarial certificate that contains material falsehoods (important statements of fact which are completely false). Generally, the most common forms of official misconduct are:

1. *Notarizing a signature where the signer did not personally appear before the notary;*
2. *Failing to exercise reasonable care to verify the signer's identity; and*
3. *Failing to ensure every word of the notarial certificate is truthful and accurate before signing and affixing a notary seal thereto.*

The notary's standard of reasonable care is simple. It is based on an understanding of what the law of notarizations is about. It consists of four fundamental principles:

1. *Always require the singer to personally appear before you; otherwise it is impossible to notarize the signature.*
2. *Always take all reasonable steps to verify a signer's identity by means of your personal knowledge, by means of a credible witness,*

or by means of what appears to be a valid form of ID (which may be defined by the notary statutes of your state).

3. *Always document every notarial act in a properly designed notary journal to prove every aspect of every notarial act was performed correctly and truthfully.*

4. *Always scrutinize the notary wording before you sign it and affix your seal.*

5. *Never allow falsehoods and serious defects to go uncorrected. Better yet, be prepared in advance with proper notarial wording to use at a moment's notice in lieu of the defective certificates handed you by document signers.*

The notary's standard of reasonable care is indeed a shield of protection. If you exercise reasonable care in every aspect of every notarial act you perform, and anything goes wrong (perhaps the document signer is later discovered to be a master imposter/forger), you cannot be held liable. You performed your notarial duty competently. The courts will assess and appoint blame to others, thus excluding you from the scope of liability.

The Case of the Notarized Real Estate Thefts

Werner v. Werner et al., 526 P2d. 570, 84 Wash. 2d 360 (1974).

In 1912, Otto and William Werner purchased a parcel of property in Sonomish County, Washington. Forty-four years later, Otto died and William deeded the property to his wife, Christine. In 1969, a Carole Albin forged Christine Werner's signature to a quit claim deed to the property, conveying it to a person named Ottie C. Werner. The forged signature on the deed was notarized by Roger Johnson, a California notary.

At the same time, a real estate agent in Sonomish County received a telephone call from a person claiming to be Ottie Werner, asking the agent to place the property on the market for sale. In no time, the agent had a buyer. In the series of transactions to prepare the necessary closing documents for the new buyer, it was discovered that Otto Werner's name remained on the title and had to be cleared off. The next month in Southern California, Carol and Alan Albin appeared before a California notary named Pomeroy to sign the names of Otto Werner and his wife, Susanna Werner, to the quit claim deed conveying the property to Ottie Werner. Notary Pomeroy notarized both signatures. The conveyance of the property to Ottie Werner was completed and closed, and the deeds were recorded with the county. Then the new "owner," Ottie Werner, sold the property to Martin Quarnstorm.

It came as a tremendous shock to the Quarnstorms when the adult son and daughter of Otto and Susanne Werner sued to quiet title to the property, claiming rightful ownership of the property and that title was stolen from them. Multiple lawsuits were filed and counter-filed. Notaries Johnson and Pomeroy, and their respective employers, were also sued. It was discovered that Ottie Werner was an alias for Alan Albin.

The court stated that notaries are "of great importance in the validation of signatories to various legal documents" and that "the notarial function has become the keystone of real estate transactions." The court pointed out that a notary's certificate is the "pillar of our property rights," and that all official records depend on the notary's certificate. "The notary is a public officer that has a duty to take reasonable precautions to assure [the notary] seal will not be a vehicle by which a fraudulent transaction is consummated." The court pointedly emphasized the joint liability of the notary's employers as well for the negligent performance of their employees' notarial duties. The Albins were criminally prosecuted.

Liability for Damages
See Liability

Limitations to Notarial Liability

See Liability

Locus Sigilli
See Placement of the Seal; Seal of the Notary Public

Latin for the phrase, "place of the seal," many traditional notarial certificates will pre-print the phrase or its initials, "L.S.," near the notary's signature line. It directs the notary where to affix the notary's seal on the notarial certificate.

No state requires by statute that the notarial certificate contain the letters, "L.S." or the word, "seal," or the phrase, "locus sigilli." It is merely a vestige of bygone eras with little or no import today.

In states where the notary is not required to affix a notary seal, locus sigilli is misleading. It cannot be construed as a mandate for a seal in such states. Moreover, a notary seal may be affixed by the notary in any clear space sufficient to render the seal legible, whether that be above, below, to the left, or to the right of the notary's signature.

Loose Notarial Certificates
See Attaching the Notarial Certificate

Lost Notary Seal
See Seal of the Notary Public

The notary seal is an official identifier of the notary's legal authority to perform notarizations. Its loss or theft should be reported in writing to the state agency that commissions notaries. Should a person find the seal and use it fraudulently, the notary is not liable for the imposter's fraudulent acts. However, a notary is negligent in failing to give the state notice of the seal's loss or theft.

Upon discovery of an imposter's fraudulent use of a notary's lost or stolen seal, the notary's written notice to the state thereof can be produced to relieve the notary of any culpability or dereliction of duty.

It is not unheard of where a notary's supervisor or co-worker removes the notary's seal from the notary's desk and uses it to "notarize a signature" while the notary is away from the office. That conduct constitutes theft of the notary seal, and a criminal fraud by means of forgery and counterfeit. When discovered, such criminality should be reported to proper authorities. However, it is understandably difficult for the notary to properly pursue the matter as it may jeopardize the notary's employment security and future. While the notary is legally protected against retaliation or sanction for remedying the criminal conduct, it may prove financially costly for the notary to enjoy such protection. For this reason, it is absolutely essential that every employee, supervisor and employer where notaries are employed be informed on the notary laws and duties of the notary.

Well-written policies outlining the procedures for reporting notarial misconduct and for protecting persons who rightfully raise such issues with management will go a long way to protect all parties and to ensure a high ethical environment in the workplace.

L.S.

See Locus Sigilli; Placement of the Seal

M

It may be questioned whether notarization is actually an improvement upon the mere signature...
- *Home Say. Of Am. V. Einhorn, No. 87C-7390, 1990.*

Malfeasance by the Notary

See Duty of Care; Liability; Official Misconduct; Reasonable Care

Notarial malfeasance is the doing of an act that the notary ought not to do at all. Misfeasance, on the other hand, is the wrongful doing of a notarial act that the notary is authorized to perform. The notary and the employer of notaries can be liable for damages caused by the malfeasance or misfeasance of the notary.

Marriages Performed by Notaries

See Authority; Notarial Powers and Authority; Statutory Authority of the Notary

Notaries in the states of Florida, Maine, Nevada and South Carolina are authorized by law to perform marriages. In bygone eras, it was common for notaries across the country to perform marriages. This alleviated the great inconvenience created by poor transportation and communication systems so the public could obtain legal marriages without undue delays. It was important to America's then agrarian society where most families lived in the country, rather than in the cities.

While performing marriages in Florida, Maine, Nevada and South Carolina are notarial functions, they are not notarizations. Inherently, notaries are official witnesses on behalf of the state to certain transactions, among which in these three states, is the entering into the oaths of marriage.

When the notary has performed the marriage, the marriage certificate is signed by the notary and is properly recorded as specified by the respective state laws. Akin to the administration of an oath to a person, the notary need not make a notary journal record of the proceeding because the journal would not be probative of the verity of the marriage.

Issues of conflicts of interest do not restrict notaries in the four states authorizing marriages by notaries. A notary may perform a marriage for a child or other family member because there are no substantive concerns one can raise regarding the familial relationship. The marriage service by a notary does not present the notary the means for self-benefit, as would the notarization of a signature. The notary may gain a son or a daughter from the marriage performed, but that does not constitute a disqualifying conflict of interest.

Material Fact
See Fraud; Material Misrepresentation

Material Misrepresentation
See False Notarization; Falsehood; Fraud

A notarial certificate contains a number of facts that are intended to induce the reader to enter into a transaction or to rely on the representations made in the document. The representations may be intended to deceive the reader into doing something he would otherwise not do, but for the false representation. The facts within the certificate are material if they are intended to induce the reader to form a decision to act in reliance on the facts asserted. For example, a notarized signature to a loan application is intended to induce the lender to feel assured the signer of the loan contract is the person for whom the loan is intended.

A misrepresentation is material if it is a *"statement or undertaking of sufficient substance and importance as to be the foundation of an action if such representation is false."* (Black's Law Dictionary, 6th Edition).

A material misrepresentation of fact constitutes an element of fraud. For there to be a misrepresentation of material fact, the asserted representations must not be mere statements of opinion. They must be asserted as true facts. It is one thing for a person to say, "John Doe robbed the bank." And, it is another to say, "I think John Doe robbed the bank."

When the notary certifies in a notarization "John Doe acknowledged his signature before me," when in fact he did not appear before the notary, the notary makes a material misrepresentation. It is material because the law requires the signer to personally appear before the notary to prove the signature on the document belongs to him. If a notary certifies falsely that such a fact occurred, the notary commits a serious violation of law.

Measuring Notarial Liability

See Proximate Cause; Scope of the Notary's Liability

Medallion Signature Guarantees

Medallion signature guarantees are not notarizations. They do not utilize the authority of a notary and are not performed in the same manner as a notarization. Rather, they are a form of signature verification performed under a program of the federal government whereby financial institutions, securities firms and other financial organizations can ensure a signature to a transaction is genuine. As part of the program, there are several levels of signature guarantees, with medallion guarantees among the top.

The primary purpose of a signature guarantee is to provide assurance a signature is not a forgery. Notarizations do the same thing. The difference is that the notary does not "guarantee" the signature is not a forgery. The signature guarantee does in fact make such a guarantee. The financial institution stands behind the guarantee and is liable if they are wrong. In law it is referred to as "strict liability." The person employed by the financial institution obligates their employer to the guarantee. If the signature turns out to be forged, and any person is financially damaged because of that forgery, the institution will pay the victim for all damages suffered.

Signature guarantees are issued at banks, credit unions, stock brokerages and any type of financial institution having fiduciary responsibility for customer's funds. The signature guarantee is similar to a warrantee of endorser or transferor in transactions of payment by check. A person who endorses a check is usually looked to as the one who will honor the check in the event of a subsequent renunciation.

Signature guarantees are created under the Uniform Commercial Code, or UCC. Under the UCC, any person (a guarantor) guaranteeing a signature of an endorser of a "certified security" (a negotiable instrument, certified check, stock transfer, etc.) is certifying three material facts:

1. The signature is genuine;
2. The signer had the authority to make the signature; and
3. The signer had the legal capacity to make the signature.

The UCC provides that any person who relies on the signature guarantee to their detriment and is harmed because the signature on the instrument was not genuine, authorized or competent, then the guarantor will be liable for the full amount of damage incurred. That is significantly different from the notary's liability for a notarization.

A notary is required to exercise reasonable care in verifying a signer's identity and to ensure the signature being notarized belongs to the person appearing before her. If the notary exercises reasonable care in making those determinations, she cannot be held liable. The principal way a notary can be liable for notarizing a forged signature is in having failed to exercise reasonable care. That is, not requiring the signer to appear, and/or failing to properly verify the signer's true identity.

A signature guarantor and their employer-financial institution will be liable regardless of the precautions taken to verify the signer's true identity. That renders the matter a "strict liability." If it happens, they are liable.

It appears that the intent of the UCC is to make the financial institution, not the employee, liable in signature guarantees. Employees performing such transactions in the routine course of their employment may wish to attain written assurance and indemnification from their employers in the event a signature guarantee performed by them turns out poorly.

As for notaries, the signature guarantee never invokes the notary's notarial authority. No notarial wording is used and the notary's seal shall not be used either.

Mental Capacity of the Document Signer
See Mental Competence; Signer's Competence

Mental Competence
See Competence to Sign; Signer's Competence; Willful, Free Making of a Signature

Many erroneously assume that part of the notary's responsibility is to determine the document signer is competent to sign. Competency of document signers lies outside the scope of the notary's purview. This is because competency, as a legal standard, requires a finding that the person possesses adequate mental capacity to fully appreciate that which they are entering into as a document signer.

The notary's obligation is to determine that the signer is signing the document willingly and freely. This standard goes to the question of intent to sign, to enter into the transaction for the purposes for which the document is signed. This lesser standard is not dependent on the signer's comprehensive appreciation for all of the contents, terms, conditions and legal ramifications of the document.

Another reason that notaries are not responsible for the measurement of signer mental competency is that such a determination requires the sophisticated, skilled judgment of highly trained, licensed mental health professionals. If the law imposed as a condition precedent to every notarization for a mentally impaired person a professional diagnosis of signer mental competence, notarizations for such persons would become unreasonably burdened with costly examinations and delays, and the notary would still have to assess whether or not the professional's diagnosis is correct. It would create an untenable burden and risk for the notary that no reasonable person could sustain.

The notary is responsible, by law, to determine that the signer signs willingly and freely. The willful free signature is found when the signer knew what the document is, not necessarily what it says. Public policy must allow for the presumption that if a person signs a power of attorney, that signer possesses a basic idea the document constitutes a granting of authority to another person to act on their behalf. Every signer of a document assumes the risks that are seen and unseen, as they are associated with the transaction. Hence, the signer must have sufficient mental competence to decide whether or not they are willing to enter into the transaction, that they are cognizant enough to decide to proceed or refuse to sign.

From "The Notary" (July 2001)

Notarizing for the Mentally Impaired

Nearly two out of every ten Americans is over the age of 65. Remarkably, the age of 65 has been until recent years the historical milestone past which a person joins the population of the elderly. Today, that milestone has been pushed way back, well into the mid to late-seventies. The miracle of medical advancements enables all of us to benefit much longer from the wisdom and companionship of our seniors, longer than any preceding generations ever enjoyed.

Seniors today are more active; more involved in community and public service, and are more self-reliant than ever before. When we notarize for seniors, there is the occasional concern over the signer's mental competence to sign a document. Every person has a legal right, regardless of age or conditions of health, to the services of a notary if they meet minimum standards the notary must evaluate.

Signer's Competence versus Signer's Willful and Free Signature

There is considerable discussion about a notary's obligation to assess a signer's competence to sign a document. There also appears, however, considerable confusion on the rule of law and its implications for the notary.

Writings and discussions on what constitutes signer competence often overlook or misunderstand the definition of signer competence. Such commentaries frequently commingle the terms "signer competence" with the "willful, free making of a signature."

There are those who readily admit that a notary is neither medically or legally competent to discern a signer's mental competence, but nevertheless assert the notary has a duty to make such assessments by employing certain helpful hints and rules of thumb. We can't have it both ways.

The American standard of law for notaries is for the notary to verify that a document signer signs a document willingly and freely. The willful, free making of a signature, as a matter of law, means that the signature was made deliberately with intent. Inherently, it requires the signer to know what the document is that they sign, and not its contents and legal ramifications. If a signer knows it is a contract to buy a house, and they proceed to sign it, their signature was made willingly and freely because it was a deliberate, intentional act.

A document and a signature that has been signed unfreely and unwillingly is not enforceable - its notarization is false.

A willful, free act is one that the person knows he is doing, and does so with the intent to achieve the results achieved by the act. Some people erroneously equate the "willful, free" portion of the equation as a complete absence of any unhappiness, hesitation, anxiety or even the slightest degree of pressure or coercion.

When we sign our tax returns, our signatures to the tax return are made willingly and freely, even though we are unhappy and reluctant to hand our hard-earned dollars to the government under threat of criminal prosecution if we do not. We do things we would rather not do, but proceed because it is required of us or because we are under an obligation to do it.

A document signature is made willingly and freely when the signer knows what the document is. In a 1972 Minnesota case, Hocking v. Guello (193 N.W. 2d 634) the court held that a notary violated the notary law by notarizing for a signer whom the notary knew "did not know what it was he was signing" and it resulted in a false notarization.

Understanding and comprehension of a document's content is not a prerequisite for a willful, free signature. What is a prerequisite, however, is the complete absence of undue influence, such as coercion or duress.

In the California case of Cameron v. Cameron (587 P. 2d 939 (1978)) the court defined what constitutes undue influence: "In determining the issue of undue influence, the court may consider the confidential relationship of the person attempting to influence the donor, the physical and mental condition of the donor as it affects his ability to withstand the influence, the unnaturalness of the disposition as it relates to showing an unbalanced mind or a mind easily susceptible to undue influence, and demands and importunities as they may affect the particular donor, taking into consideration the time, place and all surrounding circumstances."

The guidelines set forth in the Cameron case are helpful. Undue influence on a signer prevents the signer's exercise of willful, free intent to sign. The court identifies four factors to be considered when assessing whether a signer is unduly influenced:

1. *Is the person who is influencing the document signer one who is trusted or relied upon by the signer?*
2. *Is the signer mentally and physically capable of rejecting and withstanding the influence placed on him? This requires the signer to recognize the influence being imposed on him is not what he wants and is able to withstand it.*
3. *Is the document signer manifesting a natural disposition reflecting a sound mind or a mind that is easily susceptible to undue influence or demands from others?*
4. *Are there any factors such as time of day, the location where the signer is subjected to the influence of others, and any other circumstances surrounding the event? For an elderly person, as an example, the late afternoon may prove difficult for the signer because it is the usual time of day the person is fatigued and needs rest; their mind is dulled by the effects of weariness. Likewise, the ill or elderly patient in the hospital examining room dressed in hospital gowns and is surrounded by strangers. It is the epitome of*

all intimidating human circumstances. In such a circumstance, when a person barks, "sign the darn thing NOW," you do it.

A signer's incompetence to sign a document automatically invalidates that document. The signature to the document may be genuine, made willingly and freely and properly notarized if the notary had no reason to know the signer is incompetent. However, the notary is not authorized by notary statutes or by common law to determine a signer's competence. The notary may only determine a signature is made willfully and freely.

This important principle is reinforced many times in case law and by statutes. In State ex. rel. Nelson v. Hammett in 1947 in Missouri (203 S. W. 2d 115) the court held, "It [by] no means follows that the [notarial] certificate is a proper one if the execution of the instrument is not the free act and deed of the maker thereof to the knowledge of the notary and, we are of the opinion that, a certificate made where the notary knows that the instrument is not the free act and deed of the maker, is false and its making is a violation of his official duty."

A person who does not sign a document willingly and freely is not necessarily incompetent. An incompetent person may be capable of signing a document willingly and freely.

Assessing a person's competence to sign a document requires highly skilled and experienced professionals. A person's competence is almost always an issue left for the courts to decide. It usually comes up as an issue after a transaction has occurred and its validity is under attack. The attack is not on the genuineness of the signature but on the signer's comprehension of the content and legal ramifications thereof.

A properly notarized signature to a document is separate and apart from assertions that a document is void due to signer incompetence. The notarization is sustainable as evidence the signature was made willingly and free of undue influence from others. Yet, the document itself could be voided for signer incompetence.

Every average, ordinary adult has sufficient experience and awareness to be able to discern when a person outwardly manifests their mental incompetence. It is a discernment made in the context of all of the circumstances then present. It may be a statement made by the healthcare provider to the notary or it may come from the notary's observation that the signer makes no response to questions.

Another Missouri case is illustrative of the issues: In Pazdernik v. Decker (652 S.W. 2d 319), the Missouri Court of Appeals in 1983 upheld the invalidation of a signer's power of attorney due to the signer's mental incompetence to sign it. The elderly woman, who signed the power of attorney, after suffering a debilitating stroke, had been unable to communicate with anyone, had not recognized any of her relatives and was capable of only making unintelligible sounds. The notary made no effort to assess the signer's capacity to sign willingly and freely.

Notaries are under strict legal obligation to exercise reasonable care in every step of the notarial process. There are standards of reasonable care for notaries to determine that a signer signs willingly and freely:

1. *The notary should engage the signer in light conversation, such as "How's the weather?" or "What are your weekend plans?" As the notary converses with a signer, it is readily evident to any reasonable person whether the person suffers from any degree of mental impairment.*

2. *If the notary determines the signer suffers from any degree of mental impairment, ever so slight as it may be, the notary should engage the signer in some friendly probative questions:*
   a. *What kind of document is this you are signing? or*
   b. *What are you planning to have happen by this document?*

3. *Make a thorough record in the notary journal of the entire transaction, including the nature of conversation and evidence of the signer's willingness and intent to sign the document. The absence of such a record constitutes reason to believe the notary took no steps of reasonable care in the transaction concerning the signer's willful, free signature.*

Notarizing for the aged and the ill can pose vexing challenges for notaries. As long as the notary exercises reasonable care and common sense, there can be no wrongdoing. Notaries are entrusted with a high public trust to exercise good judgment based on common sense and integrity.

233

Unless the signer's incompetence is obvious to any reasonable and untrained observer, the notary may proceed to ensure the signature is made willingly and freely. The subsequent finding in court that the signer was also incompetent will not invalidate the notarization nor expose the notary to risk of liability.

Ministerial Act
See Ministerial Officer; Notary Public

Ministerial Officer
See History of the Notary Public

Although today it is an archaic distinction, historically it was legally significant that a notary was a ministerial officer and not a judicial officer. A ministerial officer is one who is neither a judicial officer nor an executive officer of government, but is one whose duties are of a ministerial nature. Ministerial duties are those that require little or no discretion or judgment.

A judicial officer, on the other hand, is one who is part of the judicial part of government, whose functions pertain to matters of the courts. Such officers exercise a degree of discretion and the authority to pass judgment.

As American notary law has evolved to what it is today, the functions of a notary have become somewhat ministerial with a loose application and interpretation. Ministerial duties are ones that are expressly imposed by law and that authorize no discretion in their performance. They must be performed exactly as outlined by law. They are set tasks for which the law prescribes the method, timing, mode and occasion for their performance.

Applying that definition to the contemporary notarial services authorized by law in all fifty states, the notary is required to exercise a modest degree of discretion in their performance. Rather than specifying every detail of the notarial process, the notary law provides the standards by which the notary shall notarize. Certain steps shall be taken, but most of the steps require a judgment call on the notary's part. For example, a notary must decide whether a signer's identification is credible and reasonably verifies the signer's true identity. The notary must determine whether the signer is signing the document willingly and freely. Most importantly, the notary must judge whether or not the signature to be notarized is genuine and belongs to the person appearing before her.

Historically, the distinction between a ministerial officer and a judicial officer directly affected the measure and scope of a notary's liability. It is irrelevant today. The legal standard of reasonable care expected of every notary inherently requires notarial judgment and decision making, all within the scope of the notary's statutory authority.

Minors
See Notarizing for Minors; Willful, Free Making of a Signature

Notaries often refuse to notarize the signature of minor children believing they are not of legal age to enter into contractual obligations, therefore are not of sufficient age to sign binding documents. A minor is a person who has not reached the minimum age at which the law recognizes a general contractual capacity. It is usually anyone under the age of eighteen.

Any person of any age can have their signature notarized, as long as they are qualified to sign and do so willingly and freely. Although not commonly done, a child's signature can be notarized. It requires no less or more concern than is required for notarizing for an adult. The transaction on which the minor signs may be invalid and unenforceable due to the minor's lack of contractual capacity, but the notarization has no affect thereon whatsoever. The notary in this case, as in all cases, takes every reasonable step to verify the minor's identity and the genuineness of the minor's signature.

Misconduct
See Liability; Official Misconduct

Misfeasance by the Notary
See Liability; Malfeasance by the Notary; Official Misconduct

Misrepresentation
See Fraud; Liability; Material Fact

A misrepresentation is the assertion of a fact that is false. It is a statement in writing, or made orally, that when accepted by the reader or listener, leads the mind to believe one thing while factually it is something else.

Multiple Document Signers

It is common for documents to require all signatures of multiple parties to be notarized. The notary can notarize all of the signatures but only the signatures of the parties who appear before the notary. As notarizations do not make a document legal or enforceable, it matters not whether there are multiple notarial certificates for different signers respectively to the same document.

When asked to notarize for a group of signers in the same transaction, the notary can use a single certificate and name each signer within the certificate. As an example, the notary can write, "Subscribed and sworn to before me by John Doe, Sara Doe, Tom Smith and Lucy Smith..." As long as the notary performed the jurat notarization truthfully, a consolidated certificate can prove thorough and efficient.

Notaries often fear that if they notarize for only one or a few of the full group of signers that the signatures of the others will be imputed to the notarial certificate, unless the notary otherwise includes a disclaimer in the certificate. A disclaimer such as, "This notarization is for John Doe only" is not necessary.

Though not specifically required by statute in a few states, it is self-evidently meritorious for the notary to name the document signers for whom the notarization is performed within the notarial certificate. The certificate should specify, for example, "Acknowledged before me by John Doe." When the certificate merely declares, "Acknowledged before me this 4th day of July..." it fails to connect the facts asserted by the certificate to the parties to whom it applies. If the certificate of notarization properly names the signer(s) whose signatures are notarized, then subsequent signers will have to obtain their own notarizations. Any attempt by a person to append his signature to a previously executed notarial certificate commits criminal fraud. The notary is not liable for the wrongful conduct of others subsequent to the proper performance of the notarial act. Moreover, the properly kept notary journal will prove dispositively that the wrongdoer has in fact fraudulently appended his signature to the executed notarization.

Multiple Notary Commissions

As a general rule, a person can possess only one notary commission at a time, except in a few select circumstances. While no state statutorily prohibits a person from obtaining more than one notary commission from the same state, such a policy is inherently requisite to the orderliness and sound administration of state notary laws. The laws and procedures for obtaining notarial commissions imply prohibitions against persons holding multiple notary commissions from a single state.

In a few states, the notary laws provide that employees of the state government can obtain limited jurisdiction notary commissions, useable only for state business. Should the state employee wish to notarize outside of the scope of state employment, that notary may apply for a regular notary commission to be used statewide on non-state business. In such a circumstance, the notary possesses two notary commissions: one restricted to state business, and the other unrestricted in its use.

A number of states permit non-residents of their states to obtain notarial commissions in their states if they are employed in their states or regularly conduct business in their states. It is not uncommon for such notaries to possess notary commissions from two states simultaneously, to be exercised only in the respective states that granted the commissions.

Holders of multiple notary commissions are few in number and are under strict limitations to their use. It is utterly dissimilar to the simultaneous holding of dual drivers licenses. The few allowances for dual notary commissions are based in public policy for the exigencies of commerce and society.

N

The officer who takes an acknowledgment acts in a judicial character in determining whether the person representing himself to be, or represented by someone else to be, the grantor named in the conveyance, actually is the grantor. He determines further whether the person thus adjudged to be the grantor does actually and truly acknowledge before him that he executed the instrument.
- Wasson v. Connor, 54 Miss. 351.

Name Change
See Identity of the Signer; Signer Identification

A continual source of concern for notaries is over a signer's change of name. The name may change due to marriage or divorce, or a person has dropped a nickname in exchange for their given name. Notaries also face an issue when a person's full, complete name is typed into the text of the document and signature block, but the signer signs by their familiar name, such as "Betty" for Elizabeth.

There is nothing unlawful or deceitful for people to go by their full name, but to sign by their familiar name. A change in marital status in no way alters a person's identity. As long as the person's variations in names used and signed are not intended to deceive or defraud others, a notary need only apply informed, common sense when notarizing in such circumstances.

From "The Notary" (July 1999)

"My Name is Guiseppe de la Avelatorno, But My Friends Call Me Gus."

Our names are really important to us. They represent our very essence; who we are, what we are. For most folks, their names are easy to get along with. They are easy to pronounce, familiar, and can be spelled with a little help. For generations, many new U.S. residents bore very foreign, strange sounding names. To get along, it only made sense for many to "Americanize" their names by making them shorter and simpler. This has been the American way for many generations of new immigrants.

Guiseppe de la Avelatorno would grow tired of having to spell his name or repeat it over and over when introducing himself. Why not simplify it to Gus Torno?

Gus signs his Americanized name on everything. Everybody knows him as Gus. But now he needs a notarization. His driver's license bears his "birth name," but he is signing his Americanized name. Obviously, the ID and the signature will not conform.

This is not a problem for Gus or the notary. Going by a shorter name is profoundly common. William goes as Bill. Elizabeth signs as Betty. And, Guiseppe goes as Gus. The only issue the notary must resolve is whether Gus is actually Guiseppe. In this matter, the notary need only exercise reasonable care in the decision.

The signer's photo ID along with a complete notary journal entry with the person's signature will constitute the foundation on which the notarization is based. Gus should be instructed to sign his two names to the document and to the notary journal. He should sign his birth name, in full, and his new shortened name preceded by the letters, "A.K.A."

In Gus' case, he would first sign "Guiseppe de la Avelatorno." Then he would write AKA and sign Gus Torno. This should be done both in the notary journal and on the document.

The notary may then complete the notarial certificate by writing Gus' birth name in the certificate because that is legally the only name the notary could verify in this scenario. When completed, the notary has successfully notarized Gus' signature with full disclosure of the signer's legal name and shortened "nick name."

Jane Doe was recently married and is signing her new name, Jane Smith. Name changes due to a marriage or a divorce is an everyday occurrence for women. It is lawful and customary. Moreover, it is a matter of public record by virtue of the marriage license. But, does it constitute an "AKA"? Not at all. A woman's identity is unchanged by marriage. Jane Doe will **always** be Jane Doe, but as Fred Smith's wife she may elect to go by her husband's last name, Smith. It may take some time to obtain a new driver's license reflecting the new married name, and it is not mandatory to do so. So, what is a notary to do if the signature and the woman's name on her ID do not conform? Relax and provide full disclosure.

Permit the woman to sign her new married name, Jane Smith, with the printed notice in parenthesis, "formerly known as Jane Doe." For purposes of reasonably verifying Jane's true identity, all of the regular rules apply. Jane Doe's ID conforms to Jane Smith's appearance, her signatures reasonably match the ones made on the ID, in the journal and on the document, therefore the notary is free to notarize.

It is an unfortunate fact that criminal impostors and forgers abound. It is equally unfortunate to suggest that notaries must double their suspicion and conspicuously raise their guard. Notaries are not elements of law enforcement or criminal investigation. Arguably it is an abuse of the notary's legal authority to approach document signers with suspicion, rather than with courtesy and warmth and an inspiring measure of reasonable care. Notaries are powerfully influential over the tone and environment of the workplace and the community. Treat the public with distrust and suspicion, and it will be visited back on the notary. Treat the public the way you like to be treated, then you will be. What goes around comes around.

We notarize to protect against signature fraud. The most successful notaries focus on the standards of reasonable care and integrity. They don't get hung up over a signer's "AKA."

Notarial Acts by Federal Authorities and Military Officers
See Fourteenth Amendment of the United States Constitution Protecting Notaries; Full Faith and Credit Clause

In nearly all states, the notarizations performed by federal officials, by notaries of foreign nations, and the notarizations performed by commissioned United States military officers are recognized and enjoy the same probative value that is accorded notarizations of their own states.

Under federal law, certain officials of the United States government, such as officials of the state department, and commissioned officers of the military, are granted notarial authority to be exercised only within the scope of their official positions within the government or military. The Uniform Recognition of Acknowledgments Act, as adopted by many states, specifies that notarizations performed by officials of foreign lands, of the U.S. government and military will be recognized within the state as if they were performed by notaries of that state.

Notarizations performed in foreign countries are usually performed under substantially different legal authority than those that are performed by conventional American notaries. For the most part, notaries in many countries are political appointees and are lawyers. It is usually their obligation not only to certify the genuineness of signatures, but also to certify the legal enforceability and validity of the transaction. The legal weight accorded notarizations in other nations is significant, but when it is received in the United States it is accorded the same weight a conventional notarization receives; that it verifies the authenticity of the signature to a document. It is not unusual for notarizations originating in the U.S. to be accorded the higher weight in foreign lands that is accorded their native notarizations, although the American notary does not intend such probative value. As a rule of law, the notary in America is under no legal duty to disclose to parties in foreign nations the relatively limited probative value American notarizations are accorded.

Notarial Certificate

See Acknowledgment Notarization; Certificate of Notarization; Completeness of the Notarial Certificate; Completing the Notarial Certificate; Copy Certification; Jurat Notarization

The notarial certificate is the written attestation of a notary that is written, signed and sealed for the purpose of authenticating a person's signature to a document. The notarial certificate is not a component part of the signer's document. To the contrary, the notarial certificate is a document separate and apart from the signer's document. It is created under the legal authority of the state that commissioned the notary. The notarial certificate enjoys great evidentiary weight in law. It is accepted on its own merits without corroborating authentication.

The notarial certificate has no effect on the substance of the signer's document. It does not render a document valid, legal, enforceable or true. No notarial certificate of any kind may make such assertions, nor is a notary authorized to certify to such representations. The notarial certificate pertains to the verity of the signature it purports to authenticate.

The notarial certificate cannot be signed and be made effective by any person other than one who has the statutory authority to do so, such as notaries. In many states, the authority of a notary is statutorily extended to other public officials, such as judges, county and court clerk to name a few.

The content of the notarial certificate is prescribed by state statute. While a certificate may reflect the stylized writing of its creator, the core component parts as enumerated by law must be included. The omission of certain information can prove fatal to the validity of the certificate, while the omission of other information is not as serious.

The certificate consists of three broad components: the declarative wording that asserts the essential facts that establish the verity of the document signature; the notary's official signature; and the notary's official seal where it is required by law. Generally, the inadvertent

242

omission of any of these required components may be cured at any time, subject to its availability and the extent to which the notarization has been relied upon by third parties.

In all states, the declarative wording of the certificate must consist of certain statements of particulars. Namely, the certificate must always indicate the venue of the notarial act, the name of the signer for whom the notarization is performed, the date on which the signer personally appeared before the notary, and a declaration of what type of notarial process was invoked, be it an acknowledgment or a jurat.

Each notarial certificate must indicate the geographic location where the notarial act was performed, usually expressed in the familiar format,

> State of _____)
>) S.S.
> County of _____)

The format is referred to as the venue. It is the state and county in which the document signer personally appeared before the notary and where the notarization was performed. Many people assume the venue is intended for the notary to indicate her county of residence, which is incorrect. In the state of Alaska, notaries indicate the judicial district or municipal borough in which the notarization is performed. In Louisiana, the state is subdivided in Parishes rather than counties. The labels may vary, but the essential purpose of the venue remains the same.

The primary notarial certificates, acknowledgment and jurat, manifest important parallel information as well as vastly different stated purposes.

The Illustrated All-purpose Acknowledgment

State of   _____   )
)   S.S.

County of   _____   )

Acknowledged before me by *signer's printed name*
this _____ day of *month, year.*

                           <u>Notary's official signature</u>
"My Commission Expires _____"

The Illustrated Jurat Certificate

State of   _____   )
)   S.S.

County of   _____   )

Subscribed and sworn before me this ____ day of *month, year,*
by <u>signer's printed name</u>.

                           <u>Notary's official signature</u>
"My Commission Expires _____"

The primary difference between the acknowledgment and the jurat is the nature by which the document signature is verified as genuine. In addition, the jurat declares the document signature was made under sworn oath before the notary.

In the acknowledgment, the signer bears the burden of proof that his signature genuinely belongs to him, and he meets the burden of proof by acknowledging to the notary the signature is his. This action can be certified to have taken place with the completion of notary journal record bearing the document signer's signature. The jurat, on the other hand, declares the signer signed the document in the notary's presence after having taken an oath attesting to the truthfulness of the document contents.

It is common for states to include within their statutes the uniform long version of notarial certificates, including special use acknowledgments, such as acknowledgments for corporations, business partners, attorneys in fact, and so forth. It is equally as common for states to provide by statute model short-form certificates which, when examined closely, are generically all-purpose acknowledgments and jurats.

Whether by state statute or by common law, the notary is granted significant latitude in the drafting of notarial certificates. In the writing of a certificate, the notary is bound by the rule of substantial compliance wherein the essential requisite elements are provided within the certificate in a writing style and order of appearance that the notary determined. So long as the certificate is in substantial compliance with the minimum requisite information prescribed by state notary law, the certificate shall be deemed valid.

> *"Unless a state statute specifically mandates the literal wording of an acknowledgment certificate, substantial compliance with the form provided in statute is widely accepted as valid. This is even true where the statute requires that acknowledgments 'must' be substantially in the form prescribed... It is unnecessary and unreasonable to apply technical rules of construction to certificates of acknowledgments. The states have conferred notarial authority to execute these acknowledgments on lay citizens who may be unlearned in the law."*
> *- Herron v. Harbour, 75 Okla. 127, 182 P. 243 (1919).*

Most lengthy notarial certificates are verbose and provide information in excess of that required by state statute. Information and content that exceeds the statutory minimums is considered "surplusage." Surplusage is not fatal to the validity of a notarial certificate, so long as all aspects of it are true and correct. Surplusage most commonly includes the name of the notary before whom the signer appeared and acknowledged his signature or signed the document under oath. It is also commonly seen where the notary certifies the signer acknowledged his signature, that he signed it willingly and freely as his own act and deed, and that the signer is in possession of the legal authority to sign the document. Technically, the notary has no authority to certify the signer's legal authority to sign.

"The general policy of the laws is to construe notarial acknowledgment certificates liberally and to uphold them if they substantially comply with the statutory requirements as to form and content, even if they contain minor errors or omissions. Likewise, words or phrases that appear in the certificate in excess of what is required by the statutory form are mere surplusages."
- *Larson v. Elsner, 93 Minn. 303, 101 N. W 307 (1904).*

The notary copy certification is not a notarization. It is a written attestation of the notary that the photographically reproduced item is a true and correct reproduction of that which is copied. A few states, either by state statute, administrative rule, or by policy prohibit notaries from certifying copies of certain documents.

<u>The Illustrated Notary Copy Certification:</u>

State of _____)
)   S.S.
County of _____)

I certify that the foregoing/attached copy is a true, correct, unaltered and complete reproduction made on *<u>date the copy was verified as true and complete</u>* by *<u>name of person who made the copy</u>* of *<u>title or name of the item that was copied</u>*.

<u>Notary's official signature</u>
My Commission Expires _____

As can be seen from the text of the certificate, the notary makes no assertion regarding the truthfulness of the document contents, or that the item that was copied was a genuine original. In a very real sense, the notary copy certification, for the purpose of evidence, is merely a written guarantee the medium by which the copy was made did so accurately.

As in the certificate of acknowledgment and jurat, the copy certification must indicate the venue where the certification was made and the date it was certified. Unlike the signer's burden of proof in an acknowledgment and jurat that his signature is genuine, the notary bears the burden of proof that the copy reproduction is a true, correct, complete and unaltered copy. The notary's burden of proof is expressed in the declared assertions the notary makes by signing and sealing the certificate.

Notarial certificates mean what they say, and are to be taken literally. They are statutory instruments of law and evidence and bear significant legal weight, under which the legal and financial stakes can be high. There is no defense in law for a false notarial certificate. Every word must be true. When a notarial certificate is signed and sealed by a notary that contains material falsehoods, the notary is personally responsible and liable. Hence, the notary must carefully scrutinize the wording of every certificate before signing it. Once it is signed and delivered, the notarization is like the opened floodgates on the irrigation ditch. It is on the loose and there is usually no retrieval thereof.

> *"The notary's complete failure to read the certificate before signing it was gross negligence and consequently a failure to faithfully perform her notarial duty as a matter of law."*
> *- Bernd v. Fong Eu, Too Cal. App. 3d 51L (1979).*

> *"If the notary read the certificate before signing it, this omission must have been known to him; if he did not, he is equally guilty of negligence, for an officer who affixes his official signature and seal to a document (thereby giving to it the character of evidence), without examining it to find whether the facts certified are true, can scarcely be said to faithfully perform his duty according to law."*
> *- Fogarty v. Finlay, 10 Cal. 239, 245 (1858).*

The courts place on notaries a substantial and heavy duty to exercise all diligence in the execution of notarial certificates.

> *"We believe that the manifest intent of the legislature in requiring a notary public to execute a certificate of acknowledgment is to provide protection against the recording of false instruments. The Sine qua non of this statutory requirement is the involvement of the notary, public officer, in a position of public trust. If the notary faithfully carries out his statutory duties, it makes little difference whether he remembers to fill in the blanks in the certificate.*

Similarly, if the notary conspires with a forger, or fails to require the personal appearance of the acknowledger, or is negligent in ascertaining the identity of the acknowledger, the statutory scheme is frustrated whether the form is completely filled in or not."
   - Idaho Farm Bureau Finance Company, Inc. v. Carney, 100 Idaho 745, 605 P.2d 509 (1990).

Under no circumstances may a person lawfully pressure or coerce a notary into signing and sealing a false notarial certificate. The notarial certificate is technically a document of the state performed by a notary commissioned by the state to perform such a function. It is never the property of the notary's employer, unless the signer for whom the notarization is performed is the employer. Even then, the technical question as to the ownership of the completed certificate is not exact.

It is common for people to be anxious over small, insignificant errors in notarial certificates. The courts have historically held such mistakes are inconsequential under basic circumstances.

"Generally, technical deficiencies in the certificate of acknowledgment will not render the certificate defective if the alleged deficiency can be cured by reference to the instrument itself, in this case, the deed of trust."
   - Pacific Coast Joint Stock Land Bank v. Security Prods. Co., 56 Idaho 436, 55 P.2d 716 (1936).

There are corollaries we can derive from the Pacific Coast case opinion. First, the omission of the acknowledger's name in the blank in the certificate will not summarily render the certificate ineffective if his name can be ascertained from other sources, as from the face of the instrument itself or from other parts of the certificate. Similarly, the omission of a pronoun, or the use of the wrong number or gender, is not usually regarded as a fatal error where the meaning and intent of the certificate are not obscured as a result.

Three early court opinions from Minnesota help frame our approach to technical flaws in notarial certificates:

"It is the policy of the law to uphold certificates of acknowledgment, and where substance is found, obvious clerical errors and all technical omissions and defects will be disregarded."
- Lloyd v. Simons, 97 Minn. 315, 105 N.W. 902 (1906).

"Where an officer has authority to take acknowledgments anywhere in the state, the addition, in the venue to the certificate, of a wrong county, or a county which does not exist, will not affect its validity."
- Roussain v. Norton, 53 Minn. 560, 55 N.W. 747 (1893).

"Where the certificate of acknowledgment of a deed identified the party as known to the officer to be the person who executed the same, the fact that the name of such party appeared in the certificate as 'Strieber,' whereas the name signed to the deed was 'Schrieber,' was presumed to be the result of a clerical error merely, and did not vitiate the acknowledgment."
- Rodes v. St. Anthony & Dakota El. Co., 49 Minn. 371, 52 N.W. 27 (1892).

Another common source of anxiety for notaries is the question of where the notarial certificate should appear in relation to the signer's document. It is well-established law that the certificate is not part of the document contents and is a transaction separate and apart from the document. The notarial certificate may appear as an attachment to the document, or may be included in blank space within the document. It need not necessarily appear in proximity to the signature to which it pertains.

"There is considerable confusion over where the acknowledgment certificate belongs in relation to an instrument. The certificate must be connected or attached to the instrument in such a way that there is no doubt that it belongs to the instrument for which it is intended. It may appear at the conclusion of the instrument, which is most commonly done, yet its location is not important. It may appear in the body of the instrument or on a sheet of paper which is attached to the instrument."
- Bridges v. Union Cattle Co., 104 Okla. 74, 229 P. 805 (1925).

Notarial Certificate in a Foreign Language
See Foreign Languages

Notarial Endorsements of Products, Contests, and Services
See Official Misconduct

In no state is a notary legally authorized to endorse products, contests, or services. Such conduct is considered an abuse of the notary's authority and in most states it constitutes an official misconduct.

The venerated reputation of the office of notary public holds a natural lure for those in enterprise to use the reputation of the notarial office to assure the public or target audience of the veracity of the claims the enterprise asserts. The office of notary enjoys worldwide respect as an office of high integrity, with unimpeachable ethics and objectivity. If the name, signature and seal of a notary were to appear in commercial advertising of products, events, contests or services the public would draw a conclusion that all claims made in the promotional piece are true and verified. Notaries have no legal authority to do so. So harmful to the reputation and integrity of the notarial office would such conduct be that it is unlawful.

Notarial Impossibility
See Impossible to Notarize

Any act performed, or attempted to be performed, that is unlawful, is a notarial impossibility. Notaries are authorized to only perform acts that are permitted by law. In every notarization of a signature, a signer must appear before the notary. Therefore, it is impossible for the notary to notarize her own signature. It is further impossible for the notary to notarize a signature where the signer does not physically appear personally before the notary.

It is legally impossible for the notary to certify a falsehood in a notarial certificate and hope or expect that the certificate will be valid and enforceable. It is a notarial impossibility to effectuate a valid notarial service unless it is done in strict compliance with the requirements of law.

It is legally impossible for the notary to certify facts the absolute truth of which the notary has no personal knowledge. The notary has no authority to make assumptions about the validity of a signer's signature, or of the signer's true identity. It is a notarial impossibility for the notary to compromise the standard of law and assert that a document signature is assumed to be true, or that a signer is assumed to be the person he claims to be.

Notarial Integrity

See False Notarization; Integrity of the Notary

The office of notary public inherently envelops the principle of integrity. The notary performs significant legal acts upon which others rely heavily. Every word the notary asserts within the notarial certificate must be factually true. The entire notarization procedure must be performed with utmost integrity, as there is no defense in law for a false notarization.

As long ago as the year 1928, legal scholars noted the concern over notarial integrity.

> *"The scandal of the reckless notary has been allowed to go too far... The notary's certificate of acknowledgment of a deed is the pillar of our property rights. All titles depend on official records; and all official records depend upon the notary's certificate of acknowledgment. And these pillars of property become a treacherous support when they are permitted with forgery. A practice which permits forgery is as dangerous in policy as it is unsound in principle."*
> *- John H. Wigmore, Notaries Who Undermine Our Property System, 22 Ill. L. Rev. 748 (1928).*

The office of the notary public is not unlike that of a sentinel, guarding the gate through which document signatures must pass, each being scrutinized for their genuineness. The notary must be expected, as a matter of law, to stand behind the facts asserted in the certification of the signature's authenticity. This well established principle was well described by the California Supreme Court in 1858:

> *"If the notary read the certificate before signing it, this omission must have been known to him; if he did not, he is equally guilty of negligence, for an officer who affixes his official signature and seal to a document (thereby giving to it the character of evidence) without examining it to find whether the facts certified are true, can scarcely he said to faithfully perform his duty according to law."*

- Fogarty v. Finlay, 10 Cal. 239, 245 (1858).

Notarial Liability
See Liability

Notarial Overkill
See Surplusage

Notarial overkill can occur in two very common ways: It can occur where the notarial certificate includes far more information than is required by statute. The other occurs where a notarization to a document signature is requested, or required, and is not necessary under the law.

Statistically, most notarizations are not specifically required by rule of law for the documents for which they are performed. Usually, such notarizations are requested as a matter of tradition or in the incorrect belief that it renders the document legal, valid, true or enforceable.

Notarizations do, in fact, add security to a transaction in that the signature thereto is verified to be genuine. Many transactions routinely bear signature notarizations for that very reason, such as parental permission forms authorizing emergency medical treatment for their child while at a camp or in the care of a babysitter. As a matter of law, they usually need not bear a notarization.

It is important for the notary to inform the document signer that the notarization has no effect on the document, but authenticates the validity of the signature. The signer should be informed that their signature renders the document enforceable and effective, not the notarization.

Notarial overkill can border on abuse of the notary's legal authority. For example, a notarization of a city mayor's signature to non-recordable city business misuses the notary's authority. It accomplishes nothing of value, as the mayor is a public official personally known to most. The risk that the mayor's signature, made before city officials, is a forgery is immensely unlikely. It is more probable that city officials in this small example assume that the notarial certificate will provide emphasis to the official nature of the transaction. In a sense, the notarial certificate for such a use is more a prop than a function of law with an appropriate purpose.

The notarization of signatures is enormously beneficial to society, commerce, law and government. It is one of the core elements of structured orderliness in our world. When it is excessively used for non-substantive purposes, its beneficial effects erode. The public begins to take notarizations for granted and begins to assume that notarizations are mere technical formalities of little substance. Hence, the reasoning goes, notaries no longer need be so concerned with procedural details and rule of law.

On the surface, notarial overkill is benign. But, when effectuated on a large scale, notarial overkill can bring about deleterious effects from which it is overwhelmingly difficult to recover. It is important that notarizations be done for correct purposes and that the parties thereto are informed of the legitimate reason for the notarization.

Notarial Ownership of the Certificate
See Ownership of the Notarial Certificate

Many incorrectly assume that authorship of the notarial certificate to a document is the property of the document preparer or of the document signer. To the contrary, the notarial certificate is the notary's written attestation to the facts asserted therein. When signed and sealed, the certificate content becomes the thoughts and words of the notary. They are written, signed and sealed under the notary's legal authority granted by the state government. The notary is personally liable for the accuracy, completeness and validity of the notarial certificate. The notary's legal authority and accountability cannot be delegated or assigned to another.

While in the preparation state, the notarial certificate is the property of the notary, under the authority of the state government. It is not the notary's personal property, but is the property of the notary's official office. Such ownership transfers to the second party upon the completion of the notarial act.

Notarial Powers and Authority

See Authority; Commission Expiration Date; Commission of a Notary; Statutory Authority of the Notary

The authority to perform notarizations is granted by the state to the notary. The notary acquires the power to perform notarial acts upon being authorized to do so. The legal authority to notarize cannot be self-appointed. In order for society, law and commerce to be orderly, secure, credible and functional there must be universal recognition of authority that is held by certain institutions, such as government, that can be conferred to individuals to act on its behalf.

If individuals could proclaim themselves a police officer, by what authority would the individual police traffic, investigate a crime or arrest a suspect? It must be the authority of the government that creates in that person the power to engage in law enforcement services. The same applies to notaries.

The statutes of the states provide procedures by which the public can be made notaries. The statutes specify the state official who is authorized to commission notaries and the procedure by which it is done. A person's authority and power to perform notarial services transfers from the state to the individual by the issuance of a certificate of commission or appointment. The person shall not perform notarial services before the certificate is issued, and shall cease performing after the appointment has expired.

It is not unheard of where persons are under the misguided impression that all that is necessary to become a notary is to purchase a notary seal. Any person who performs notarial acts without being legally empowered to do so through a notary commission from the state commits serious criminal violations of law. The penalties can be severe.

Notarial Translations
See Documents in a Foreign Language; Foreign Languages

Notaries commonly face the issue of notarizing on documents that are written in foreign languages. Also, notaries are often asked to certify that documents have been correctly translated from one language to another. A third situation arises when the notary is requested to translate the notarial certificate from English to a foreign language.

Notaries do not have the legal authority to certify the correctness of document translations. Notaries may, however, notarize the sworn affidavit of a translator who has translated the document from one language to another. If the notary is the translator, the notary cannot make any notarial certification about the translation. Another notary could be used to notarize on an affidavit pertaining to the translation.

There appears to be a general implication in law that notaries shall execute their notarial certificates in the English language. Occasionally, when a document is destined for a foreign nation, the notarization is requested to be written in the language of the intended country. In such cases, the English version of the notarial certificate must be used, and it constitutes the legally enforceable notarization. It can be subsequently translated to the foreign language in a place adjacent the English version, or attached to the signer's document. It is inappropriate for the notary to sign and seal the translated version of the certificate, as it may violate the notary law.

From "The Notary" (May 1998)

Notaries Can't Certify Their Own Translations

It is impossible to notarize your own signature. It is also illegal.

When a document is translated from one language to another, the translator usually certifies the translation is true and correct. When it is the notary who also performs the translation, then a small problem arises. The certification of translation requires a notarization and the bi-lingual notary cannot perform both.

The correct and easy solution is to have another notary notarize the translator's signature by jurat. The translator can write a simple *statement, "I, Jane Doe, certify that the foregoing is a true and correct translation of Fred Smith's document from English to the Portuguese language." Jane Doe will sign her name under oath in the presence of the notary, and the notary will notarize with, "Subscribed and sworn to before me by Jane Doe this 4th day of July, 1998."*

The notarial work product created here to certify a translation of a document consists of four items:

1. *The document being translated;*
2. *The document in the new language;*
3. *The translator's affidavit that the translation was true and correct; and*
4. *The notary's jurat notarization of the translator's affidavit attesting to the correctness of the translation.*

Notaries often wear more than one hat, especially when they are multi-talented and skilled. Yet, under no circumstance may notaries notarize their own signatures. When in doubt, write up a simple affidavit declaring what you are certifying and have another notary notarize your signature by jurat. You can never go wrong as long as every word is true.

Notaries in Foreign Countries

The United States may be the only nation where the average resident may acquire a notary commission, regardless of profession, political position or influence in the community. Generally, notaries across the world are part of the legal community as attorneys. They are commonly known as "common law notaries." Not all attorneys are notaries in such places, but the license to practice law is usually required.

The title, Notary, is used universally in all languages, albeit translated to each respective tongue. Wherever law offices are found, some identifiable variation of the word, notary, is seen on the brass nameplates and office building directories.

The notaries of foreign nations exercise substantially more authority and responsibility than do the notaries of America. The notaries of the United States are not responsible for the legality, or enforceability of signer's transactions. However, the notaries of most other nations are responsible for the signer's transactions to ensure they are complete, valid and enforceable. In a very real sense, the notarial act in other nations is integral to the practice of law. Their obligation to exercise professional competence and diligence is commensurately higher than that held by notaries of the United States.

Notarius
See History of the Notary Public Office

Under ancient Roman law, a notary bore the title, "Notarius." In old English law, the notary was also referred to by the Latin, "Notarius." The term translated literally refers to a "rapid writer" or a shorthand writer.

Notarization
See Certificate of Notarization; Notarial Certificate

The term, notarization, is used broadly in many contexts, often leading to confusion. A notarization is the authentication of a signature on a document. The only thing that can be notarized is a signature. The document on which the signature appears is not made legal, valid, enforceable, or true by a notarization. Although, it is common for people to refer in the vernacular to the "notarized document," it is also common for people to request that they "be notarized," even though it is their signature that will be notarized.

A copy certification is not a notarization, as it has nothing to do with the verification and authentication of the genuineness of a person's signature. Surely, the broad usage of the word, notarization, is due in large part to the public's high regard for the value of the notarization. It provides considerable security and relief to parties to transactions, although often times misdirected.

Notarizations are official acts performed under government authority. They can be performed only by those holding such authority through appointment by their state government, or in limited cases by virtue of their government position. A notarization must be performed under strict compliance with specific procedures and standards. A notary who negligently or falsely performs a notarization, or does so in violation of state notary law is personally liable for the damages caused by the notarization. Such conduct is often punishable in most states as a crime.

Notarizations While in a Foreign Country

Americans traveling abroad can obtain notarizations performed under the authority of the federal government by contacting the U.S. consulate or embassy. In all fifty states such notarizations enjoy full recognition as they are performed by State Department officials holding legal notarial authority by virtue of their federal positions.

United States commissioned military officers also hold notarial powers. Military officers and State Department officials may exercise their notarial powers worldwide. Their notarizations are given the same accord as notarizations performed by stateside notaries.

United States citizens may obtain notarizations from foreign notaries abroad. However, the procedures and costs for such services are more formal and expensive for the signer. Notarizations performed abroad by local notaries will be recognized in the United States. Matters pertaining to English translations of foreign notarizations may complicate the signer's objectives, as might the notary's obligation to conduct a legal analysis of the document. Notaries in foreign lands are not notaries "public" as they are in the United States. The public does not usually enjoy the same legal rights of access to a notary's services abroad as we do in America.

Notarize
See Notarization

Notarizing a Blank or Incomplete Document
See Blank Documents; Completeness of the Signer's Document

Notarizing by Telephone
See Notarial Impossibility; Personal Appearance of the Signer

It is legally impossible to perform any form of notarization over the telephone. The document signer must personally appear before the notary, for which there is no substitute. The personal appearance of the signer before the notary is absolutely requisite to the notary's duty to verify the validity of the signature being notarized. The new technologies of video-conferencing and Internet live video access do not constitute the requisite personal appearance of the signer before the notary.

In some jurisdictions and under certain provisions of the federal rules of procedure, a witness's testimony may be taken under oath over the telephone. Occasionally, trial lawyers will erroneously assume that the same may apply to notarizations as well. It does not. It is absolutely impossible to legally notarize a signature unless the maker of the signature physically appears before the notary. No exceptions.

The Federal Rules of Civil Procedure, amended as of December 1, 1993, authorize telephone depositions.

> *"The parties may stipulate in writing or the court may upon motion order that a deposition be taken by telephone or other remote electronic means. For the purposes of this rule and Rules 28(a), 37(a) 1 and 37(b) 1, a deposition taken by such means is taken in the district and at the place where the deponent is to answer questions."*
> - Fed. R. Civ. P. 30(b)(7).

While this rule recognizes depositions taken over the telephone and by other electronic means, it does not, of course, grant notarial authority to take such depositions, nor does it address the questions of whether an oath may be administered over the phone, or whether a phone-in deponent may be outside the notary's jurisdiction.

There has been little written on the question of whether or not it is proper conduct for a notary to administer oaths to persons over the telephone. This Florida Attorney General addressed this issue in a 1992 journal opinion that is helpful.

> *"The purpose of requiring the personal presence of the affiant appears to be that the officer administering the oath can identify that individual as the person who actually took the oath, not that the officer knows him to be the person he represents himself to be. This*

purpose would not be satisfied by the interested parties stipulating as to the person's identity. Accordingly, I am of the opinion that a notary public may not administer an oath to a person over the telephone even though the attorneys for all interested parties stipulate as to the person's identity."
        - 92 Op. Fla. Att'y Gen. 95 (Dec. 23, 1992).

The Florida Attorney General also addressed the question of whether or not a notary may administer an oath over the telephone or by video-conferencing to a person located outside the state in which the notary is commissioned. He wrote,

"Inasmuch as the powers of a notary public, as an officer of the state, are coextensive with the territorial limits of the state, the participants using such an interactive video and telephone system should be located within the state."

From "The Notary" (September 1999)

Notarizing a Signature over the Phone

"Alice, this is Harvey Smith calling from Ajax Bank. Yesterday you signed a deed of trust here at the bank and it has to be notarized. Can you confirm that you signed it so I can go ahead and notarize this for you?"

This is not unusual. Just get on the phone and confirm with the customer they signed the document so you can notarize it. It is convenient, quick and friendly. It is also 100% illegal!

It is absolutely impossible for a notary to notarize any signature for any person without that person personally appearing before the notary. But requiring the signer to appear personally can cause great inconvenience. Signature confirmation by telephone may seem appealing. In a legal sense, it is a potential liability trap with terrible legal consequences for the notary.

260

The temptation to notarize over the telephone has been around since telephones became commonplace across America. In 1920, the Idaho Supreme Court ruled that the "person acknowledging the execution of an instrument must be personally present before the notary. An acknowledgment over the telephone is insufficient" (Myers v. Eby, 193 P. 77).

In 1955, a Texas court ruled the same way: "A notary cannot perform by telephone those notarial acts which require a personal appearance... A wife's personal appearance before the notary who purports to take her acknowledgment to a conveyance of her homestead is necessary to the validity of the document. The argument is made that the telephone conversation invokes the power of the notary, which is enough to breathe life into the instruments. It is conceivable the notary can make an explanation by telephone, but a notary must also be in a position to know and certify that the signer is examined to be signing willingly and freely. These matters require the (signer) to be in the presence of the notary. Knowledge of the identity of the signer is required by (state statute) when it declares that the certificate must show that the person 'personally appeared' before the notary. The words 'personally appeared' are simple and have a common meaning. The temptation to construe them differently pushes the law beyond its meaning. The notary in this case is unable to identify either (of the signers)."

This Texas court went on to say, "If a famous actor or artist should advertise that he would personally appear at a concert on a given date, and then should in fact perform for the audience by telephone, that audience would have no difficulty in concluding that the performer had not 'personally appeared.' A notary can no more perform by telephone those notarial acts which require a personal appearance than a dentist can pull a tooth by telephone. If a telephone conversation is a personal appearance, we must suppose that a letter or telegram to a notary would also be as good or maybe even better" (Charlton v. Gill, 285 S. W. 2d 801).

When an employer challenges a notary's sound and wise judgment on issues like these, it puts the notary in a terrible position. The employer is already in a similar position. Employers do not want to inconvenience clients and customers by having them return at a later time so they can personally appear before the notary. Employers want to impress their customers with their efficiency and business skills. Proper notarizations are not designed to accommodate expediency and customer convenience.

George and Martha Smith have co-signed a document that needs notarizing. Poor Martha is home ill, so George brings in the document expecting the bank or lawyer to have it notarized. The deadline is today, so there is no time for dilly-dallying. Lots of competing wants, needs and legal issues come into play here, and the notary is too often made to be the "bad guy."

George is truthful when he claims his wife signed the document, and he expects to be believed. George wants this transaction signed, sealed and delivered by today's deadline. George also wants to be treated with respect, courtesy and professionalism. The boss wants George to be happy and pleased with the services being provided. The boss wants no delays or embarrassing slip-ups. The boss believes George's wife truly signed the document, that George is an honest man. The boss and George both believe that the only thing a notarization is good for is to indicate the signatures are not forgeries.

The notary wants to please George and the boss. Job preservation is important here. A happy customer means a happy boss, and a happy boss means a more secure employment future.

Now all eyes are on the notary. Will she or will she not notarize Martha Smith's signature on the mere belief that George and the boss are telling the truth that Martha signed it? The notary hesitates and points out with utmost diplomacy, "the law requires the signer to appear before the notary. If I notarize Martha's signature without her being in my presence, I notarize falsely and it could invalidate the entire transaction. Only a fool would want that, and you two upstanding gentlemen are not fools."

George proffers, "well, let's just get Martha on the phone and she can tell us she signed this document, then you can notarize it. Isn't that what you want? For Martha to confirm to you that the signature is hers?"

Now the notary really has to put her foot down and exercise leadership. "Gentlemen," she blurts out, "how can my boss or I be certain that the voice on the phone belongs to Martha and not to some imposter George is seeing behind Martha's back? How can we be sure George hasn't forced Martha to sign against her free will? How can we know that Martha is not dead or lost in the wilderness of Alaska and George is not pillaging Martha's estate?"

In stunned amazement, George and the boss glare at the notary and ask meekly, "How can Martha's signature be notarized correctly? We are men of character and integrity and seek to have this done properly!"

The notary replies, "I will notarize for you, George, here and now. Then I will gladly drive to your home to see Martha and notarize for her there. I am sure my boss will approve of this because he can clearly see that I am saving his bacon from total disaster. That's what we notaries are for!"

Notarizing Falsely
See False Notarization; Fraud; Liability

There is a small distinction between notarizing falsely and false notarizations. In both cases, the conduct is illegal and carries criminal penalties in every jurisdiction. Notarizing falsely occurs in any notarial conduct that is in violation of state law that results in a false representation of an asserted fact within the notarial certificate. For example, a notary notarizes falsely when she fails to require the signer to personally appear before her, or fails to identify that signer.

A person also notarizes falsely when they perform a notarial act without being a commissioned notary. Acting in any official notarial capacity without the legal authority to do so constitutes a false act.

In Territory v. Gutierrez, 13 N.M. 312, 84 P. 525 (1906), the court held,

> *"The distinction between falsely making a certificate of acknowledgment and making a false certificate is that the former term contemplates a certificate which is not genuine while the latter*

imports a genuine certificate the contents or allegations of which are false."

Notarizing for Elderly
See Willful, Free Making of a Signature

Notarizing for Minors
See Minors; Willful, Free Making of a Signature

There are no limitations on the minimum age a person must be to qualify for having their signature notarized. Rather than imposing an arbitrary fixed minimum age, the standard of law is whether or not the signer is signing their document willingly and freely. That is to say, does the signer understand what the document is that they sign? Do they sign it voluntarily without undue coercion or duress?

A person's capacity to formulate intent to agree with a document's contents or be bound by the terms of the document by signing can develop at an early age. A person's right to have their signature notarized has nothing to do with the statutorily set "age of majority," which is usually 18 years in most states.

Minor children are generally held immune from entering contractual obligations until they reach majority age. Although a child might not be legally bound to the document he signs, a notarization of his signature thereto would have little consequence in law either way.

Notarizing for the Physically Impaired
See Physically Impaired Signers

Notarizing for Relatives
See Conflict of Interest; Consanguinity; Disqualification

A number of states prohibit notaries from notarizing for their spouses or for people to whom they are related by blood or marriage. The majority of states make no such restriction by law. In all states, the widely accepted principle is that the notary should be completely impartial to the transactions for which notarizations are performed. However, law and policy may bear contradictions and inconsistencies that have to be considered objectively and balanced rationally.

The most frequently cited justification for prohibiting, or for teaching, notaries not to notarize for a family member is that such constitutes a conflict of interest. Indeed, the notary probably does possess an interest, albeit very small or substantial, in the affairs of their family members.

The issue of notarizing for family members is more sensitive where such acts are not statutorily prohibited, but notaries are nevertheless taught under the color of "official state policy" that such acts are wrongful. In order for a notary to be prohibited from notarizing for family members, it is necessary for state statutes to impose the prohibition. The state law, therefore, needs to disqualify the notary from notarizing for relatives. It is otherwise left as an assumed power of the notary, subject to limitations created by disqualifications.

Law cannot be practically constructed to disqualify notaries from notarizing in any circumstance in which the notary might have a conflict of interest. Conflicts of interest are too ubiquitous and ambiguous to constitute universal disqualifications for notaries. To that end, law must look to clear standards for disqualifying notaries from acting.

As long as the notary is not disqualified by statute from notarizing for a family member, the notarization has significant merit and strength. The primary reason a signature is notarized is to ensure the signature is not a forgery. Forged signatures are made by imposters, and few people can positively prove a signer's true identity better than a family member. Hence, in that context, the notarization of a relative's signature constitutes a solid and compelling authentication of the signature. But, it can be argued that it conflicts with the policy objective of complete notarial impartiality. It is an issue that merits thoughtful consideration by the notary to be approached with an ethical attitude.

Notarizing a Power of Attorney
See Power of Attorney

Notarizing Signatures Made Under the Power of Attorney
See Authority of the Document Signer; Power of Attorney

Powers of attorney have been part of the mainstream of business and law for centuries. They are essential to the successful flow of commerce, without which society could easily bog down because transactions cannot be conducted in the absence of a principal player.

Powers of attorney are a form of contract between a principal granting to his agent certain powers to act in the principal's behalf. The actions of the agent are binding on the principal. What the agent (attorney-in-fact) agrees to on behalf of his principal is binding on the principal. The agent must be absolutely loyal to his principal and be vigilant for anything that might harm his principal's interest.

A power of attorney cannot be created orally. It must be created in writing, signed by the principal. In most states it must be notarized or witnessed. The power of attorney is a powerful document in which commitments of great loyalty and fidelity are founded.

One of the most vexing problems for notaries comes when the attorney-in-fact asks for a notarization to a transaction. What should be a simple process can turn horribly complicated because there are few clear guidelines and rules to follow.

If the document signer, Alice Cordova, signs the name Laura Bush to the document, Alice is in violation of law and it is unlawful for the notary to notarize the signature. If Alice gives truthful and full disclosure when signing, such as, "Laura Bush by Alice Cordova," then Alice clearly discloses the truth of the signature and has not intended to deceive. Yet under this variation the Laura Bush signature is not eligible for notarization. The only way a Laura Bush signature can be notarized is for Laura Bush to make the signature herself and appear personally before the notary.

The most appropriate solution is one that provides for full and honest disclosure, and permits the notary to perform in full compliance of the notary law. The key to the correct answer lies with the manner in which the attorney-in-fact signs the document.

There is no fixed rule on how the attorney-in-fact should sign for the principal. This may be viewed by some as a serious flaw in the context of

266

powers of attorney. Some lawyers instruct the client to merely sign the principal's name. That is a poor, and deceptive practice, as it gives no disclosure that the signature was not made by its purported owner. It is passed off as an "original signature of its owner."

Other lawyers direct the attorney-in-fact to sign the principal's name, "Laura Bush, by Jane Doe under power of attorney." This format is laudable because it fully discloses the signature is not genuinely Laura's but that it was made by Laura's attorney-in-fact under the power of attorney. The problem with this format, though, is that the notary cannot notarize the Laura signature because its owner, Laura is not appearing before the notary as required by law.

Perhaps the most appropriate manner for attorneys-in-fact to sign on behalf of their principals is to sign their own names with disclosure of their authority. For example, a notary could notarize this signature, "Jane Doe under power of attorney for Laura Bush." Jane Doe personally appears before the notary, proves her identity to the notary and proves the signature belongs to her.

In this alternative "POA signature" format, the important objectives of full and truthful disclosure are fulfilled, and there is a genuine signature of the attorney-in-fact that the notary can notarize.

Notaries are often asked to notarize a transaction where the signer appearing before them has power of attorney to act on behalf of another person. The key is in the signature wording. It is one thing, for example, to sign one's elderly mother's signature to a title deed. It is quite another to sign one's own name on behalf of one's mother under power of attorney.

When an attorney-in-fact throws caution to the wind and signs the principal's name without full disclosure of having power of attorney, it comes awfully close to the commission of a forgery. It is not their signature and it is made with the deliberate and calculated intent to induce others to incorrectly believe it is the genuine signature of the principal. To notarize such a "forged" signature brings about dark and foreboding consequences.

Powers of attorney are peculiar. They are powerful. They must be in writing. They can be general and broad in their scope of granted authority, or they can be very narrow and specific in scope. They can have a short life span with an early expiration date, or they can be enforceable for many years. The written power of attorney merely documents a relationship between two people: the principal and the agent. That relationship can be terminated at any time, even though a written power of attorney between them is still circulating around town. The power of attorney instantly expires upon the death of the principal. The attributes and characteristics of powers of attorney go on and on. They are complex and rife with potential legal problems.

If we can apply these legal principals to the signer's invocation of a power of attorney, a notary can establish a high standard of care and ethical conduct. The notary can take several steps when notarizing signatures made under power of attorney. The notary should cause the attorney-in-fact to:

1. Sign their own given name;
2. Disclose in writing at the signature line the name of the principle for whom he signs;
3. Disclose in writing the date of issuance of the power of attorney, its date of notarization (if any) and the statement that "this transaction is entered into by the attorney-in-fact, John Doe, in compliance with the terms and limitations of the power of attorney and is done with utmost good faith and fidelity to the principal."
4. Proceed to notarize the attorney-in-fact's signature, having made full record thereof in the notary journal.

The level of risk when dealing with powers of attorney is minimized when:

1. The notary personally knows the principal and the attorney-in-fact and is familiar with the circumstances of the two persons;
2. The power of attorney was created by the notary's employer and is to be exercised only within the notary's company; and
3. The power of attorney is professionally prepared on the letterhead of a law firm enabling the notary to telephone the preparer of the document (the lawyer) to confirm its validity and the appropriateness of the transaction at hand.

Notarizing Witness Signatures
See Witness; Witness Signatures

Signature witnesses are persons who sign their names to documents as witnesses having seen a principal signer sign his name to the document, such as in a will. The laws of each state provide the requirement for signature witnesses, and they may vary from state to state. It is not the notary's responsibility to know and identify when witness signatures are required for a transaction. It is up to the document preparer or signer to inform the notary of such a need.

Although perhaps required by state law, witness signatures are functionally redundant when a notarization is added to the transaction. While they essentially accomplish the same objective, the notarization is legally stronger and more compelling in its probative value.

In the event witness signatures are required to be notarized, the notary notarizes the principal signer's signature separately from the signatures of the witnesses. The witness signatures can be notarized with a combined notarial certificate for both persons.

The notarization for signature witnesses must be performed with the same standard of care and procedure as the notary would utilize in notarizing for any person.

Notary Application Tests
See Qualifications for Appointment to the Office of Notary Public

A number of states require the notary to successfully pass a written exam in order to qualify for a notarial commission. Such examinations are useful tools to help ensure the notary makes a reasonable effort to learn the fundamentals of notarial rules and procedures. The exam is often an open-book test, rendering the exam an effective training tool rather than a static measurement of notarial knowledge.

Effective notary testing cannot credibly function if done amateurishly. Testing of this nature requires considerable skill, review and field-testing. Most states that test their notaries have mastered this process.

An effective notary test will focus on rules and procedures for notarizing and not test on the requirements of notarial qualification or the process to become a notary. Especially helpful to notary applicants are test questions that require the notary to solve commonly faced notary problems, such as notarizing under duress or for people who have no identification cards or papers.

Testing notary applicants in the application process can be a highly effective tool that benefits the notary and society. It is also cost-effective.

Notary Bond
See Errors and Omissions Insurance

The majority of states require notaries to post a notary bond as a condition precedent to their being appointed as a notary. Bond amounts vary from under $1,000 up to $25,000.

Many notaries incorrectly assume the notary bond is insurance. It is not. Rather, a bond is a contract between the notary and the bond surety. Anciently, a bond was a promise made under wax seal, bonding the written agreement to the parties. The promise was for one party to pay a sum of money to another party under specified conditions and terms. The obligor, the bond surety, binds himself to pay the certain sum of money to the obligee when terms and conditions are met. In the case of a notary bond, the obligor is the bond surety company, and the obligee is the victim of a wrongful or negligent notarization.

When purchasing a notary bond, it is generally assumed the notary signs a contract with the bond surety company (the obligor). For the fee the notary pays to purchase the bond, the surety promises to pay to harmed victims of the notary's misconduct (the obligee) compensation for their losses up to the face value of the bond. If the bond amount is $1,000 the compensation to the obligee will be nominal. If the bond amount is $25,000 the compensation may prove more helpful. However, a victim's recovery of any money from the bond surety does not restrict or prevent the victim from suing in court for the full amount of their losses.

As the bond is not insurance, the notary is bound by contract to reimburse the bond surety for money disbursed to claimants against the bond. The surety is legally obligated to take every reasonable step to acquire all the facts of the complaint and claim on the bond prior to any decision concerning payment on the bond to the victim. The surety must follow due process of law, including notice to the notary a claim has been made and a procedure for the notary to respond and defend against the allegations made.

In the past decade, a few states eliminated the notary bond requirement from their statutes. However, the notary bond industry asserts that the purpose for the bond is to protect the public in several ways:

1. A notary bond can effectively impress upon a notary the imperative that the notary performs official duties in faithful compliance with state law. The bond is a contract between the notary and the surety that the notary will perform all official duties with reasonable care and integrity;
2. A well prepared notary bond puts the burden of proper performance squarely on the notary because the surety is trusting the notary not to breach their duty of care; and
3. The notary bond process helps reduce traffic in the court system by resolving disputes out of court through the bond surety. It is asserted that this favors the public at large because seeking recovery on a notary's bond is not as arduous, complex and lengthy as seeking recovery in a court trial.

In the structure of the notary bond contract, there are three players: the "principal," the "beneficiary," and the "surety." The principal is the person who is liable for the performance of a duty or obligation to another party. In notarial services, the principal is the notary. The notary is obligated to perform notarial services for another person, and is liable for doing so wrongfully.

The beneficiary is the person to whom the notary owes a duty to perform a service or action with competence and correctness. The beneficiary has the comfort of knowing that if the principal performs her duty wrongfully, thus causing the beneficiary harm, the surety will step in and pay him a fixed sum of money, for which the principal will reimburse the surety later. In a notarial transaction, the beneficiary will be the document signer or any other person harmed by the wrongful notarization.

The surety is usually a corporation and is under the same legal duty to the beneficiary as it is to the principal. The surety becomes liable only upon the principal's wrongful performance of duty. The beneficiary may require the surety to pay for the damages caused by the principal. The principal is contractually obligated to reimburse the surety for such payments made.

The contract or document that sets forth the terms and conditions of these relationships and duties is called the "bond." It is literally a guarantee from the surety to the beneficiary that the principal will perform her duty with correctness and competence. If the principal breaches her duty, the surety will pay to the beneficiary monies up to the limit of the bond amount. Every bond has a bond limit to the amount the surety is liable to the beneficiary. The surety cannot be held liable in excess of this specified amount in the bond. Both the principal and the surety must sign the bond in order for it to be effective.

It is believed that most of the public has little or no idea that notaries are bonded. If they are aware, like the notary, the public tends to assume it means the notary is insured. Again, this is incorrect. Bonds are not insurance. In the 19th century, when notary bonds were first introduced, their bond limits were set between $500 and $5,000. Over a century later, bond limits in most states remain relatively the same as they did in the horse-and-buggy age.

While the nation's economy and legal system have evolved dramatically in 100 years, so have the measurement of damages from negligence and wrongful conduct by notaries. They run into the tens and hundreds of thousands of dollars. It can be justifiably argued that notary bond limits this day and age are negligible and relatively meaningless. The merits for requiring notaries to post bonds in any of the many states that require them are difficult to identify. Court awarded damages for wrongful notarial acts routinely far and away exceed the notary bond limit, rendering the notary bond essentially ineffective. As the disparity grows between the value of damage claims and the value of the bond limit, little or no attention is paid by state officials or the notary bond surety companies.

Economically, it is advantageous for bond surety companies to keep the notary bond limits low because they constitute a disincentive for victims (the beneficiaries) to trifle with such small amounts. If bond limits were set at one or two hundred thousand dollars, there would surely be an increase in claim activity by beneficiaries, and an equal increase in the surety's inability to recover the funds from the principal. That is a bad scenario for notary bond sureties.

According to the Surety Association of America, notary sureties are making an approximated 97% profit margin on notary bonds sold in America. It is estimated that there are over 2.3 million notaries in states requiring notary bonds, each paying an average four-year premium of $50 to $75. The 97% profit margin on those sales is made from the surprisingly low volume of claims made and paid out nationally on the notary bonds. With a financial picture this strong, there is no incentive for notary bond sureties to seek increases in bond limits through legislation in the various states.

It is self-evident that the intended purpose of notary bonds is not being met. So few claims are made on notary bonds, and the bond limits are set disproportionately low compared to claim amounts. The public is not benefitted. The millions of dollars spent on notary bonds as required by the laws of most states are wasted, as less than 3% of those dollars are paid to the public on notary bond claims.

Notary bond efficacy presently receives little public or governmental scrutiny. However, it eventually will. It is overdue.

Notary Errors and Omissions Insurance
See Notary Bond; Errors and Omissions Insurance

Notary Fees
See Fees

Notary Journal
See Journal Recordation; Notary Journal as Evidence; Notary Journal Contents and Format; Notary's Duty to Maintain Journal Records

Notary journals are commonly called "journals," "logs," or "registers." In all cases, they are complete records of every notarial act. The notary performing the notarial act should make the journal record, as it is the personal record of the notary and is not delegable. Great presumptive weight is accorded the probative value of the journal contents by the court system.

The large majority of states do not require by their statutes the keeping of notary journal records by their notaries. However, implications that every notary should journalize each notarization performed are compelling and persuasive. Properly designed, the journal can effectively guide the notary through every required step of performing a notarization without risk of material errors. Moreover, a record documenting each material fact asserted in the notarial certificate will satisfy valuable evidentiary burdens for the notary in defending a recorded notarial act.

The notarization is a function of government and constitutes a valuable function of law. It is a form of evidence in all courts that establishes the verity of a signature. As evidence, outside the courtroom or inside, there is great reliance placed on the notarization. It is the certificate by which third parties can reasonably conclude that the document signature is genuine and binding.

The old cliché, "if it isn't written, it didn't happen," is a fundamental principle. Appropriate and consistent record keeping is the surest form of evidence that a notarization was performed truthfully and correctly.

In the law, the courts look to "evidentiary facts" to prove the primary facts of a matter, or "ultimate facts." In notary law, the ultimate facts are whether or not a signature is genuine, made willingly and freely by its maker. Under the law, the maker of the signature has the burden of proof of these ultimate facts. The notary is the vehicle established by law for the signer to use in proving these facts. The notarial certificate is accepted in law to satisfy the signer's burden of proof of signature authenticity.

The ultimate facts are proven in law by evidentiary facts; facts that are probative to prove the ultimate facts. The notarial certificate is the ultimate fact that the document signature is genuine. The notary journal provides evidentiary facts to prove the notarial certificate is true and correct.

It is unwise to assume that because a state may not require a notary journal to record notarizations, one need not keep a journal. The failure to keep such a record is a frustration to the system of law, in which the notarial process is immersed. The failure to provide the evidentiary facts to prove the ultimate facts in notarizations is serious. Such a failure is deleterious to the document signer, to the parties relying on the notarization, and to the system of law.

The prudent rule of thumb is simple: when one notarizes, document it. There is no substitute for the value of a properly kept notary journal.

Notary Journal as Evidence
See Notary's Duty to Maintain Journal Records

From "The Notary's Duty to Meticulously Maintain a Notary Journal,"
 - By Peter Van Alstyne, 31 J. Marshall Law Rev. 779-782.

The Evidentiary Value of Notary Journals

In most jurisdictions, notary journal entries are clothed with a presumption of genuineness or authenticity as to their contents.

In Prudential Trust Co. V. Coghlin, 144 N.E. 283, 284 (Mass. 1924), the court held, "Notaries public hold office under our Constitution... and entries made by them in a book kept in the regular course of business are deemed original acts, and are admissible to the extent that the facts stated are within the scope of their duty as defined by custom or statute."

In most states, the rules of evidence allow certain documents and writings to be admissible without extrinsic evidence of their genuineness or authenticity. Additionally, the routine keeping of a notary journal constitutes evidence of habit or routine practice on the part of the notary.

Under the Federal Rules of Evidence, notary journals are admissible into evidence under the business records exception to the hearsay rule if the journal entries are made in the regular course of the notary's services and at the time of the notarial act. The admissibility of business records and notary journals is necessitated by the record's presumed reliability. Like businesses, notaries rely on their records in order to manage their affairs and have a motive to see that their records are accurate. Moreover, such records are routinely relied upon to prove a business transaction, sale, receipt or other matter. Under the business records exception, the business record must be in writing, thus eliminating photographs, audio or videotape recordings.

It is common for some notaries to retain photocopies of notarial certificates and signers' identification cards in the belief it constitutes a valid substitute for a proper notary journal. There is no worthy substitute for the properly maintained notary journal. The value of photocopies of executed notarization certificates and signers' identification cards pales in comparison to the supreme value of a notary journal. Photocopies will fail to demonstrate consistent proper performance on the part of the notary. They do not prove the signer personally appeared before the notary, and they show nothing concerning the signer's willful making of the document signature. Depending upon what appears on the photocopies of the notarial certificates and signer identification, questions regarding the signer's privacy can also be raised At best, such photocopies saved in a folder or a file will merely show the good, but naive, intentions of the notary and little else.

Rule 803(6) of the Federal Rules of Evidence provides that the written record must be made in the regular course of business. It is those books and records that are regularly relied upon in the operation of the business. The rule does not apply to records of "businesses" only. The rule may also apply to household records, government records, records of non-profit entities and individually kept records. To be admissible, the record must document an act, condition or event and may even contain opinions or diagnoses. The record must be made "at or near" the time of the event or act recorded. This is essential to reduce the risk of inaccurate recollection. Every notary journal entry should be made contemporaneously with the performance of the notarization.

The notary's journal will be admissible as a business record if it is faithfully utilized to document every notarial act performed. Ad hoc and irregular recordations in a notary journal jeopardize the admissibility of that journal under the business records exception. Journal recordations must be made consistently. Under the Federal Rules of Evidence, a business record is inadmissible if it is not trustworthy because of substantial flaws in the method or timing of its preparation.

In McCormick v. Mirrored Image, Inc., 454 N.E.2d 1363, 1365 (Ohio Ct. App. 1982) citing rule 803(6) of the Federal Rules of evidence, the court discussed the four conditions set forth in 803(6) and stated that the failure to "satisfy any one of these fundamental conditions" would lead to inadmissibility of the evidence.

Likewise, the notary journal can protect a notary from accusations of having performed a notarial act that the notary had never, in fact, performed. Too frequently a notary's employer or associate will take the notary's official seal to "notarize" a document in the notary's absence. The perpetrator usually has no malicious intent. Rather, they are foolishly attempting to expedite business procedures in the seriously flawed belief that the notarization "doesn't matter anyway." As most perpetrators will not realize that a journal entry must accompany every notarial act, the absence thereof will be the smoking gun pointing to the perpetrator's misdeed.

Under the "Silent Hound" exception to the Federal Rules of Evidence, the absence of a journal entry can be used to prove false an accusation that a notarization occurred. If an event or procedure would have normally been recorded had it taken place, the fact that there is no record of the event or procedure in the notary's journal can prove the event never occurred. If a notary thoroughly and properly journalizes every notarial service performed, the "Silent Hound" exception will render valuable protection against false accusations of journalization. Suppose the notary is meticulous about his or her record keeping and always indicates in the journal the method used to verify a signer's mental capacity to sign an instrument when the signer is elderly, severely ill or suffering from diminished capacity. The absence of any written comment to that effect, under the "Silent Hound" exception, will protect the notary if a signer's family claims the signer was legally incompetent to sign the instrument and it was therefore notarized fraudulently.

When a notary faithfully keeps a journal, the Federal Rules of Evidence afford an extraordinary level of protection. It is so remarkable that it makes no sense for any notary or employer of a notary not to insist on the meticulous keeping of such a record. The courts hold the notary as the guarantor of the probative force accorded the notarial certificates. Notaries are personally responsible for the truthfulness of every word of the notarial certificate they execute. For this reason, the notary and his or her journal should be inseparable.

Notary Journal Contents and Format
See Notary's Duty to Maintain Journal Records

Only a few states specify by statute the contents and format of the notary journals they mandate. For the most part, the standards are relatively similar. Regardless of the state's position on journal record keeping, the notary should maintain a complete record of every notarization performed.

The journal has profound evidentiary value to the notary, to the document signer for whom the notarization is performed, and to the finder of fact in any dispute. Its durability and integrity are important. The journal should be a permanently bound book that cannot have pages removed or altered easily without detection thereof. As a general rule, the book should have a sown binding, rather than stapled. It should not be a loose-leaf or spiral notebook.

One of the intrinsic values of the journal is its proof of a consistently proper and competent notarial performance by the notary. The journal should have pre-numbered pages and entry spaces for the notary to utilize in chronological order with each notarial act.

The journal should provide for documentation of every material fact asserted within the notarial certificate. The most important of these is the signature of the person for whom the notarization is performed. The notary should always require the signer to sign the journal first, before requesting identification and before identifying what the signer's transaction might be. It is a condition precedent to the decision whether or not the notary should proceed with the notarization.

In addition to the signature of the person for whom the notarization will be performed, the journal should also indicate:

1. The signer's name;
2. The date and time the signer appeared before the notary for the notarization;
3. The type of notarial service the notary is performing for the signer;
4. The type of document for which the notarization is intended;
5. By what means the notary identified the signer's true identity;
6. The signer's address;
7. The date of the signer's document and the fee, if any, the notary charged; and
8. Sufficient space for the notary to write notes that might be relevant to the transaction.

It is human nature for people to avoid certain procedures if they are burdensome and onerous. The notary journal is too important to disregard or to use selectively. It must be used consistently. The design of the journal should be one that is user-friendly, convenient for both the notary and the document signer. It should be easy to understand and quick to locate a specific journal entry from the past.

The traditional notary journal design has been like a ledger book, with a single entry extending the full length of two pages across the spine of the book, and divided into columns. Such a format is considerably cumbersome and an aversion to dutiful record keeping. Moreover, it fails to accommodate the common situation where the notary notarizes multiple times daily for the same signer.

A competent notary cannot afford to cut corners in journal record keeping. The notary journal format and content must be equally competent. It should be one that is designed around the key principles of notary law, and not around the idea of record keeping for its own sake.

Notary Law
See Case Law; Common Law; Notary Statutes; Statutory Law; Statutory Provisions Every Notary Should Know

Notary Law Institute

See Notary Training

Notary Public

See Agent of the State; History of the Notary Public Office; Impartiality; Integrity of the Notary; Why Notarizations are Performed; Witness

The notary public, also simply called a "notary," is an impartial agent of the state government that has appointed that person. The office of notary public is governmental in nature. The notary attests to the genuineness of writings and signatures in order to render them available as evidence of the facts therein contained.

When a notary performs an official act, the notary exercises a delegated state power. Every notarial act is a function of state government. There is no such thing as a "private" notary or notarization. The notary is an agent of the state exercising delegated state powers. The notary's certificate of notarization is a government certificate prepared on behalf of the state. In no circumstance is the notary's authority and power to act subject to the jurisdiction or control of a private company or entity. The notary is personally accountable to the state government by the authority of which the notary functions.

The office of notary public is highly venerated, esteemed position. Notaries are long respected for their integrity, their commitment to ethical conduct, and for their willingness to serve the public. Notaries have played important and significant roles in historical events. Moreover, the office of notary has existed with nearly every society, empire, regime and nation since the ancient Roman Empire.

The function of the notary is crucial to the security, orderliness and functionality of government, law, and commerce. It has never been substituted with another system, and has never been eradicated as a tool of law. It is through the use of notaries that persons can mitigate their risks when engaged in transactions with parties they do not know, or are unseen. The notarization serves as the "third pillar" that supports the orderly and secure legal structure of property ownership.

In one of America's more significant cases concerning the role and duties of notaries, Farm Bureau Finance v. Carney (100 Idaho 745, 605 P.2d 509), we find important instruction.

> *"We believe that the manifest intent of the legislature in requiring a notary public to execute a certificate of acknowledgment is to provide protection against the recording of false instruments. The Sine qua non of this statutory requirement is the involvement of the notary, a public officer, in a position of public trust. If the notary faithfully carries out his statutory duties it makes little difference whether he remembers to fill in the blanks in the certificate. Similarly, if the notary conspires with a forger, or fails to require the personal appearance of the acknowledger, or is negligent in ascertaining the identity of the acknowledger, the statutory scheme is frustrated whether the form is completely filled in or not."*

The court continues,

> *"A notary betrays the public trust when he signs a certificate of acknowledgment with knowledge that the blanks will be filled in later or when he signs a completed certificate of acknowledgment but without requiring the personal appearance of the acknowledgers. Whether the certificate blanks are empty or full is not the significant fact. The key to the statutory safeguard is the integrity of the notary in the proper discharge of the notarial duties by requiring the signatories to personally appear before him and acknowledge that they did in fact execute the document."*

Additionally, the Idaho court stated,

> *"In taking acknowledgments a notary properly discharges his duty only when the persons acknowledging execution personally appear and the notary has satisfactory evidence, based either on his personal knowledge or on the oath or affirmation of a credible witness, that the acknowledgers are who they say they are and did what they say they did."*

Because the office of notary public is governmental, every qualified individual has a constitutional right to serve as a notary. Likewise, all persons have an equal right to obtain a notarization without discrimination. As a matter of law, the only restrictions a state may impose on the qualifications to become a notary must have a direct relationship to the authority of a notary and the functions a notary performs. The states require the notary to be a legal resident of the state. It is unconstitutional for a state to require residency of an excessive period of time, usually anything longer than several months. The states shall not require the notary to be a U.S. Citizen or a registered voter. Such restrictions violate a number of constitutional protections accorded all people.

The U.S. Supreme Court struck down the requirement that notaries be U.S. citizens in 1984. In Bernal v. Fainter (467 U.S. 216) a Mexican native and long-time resident of Texas applied to become a Texas notary. Texas denied his application solely because he was not a United States citizen as required by Texas statute. In reversing the Court of Appeals the U.S. Supreme Court used a strict scrutiny test since the constitutional question was one of alienage. Since there was no relation "to the achievement of any valid state interest" the statutory limitation was declared an unconstitutional restriction under the Equal Protection clause of the 14th Amendment. Any statute or administrative rule restricting the office of notary public to citizens of the United States cannot stand, unless it advances a compelling state interest by the least restrictive means available.

Requirements that applicants to become notaries be honest and have a reputation for their integrity, that they are literate in English and are free of criminal record, are defensible and essential to the integrity of the notarial office.

Notaries, in most states, are required to take an oath of office, which commonly references the notary's attestation that they have read and understand the notary laws of the state and will obey them faithfully.

The entire process governing the appointment of notaries must be conducted entirely without regard to the applicant's race, religion, national origin, political persuasion, age, or gender. These are the constitutionally protected rights of every American and shall not be abridged in the slightest degree by the application to become a notary.

Serving as a notary is a sacred trust the state places in the notary. It is to be taken seriously with a good understanding of the reliance people place on notarial acts. Every person who serves as a notary has a duty not to harm the public trust placed in them. Integrity and ethical conduct is everything in the service as a notary. As long as that remains so, notaries will continue to hold a venerated status for generations to come.

Notary Statutes

See Statutory Law; Statutory Provisions Every Notary Should Know

From "The Notary" (May 1998)

Reading State Notary Statutes: It's No Thriller

When is a law really a "law?" Occasionally we hear about silly laws that are still on the books. For example, it is illegal to whistle a happy tune on the city sidewalk in New England.

Of course, such laws seem silly (although at the time they were written, they must have been awfully important to their sponsor in the legislative body where they were passed into law)! Fortunately, notary law is not fraught with silly off-the-wall requirements. In fact, the notary law in nearly every state is relatively simple, clear and understandable.

State statutes are not written to be read only by lawyers. They are written for everybody to read and to understand. Only sometimes, they aren't very understandable.

We don't need a law degree to be a notary expert, just as we don't need a zoology degree to be an expert in ornithology (the study of birds). Our expertise in notarial law and procedure is achieved through ongoing study and practice of notarial services. It requires straight thinking and clear reasoning.

On occasion, the law can be a fog. It is not always clear. The law is often contradictory, incomplete, ambiguous and just plain confusing. Even

worse, just because it is written in the law, it is not always saying what it means. The writing of law is in art. Some people have it, and others don't. The writing of law requires extensive homework. Some people do their homework, others don't. Every time a new law is enacted, somebody's "dominos" will be knocked down.

It is often impossible to foresee or anticipate all of the ramifications from a new law. Unexpected results can happen. It's all part of the system in our representative form of government.

As notaries we are often alone on the front lines having to decipher and interpret what the governing authorities of our states have written into law about our notarial duties and authority. Have they told us everything we are permitted to do? Have they put into law everything we are forbidden from doing? Have our legislative leaders cleared away the ambiguities or gaping holes in our notary statutes leading us with crystal clear directions and rules to follow? Likely not, in fact, it is unreasonable for us to expect our laws to be perfectly clear, exact and 100% thorough. There is not paper enough on earth on which to print such laws, let alone enough man-hours available to read and understand it all.

Our society and system of law is premised on a very crucial principle of self-governance. That is, as participants in our society it is incumbent upon each of us to learn for ourselves correct basic principles and then to govern ourselves accordingly. To be directed on every small detail of our laws is to foster slothfulness and an unmindful society. We must learn to study out in our own minds the basic principles and to draw our own informed and prudent conclusions concerning correct and proper conduct.

Notaries are generally subject to three bodies of law: state notary statutes, state administrative rules, and the common law or decisional law. As a general rule of thumb, the order in which these three categories are listed is also the order of strength they have when it comes to governing the notary.

The state's notary statutes are usually the "base line" by which the administrative rules and court cases are decided. Occasionally, the statutes are amended because of a court case decision that holds a provision of the statute is not legally permissible.

284

The administrative rules are written and enacted to provide the notary and the government better understanding about the statute's meaning. Oft times, the state statutes will merely set forth broad policy or legal parameters and direct the state agency to write detailed rules to implement and enforce those policies and legal parameters. Then, of course, such rules can end up in court and be tossed out because they are also not legally permissible. When that happens, it's back to the drawing table for either new statutes or new rules.

The common law, on the other hand, is a system of elementary rules and general declarations of principles from the courts which are handed down over the generations. It has been described as "that great body of unwritten law, founded upon general custom, usage and common consent." The courts in your state are not strictly required to follow the common law. However, the common law is given great weight in most cases.

By knowing that these are some of the characteristics of how laws are created, and often evolve through trial and error in court, we are better able to interpret and understand our notary laws. The more you know about the notary law, the more valuable you are to your community.

A Final Word: The ability to read and correctly interpret the notary statutes of your state is valuable. It enables you to make better-informed decisions in any situation. Never let the notary statutes intimidate you. They are a valuable resource and tool. Exercise your own skills of logical thinking and clear reasoning. You will be a valuable information resource!

Notary Training

Every notary public is legally obligated to attain a competent level of understanding of the legal duties and standards notaries must abide by. The old cliché, "ignorance of the law is never a defense" is directly applicable to notaries. In all states, a notary takes an oath of office, in one form or another promising to perform all notarial duties correctly and in accordance with law. Implicit in that oath is the understanding that the notary has taken the initiative to study the fundamentals of notary law and procedure prior to entering into the oath.

A few states require classroom training before a person can become a notary. A larger number of states require the notary to study state-issued manuals and to take a test on notarial rules and procedures as part of the application to become a notary.

Competent, quality notary training will be based in rules of law rather than in traditions and oft quoted helpful hints. The training should comprehensively examine the state's notary code and pertinent case law authority. The notary is appointed as a responsible, experienced, honest adult who is fully capable of making correct decisions on notary maters, if she understands the core basic principles of the notary law. Optimal notary training will be that which teaches the notary correct principles and then entrusts the notary to govern herself accordingly.

The notary must learn from the training that the rule of law governs. Some notaries are inclined to gravitate towards overly simplistic, and often incorrect, "rules of thumb" and dogmas. Too often, such teachings are unsupported by rule of law but are taught as "law." Too frequently such teachings are contrary to the rule of law. It is essential that the notary learn to verify such matters, and to discern when such is necessary. Notaries have a right to be entrusted with the rules of notary law. Notary training should be appraised by how effectively the notary law is used as a tool for the notary.

The notary's failure to obtain competent training early on can lead to disastrous results. The notary is entrusted with profound legal powers. The exercise of those powers in the absence of adequate training constitutes negligence for which liability might accrue. The employer of a notary may be equally liable for failing to ensure the notary is properly trained. The employer's silent acquiescence to the notary's wrongful conduct will be evidenced by his failure to have the notary trained.

The Notary Law Institute has trained many tens of thousands of notaries nationally following these principles. It is the only notary training program of its kind in the United States and is often cited as the most effective notary education by legal, business and government leaders.

The Notary Law Institute is based in the Orem, Utah area and was founded in 1991 (Notarylaw.com).

Ignorance of the law is never a defense. Failure to obtain competent notary training is indefensible.

Notary's Duty to Maintain Journal Records
See Journal Recordation; Notary Journal as Evidence

The Notary's Duty to Meticulously Maintain a Notary Journal

By Peter J. Van Alstyne, 31 J. Marshall Law Rev. 777-802.

The idea that notaries should diligently maintain a journal record of every notarial act they perform is not new. It has been around for centuries. In fact, one of North America's earliest notaries, William Aspinwall of the Massachusetts Bay Colony, argued strenuously against having to turn over his notary records to his successor in office. He told the General Court in 1652, "The bookes are mine own, bought at my owne chardge & register therein my owne voluntary & handy worke, and is a proply mine as anything I possess is mine."

Notary journals have been in various degrees of use across the country for decades. For the most part, the value and importance of notary journals has been widely underestimated. Notary journals are often referred to as "notary records," "notary ledgers" or "notary logs." The most commonly used term is "notary journal."

The notary's journal constitutes independent physical evidence that an instrument was signed or acknowledged on a particular date by an individual who was positively identified by a public official - the notary. The notary journal is an official record whose purpose it is to protect the instrument signer, the notary and the public.

Most states do not require notaries to keep a journal. The keeping of a notary journal is statutorily required in fourteen states and the District of Columbia, and is recommended by state officials in another fourteen states. It is reasonable to assume that the majority of American notaries do not journalize their notarial services. Much of this is due to a lack of awareness that such a practice is encouraged or expected of the notary. For some, record keeping is viewed as an added burden and tends to be avoided

It is not uncommon for employers of notaries to discourage notary journal keeping because it might inconvenience them or their clients. When the purpose of notary journalization and its extensive legal protections are understood, it is reasonable to conclude that every notary should keep a notary journal, even if it is not required by state law.

Notaries hold a public office. The records they maintain as to the exercise of their legal powers and authority are the official records of that office. The importance of such record keeping is so great that it cannot be overstated. It is every notary's inherent duty of reasonable care to make a careful and complete record of every notarization performed. If properly maintained, the notary's journal will demonstrate that reasonable care was exercised in every aspect of a notarial act. It will further establish that the notary routinely exercises reasonable care in the performance of his or her notarial duties. The notary journal guides the notary through correct notarial procedures for every act, thus minimizing any potential for serious mistakes. As a result, the notary journal is a valuable protection for the notary against groundless accusations of wrongdoing. It is especially useful for refreshing the notary's memory about a notarial act that took place years ago.

The keeping of certain records is an inherent responsibility of nearly every responsible adult. Record keeping is vital to the survival and legal protection of any business enterprise, for example. As taxpayers we must be prepared to produce personal financial records in the event of a tax audit. In many ways, the failure to maintain a minimal set of records is negligent behavior.

As a public official, the notary is under a duty to the signer, for whom he or she notarizes, to exercise reasonable care in notarizing signatures and safeguarding the notary journal. The document signer has every right to expect that the notarization is being performed correctly and that it will withstand challenges to its validity. The signer has a right to expect the notary to be able to show by documentation that the signature on the instrument was notarized in accordance with prescribed notarial procedures.

A properly maintained notary journal record will provide invaluable documentation in four respects:

1. *It shelters the instrument signers and other parties from risks if the instrument is lost, wrongfully altered or challenged,*
2. *It shelters the notary from groundless allegations of wrongdoing by documenting that reasonable care was exercised in performing the notarization;*
3. *It discourages groundless threats of litigation, and facilitates quicker resolutions of disputes outside of court; and*
4. *It aids officials in investigating and prosecuting acts of fraud.*

The journal documents key information showing for whom the notarization was performed, when it was performed, on what type of transaction it was performed and how the signer's identity was verified. The journal will indicate the signer's address, evidence the signer's mental capacity to enter into the transaction, and provide other valuable information about the notarial procedures followed in a particular notarization. The rules of evidence clothe notary journal entries with an invaluable presumption of truthfulness. The old cliché, "If it isn't written, it didn't happen," is especially true for notaries and their notary journals.

Contents and Form of a Journal Entry

Because journal entries should document every material aspect of the notarial certificate, the contents of the journal entry are important. Superficial, vague notations will not suffice. Only six states statutorily define what information shall be recorded in a notary journal. The journal entry should document nine material items about the notarization:

1. *The document signer's signature. This feature evidences the personal appearance of the document signer before the notary. It also establishes that the signer's ID card presented the notary was reasonably reliable because the signatures in the journal and on the ID match. The journal signature will also match the signature on the document to be notarized. Because acknowledgment notarizations do not require the signer to make their signature to the instrument before the notary, having the journal signed by the person enables the notary to verify its genuineness. The journal signature also helps to substantially demonstrate the signer's intent and mental capacity to execute the instrument on which the notarization is to be performed*
2. *The signer's printed name adjacent to the signature;*
3. *The address of the person for whom the notarization is performed;*
4. *The date and time of the notarial act;*
5. *The date, if any, of the instrument;*
6. *Identification of the type of instrument on which the notarization is performed;*
7. *What notarial service was performed on the instrument;*
8. *A statement on how the notary verified the signer's true identity; and*
9. *Additional comments by the notary, which clarify important aspects or determinations the notary, had to make in the course of performing the notarial act.*

The heart of the importance of the certificate and the notarial act documented thereby is three fold: the certificate asserts that the signer personally appeared before the notary, the notary took reasonable care to verify the signer's identity and the signer either signed the instrument or acknowledged his signature on the instrument willingly before the notary. Each of these material facts is documented to be true through the recordation of the nine items of information found in the journal entry.

All of the benefits of journalizing notarial acts can be lost if care is not taken to utilize a secure, well-designed notary journal. Not all notary journals are alike. Just because it is labeled "Notary Journal" on the cover does not assure that it passes muster. The journal record pertains to services and instruments that may be in effect and have enforceability on the notary for many years. The journal must be permanently bound, constructed of quality materials and be tamperproof.

The meticulously maintained notary journal is most useful in demonstrating a notary's consistency, especially with regard to proper performance of notarial act. Since it documents the notary's habitual exercise of reasonable care, the journal should provide an uninterrupted chronology of services rendered. Journal pages and entry spaces should be in permanent sequential order. The notary journal should be permanently bound with a sewn binding. Journals in the form of a loose leaf or spiral notebook do not meet the requirement. Pages can be easily removed without a trace, leaving open a question of the record's completeness.

Conventional wisdom suggests that a notary carefully select a journal for use. Design and format can vary widely, and user friendliness is important. It is often tempting to skip a journal entry or cut corners when the notarization is rushed. That is when serious mistakes are often made. The journal should be designed in such a manner so as to guide the notary through the correct notarial steps, where the recordation is thorough yet simple.

The Notary Journal as a Public Record

In every state where journal record keeping is statutorily mandated, the journal is also designated a public record. Elsewhere, the voluntarily kept journal is impliedly a public record. The office of the notary is a public office, ministerial in nature. The official records of public offices and officers are inherently public records, including the journal of the notary.

The notary's journal should be available for inspection by interested parties. As a general rule, where journals are mandated by statute, the notary is required to provide photocopies of journal entries upon request. Of course, a notary is entitled to reasonable notice for such requests and he or she is permitted to charge a nominal fee for supplying photocopies of the journal pages. However, the notary does not enjoy a right to withhold the journal from public inspection. There is no protected right to privacy accorded a notary journal. In a number of states, the notary's refusal to provide copies of journal entries upon reasonable notice and payment of a fee can result in the notary's personal liability for damages sustained as the proximate result from such a refusal.

While the journal is deemed a public record, it may be appropriate for the notary to invoke his or her discretion when it comes to honoring a request to view the journal. A vague request to view a journal for the purpose of conducting a "fishing expedition" may warrant the notary's refusal to honor a request. The notary's journal will contain information pertaining to matters that are often considered very private by the signers and owners of the documents serviced by the notary. Hence, there is a conflict between two public policies. First, the authority and actions of a notary are public and, therefore, the records are public. However, the second public policy issue concerns the transactions on which notarial services are provided. These transactions are often profoundly confidential to the document signers. The parties to any transaction required to undergo notarization and journalization do not and should not have to forfeit their rights to privacy by risking public disclosure of the transaction.

The public's right of access to the notary's journal must be weighed against the document signer's right to privacy. The public policy objectives for requiring journal recordations are three-fold:

1. *To provide a means whereby, at a subsequent date, the validity of a notarization can be verified;*
2. *To protect the notary, the document signer and the public from baseless accusations of notarial wrongdoing; and*
3. *To guide the notary to perform every notarial service accurately and truthfully.*

Broadly speaking, a notary journal is intended to facilitate resolution of disputes by providing accurate records of events and transactions. They are not intended for public reading per se. Unless a person seeking to view a notary journal and its entries is doing so with a purpose concerning the validity of or a challenge to a specific notarial act, then the request to view the journal is suspect. Such requests should not supersede the right to privacy of the parties who are referenced in the journal entry.

When responding to a request to view a journal entry or for a copy of an entry, the notary should exercise reasonable care in accommodating such a request. First, the notary should take steps to verify the request is legitimate. Second, the notary can take simple steps to obscure other entries in the journal with blank sheets of paper, if it is warranted, to protect the privacy of the parties to those recordations.

Notaries are under a duty of care to safeguard their notary journal from loss, unauthorized alteration, destruction and theft. In several states, statutes provide sanctions for the intentional destruction of a notary's journal record. The legal standard by which the notary is judged is the exercise of reasonable care. Accidents may happen; journals can be lost or destroyed for reasons beyond the control of the notary. The notary's legal defense is showing that reasonable care was taken to protect the journal from such a mishap. However, some suggestions for safeguarding a journal can exceed basic tenets of reasonable care and deserve thoughtful review. For example, some commentators have suggested that notaries keep journals under lock and key and away from children and pets.

The State of California, effective January 1, 1998, statutorily mandates that a notary's seal and journal "must be kept in a locked and secured area under the direct and exclusive control of the notary." This unique provision, the first of its kind anywhere, is a quantum shift in public policy with potentially significant ramifications. The California law holds the notary personally liable for damages proximately caused by the notary's failure to keep the seal and journal under lock and key.

The requirements in California serve as direct notice to employers and coworkers of notaries that notary seals and journals are not to be tampered with. However, it imposes the burden of notarial crime prevention on the notary, the private individual in public service to the community. Proponents may not view the requirement of keeping notarial tools under lock and key as onerous. After all, locked liquor cabinets and gun cabinets are obviously essential for public safety. However, requiring the same safeguarding for notary seals and journals may be going too far. For every new regulation passed, there are often some unforeseen, negative ramifications. In this case, the regulations will, at the very least, foster distrust and ridicule in the working environments of thousands of

California notaries. Instead of placing the onus on the notary, state governments could impose stiffer criminal sanctions for tampering with a notary's seal and journal, including substantial fines and damages payable to the notary and the state.

The requirement of lock and key under the exclusive control of the notary will foreseeably pose practical challenges for many. For example, will the single notary living alone easily satisfy the regulation every time the front door to the home is locked? Will the journal have to be locked in a cabinet if the housecleaner has been entrusted with a copy of the house keys? Likewise, notaries in many workplaces may have no practical means of exclusively securing their seal and journal without considerable expense for the notary or their employer. Contemporary principles of employee and business management are premised on concepts of trust, integrity, teamwork and openness. Forcing notaries to keep their seals and journals under lock and key in the modern workplace is anathema to those principles.

Retention of the Notary Journal

No state has enacted a statute of limitations pertaining to the enforceability of notarial certificates. Certificates are generally binding on the transaction and the notary who executed it for as long as the transaction it appears on is in full force and effect. The notary journal documenting the execution of the notarization is an especially valuable protection to the notary, the signer and the parties relying on the notarization for indeterminate lengths of time. As a matter of public policy, the notary's journal should be carefully preserved and safeguarded to ensure its availability for resolution of disputes and validation of notarizations performed long past. But, who should have the duty of preserving the journal to ensure its availability - the notary or the government? Furthermore, how long should a notary's journal be preserved for public access?

Throughout the middle and late 1980s, numerous states responded to this question by adopting certain provisions of the Model Notary Act, promulgated by the National Notary Association on September 1, 1984. The Act provides for the mandatory delivery of the notary's journal to a

294

designated government office "upon the resignation, revocation, or expiration of a notarial commission, or death of the notary."

Presently, twenty-four states require their notaries to convey their notary journals (although not required to be maintained in many of these states) to a government agency upon completion of notarial service. In some states, the journal is filed with the Secretary of State, while in others it is filed with the county or court clerk. Where mandatory filing of the notary journal with a government entity is required, conflicts in public policy can be found.

The journal is the notary's official record of notarial services performed. Under the business records exception in the Federal Rules of Evidence, the journal is admissible if the person who is a personal witness to the events documented therein prepares it. The notary has a very immediate and direct personal interest in the accuracy of the journal, its long-term protection and safekeeping, and in its immediate availability for reference should questions arise over a notarial act documented therein. Compulsory filing of the journal with the government upon completion of notarial service denies the notary the opportunity to protect these interests. Moreover, such requirements may actually be detrimental to the larger public purpose for maintaining a notary journal. The necessity for the journal and its invaluable benefits do not diminish, let alone expire, upon the termination of a notary's commission to serve. The individuals and parties to the transaction on which the notarization is performed have a stake in the validity of the notarization and a right to expect that it can he readily documented at an indeterminate future date. The first point of contact to check a notary's journal will most likely be the notary. After all, it is the notary's name, seal and signature appearing on the notarization certificate. It is far easier to track down "retired notaries" than it is to locate their old journals. This is especially true in many jurisdictions where the government entity receiving the notary's journal has a short retention schedule or none at all.

Arguments in favor of having government serve as the official repository of notary journals to better serve the public's interest are difficult to justify. A 1985 report on the issue concluded that fewer than ten percent of local government entities required to receive notary journals for filing do not comply with the law. Few notaries comply with the requirement by turning their journals in to the government, and they are readily discarded because there are so few requests by anyone to see them. This alarming fact no doubt has our seventeenth century Massachusetts Bay Colony notary, William Aspinwall, trundling in his sempiternal sepulcher.

One of the primary reasons government entities are not generally dependable archivists and repositories of notary journals is due in large part to a lack of understanding regarding the journal's purpose and value to the public. In addition, governmental retention of any public documents and records is costly, and state and local government political winds blow in favor of reducing government paperwork and expense. Appropriations for notary journal repositories for a meaningful length of retention have very low political priority. It is surely a disservice to the notary and the public for statutes to require the notary to turn over the journal to the government and then fail to retain it for a period time which reasonably coincides with the foreseeable number of years in which a notarization may come into question.

The policy reasons behind compulsory governmental repository of notary journals in generations past were soundly rooted in a society lacking modern technological advances. Until some seventy-five years ago, America's population was primarily rural. Communication, travel and the mail were slow. The ability to hunt down a notary's journal for any reason would have been an enormous endeavor, especially if the notary had kept possession of it and had moved from the community. Requiring the notary to file the journal in a central repository made sense. There were fewer notaries serving a much smaller population, and the pressures on government for services were fewer. The costs for archiving relatively small volumes of public records were nominal. By virtue of the statute, the community was on notice that the office of the clerk of that county or the office of the Secretary of State kept journals of former notaries from that county. Modern technology has eliminated the practical justifications for filing notary journals with the government.

Today's telecommunication technology and document transmission capabilities enable us to access, photocopy and transmit the copy of a notary journal entry, regardless of location. Moreover, with that same technology it is far easier to locate people and former notaries than it was generations ago. Indeed, America's population is much more mobile today than only a few decades ago. Nevertheless, unless state and local governments can begin to commit significant resources to proper archival procedures and facilities for America's millions of notary journals, the public is far better served by requiring the notary to personally retain his or her journal for life.

The rules of evidence grant a valuable presumption of truthfulness to the contents of a notary's journal because the notary presumably seeks to protect himself or herself by making truthful and accurate recordation. The same can be said about the notary's incentive to safeguard the notary journal. It is self-evident that a notary who personally retains the journal in perpetuity will presumably have nearly instantaneous access to the journal for any reason.

It is not at all unreasonable to impose the responsibility on the notary to safeguard, keep and make available for public review the notary journal. It involves very little expense to the notary. And, as a matter of policy, the journal should be viewed as it is under California's notary journal protection requirements. The statute declares the notary's journal to be "the exclusive property of that notary public."

There is a propensity for some employers to feel justified in requiring a notary to deposit the notary's journal with the employer upon change of employment. The tendency towards this view is based upon the employer's assumption that a journal purchased with the employer's funds is "company property." Moreover, if the notary has been recording notarial services performed while in the scope of employment, then it would stand to reason that the journal constitutes an official company record belonging to the company. In states where the journal is required to be deposited with a government entity, the employer's claim on the notary journal directly conflicts with statute and places the notary in a difficult position.

The Oregon notary statutes address the matter by allowing the notary to enter into an agreement with the employer for the retention and final disposition of the journal. This compromise may be comforting to employers of notaries, but does not address the public's need to readily access the notary's journal. Unless a third party has notice that the journal documenting a particular notarial act in question is in the custody of the notary's former employer, it may never be found.

Typically a person's first step in tracking a notary's journal is to reference the notarial certificate in question. The certificate will provide the notary's name, the state in which the notary is appointed and very often the county in which the notary resided while serving as a notary. It will also indicate the county in which the notarial act was performed. If the state is one in which the journal must be archived with the government, then the search for the journal would begin with the appropriate governmental repository. Otherwise, the inquiry can be made of the state agency that appointed the notary for the notary's last address of record. If the notary journal is ultimately located in the possession of a notary's former employer, that employer may feel no obligation to provide the journal for inspection, if it has not already been discarded.

An employer's retention of a notary's journal raises considerable public policy issues and several legal concerns. Although a state can legislate retention schedules and public access standards for employers of notaries who keep the journals of their employee-notaries, it is not as effective and beneficial to the public as it is to require state or local government or the notary to retain the journal in accordance with certain standards. Employer retention of the journal complicates and impedes the public's access to the journal. Moreover, an employer's claim to the journal based on proprietorship, company confidentiality or protection against potential claims of liability for notarial misconduct are outweighed by the compelling need to make the journal readily available for public access as a public record.

The best strategy for protecting the notary and the public's need for access to the notary's journal is to statutorily require the notary to permanently retain the journal. Placing the burden on the notary is not especially onerous, particularly as it serves to provide the notary the advantage and protection of immediate access to the record to refute any questions or allegations of wrongdoing.

298

Maine's notary statute provides an excellent model for the retention and safekeeping of a notary's journal:

> *The notary shall safeguard and retain exclusive custody of these records. The notary may not surrender the records to another notary or to an employer. The records may be inspected in the notary's presence by any individual whose identity is personally known to the notary or is proven on the basis of satisfactory evidence and who specifies the notarial act to be examined.*
> *- Me. Rev. Stat. Ann. tit 19, § 955-B (West 1993).*

In statutorily mandating the notary's retention of the journal, the statute should also define several procedural standards for compliance. As in the Maine model, the notary should be permitted to require the inquiring party to provide proof of identification and to specify the journal entry sought. The notary should be entitled to reasonable prior notice of the request and be permitted to charge a reasonable fee for providing a certified photocopy of the journal entry requested. The notary should be expected to take reasonable safeguards to protect and conceal from view other unrelated journal entries.

The most effective way to inform notaries of the obligation to retain journals is at the time of making application to become a notary. As part of the application material and oath of office, the notary can be given clear instruction on the requirements to maintain the journal during and after service as a notary.

As there is no defined statute of limitations on liability for the performance of a notarial act, there are no instructions as to how long a notary ought to personally retain the notary journal. Every transaction for which a notarization is performed and journalized is potentially unique. Every situation in which a notary notarizes is potentially unique. The effective life of a living will or durable power of attorney will vary with each individual. Notarized vehicle titles will probably be short-lived in comparison to the notarized quitclaim deed to a person's home. As it would be bad public policy to arbitrarily affix a statute of limitations on the notarial act and the notary's liability for negligently performing it, it is likewise imprudent to arbitrarily affix a term of years over which a journal should be retained.

The notary should be required to retain the journal for life. The notary should be held liable to parties damaged as the result of the notary's negligent or intentional concealment, destruction or alteration of the journal, as is already statutorily provided in seven states.

Of the twenty-one states requiring the notary to surrender the journal to the government upon termination of notarial service, eighteen states require this to be done even upon the death of the notary. While a number of these state requirements do not specify who bears the burden to convey the decedent's notary journal, it can be safely assumed the burden lies with the decedent's family or employer. In some cases, punitive sanctions may be imposed for noncompliance.

The issue of whether the public is best served if the journal of a deceased notary is deposited with the government is relatively unexplored, and it is not widely discussed in legal literature. The value of the journal to the public verifying a notarial act or resolving a dispute is not diminished upon the death of the notary.

It is not even settled whether a cause of action for notarial negligence can be maintained against the deceased notary's estate. The journal may offer little insight into the deceased notary's possible liability for prior negligent acts. The need for long-term retention may be less compelling in this kind of situation.

There are inherent and often unforeseeable risks in the long-term keeping of any public records. Acts of God and negligent acts of mankind inadvertently destroy records of profound importance. Notaries should be entitled to statutory relief from liability if their notary journal is lost, destroyed or stolen. The notary should always be responsible for the reasonable safeguarding of the journal, subject to limited liability for its loss or destruction due to gross negligence. However, if the notary can establish that reasonable care in safeguarding the journal had been exercised and that the journal's loss or destruction was the result of some cause not directly related to the negligent safeguarding of the journal (such as a house fire or flood), the notary should be absolved of liability for loss. Moreover, since the journal serves as the notary's first line of protection against accusations of notarial misconduct, the loss of the journal should not unduly expose the notary to such accusations.

Upon loss, destruction or theft of a journal, the notary should be statutorily required to provide written notice thereof to the office of the Secretary of State. By giving such notice, the notary should be granted a presumptive benefit of the doubt concerning accusations of misconduct involving a notarial act in the journal. The burden of proof, on the part of the accuser, would thereby be heightened. If in fact the notary committed notarial misconduct during the time period covered by the destroyed notary journal, there would be a presumption in favor of the notary providing that if the journal had not been destroyed, the notarial act in question would be documented by journal entry. Also, because the notary maintained such a journal, there would be a refutable presumption that the notary was neither inclined nor likely to engage in misconduct because the journal would have exposed such conduct and implicated the notary.

Conclusion

Notary journals have been in use for centuries, but are only recently making a comeback. A number of states require their use and the notary's awareness of their benefits is increasingly taking hold. A properly designed and maintained notary journal can direct a notary in correct notarial practices, virtually assuring error free service every time a notarization is performed. It is indeed the notary's most important notarial tool.

An important reason the notary journal has no peer in comparability of protection to the notary and the public is because it is the least intrusive solution, for the greatest good, for the greatest number of people. If in fact American society is experiencing a continued upswing in document fraud and forgery, the increased usage of the venerated notary journal is an ideal solution for solving the problem. The notary journal has a clear and permanent place in American jurisprudence. The real challenge today is to encourage every notary and every employer of notaries to require the proper and diligent keeping of the notary journal. Furthermore, the public served by the notary should come to expect that a signature in the notary's journal is required, to provide identification and to assist the notary to complete an accurate recordation of the notarial act in a matter of a few quick moments.

The properly maintained notary journal is indeed the notary's most valued tool of the trade. William Aspinwall of Massachusetts Bay Colony in 1652 had it right.

Notary's Role in Society
See History of Notary Public Office; Why Notarizations are Performed

The process of witnessing signatures and transactions has been among humankind over two millennia, and probably longer. This process, provided by notaries, is surprisingly essential to the functionality of law, government, human rights, commerce and trade. Without the notary public, the security needed to ensure that parties to transactions are as they represent themselves to be, would be nearly impossible to attain.

There must be a reliable ascertainment that the sellers of commodities or property are the ones who enter into the transaction, and are not imposters.

Notaries public are found in nearly every work place in America. They are most common in financial institutions such as banks and credit unions, hospitals and nursing homes, government agencies, real estate businesses, law offices, and the list goes on. They are there because they provide their constituencies' convenient access to the important government function of notarizations. Notarizations play such integral roles, established by law in most cases, to the finality of transactions and their legal perfection preparatory to filing with government or courts.

The essence of the notarial officer is integrity and a commitment to complete honesty in the performance of notarial duties. Notaries are universally recognized as ones who stand for integrity and honesty.

It is often said that there may be too many notaries in America, approximately 4.5 million. Arguably, in the context of the standards notaries represent, there could never be too many competent notaries. Perhaps, in some small part, this is one reason it is relatively simple to become a notary in most states. Society as a whole benefits from the presence of competent notaries of integrity in the community. The more, the better.

O

In order for an acknowledgment to be effective, it must clearly identify; the person or persons who executed the conveyance and the person signing the instrument must have appeared before the notary and acknowledged that he signed the instrument.
- Alabama Supreme Court, 1985.

Oath and Affirmation
See Affidavit; Credible Witness; Jurat Notarization

Notaries in all states are authorized by law to administer oaths and affirmations to individuals. It is most commonly done in the performance of a jurat notarization, or in the use of a credible witness to identify a signer. Many states authorize the notary to administer oaths and affirmations in all matters, even in transactions beyond the performance of notarizations.

The terms, "oath" and "affirmation," are used interchangeably. They constitute the same meaning and legal importance. While oaths imply a reference to the judgment of a divine being, affirmations are neutral. Notaries should be aware and respectful that some religions and cultures do not permit a reference to deity. When administering an oath, the notary asks the questions, "do you swear…" while in an affirmation the notary asks, "do you swear or affirm…?" It is widely accepted practice to commingle the two by asking, "do you swear or affirm…?"

For an oath and affirmation to have any legal validity, officials having the legal authority to do so must administer it. Notaries bearing this authority place the respondent, also called an affiant, under the penalty of perjury for falsehoods to which they attest are true.

The administration of an oath or affirmation is serious business and must not be taken lightly. Great weight is placed on the affiant's acceptance of criminal penalties for their document contents, should they prove false. The notary must administer the oath and affirmation with clarity and sobriety. The respondent must reply affirmatively, without hesitation or ambiguity. When administering the oath and affirmation, the notary must discern whether or not the affiant comprehends and appreciates the nature of the obligation he takes upon himself.

From "The Notary" (September 1996)

"Do You Swear Under Penalty of Perjury?" Administering Oaths: A Notary's Greatest Legal Power

Nothing intimidates a notary more than having to administer an oath. After all, we see this done on TV shows and it looks downright serious! The uniformed courtroom bailiff sternly asks the witness, with stiffly raised right hand, if they swear the testimony they are about to give is true. In the background, the judge and attorneys scowl as they watch this proceeding. It is little wonder notaries are uncomfortable with this very important notarial power and duty.

A notary's authority to administer an oath is highly esteemed by the law. It is an indispensable step in jurat notarizations and in using credible witnesses to verify a signer's identity. Most importantly, oaths, by law, are taken literally. If an oath is required to be administered in a notarial procedure, when in fact it has not been done, that omission is usually, fatal to the notarial act.

An oath is any form of attestation by which a person signifies that he is bound in conscience to perform an act faithfully and truthfully. It involves the idea of calling on God to witness what is averred as truth, and it is supposed to be accompanied with an invocation of His vengeance, or a renunciation of His favor, in the event of falsehood.

304

When a notary administers an oath to a document signer, the notary is placing that person under the criminal penalties of perjury for falsehoods contained within that person's statement, testimony or document. Not just anybody has the authority to administer in oath. The authority to do so must be specifically created by state law and then be specifically appointed or commissioned to the official administering the oath. That is exactly how notaries receive this very important authority.

The word, "affirmation" is synonymous with the word "oath." The key difference being that an oath requires the signer to attest to the truthfulness of his statements or document by swearing to a Supreme Being. Historically, the solemnity of the signer's intent is demonstrated by raising the right hand while placing the left hand on a Bible.

Ancient Christian tradition required oath-takers to kiss the Bible. In previous centuries, religion played a higher role in society and law. The oath was a means for assuring truthfulness in statements and documents. The oath to a Supreme Being was viewed as the most certain form of truth-enforcement because the penalty for lying was eternal damnation.

In other cultures, oath taking historically attached to items of culturally significant value. In many early Middle Eastern cultures the oath-taker sealed the oath by placing one's hand on a man's body. In these societies, the oath was conclusive. Fear of retribution was profound motivation to deliver the truth.

Oaths found their way into the 15th century English law with its strong religious influences. Religion also raised objection to swearing to God under oath, as did the 17th and 18th century Quakers. Oaths before God conflicted with their doctrines on swearing. After all, a person is obligated to tell the truth at all times even without an oath. Thus, the common use of affirmation was introduced into the legal system as an alternative to the oath, carrying with it the same legal weight as an oath.

Notaries are uncomfortable with administering oaths because it seems so formal. Is the formality necessary? Can't simple spoken statements be enough? After all, the formalities do not guarantee the oath-taker is telling the truth. The answer to this question lies in the mind and intent of the oath-taker. The oath-taker must signify to the notary that he is bound in conscience to the truthfulness of that which is attested and that he knowingly and willingly accepts the threat of criminal penalties for untruthfulness. As a state official, the notary is fully authorized and capable to judge and certify whether or not the signer measures up to this legal standard.

Most states do not legislate what wording or procedures to use when administering an oath or affirmation. While a number of states specifically mandate certain wording and formalities (be sure you refer to your own state's statutes to learn what your state requires), these three requirements are mandatory in every state:

1. Orally ask the oath or affirmation in question form. Example: Do you swear or affirm the statements in your document are true?
2. The oath-taker must respond orally in the affirmative to the notary. A mere nod of the head is not enough.
3. The notary must determine if the oath-taker understands their moral and legal obligation to truthfulness in their document or statement.

Notaries may be asked to administer an oath to a witness in a law office where a deposition will be taken. Administering an oath is not a notarization. It is the exercise of notarial authority granted by state law to place a person under legal penalties of perjury. The most common usage of oaths are: jurat notarizations (also called "verifications upon oath or affirmation"), affidavits, depositions and other sworn documents, for credible witnesses to identify document signer, for subscribing witnesses to identify document signatures, and for swearing in elected and appointed officials.

Not all oaths are associated with a signature upon a document. If signing a document requires an oath and notarization, it will always be a jurat notarization. The typical jurat wording includes, "Subscribed and sworn to before me..." Remember to always first verify the signer's identity and to complete a notary journal entry for the jurat transaction.

Officer

See Impartial Agent of the State; Notary Public; Notary's Role in Society; Public Ministerial Officer

Notaries public are officers of the state. An officer is a person who holds an officially designated position created by law or rule. It is a person on whom is placed a public trust. An officer is also endowed with specific powers and duties. The notary public is a public office which is created by law, and whose powers are prescribed by law.

An officer will act on behalf of the needs and benefit of the organization or constituency for which the position is created. The notary public performs public service. As an officer of the state the notary shall perform in a manner that protects the interest of the public and the state, and shall place all personal interests aside in the exercise of official duties.

Official Misconduct

See Abuse of Notarial Authority; Liability

Whenever a notary violates state notary law or breaches the requisite duty of care, that notary has committed official misconduct. The term, "official misconduct" is often applied by the courts because the notary holds a position of high public trust and responsibility. The notary is an official whose duties are specified by law.

Breach thereof is misconduct by an officer. It is misconduct performed within the auspices of the notarial office.

The notary is personally liable for official misconduct. The notary generally bears the burden of proof that each notarial act is performed properly in the complete absence of misconduct.

"A notary who willfully and knowingly violates his official duty is liable to one injured thereby. Deliberate misfeasance of a notary public occurring during the course of his official notarial duties will subject the notary to liability for all damages sustained by the aggrieved party which are proximately caused by the misfeasance.

Acts of misconduct upon which the liability of a notary or his surety may be predicated include the making of false or fraudulent certificates

of acknowledgment. A notary who knowingly purports to authenticate a document which, in fact, has not been properly authenticated, to the detrimental reliance of innocent third parties, is liable for fraud."
- *Ware v. Brown (CC Ohio) F. Cas. No. 17170.*

Official Seal
See Seal of the Notary Public

Official Signature
See Signature

Every notarization performed in the United States must, by the law of each state, bear the official signature of the notary who executed the notarial certificate. The notary's signature is designated "official" if it represents the full name by which the notary is commissioned by the state. If the notary is commissioned and is of record by a name bearing a middle initial, the official signature must include that initial. If the notary's full given name appears of record, then it is inappropriate for the notary to sign the familiar version of that name, such as "Betty" for "Elizabeth."

The concern over the validity of the official signature is heightened when the signature is written clearly and legibly. If the notary's customary signature is freestyle and artistic, rather than legible, its completeness can't be determined. Ironically, a free-style signature will usually receive less scrutiny for completeness than will a legible signature.

A number of states require the notary to file with the state a sample of their official signature along with an impression of the notary seal. It can be assumed that the signature an applicant makes to a notary application constitutes a valid sample of the notary's official signature for the public record.

The standard for a notary's official signature is not measured by legibility. Its purpose is to establish a fixed means by which a notary may evidence her assent to the contents and terms of a notarial certificate. An official signature of a notary made by any person other than the notary constitutes a forgery. But for issues causing reasonable doubt about a signature's validity, the notary's official signature to a certificate will almost always be presumed to be official.

Notaries are not permitted to affix an ink-stamp facsimile of their signature. It must be an original hand-made inscription on the paper on which the certificate appears. It is not uncommon to find pre-printed notarial certificates generated by computer, or otherwise, that bears the pre-printed notarial signature. Such a signature is inherently and completely invalid. Such a practice constitutes an abuse the notary's authority and is an official misconduct.

Omissions in Notarial Certificates
See Completing the Notarial Certificate

Original Copy
See Copy Certification

In jurisdictions that permit notaries to make copy certificates, discussions often invoke the term, "original copy." This inevitably leads to confusion, as it is a bit ambiguous.

The notary certifies that a reproduction of an item is a true, correct and complete reproduction of that which was copied. When referring to the item that is copied as the "original," people assume that the item must be the first, original version of that item. For example, a pencil sketch by Picasso may be photographically reproduced and sold as a print of Picasso's drawing. A photocopy of that print is not a photocopy of the original. Yet, a notary could certify that the photocopy is a true, correct, complete photocopy of a print reproduction of a Picasso drawing. For conversation purposes, one could say that the print is the original. For certification purposes, the notary cannot truthfully declare the photocopy is made of the original.

In the making of copy certifications, the notary must take care to fully and truthfully disclose exactly what it was that was copied. The notary never has to see or examine the "original copy" of the document if they have witnessed the copy being made that is to be certified. If however, both the "original copy" and the claimed copy are presented for certification the notary is obligated to see and compare the "original copy", even if it is a "copy" or print of the genuine original.

Original Imprint of the Notary Seal

See Pre-Printed Notary Seal

Original Signature

See Official Signature; Signature; Signature Made by a Mark

The only signature that a notary may notarize is an original signature. By definition, a signature is a hand-made inscription on a piece of paper that evidences and manifests the signer's intent to be bound by and to assent to the terms of the document that is signed. It is an extension of its maker's identity.

Notaries have no authority or cause to be concerned with a signer's penmanship. The notary is required by law to attest to the genuineness of the signature, that it was made by and belongs to the person who appeared personally before the notary.

Often, notaries erroneously concern themselves with the correctness of the signature. For example, if the signer's name in the document text is the complete, formal name of the person, but he signs using the familiar version of his name, the notary feels that it cannot be notarized. If Abraham Lincoln were to sign his name, Abe Lincoln, it is not the notary's authority to be concerned.

In the conveyance of real estate and in the execution of testamentary documents, the signer must as a matter of law sign his name exactly as it appears printed in the document text. This would be an issue only if the signature is clear and legible. But if the signer signs with an artistic flourish, it will be indecipherable. This illustrates a principal reason why notaries are involved in such transactions to authenticate the signature, regardless of its legibility.

Persons who are physically impaired, or are legally blind, are known to sign their names with ink-stamp facsimiles of their signatures. Such signature can be notarized. It is a form of hand-made inscription on paper manifesting the maker's intent to be bound by and to assent to the terms and content of the document. The ink-stamped signature must be affixed to the document by its owner, and never by another person. While this form of signature making is customarily not viewed as appropriate for those who are physically capable of making their signature by ink pen on paper, it is traditionally accepted for the impaired.

A few states permit, or require, the notary to write the signer's name and to provide for signature witnesses. This procedure is intended for circumstances where a signer is so impaired that they could not hand-make a mark or ink stamped signature to the document.

From "The Notary" (July 1998)

Original Signatures Only

Fax machines are convenient and their transmissions are becoming clearer all the time.

But the rule of law is even more clear - the only signature a notary may notarize is an original signature.

Thanks to fax machines, documents can be transmitted to numerous cities around the country in the same day for multiple signatures to the same transaction. The first "original" document is written and signed by Joe in Los Angeles. Then it is faxed to Jane in Denver for her to sign. Then it is faxed to Steve in Atlanta for him to sign. Finally it is faxed back to Joe in Los Angeles. The document Joe takes out of his fax machine has the signatures of Joe, Jane, and Steve at the bottom.

Yet, not any of these signatures are originals. And the document may be fully enforceable.

It gets a little perplexing sometimes when you are asked to notarize on a faxed or photocopied document. Is it legal to do because the document itself is not the original? The only issue the notary must address is whether the signer is physically in the notary's presence and the signature to the document is made originally on that document. It matters not if the document itself was faxed to the signer, or is a photocopy of some other document.

When we notarize, we are not affecting the truthfulness of a document. We do not even make if legally enforceable. We are only certifying the signature to the document (regardless of how the document was created) is the signature of the person who appeared before us.

There are some practical limitations to the notarizations of signatures on faxed or photocopied documents. If the document is a title deed or real estate conveyance for government recording, there are good reasons why a faxed document bearing an original signature and notarization might not be accepted for filing. Because the stakes are very high in real property transactions, there must be exactness in the paperwork documenting the transaction.

One's only proof of ownership to a home or piece of land is a written document. Documents can be tampered with, forged, lost and destroyed. The notarial act to these transactions is one of the cornerstones to secure America's cherished right to own property.

Another area of common concern is the notarization of signatures to multi-page document packs, usually made from NCR paper or carbon paper. The signer is instructed to press hard when signing so the signature appears on the yellow and pink copies below.

May a notary affix her notary seal to the yellow and pink copies to show that all three copies in the pack were signed and notarized? No, she may not. The only signature a notary may notarize is an original signature made by hand with a writing instrument from which ink flows onto the paper. A genuine signature can be made only one at a time (unless you are fully ambidextrous and able to write with both hands simultaneously).

If all three copies of the NCR form must be signed and notarized, the signer must sign the white, yellow and pink copies separately and have them notarized individually.

Out-of-State Forms

See Correcting Notarial Certificates; Full Faith and Credit Clause; Venue

Business and legal forms commonly include notarial certificates for the notary to execute. When the form originates in another state, it often includes the preprinted name of that state, along with the county in which it was drafted. This most often appears in notarial venues and near the notary's signature line to indicate the county in which the notary resides.

The notary shall not permit incorrect state and county names to appear in the notarial certificate. The notary is obligated either to use a new, correct notarial certificate, or amend the one provided on the form. The notary may line out the incorrect state and county names and write in correct information. The notary can initial the deleted information, if deemed necessary.

Some states legislate certain types of notarial certificate formats that are unique to their state. When such a format is sent to another state for its execution by a notary, the notary is not under a legal obligation to use the format prescribed by the originating sate. The notary is subject to the jurisdiction and laws of the state in which she is commissioned, and is not subject to notarial requirements of other states. As a matter of law, the notary is not obligated to execute an out-of-state certificate, but may substitute it with one of her own.

Preparers of documents in other states have no authority or legal standing to require or compel a notary to execute a particular certificate that has gone out of their state for completion. For that matter, no person has the authority or standing to compel a notary to complete a given notarial certificate in any circumstance. When the notary affixes her signature and seal to the certificate, she is the guarantor of the facts asserted within the certificate. Therefore, the ultimate authority for certificate wording rests with the notary, within the bounds of her state's notary laws. Were it not so, the integrity of the notarial process would be compromised. There could be no reasonable assurance that certificates are true and comply with state law if all must be signed and sealed indiscriminately by notaries, as directed by their authors.

As guarantor of the certificate contents, the notary inherently must have judgmental authority over the appropriateness, correctness, and truthfulness of the certificate. Otherwise, all notarial certificates will be potentially questionable as to their content and to the notary's accountability thereto.

Out-of-State Notarizations
See Full Faith and Credit Clause; Venue

Notarizations performed in other states will be honored in the state in which it is received. This is provided by the Uniform Recognition of Acknowledgments Act and by the protections granted by the Full Faith and Credit Clause of Article IV, Section I, United States Constitution. If the notarization was performed legally and in compliance with the notary laws of the state in which it is executed, it shall be honored in the state it is received.

Ownership of the Notarial Certificate
We are a nation of ownership. Among our most cherished constitutional rights is the right to private ownership. The concept of private ownership is so important to our society that it is the essence of our freedom. It lies at the heart of our democracy. Each of us are expected to respect the ownership rights of others, and to do nothing to impede them.

Notaries face a bit of an issue when it comes to the question of ownership over notarizations. Does the notary own the notarization, or does the owner of the document to which the notarization belongs? Because notarizations are performed under the authority of the state government, do they actually belong to the state rather than to the notary or document owner?

Ownership of the notarization matters because ownership denotes responsibility for its integrity, for its protection from loss or abuse, and for its delivery to the parties for whom it is intended. The important thing to recognize is that ownership of a notarization is not permanent and that it is usually shared. Ownership can shift from one party to another.

Notarizations are not performed spontaneously on a whim. They are the result of a person's request that it be performed. It is understandable that a person who is having a notarization be performed to assume that the notarization belongs to her. Yet, the notarization is a governmental function that is performed by legal authority conferred on the notary. The notarial certificate is literally a document of state government created by the notary as an agent of the state government. The certificate authenticates the verity of the document signature, and is not part of the signer's document.

The notary is personally liable for every word of the notarial certificate. It must be true, accurate, and complete. As to the ownership of the certificate while in preparation, the certificate clearly belongs to the notary. It is the notary who is accountable for its validity. It is the notary who attests to the facts asserted within the certificate. It is the notary who must create the certificate in strict compliance with state law. As the agent of the state government, the notary certificate under preparation belongs to the notary acting as that agent. When the certificate is completed and is conveyed to the signer, ownership of the notarization begins to shift away from the notary. The receiving party begins to assume the duty to protect the certificate from loss, abuse and misuse.

No person has any right, authority or legal cause to direct a notary to perform the notarization and to certify it in a manner that conflicts with the notary's standard of care and with the rule of law. The notarization is the notary's to perform and is shared with no one.

The intended use of the notarization is to provide all persons receiving the document security that the signature is genuine and can be relied upon. When taken with the notarial certificate, the document may become qualified for filing and recording with a government agency or with the courts. It is intended for the document to which it pertains, a document that is privately owned. When the notarial certificate is properly completed, signed and sealed, the "ownership" of the notarization passes from the notary to the signer of the document for whom the notarization was performed. However, this form of ownership is not the kind of ownership we are most familiar with. It is not absolute ownership.

When we think of ownership, we include the notion that the owner of something can do whatever he wants with his property. Ownership of a notarial certificate is never absolute. It is created by legal authority and it binds the state government to the genuineness of the document signature. This is the product of agency law.

The notary is the agent of the state. Agents bind their principals to the actions they are legally authorized to perform on behalf of the principal. Hence, notarizations are created by agency from the state and are therefore always partially "owned" by the state, albeit modestly.

As owners of property, we assume the right to paint our homes any color, to landscape as we desire, to write notes in our books, or to make changes as we deem appropriate. Under no circumstances may a person make any changes, corrections or additions to notarial certificates, even if they are in partial ownership thereof.

Some people assume they have complete ownership of a completed notarial certificate and are authorized to modify it. They are very wrong. The certificate, by definition, is the certification of facts, the truth of which is attested to by authority of the official making the certification. Any alteration to such a certificate constitutes unlawful conduct, and is possibly fraudulent.

The only way for a notarial certificate to be changed, corrected, or expanded to include additional signers is for the notary to perform the changes under legal authority. The notarial certificate is intended for the document to which the signature being notarized belongs. The document signer has no authority to appropriate the certificate from its intended use to another transaction altogether. Under normal principles of ownership, an owner could do such a thing so long as it is not done to deceive or defraud another.

The right to personal ownership is a wonderful freedom. Ownership still applies, but does so in a different way. It is shared ownership and is not the exclusive property of any one person or entity. It is not available for treatment like other personal property. It is strictly subject to the rule of law and permits no one to singularly dominate over it.

The completed notarial certificate is legally unalterable by all persons other than by the notary who prepared it. Ownership of the notarization doesn't allow for tinkerers and renovators.

P

Party to the Transaction
See Conflict of Interest; Disqualification; Notarizing for Relatives

Notaries shall not perform notarizations on transactions in which they are a party. A party to a transaction is any person who is named in, or appears as a signator of, a document from which they will receive some benefit or gain. A notary in such a position is strictly disqualified from notarizing for that transaction.

The notary is also strictly disqualified as a party to the transaction when the notary has or will receive a property right as a result of the transaction. It is not essential for the notary's name to appear in the document text for the notary to be disqualified. Property right interests are not always evidenced with the notary's printed name in the document text.

The notary is under a legal duty to determine whether or not she is a party to a transaction prior to notarizing. Most often, the notary will either know or be informed of a property right in the transaction. If in the most unusual circumstance such information is withheld from the notary, the notarization may be subject to invalidation without prejudice against the notary. The notary cannot be held liable for such a situation if the notary performed all official duties with integrity and reasonable care.

Penalties for Notarial Misconduct
See Liability; Notarial Integrity; Official Misconduct

Notaries are personally responsible for the truthfulness, completeness and validity of the notarial certificates they sign and seal. They are the guarantors of the probative value accorded the notarial certificate.

Notarial misconduct of any nature will always affect the integrity of the notarial certificate. The notary is financially liable for all damages caused by the misconduct, as it affects the notarial certificate. There is no limit to the dollar amount of the notary's liability. If the misconduct takes place in the workplace, it is possible for the notary's employer to be jointly and severally liable for the damages the notary caused.

Notaries can also be fined by the state government for their misconduct in a number of states. In all states, the notary's commission can be restricted or revoked by state officials upon a finding of misconduct.

Where the misconduct is deliberate, willful or the results of wanton disregard for the rule of law and the truthfulness of the certificate, the notary may be subject to criminal penalties as well. The legal standards of proof a prosecutor must prove for criminal liability to attach is significantly higher than the standard applied to find financial liability on the notary's part.

It is one thing for a notary to commit misconduct. It is another thing to hold the notary liable for the misconduct. Generally, the notary is liable only for the damages proximately caused by the notary's misconduct. A plaintiff has to prove the notary committed misconduct and that the misconduct proximately caused identifiable financial harm.

A notary cannot be held liable if a signer's document is found to be invalid. If the document was inherently invalid to begin with, the notary's misconduct in notarizing on the document will unlikely produce harm for which the notary is liable. The notary's liability most often must come from a finding that had the notary not committed misconduct, there would have been no harm suffered. There has to be a proximate connection between the notary's conduct and the resultant damages.

A notary standing accused of liability for misconduct, if the circumstances permit, may raise a defense that the harmed party did nothing to minimize the damages. If a person discovers that the notarization is not true or valid,

318

that person is not entitled to take undue advantage of the problem and attempt to maximize potential financial compensation. The harmed party is duty-bound to make a reasonable effort to mitigate against such damages if they know or have reason to know the defect exists and damages could result.

Penalties for Perjury
See Liability; Perjury

The crime of willful and corrupt swearing or attesting under oath is punishable by fines and imprisonment.

Perjury is a serious crime, often prosecutable as a felony.

The seriousness of the nature of the false testimony will be highly determinative to the level of criminal sanction imposed. The standards are not fixed or consistent, often left to the court's discretion. In the Clinton White House scandals in the late 1990's, the President was accused of several counts of perjury. While Clinton made false statements under oath, legal scholars wrangled over applicable criminal issues concerning the gravity of the falsehoods and the respective contexts in which they were made.

One immutable fact concerning the crime of perjury remains undiminished by the Clinton perjury scandal. That is, the system of law and criminal justice absolutely depends on truthfulness. There can scarcely be the slightest degree of tolerance for false sworn and attested statements. False swearing and attesting gravely jeopardizes the functionality of everything it affects. Absolute truth is important. It is everything.

Performing Marriages
See Marriages Performed by Notaries; Statutory Authority of the Notary

Only three states currently authorize their notaries to perform marriages: Florida, Maine, Nevada, and South Carolina. A few generations ago, notaries in many states held the authority to performing marriages, but with the course of time the legislative bodies of the states repealed this notarial function.

In the states where a notary may perform a marriage, the function is a notarial act performed by an official of the state. Similar to being married by a justice of the peace in many states, the notary exercises government powers by certifying the exchange of marriage vows and the execution of the marriage certificate. When completed, the notary is a witness of record of the marriage contract rendering the marriage certificate eligible for filing in the offices of the county or state government.

The states do not prescribe the formalities of the marriage ceremony, but for the key basics of the exchanged vows of marriage. Many notaries in Florida and Maine are particularly active in the wedding business, providing all manner of wedding planning and consulting services along with their legal authority to officiate over the marriage.

The performance of a marriage is not a notarization. It is not subject to the issues notaries face concerning conflicts of interest. Notaries are authorized to, and find great joy in, performing marriages for their family members. It is, however, an impossibility in law for a notary to perform his or her own marriage.

Perjury
See Affidavit; Affirmation; Jurat Notarization; Oath and Affirmation; Penalties for Perjury

The crime of perjury is the willful and corrupt false swearing, or affirming, after taking an oath that is lawfully administered in the course of a judicial or legal proceeding, to some matter that is material to the issue or point in question. Generally, the false swearing and affirming must be knowing, deliberate and with intent to deceive others. One cannot commit perjury inadvertently. Nor is expressing an opinion or a belief grounds for perjury. It must pertain to the false representation of material facts.

Notaries in all states are legally authorized to administer oaths and affirmations to persons on nearly any matter. False statements made orally or in writing before a notary, after having taken an oath or affirmation administered by the notary, will constitute a perjury. When a document signer's signature is notarized by a jurat, the signer has attested to the notary that the contents of the document are true. Should it later be found the document contains material falsehoods, that signer is subject to criminal penalties of perjury.

Credible witnesses to the identity of document signers are under penalties of perjury for their attestations to notaries, made under oath or affirmation, as to the true identity of the document signers. As a matter of law, there can be no tolerance for false testimony and statements made under oath and affirmation, when properly administered. The system of law is absolutely dependent on the integrity of society, that a person's word is truthful. While the degree of severity of the crime of perjury can vary according to the circumstances, it is serious business. Lying under oath in any matter, regardless of one's position (even the President of the United States), is corrosive to the judicial process and to the integrity of the community.

A person accused of perjury cannot use as a defense that the oath was not properly administered, or that it was superfluous and unnecessary. The crime of perjury is correlated to the crime of fraud. In the event a court were to hold that the defendant was not under an oath or affirmation, the defendant may yet have to answer for the crime of intent to deceive.

Permanently Bound Book
See Notary Journal Contents and Format

Notary journals should be permanently bound books that cannot be easily tampered with or altered. A loose leaf or spiral notebook will generally not hold up to scrutiny when challenged for its physical integrity. The journal should be able to withstand the inevitable wear and tear that comes with time and usage. The journal is so vitally important as a record that some states require by law that the journal be permanently bound. It is faulty to cut corners and a little expense by accepting a journal with inferior binding.

Some notary journals are manufactured with a "saddle stitch" binding, one that is done by two staples in the spine of the book. While it may be difficult to remove or substitute a phony page into such journal, it is less likely to hold up to average wear and tear for the years of life the journal will be needed.

Person Acknowledging
See Acknowledgment Notarization; Personal Appearance of the Signer

It is quite common for people to mislabel the notary and the document signer in an acknowledgment notarization. Some incorrectly state that the notary is the person who is acknowledging, when in fact it is the document signer who acknowledges their signature. The document signer must personally appear before the notary to acknowledge their signature to the notary. Hence, the person acknowledging is the document signer.

Personal Appearance of the Signer
In every notarization of any signature, the document signer must personally appear before the notary. This is the rule of law for every notary and every notarization in every state, and always has been. This means the signer must be in the notary's physical presence. Merely being under the same roof or in direct voice contact is never enough to satisfy the law. There is no substitute for physical presence.

It is legally impossible to notarize without the personal appearance of the signer before the notary. It is not only a required component of the notarial certificate, but it is also a requisite to the proper verification the document signature belongs to the person claiming it. The personal appearance of the signer before the notary is utterly inseparable and indispensable to every notarization.

Every notarial certificate, be it an acknowledgment or a jurat notarization, specifically declares the signer personally appeared before the notary. The false certification of this material fact by a notary constitutes a serious violation of law and public trust. It cannot be defended by claiming it was inadvertent or done unknowingly.

A notary who notarizes a signature without first having the signer personally appear violates state law, notarizes falsely, and notarizes fraudulently. The notary is strictly liable for such conduct. There is no defense in law for a notarization without the signer appearing before the notary. The notarization is invalid and unenforceable. The signer's transaction may also be jeopardized as well. The notary squarely bears full liability for the damages caused by such conduct.

322

It is an unfortunate common occurrence for employers and supervisors of notaries to request them to notarize signatures where the makers thereof do not appear personally before the notary. Such requests are illegal and are potentially actionable in court. While such requests may be well intended, to avoid inconveniencing the customer or to expedite an urgent matter, they can never be honored.

The requirement that the signer personally appear before the notary is the key to the mitigation against signature fraud. A signature forger is far less likely to obtain a notarization on a forged signature if they must personally appear before the notary to be positively identified. Personal appearance of the signer before the notary is so vitally crucial to the protection of the public and to the parties to the transaction that there can be no exception or exemption granted to the requirement. It is never discretionary.

A notary, and the employer of the notary, cannot be held liable for a notarization performed in accordance with the rule of law and with reasonable care. There is no instance where a notary is exculpated from liability for failure to have the signer personally appear.

Some people erroneously assume that a telephone call between the signer and the notary can substitute for personal appearance before the notary. It does not. Likewise, many assume that because they are so familiar with the signature they may waive the requirement the signer appear personally. It is legally impossible to waive this requirement.

The notary has no authority to certify that they are familiar with the likeness of the signature. Besides, such an assertion does not establish that it is genuine. The signer has the burden of proof to establish for the notary the signature belongs to him. It can be done only in the notary's physical presence.

Personal Knowledge
See Credible Witness; Signer Identification

When a notarial certificate declares, or a notary journal entry records, the document signer is "personally known" to the notary, it means that the notary has first-hand knowledge, or "personal knowledge," of the signer's factual identity. Such knowledge is derived from an acquaintance and interaction with the person over a period of time sufficient to eliminate all reasonable doubt as to the person's true identity. Such an acquaintance cannot be based on the word of other persons. It must be based on a chain of circumstances surrounding the person, all of which tend to show that he is what he purports to be. Something affirmative in the nature of evidence must appear during the course of the acquaintanceship.

One particular case opinion is very helpful in setting forth the legal test of what constitutes personal knowledge:

> *"Such knowledge, in our opinion, involves such an acquaintance, derived from association with the individuals in relation to other people, as establishes their identity with at least reasonable certainty. Such an acquaintance cannot in its very nature depend upon the mere word of one or two or three individuals, but must be based upon a chain of circumstances surrounding the persons in question, all of which tend to show that they are what they purport to be. That there is nothing to arouse suspicion is not enough. Something affirmative in the nature of evidence of identity must appear during the course of the acquaintanceship which would not normally appear if the persons were other than they purport to be, before it can be said that their identity has become a matter of personal knowledge."*
> *- Anderson v. Aronsohn, 181 Cal. 294, 184 P. 12 (1919).*

Knowledge is not personal if it is knowledge acquired from the statements of other persons. A person who read about an automobile accident cannot be a witness to that accident. However, a person who saw the accident occur has personal knowledge as to its occurrence and how it proceeded.

Personal knowledge is powerful legal evidence. It is quite resistant to impeachment of credibility. It is usually taken at face value.

Personal knowledge cannot be faked nor contrived. A notary claiming to personally know a document signer may have the burden of proof to show her knowledge of the signer's identity is based on sufficient acquaintanceship and interaction. The standard by which personal knowledge of another's identity is measured is subjective, and will vary in each circumstance. The notary must exercise a high degree of objectivity and candor when deciding they personally know a document signer.

"It is not easy to give a definition of what will constitute "personal knowledge." Everyone knows that two intimate friends, who have known each other from childhood to mature age, living in the same neighborhood all that time, may, in the fullest and most unreserved sense, be said to have such "personal knowledge" of each other. But, if a stranger be introduced by a respectable person into any company, it is generally safe to assume that he is what he professes to be, although the person making the assumption has nothing for it but his reliance on the habits of accuracy of the introducer; who, in his turn, may be relying on similar habits in someone else, on whose information he had made the last introduction. It is obvious that, when an officer taking an acknowledgment and making a certificate assumes any such fact, he does it at his own risk. The law warns him, when he has not "personal knowledge" of his own, to resort to certain observances which the law supposes to be sufficient in practice to prevent imposition. It may be very courteous to waive all such formalities; it may be disagreeable to speak plainly, and tell a party that one is not willing to assume that he is not falsely impersonating another; but no one is at liberty to practice courtesy or gain popularity, to indulge his own indolence, or avoid unpleasant things at the expense of others. If these others sustain loss by his laxity, it is impossible to listen to assurances from him that he meant well, and really did not know better, where it was his plain duty to probe the matter to the bottom, and not to certify at all until he knew what he was talking about. It is perfectly idle for him to protest that he did not know or suspect that his certificate was false. That may be granted; but it is nothing to the purpose. His business was to know that it was true."
    - Joost v. Craig, 131 Cal. 504, 63 Pal. 840.

Some notaries may consider personal knowledge of a signer's true identity too tenuous. They are inclined to require the signer to produce photo identification, even if they genuinely know the signer personally. That sort of conduct is inappropriate, and is based on emotional insecurity, rather than logic. Personal knowledge of identity of a document signer is a function of reasonableness.

While introverts may ask, "do we really know ourselves?" there are no guarantees that our best friends or neighbors are who they claim to be. People fall in love and marry criminal imposters. Thousands in our country live under aliases, even hiding from the law. If in our hearts and minds we know the person personally to be whom they claim to be, there isn't any higher standard. It is sufficient for purposes of notarizing.

Personal Liability
See Liability

Personally Known to Me
See Personal Knowledge

Photocopies of the Notarization
Making a photocopy of a notarization is permissible, and is done occasionally for the files accompanying the transaction. Such photocopies have little probative value.

From time to time, notaries assume that if they make photocopies of all their notarizations and keep them in a file it will prove the validity and correctness of their notarization. This is false and has no merit to it. It is impossible for the photocopies to adequately substitute for the probative value of notary journal entries. The photocopies do not evidence the notary performed truthfully and correctly.

Photocopies of the Signer's ID
See Notary's Duty to Maintain Journal Records; Signer's Right to Confidentiality and Privacy in Notarizations

Some notaries incorrectly assume that by making photocopies of their signer's ID for their files, they will satisfy the necessity to document how the notary identified the signer. While at first blush the concept sounds reasonable, further consideration presents important problems.

The photocopy of the signer's ID contains personal data about the signer which may be legally protected data, which the notary has no authority to possess. The photocopy is detached from the notary journal and offers no connection between the signer's personal appearance before the notary and the proper verification of his identity. Making and keeping photocopies of signer's ID is inappropriate and futile. It offers little probative value establishing the signer was properly identified in the notary's presence by the notary.

Photograph of the Bearer
See Identity of the Signer; Reasonable Care; Signer Identification

While a number of states mandate by law that a signer's ID card or papers must contain a photograph of the bearer, such a requirement is reasonably implied on all notaries nationally. How could an identification document reasonably evidence a bearer's identity if it does not contain a photo of the bearer?

Notaries must exercise a high degree of care when identifying a signer. However, some forms of ID do not contain photographs of bearers. Even a few states do not require a photo of the licensee on their state driver's licenses. When in the performance of a notarization, the signer bears the burden of proof that they are who they claim to be. While it may be legal in many states to accept a signer's ID without a photo thereon, it marginalizes the notary's efficacious verification of the signer's true identity. The burden of proof may not be met.

Unusual circumstances may arise where there is a preponderance of evidence as to a person's true identity, but it does not include a photo ID. In states where notarial discretion has not been removed, notaries may take into account other corroborating and convincing evidence of a person's identity. The elderly, patients in hospitals, and residents in nursing homes constitute a large population base without the customary photo ID. They are entitled to notarial services and to the notary's careful assessment of evidence that establishes their identity without a photo ID.

A photograph on identification cards and papers is merely a printed image of the bearer's likeness, and is accompanied by the bearer's name and other pertinent information. While extremely valuable, the ID photo is not the only printed information that evidences a person's true identity. Unusual circumstances can be satisfied with clear thinking and reasonable care. Understanding that principle, some states are comfortable with issuing driver's licenses without a photograph of the licensee. Information such as detailed physical descriptions of the bearer, a signature of the bearer, and the nature of the source of the ID can be highly probative of the bearer's identity.

Identification without a photograph issued by a vending machine illustrates the extreme unacceptable form of ID. Photo-less ID issued as a state's driver's license will enjoy full credibility for legitimacy and for the standards by which the state identified the bearer prior to issuing the license. In states where the statute specifically requires the signer's ID to bear a photograph, the notary has no options. The ID must comply or the signer cannot have his signature notarized by a notary he does not personally know.

Physically Impaired Signer
See Original Signature; Signature; Signature Made by a Mark

Every person has a legal right to have his or her signature notarized. The physically impaired enjoy equal rights protected by the Constitution, including the right to enter into transactions and agreements, to execute testamentary documents, to swear affidavits and depositions. So long as they are mentally qualified to enter into the transaction, their physical impairment shall never constitute grounds for refusal to notarize.

A signature is a written name or an inscription on a document evidencing the maker's intent to be bound by, to concur with, or to assent to the content or terms of the document. Penmanship is irrelevant. The signature, in whatever stylized form it may appear, is an extension of the signer's identity. It is the role of the notary to certify the inscription was the willful act of its maker and that it belongs to the maker.

For many generations, it has been customary for the impaired to write the letter "X" or to place their thumbprint on the signature line in lieu of a signature. Often, it is required that the notary writes the person's name adjacent their mark, and even provide for witnesses to sign their names as well.

328

The mark or thumbprint inherently, by definition, constitutes a valid signature. Adding the printed names of the signer and witnesses to the thumbprint may be surplusage, albeit required in some states. It is useful for clarity and full disclosure of the nature of the execution of the document by the physically impaired signer.

It is ironic, however, that little fuss is made over signatures that are creative, artistic, and bear no likeness to any letter of the alphabet. Medical physicians are especially noted for their atrocious writing, often leading to serious medical mistakes. It stands to reason that if a physically impaired person has the slightest means of writing a letter "X" on their signature line, they are equally capable of making a stylized signature similar to that of a medical doctor's. A person's signature is not a fixed, permanent design or logo. It evidences a signer's intent. If that standard is satisfied and verified by a notary, the physically impaired are entitled to a broader selection of choices on how to sign their documents. When the signer has made a similar mark in the notary's journal, the validity of the signature is unimpeachable.

Placement of the Seal

See Completeness of the Notarial Certificate; Completing the Notarial Certificate; Seal of the Notary Public

The notary seal, where required by state notary law, should be affixed in a clear and legible manner near the notary's signature. The seal represents and declares the notary's legal authority. Its legibility is important.

The affixed notary seal should not overlap the notary's signature, or any other signature. It should not overlap any text of the signer's document or of the notarial certificate. Old traditions seem to die hard, and one of them is for the notary seal to affix to the notary's signature. This improper practice does not necessarily invalidate the notarial certificate, but in a few states it may.

There is no specific place the seal should be affixed, as long as it appears near the notary's official signature on the notarial certificate. In order to affix the seal legibly, it may affix perpendicular to the text, in an angular manner, and upside down. Embosser seals will naturally appear right side up on one side of the page and inverted on the other side. It matters not, as long as it is legible and complete.

The seal should affix completely. Ink stamp seals might partially miss the page if the work surface is uneven. It is not a concern if the substantive portions of the seal are legible. If the seal is substantively complete the intent of the statute is fulfilled. That is to say, if the information required to appear in the seal is discernable, although fragmented or faded, it need not be affixed again. If the ink stamp seal smudges but the key information remains discernable, it doesn't have to be reaffixed.

If the seal is not substantively complete and legible, the notary need only reaffix the seal in a clear space adjacent the first attempt. Only the notary has the authority to rule on the adequacy of the image her seal has made during a notarization. In making such a finding, the notary must invoke common sense and reasonableness. The notary can redo the flawed placement of a notary seal image at any time while the document remains available. If the document is filed with a government recording office bearing a questionably flawed seal impression, the acceptance by the government of the notarization most often legally "perfects" the seal impression, meaning that the defective seal is approved as if it were not flawed.

Power of Attorney

See Acknowledgment by Attorney-in-fact; Attorney-in-fact; Notarizing a Signature Made Under Power of Attorney

Powers of attorney are written authorizations, by a "principal," to another person, called an "agent," enabling the agent to act on behalf of the principal. Powers of attorney must be written and signed by the principal. In many states, the principal's signature must also be notarized. Usually, the principal's signature is notarized by an acknowledgment. The letter that represents the power of attorney is called a "letter of attorney."

Powers of attorney are ancient in origin and powerful in their use. They can be written to grant the agent, who is also called an "attorney-in-fact," very broad, generalized powers. They can be very restrictive, limited to a single act or function.

It is not the notary's authority to be concerned over the validity or appropriateness of a power of attorney document. It can be notarized without undue concern. The notary is obligated to ensure the signer understands that the document he signs is a power of attorney. Powers of attorney can be handwritten or typed. Because of the complexities and legal ramifications powers of attorney present, it is extremely important that they be drafted by competent legal counsel. Do-it-yourself kits are usually defective and risky.

The attorney-in-fact as a matter of law are agents of the principal. The agent can do anything permitted under the scope of the written power of attorney. That which the agent does becomes binding upon the principal. Businesses and estates have been ruined by attorney's-in-fact and the contracts, conveyances and expenditures they make and bind to the principal. It is reasonable for a notary to refuse to notarize a power of attorney if it has not been prepared within the notary's own workplace in the regular course of business. Powers of attorney brought in off the street by a person unknown to the notary duly belong in the offices of a lawyer for review, rewrite and notarization.

Unfortunately, elderly, ill and incapacitated persons in hospitals and nursing homes execute large volumes of powers of attorney. Their competence to execute such documents is highly suspect and they are under extreme duress as their families panic over the potential estate problems if the document isn't signed and notarized immediately. The old adage that we should plan and prepare our estate documents under the guidance of a competent attorney while we are young and healthy cannot be over emphasized. Notaries can serve as valuable examples of prudent living by taking care of such matters for themselves early on.

Practice of Law
See Unauthorized Practice of Law by Notaries

Notaries are warned often to avoid the unauthorized practice of law. The unauthorized practice of law constitutes a criminal act in every state. The problem is that the definition of the practice of law is vastly misunderstood and is often spun to create an exaggerated picture. The notary is too often taught false principles about the unauthorized practice of law. These false dogmas harm the notary profession and the public notaries serve.

The practice of law consists of the preparation of pleadings and other documents incident to actions and special proceedings, and the management of such actions and proceedings on behalf of clients before judges and courts. It also includes the preparation of legal instruments of all kinds, and, in general, all advice to clients and all action taken for them in matters connected with the law.

Notarial acts are functions of law. They are legal in effect and have important roles in transactions, conveyances and proceedings. However, as a matter of law, performing notarizations does not constitute the practice of law.

There is very little in life we do that does not have some sort of legal implication. It is unlawful to drive over the speed limit. But if we tell our teenager to avoid speeding tickets by obeying speed limits, we are in effect giving legal advice.

A licensed real estate agent will give considerable advice regarding conveyance documents, financing instruments, contracts to buy, and so forth. It is all steeped in property law and it is all legal advice.

Too often notaries are handed platitudinous dogmas that they must not give legal advice. But, they are not taught what constitutes the unauthorized practice of law and what forms of legal advice are off limits. Untrained and unqualified spin-masters effectively lead many notaries to believe that it is the unauthorized practice of law for a notary to write a notarial certificate, to make corrections to pre-printed certificates, and to decide whether to use an acknowledgment certificate or a jurat certificate.

Most notaries are trained, experienced professionals with expertise in their chosen field. Within their expertise, they possess considerable legal knowledge regarding rules and procedures about their functions, services or products. Giving a customer guidance or advice within the scope of their expertise does not, and cannot, constitute the practice of law.

Within the scope of the notarial services, notaries have no authority or need to address the statutory completeness or enforceability of the signer's document. Selecting and writing a notarial certificate, be it acknowledgment or jurat has no legal bearing on the signer's document. Making corrections to a notarial certificate is absolutely the notary's legal duty, having utterly no connection to the practice of law.

Very often signers will ask the notary if their document is legal or will hold up in court. If the question pertains to a transaction in which the notary has expertise by virtue of her profession, she is completely free to offer an opinion. If the notary has no such expertise, the standard of integrity mandates the notary to decline an answer and advise the signer to consult legal counsel. Ironically, advising a person to consult legal counsel on legal matters constitutes giving legal advice.

The line between competent notarial service and the giving of legal advice and the practice of law consists of varying shades of grey. Notaries most frequently face the lightest shades of gray, such as informing a signer that witness signatures are needed in addition to the notarization. Giving such information is never wrongful or unlawful. The darkest shades are unmistakable. A non-attorney notary must never advise a person on the creation of a trust or will.

Notaries must be informed on the limitations on what advice they may offer their clients. But, it must be information that is based in law rather than in false dogmas. Notaries are very important to the legal system. The more notaries know and accurately understand about legal matters, the more valuable they are. Effective notaries understand that the unauthorized practice of law is not a gag order with shackles. Rather, it is a guideline intended to raise the level of competence of all people who function with it.

Pre-Numbered Notary Journal Pages and Entry Spaces
See Notary Journal; Notary Journal as Evidence; Notary Journal Contents and Format

A notary journal must show consistent, uninterrupted reasonable care and thoroughness by the notary for every notarization performed. The notary journal must consist of pre-numbered pages and entry spaces to evidence such a pattern.

Moreover, a fraudulent alteration or concealment of information will be readily self-evident as gaps in the chronology of pages and entries appear.

Pre-numbered pages and entry spaces also effectively remind the notary of the absolute need for consistent proper performance and recordation in every notarization performed.

Pre-Printed Notarial Certificates

See Certificate of Notarization; Completeness of the Notarial Certificate; Legalese; Notarial Certificate; Probative Value Accorded the Notarial Certificate

The notarial certificate is not part of the content of the document for which it is created. It is a separate document giving certification of the facts declared therein. It certifies the signature to the signer's document is genuine. The notarial certificate is not required by law to share the same sheet of paper of the document. It can be an attachment.

It is very common for notarial certificates to be pre-printed on the signer's document, usually at the end of the last page. The notary must be cautious before signing and sealing a pre-printed notarial certificate because it is highly common for such certificates not to comply with state notary law and to make statements that are false. In such certificates, the notary has no option but to refuse to use it. When the notary signs a notarial certificate, regardless of who drafted it, the notary becomes the personal guarantor that every word of the certificate is true. This is especially perilous when the certificate is written in cumbersome "legalese."

It is prudent for a notary to have pre-printed notarial certificates ready for use that the notary understands thoroughly and can readily attest to its truthfulness and completeness. Pre-printed certificates can be in the form of full-sheet or half-sheet attachments, or ink-stamp, or in the form of gummed labels that affix to blank space on the signer's document or as an attachment thereto. (The Notary Law Institute produces these types of instant notarial certificates that are used by thousands of notaries nationally. Visit Notarylaw.com.)

334

Many people assume that the notary is legally obligated to use the notarial wording that is provided on their document, especially if it is created by an attorney for a transaction. No person has the right or authority to dictate to a notary the wording the notary shall certify by signature and seal on a transaction. The notary is inherently empowered by virtue of the notary commission to take responsibility for the notarial wording and provide it in the form of a separate page of paper or by other written form.

It is a wise rule of thumb for the notary to use her own pre-printed certificate whenever in doubt about the pre-printed certificate accompanying the signer's document. Moreover, if no certificate wording accompanies the signer's document to begin with, a notary avoids any risks by using a certificate she has ready to use spontaneously. A prudent notary is a prepared notary.

From "The Notary" (July 1997)

Pre-Printed Forms Do Not Supersede Law

Visitors to the Republic of Russia tell about very startling contrasts between "the old world" and modern technology. When making a purchase at a store, the purchase will likely be run up on a state-of-the-art computerized cash register. The cashier will then verify the total purchase amount by hand on an abacus and then write a lengthy, multi-copy receipt. Old habits die hard in some societies.

This scene illustrates human nature's complacent acceptance of "form over substance." That is, procedures and format are too often more important than the substantive objective sought. It is visible most everywhere. Consider, for example, the massive volume of forms and documents you must sign to be admitted to a hospital for a simple tonsillectomy. Can't they be consolidated into a single form, perhaps done on a computer? The likely answer could be that too many departments within the hospital must have their own forms completed and signed. Therefore, consolidating isn't in each department's own interest. Hence, form overrules substance.

When it comes to notarizing on business or government forms and applications, form can heavily outweigh substance. One of America's most common notarial complaints is that pre-printed forms and documents contain defective notarial certificates. There is usually insufficient space for a notary seal or signature. Too often, the pre-printed certificate contains defective notarial wording. Attempts to correct the problem on the form or document is often met with umbrage. Any attempt to correct the defective notarial certificate is often, and erroneously, viewed as grounds for voiding the document.

The design of a form usually comes in response to a new law or solution to a problem. In government, often the form is designed not by the policy-makers but by the print shop. If a notarization is required for the transaction, the form will include the notarial certificate. Unfortunately, the form designer does not understand the notary law, but attempts to piece together something that "looks like a notarization." It is utmost ironic when the forms of a state government contain notarial certificates that fail to comply with the state's own notary laws.

Of the few states that still require a notarization on a motor vehicle title, none of the state-mandated titles provide for correct notarizations. Either the wording is inadequate or there is insufficient space for a notary seal. Any attempt by the notary to notarize correctly thereon will almost certainly result in rejection from the motor vehicle department.

Form does not supersede substance. Form does not overrule law. The notary law is neither repealed nor excused simply because a form design is defective. To the contrary, a notary is not granted legal waivers from the requirements of the notary law.

A notary is required by law to refuse to violate any aspect of the notary law. A notary is forced into a tough spot when the form design provides a defective notarial certificate. It's especially frustrating when the defective form comes from the government of the state that also sets forth the very notary law we are required to obey. The left hand does not know what the right hand is doing.

The notary law does not permit form to supersede the requirements of the law. Instead, we must place substance of the law over form.

336

Pre-Printed Notary Seal
See Seal of the Notary Public

In every state where a notary seal is required, or used voluntarily by a notary, it shall be affixed to the notarial certificate at the time the notary signs it. Under no circumstance may a notary seal be pre-printed on a certificate for subsequent execution.

The notary seal represents the notary's authority to perform notarial acts. It affixes near the official signature the notary makes to the certificate, and the seal stands as the official emblem of authority. To pre-print the seal on forms and certificates is an abuse of the notary's authority and official seal. Such a practice would invalidate the notarization, and the notary would be liable for damages caused thereby.

Pressure to Notarize
See Duress; Employer and Notary Relations; Employer Liability for Notarizations; Employer's Legal Duty to the Notary

In the request for a notarization, it is unlawful to pressure the notary to perform the notarization. The notary is required by law to exercise objectivity and reasonable care. The notary inherently must be free to evaluate the facts of the request and the procedures to be fulfilled in order for the notarization to be valid and defensible.

Occasionally the public is under pressure, due to time constraints or the fear the notary will refuse to notarize. Pressure asserted against a notary automatically raises a warning flag for the notary to investigate more closely why the pressure is asserted. The signer's fear the notary might refuse to notarize is a common indicator of wrongdoing on the signer's part because the signer fears it will be discovered if the notary performs in accordance with law.

Pressure on a notary, like pressure on a person to sign a document, mitigates against, and possibly eliminates, the notary's legally required objectivity and impartiality. The notary is an official of the state and performs strictly as an agent of the state and not as a free, independent person. Pressuring a notary to notarize under any circumstance is an unlawful interference with the notary's authority to perform. It is actionable in court civilly and, possibly, criminally.

It is an unfortunate commonality in America's workplaces for employers of notaries to apply extreme pressure on their employee-notaries to notarize. It is usually born out of the misinformed belief that the notary's authority belongs to the employer and is subordinate to the employer's demands. If the notary is pressured in the work place to notarize in violation of state law, the employer is criminally liable for such conduct.
It can be conclusively stated that those who pressure notaries to notarize usually do so for non-sinister reasons. However, it demonstrates a deep lack of knowledge and poor personal behavior. Pressure applied to a notary is never justified and is never excusable.

Pressure to Sign a Document
See Willful, Free Making of a Signature

Prevention Against Notarial Misconduct
See Employer's Legal Duty to the Notary; Ignorance of the Law; Notary Training; Notary's Duty to Maintain Journal Records; Official Misconduct

The best prevention against notarial misconduct is proper notarial training and supervision. Every notary, every supervisor of notaries, and every employer of notaries is legally obligated under their duty of care to understand the rules and procedures for correct notarial services. Both the employer and supervisor are obligated to create a work environment that fosters correct, truthful notarizations. The employer and supervisor are in the best position by virtue of their authority over employees to foster a sound notary-ethic. It is true that the manner in which notarizations are routinely handled in a work place is a reflection of the ethical standards that are cultivated by its management.

Clear, comprehensive and well taught notarial policies and procedures in the workplace will be highly effective against notarial misconduct. Notaries are owed appropriate supervision for compliance and positive reinforcement for their notarial services. For the most part, the employee becomes a notary at the direction of the employer. Were the employee assigned to a new position, the employer would make a reasonable effort to ensure the employee is trained and competent in the new assignment. Otherwise, the employee is destined to make costly mistakes and risks being terminated from her employment. Employers who place responsibilities on their employees without training or supervision are on a path to overall failure.

Effective training, management and supervision are the surest preventative against official misconduct by notaries and colleagues in the workplace. It creates an environment of competence and accountability. It manifests a respect for integrity and ethical conduct. It evidences respect for the notary law. Commitment to effective training, management and supervision is a paramount requirement for honest performance.

Prima Facie Evidence
See Probative Value Accorded the Notarial Certificate

Evidence that is sufficient to establish a fact and is not rebutted is called "prima facie evidence." It is evidence that stands on its own. The facts it proves are self- evident.

Prima facie evidence becomes the controlling evidence of a fact when no discrediting evidence or circumstances is introduced. For example, the fact that a document signer is out of town on the date and time his signature is notarized is prima facie evidence the notarization is false.

Principal
See Agent of the State

Probative Questions
See Competence to Sign; Willful, Free Making of a Signature

A question will be probative in nature if it is open-ended and the answer to which will have a tendency to prove or establish a fact. A question that can be answered "yes" or "no" is generally not considered probative.

The open-ended question forces the respondent to ponder a response, to formulate a thought or series of information in order to answer the question. Probative questions are highly effective tools by which accurate and factual information is procured from people.

Notaries are considered under obligation to ask probative questions when notarizing for aged or ill individuals to ensure they are signing a document willingly and freely. An effective notary will ask the signer to state why they are signing the document, or state what they want the transaction to achieve. The signer's answer to the question, if relevant, will establish the fact the signer is capable of formulating the intent to sign the document and therefore does so willingly and freely. The signer's answer can just as well establish the fact the signer is not competent to sign the document.

Probative Value Accorded the Notarial Certificate
See Notarial Certificate; Prima Facie Evidence

The notarial certificate asserts a series of material facts that establish the genuineness of a person's signature. In every state, the notarial certificate is considered prima facie evidence of those facts asserted therein. The notarial certificate has significant probative value that automatically attaches to it as a matter of law.

American society as a whole tends to attach great expectations to notarizations. It is common to find notarizations on signed documents performed in the belief that the notarization legalizes or validates the document, or makes it "legal." Most frequently, American society assumes that because a notarization is affixed to the instrument, it guarantees the truthfulness of its contents. These assumptions are groundless, yet this occurs in government, law enforcement, banking, insurance, real estate and in nearly every other industry throughout the United States today.

When the validity of a signature to a document is questioned, the probative value accorded the notarial certificate prevails unless it is otherwise shown to be falsely made. If evidence is brought forth proving the notarization was made falsely, the false certificate is then probative of the notary's violation of law and liability therefore.

Proffered Copy
See Copy Certification; Original Copy

In the discussion of copy certifications by notaries, and in the statutes authorizing notaries to perform copy certifications, the document that is copied is often referred to as the "proffered copy." The proffered copy need not be the "original" of the document.

When a person gives a document to a notary to copy and certify, that person "proffers" the document, meaning the person offered or presented the document to the notary for copying and certifying.

Protests and Protestations of Negotiable Instruments
See History of the Notary Public Office

In most states in America today, a notary still retains the legal authority to execute a protest.

A notarial protest is a long ago business and legal procedure for collection on bills and invoices, or for refusal of payment thereon. There hasn't been a notarial protest in decades, yet they still appear as a legal function in the state statutes.

> *"A protest executed by a notary means the formal declaration drawn up and signed by the notary that he has presented the bill for acceptance or for payment, and it was refused. But according to popular usage of common men, the term has acquired a more extensive signification and includes all the steps necessary to charge an endorser. If a bill has been protested for nonacceptance and due notice has been given to the drawer and endorsers, it is not necessary to protest it for nonpayment. But a bill which has been protested for nonacceptance may be subsequently protested for nonpayment."* - 8 Am. Jr. 382.

Historically, notaries played vital roles in the transoceanic shipment of cargo through marine protests. One observer commented:

> *"In the nineteenth century, notaries were routinely called upon to issue marine protests and banking protests. Although the laws of every state still provide for protests, today protests are mainly of historical interest... A marine protest was a formal document, sworn to by the master, first mate, and a portion of the crew of a merchant vessel, that stated that any damage suffered by the ship or the cargo was caused by bad weather or other perils of the sea beyond their*

control. The purpose of such protests was to protect the ship's owner from being held liable for damages."
- Source Unknown

Almost always, the notary's execution of a protest was carefully logged in a book, the contents of which the notary would certify as true and correct.

Prothonotary

A prothonotary is a clerk or ministerial officer of a court of justice. It is the person who is responsible for the keeping of the court's records and official seals. The prothonotary has authority to certify the correctness of transcripts or copies of such records and to perform certain ministerial duties for the court, such as issue notices, set calendars and other duties court clerks normally perform.

The office of prothonotary is not the office of notary public. While the prothonotary performs some functions the notary public performs, the scope of their authority is narrower than a notary's. Their purpose is to facilitate the public's access to accurate, complete and unaltered court records and to an orderly court.

The office of prothonotary is found in only a few states and is nearly identical to the office of a court clerk. It is a vestige of generations past before the conveniences of electronic reproduction of documents, recordations of court proceedings, and their ready availability to the public.

Proximate Cause

See Breach of the Notary's Duty of Care; Liability; Reasonable Care

A notary is liable for only those damages that are proximately caused by the notary's official misconduct. For there to be proximate cause the injury must be the result of a natural, continuous sequence of events set in motion by the notary that is unbroken by any intervening cause, and without which there would have been no injury.

Proximate cause can also be the act or omission that immediately causes or fails to prevent the injury. The injury suffered need not be the immediate and direct result of the wrongful act, although it is highly indicative of liability if it is.

One way to examine proximate cause is by the "but for" rule. In the context of a notarization, one would ask, "but for the notary's misconduct, would the injury have occurred anyway?"

Notaries are in the position of expertise and trust. They are entrusted with the duty to scrutinize the notarial certificate for flaws or defects before signing and sealing it. The notary is the only one with the last clear chance to ensure the notarization is done properly so no injury can result from misconduct. Failure to carefully perform that duty can be the proximate cause of injury.

Assignment of liability against a notary by proximate cause of injury can be defeated by showing there was an intervening cause that disrupted the natural flow of events. For example, a notarial certificate is discovered to be false and that fact is disclosed to the party receiving the document on which it appears. The receiver is informed not to rely on the notarization because it is invalid. If the receiver disregards the disclosure of invalidity, and subsequently is harmed by their reliance on the invalid notarization, the injury suffered is no longer the proximate result of the notary's misconduct. The injury did not result from the natural and uninterrupted flow of events set in motion by the notary. Rather, it was suffered as the result of accepting the risk the invalid notarization would pass as valid without jeopardizing the transaction.

The "but for" test can be applied to the injury after the intervening event occurred. "But for the notary's misconduct and the full disclosure to the injured person that the notarization is invalid, would the injury have resulted anyway?" The answer is clearly no. A reasonable person would not rely on an invalid notarization to their detriment if they were informed it was invalid. Therefore, the injured person caused his own injury by acting unreasonably and, in the context of notary law, dishonestly, by pursuing the transaction while knowing its notarization was invalid.

Prudent Person
See Reasonable Care

There may be an infinitesimal slight shade of difference between being "cautious" and being "prudent," but they are essentially the same. They carry the same legal significance for all practical purposes.

A prudent person is one who exercises the same degree of care and caution as a reasonable person would exercise under the same circumstance or situation.

The notary public is required by law to be prudent, to exercise reasonable care, while performing the steps of a notarial service and thereby not commit negligence in the performance thereof. The notary shall be personally liable for all damages proximately caused by her negligence while performing official duties.

Public Ministerial Officer
See Notary Public; Officer

The office of notary public in all states is a public ministerial office. The notarial act is a ministerial act.

An official act or duty is ministerial if it is imposed expressly by law, and not by contract or as an incidental matter that happens to come along with the office. It is an act and duty that provides no discretion in its performance. The ministerial act and duty is defined and created by mandate of law to which no discretion is left to the officer on whom the duty is performed. It is the execution of a set task on which the law imposes the mode, the means, the time and occasion when it will be performed. Nothing is left for judgment or discretion.

The notary laws of the states define the conditions and qualifications for a person to become a notary. The laws define how the notarization shall be performed and the term of office the person is authorized to exercise notarial authority. The notary law, for example, does not grant the notary unlimited discretion to decide what means are acceptable for verifying a signer's true identity. Such methods are prescribed by statute or case law in all states. A notary has no discretion on whether or not to require the document signer to personally appear before the notary. And, a notary is not granted discretion on whether or not to perform a notarization for a person based on the person's race, gender, age, national origin, and so forth.

By protecting the notarial office as a ministerial office, the public interest is protected against abuses of authority and unchecked misconduct. The very nature of the ministerial office creates the legal requirement for accountability by the notary for her official conduct. It creates a strict liability for misconduct wherein there is no valid defense for official misconduct. If the signer fails to personally appear before the notary, as required by law, there is no defense the notary can raise to mitigate against that unlawful notarial act.

The notion that the notarial act is without any discretion or judgment on the notary's part is not altogether correct. The limit on discretion pertains to the core of the notary's authority and primary notarial procedures. It is not discretionary for the notary not to identify the document signer. However, the notary must exercise judgment and discretion when examining the signer's ID cards or papers to ascertain they are valid and credibly represent the bearer. The notary must exercise judgment on whether or not the signer is signing the document willingly and freely, but it is not discretionary to disregard that issue. While the contents of a notarial certificate may be prescribed by statute, the notary has some discretion to phrase the certificate in a different manner as long as it substantially complies with that which is required by statute.

The ministerial office of notary public is very tightly regimented as to its duties and authority. However, the notary must exercise a high degree of care and prudence when performing those duties, as they require a degree of judgment by the notary. The notary should not be held liable for a misjudgment made reasonably. A misjudgment made negligently, with reckless abandon for the standards of care imposed on the notary, is not defensible for it was made outside the scope of the ministerial authority of the notary.

Public Misunderstanding of Notarizations
See Public Perception of the Notarial Office

Public Official
See Agent of the State; Public Ministerial Officer

The notary public is an office created by law and is overseen by the state government. Employers do not make their employees notaries, nor may a person appoint herself as a notary. The authority and power to perform notarial services extends from the state to the notary. The state must follow specific procedures to commission a person as a notary.

As a governmental position, the notary is inherently a public official vested with legal authority to act on behalf of the state that appointed her. Although the notary is not an employee of the government and enjoys no rights of protection or legal defense by the state for her notarial acts, the notary is an agent for the state and has no property right interests in the office of the notary.

Public Perception of the Notarial Office

See Notarial Certificate; Notary Public; Purpose for Notarizations; Why Notarizations are Performed

The perception the public holds for the office of notary public has rarely, if ever, been empirically measured. The most reliable observations about public perception come from personal and anecdotal experiences by notaries and students of the notary law.

The office of notary public is widely held in high esteem by the public. It is generally considered a symbol of integrity and respect for law and truth. The public tends to consider the notarization important and of worth, but does not understand the legal implications of notarizations. There is a generally held assumption that somehow the notarization renders the document for which it is prepared more legal or enforceable. In a sense, many believe the notarization is the official "seal of approval" ensuring all will be well with the transaction.

A disturbingly high number of people consider the notarization as a trivial technicality requiring the notary to do nothing more than to sign and seal the certificate where indicated. Overall, however, the public is respectful of the notary's meticulous exercise of reasonable care and dutiful compliance with law.

There is a likely correlation between the public's belief that the notarization validates their transactions and the public's expectation that the notary will not jeopardize their transaction by performing the notarization in non-compliance with law. The public at large places great trust in the notary to perform competently and to do nothing that would place their transaction at risk.

Notarial services provided in a competent, expedient and cheerful manner have a profound effect on the public. Undoubtedly, the public judge the notary according to the manner by which the notary performs. Notarial performance is a direct reflection on the notary's knowledge, competence, and integrity. It reflects indirectly on the notary's employer as well. Little things tend to say a lot about big things. When the notary service is done with utmost integrity and competence, it tends to indicate that all of the services and products provided by the workplace are handled with the same degree of integrity and competence.

Competent delivery of notarial services within an organization can be a significant credibility and reputation enhancer for that organization. It holds the potential for being a valuable asset for any organization to whom the public comes for service of any kind.

Public Trust
See Agent of the State; Impartial Agent of the State; Public Official

The notary holds a public trust to perform all notarial duties in strict compliance with the law, with unfaltering integrity. The notarial office is a public office created by law to provide a means by which the public may have their transactions made secure against signature fraud. The law provides specific procedures and standards of care by which the notary shall perform. The state and the public place their trust in the notary not to breach the duty of care and thereby jeopardize the security of the signatures to documents that are notarized.

It is a potentially grievous error to assume the act of notarizing is a technical detail of little consequence. The entire system of notarial services depends on the individual integrity of each notary. Having placed its trust in each notary, the public, through the state government, is legally entitled to rely on each notary to serve competently and honestly.

One of the greatest harms a notary inflicts by failing to notarize with integrity is the breach of the public trust. Trust and integrity are fragile. There is no limit to their value. The public trust placed in notaries is a sacred trust never to be underestimated.

Purpose for Notarizations

See History of the Notary Public Office; Notarial Certificate; Why Notarizations Are Performed

Notarizations are authorized and recognized by law for one reason: to ensure that signatures to documents are genuine and valid, and are made willingly and freely for the purposes provided within the document. Notarizations have nothing to do with the signer's document per se. The document content is utterly irrelevant to the notarization. The notary has no duty, or legal right, to scrutinize the content of the signer's document. To do so, without the signer's consent, raises serious issues of signer's privacy. Moreover, such conduct by the notary has no plausible defense. It does nothing to enhance the security of the notarization.

For centuries the notarization has been an effective preventative against signature fraud. A fraudulent signature is either a forgery or one made under coercion or duress as the result of some threat of harm. The only manner in which a signature can be valid is if it is the true signature of the person who claims it, and that he made it willingly and freely. Imposters make forged signatures. Hence, in every notarization, the signer must personally appear before the notary because the notary must verify the signer's true identity. The notary must verify the signature to the document is the genuine signature of the person claiming it, and does so by causing the signer to sign the notary's journal. The notary must eliminate any reasonable doubt the signer made the signature willingly and freely. Each of these procedures must be documented in writing within the notary's journal.

The public tends not to understand the purpose of notarizations. Unfortunately, it is common for people to assume the notarization validates, legalizes or proves the document to be true, when it has no such effect. The trained notary has superior knowledge about the law of notarizations and is in the best position to inform the signer that the notarization addresses the validity of the signature only. The notary can provide a valuable service by informing each signer for whom a notarization is performed that the notarization has no effect on the document's validity. It merely authenticates the signature appearing on the document. Such a kindly gesture by the notary aids the signer with the knowledge that perhaps further scrutiny or review by legal counsel may be warranted on the transaction, and not to assume the notary has done just that.

Q

Everything must be made as simple as possible, but not one bit simpler.
- *Albert Einstein*

Qualifications for Appointment to the Office of Notary Public

See Appointment to the Office of Notary; Commissioning Process

Each state's notary statutes provide a set of minimum qualifications a person must meet in order to be commissioned as a notary public. At the least, a notary must meet minimum age and residency requirements, along with full disclosure of the person's name, address and other personal data the state deems important. Many states prohibit persons with criminal records, and those who are not competent in the English language, from serving as notaries.

The office of notary public is premised in individual integrity. A number of states require the applicant to submit with their application the signatures of endorsers of their good character. In addition, most states require the submission of a surety bond that, in a sense, is a form of endorsement by the surety of the notary's good character as well.

The statutes of a few states require that the notary be a United States citizen. This requirement is unconstitutional, according to the U.S. Supreme Court ruling of Bernal v. Fainter. Such a requirement violates the applicant's guaranteed protection against discrimination on the basis of alienage. The few states that require their applicant's to be registered voters fall under the same constitutional scrutiny. U.S. citizenship is requisite to register to vote and cannot be sustained as a qualification for a notary commission.

The information provided on a person's application to be a notary must be treated objectively without prejudice or predisposition aforethought. A state may ask the applicant for information that extends beyond the statutory minimum requirements for eligibility to be a notary, but the state may not use such information as disqualifiers of the application. Likewise, the applicant's failure or refusal to provide such requested information may not disqualify the applicant as well. Requested information that goes beyond the statutory minimum is surplusage and has no substantive value to the qualifications of the applicant. It is valid only for the state's administrative purposes in maintaining an orderly registry and regulation of the state's notaries.

Qualified Elector

See Equal Protection; Qualifications for Appointment to the Office of Notary Public

A few states require that persons applying to serve as notaries be qualified electors of the state. The term, qualified elector, is occasionally misunderstood with unfortunate consequences. The term is a generic, technical description of a person having constitutional and statutory qualifications that enable him to vote. This term applies not only to persons who do vote, but also to persons who choose not to register to vote but are qualified to do so.

Courts have held that an elector is not necessarily a United States citizen. Rather, a qualified elector is given broader meaning to include all persons who enjoy legal residency within the state. Though not qualified to vote, they are entitled to the same Constitutional rights and protections citizens enjoy. They may own property, participate in the political process, have their concerns heard by government, and serve as notaries public.

A state cannot defend a denied notary application on the basis the applicant would be ineligible to vote for lack of citizenship or voter registration. Such indifference to the applicant's protected rights could result in a potentially costly liability to the state.

Quiet Acquiescence

See Employer and Notary Relation; Employer's Legal Duty to the Notary; Notary Training; Respondeat Superior

An important principle of law is the concept of quiet acquiescence. That is, a person is viewed to consent to, or encourage, an action or conduct by merely keeping silent about it. It may constitute tacit approval on the part of the observer.

In order for there to be acquiescence, certain conditions must first be met. There must be a person who is entitled to object to, control, prohibit or prevent certain conduct by others, such as supervisors over their employees. There must be conduct that is wrongful, unacceptable, or in violation of policies or rules. The person in authority must know, or should know, the wrongful conduct is ongoing. The person in authority acquiesces to the conduct by permitting it to continue unabated for a period of time. In the end, the supervisor has tacitly approved of the wrongful conduct by the employee.

Employers and supervisors of notaries can be liable for the wrongful notarial conduct of their employees under the theory of quiet acquiescence. They cannot defend themselves by asserting that the wrongful conduct was the independent act of the employee and not subject to the managerial preview of the supervisor. It is a well-established principle of law that employers and supervisors are responsible for the actions and conduct of their employees under their authority, even those actions that are not pertinent to the business of the employer. For example, employers are obligated to supervise their employees with sufficient competence to protect against and prevent the use of, the storage or distribution of controlled substances in the workplace. This doctrine is applied to establish employer liability for harassment in the workplace.

The employer and his supervisors are in the best, and often only, position to watch for, prevent and punish wrongful behavior among employees. Employers and supervisors are deemed by law to have the duty to know all that goes on under their supervision. They cannot assert a defense that they "did not know what was going on." To the contrary, concerning employee actions and conduct, the law imputes knowledge thereof to the employer and supervisor.

Hence, the law provides the employer and supervisor either knew or should have known the conduct was occurring.

Because the law imputes knowledge of employee conduct on the employer and supervisor, the failure to prevent, to discover and to terminate the conduct constitutes the employer's and supervisor's quiet acquiescence to that conduct. In other words, it is legally implied that the employer and supervisor tacitly approve of the wrongful conduct and are therefore fully liable therefore.

Employers and supervisors of notaries will be liable by quiet acquiescence for the wrongful notarizations their employees perform in the workplace. If it is routine for co-workers to bring documents from home bearing signatures of spouses or family members needing notarizations, and routinely they are illegally notarized because the signers do not appear before the notaries, the supervisor's failure to discover this and cause it to cease constitutes quiet acquiescence. If he in fact knows it is ongoing and does nothing, he likewise quietly acquiesces to the illegal notarial activity. While liability by acquiescence renders the employer and supervisor liable for the wrongful acts of employees, it does not release the notary from personal liability.

The Restatement (Second) of Agency, a venerated source of legal principles, sets forth helpful standards that apply to employers in their hiring, supervision and training of employees.

> "*§ 213. Principal Negligent or Reckless*
>
> *A person conducting an activity through servants or other agents is subject to liability for harm resulting from his conduct if he is negligent or reckless:*
> a) *in giving improper or ambiguous orders of (sic) in failing to make proper regulations; or*
> b) *in the employment of improper persons or instrumentalities in work involving risk or harm to others;*
> c) *in the supervision of the activity; or*
> d) *in permitting, or failing to prevent, negligent or other tortious conduct by persons, whether or not his servants or agents, upon premises or with instrumentalities under his control.*"

Protection against liability by quiet acquiescence in the workplace is a matter of proper managerial principles - doing the job the supervisor and employer are paid to do: competently supervise their employees.

Implementing four key procedures may attain employer and supervisor protection against notarial liability:

1. Adopt clear, comprehensive policies and procedures regarding the correct performance of notarial services, the standards of care to be followed, and the criteria by which notarial decisions will be made;
2. Provide thorough and on-going training on the policies, procedures and standards for notarial services;
3. Competently supervise the notarial services of the employees to ensure they are performed in accordance to policy and training, to identify where further training or correction is needed; and
4. Terminate the wrongful conduct; take remedial action or disciplinary action against the violator in a predefined procedure for violations of the policies and standards.

If these managerial duties are faithfully met, and are documented to the court, employer and supervisor liability for their employee's bad conduct can be significantly mitigated, if not eliminated. Employers and supervisors are in the best position to prevent wrongful employee conduct. Implementation of preventive management principles is not discretionary. Employers with notaries in their employ are squarely obligated to ensure all notarial services are done in strict compliance with law. An employer's ignorance of the notary law and of their notary's misconduct is not a defense. It is an admission of malfeasance.

R

"A notary betrays the public trust when he signs a certificate of acknowledgment with knowledge that the blanks will be filled in later or when he signs a completed certificate of acknowledgment but without requiring the personal appearance of the acknowledgers. Whether the certificate blanks are empty or full is not the significant fact. The key to the statutory safeguard is the integrity of the notary in the proper discharge of notarial duties by requiring the signatories to personally appear before him and acknowledge that they did in fact execute the document."
- Idaho Supreme Court, 1980.

Rationalization for Notarial Misconduct
See Pressure to Notarize; "We Have Always Done It This Way"

Reading the Signer's Document
See Completeness of the Signer's Document; Signer's Right to Confidentiality and Privacy in Notarizations

The content of a signer's document is impertinent to the notarization. Document content is entitled to privacy protection that the notary has no authority to breach. The notary has no need to read the signer's document in order to notarize properly, as the notarization pertains to their signature to the document only. Some notaries acquire the idea that they must read the document to ensure it is complete and to give the notary a basis by which she can determine the signer is competent to enter into such a transaction. Such conduct by a notary is improper and misguided. Such behavior is wrongful and potentially actionable by the signer if privacy is invaded and confidentialities are divulged. The notary's reading of the signer's document can only be justified if the signer, for whatever reason, directs the notary to do so. And, even then, the notary should exercise a high degree of caution before consenting to do so. If electing to do so, a notation of the matter should be noted in the notary journal.

Reasonable Basis for Refusal to Notarize

See Public Ministerial Officer; Public Official; Reasonable Request for a Notarization

A notary is under legal obligation to be willing to perform notarial services for persons making a reasonable and lawful request for such services. Inherent within this obligation of law is the notary's duty to discern notarial requests that are unreasonable or unlawful and to decline to serve in response thereto. An unlawful request for a notarization is by definition an unreasonable request.

An unlawful request for a notarization would be one that would cause the notary to violate state notary law or to create a notarial certificate containing a false statement. It would also be a request that would have the notary breach her duty to exercise reasonable care in any step of the notarial process.

It is irrefutably unreasonable, and unlawful, to request a notary to notarize for a signer who cannot be reasonably identified, who is unable to sign a document willingly and freely for the purposes stated within the document, and who refuses to sign a notary's journal. Likewise, it is unreasonable to coerce or pressure a notary to notarize where the notary feels uncomfortable or doubtful about the transaction. The notary is authorized to refuse to notarize any time she has reason to doubt the appropriateness of any aspect of the request or transaction.

The first step in every notarial service is to cause the document signer to sign the notary journal. This occurs before the notary is informed what the signer's request may be. Upon deciding the request is unreasonable, and after the notary declines to perform the notarization, the notary should record in the journal the basis on which she refused to notarize. As long as the basis for refusing to notarize is reasonable, the notary's conduct is meritorious and defensible.

Reasonable Care

See Common Sense; Duty of Care; Integrity of the Notary; Prudent Person

The standard by which a notary's official conduct is judged is by the standard of reasonable care. Reasonable care is the level of care an ordinary prudent person would exercise under the same or similar circumstances the notary is under. What is reasonable depends on a variety of considerations and circumstances. Reasonable care is also referred to as ordinary care.

The legal principle of reasonable care plays a key substantive role in law. It is a corner stone to an orderly, safe and responsible society. It is also the corner stone to notary law. The notary must exercise reasonable care in every aspect of the performance of every notarial act. This standard of law is not only an imposed duty but is also an essential protection for the notary against legal liability.

When notarizing a signature, the notary must verify a set of facts that will be certified in the notarial certificate. The notary must exercise reasonable care in verifying each fact, such as the document signer's true identity. If the notary has exercised reasonable care in verifying the signer's identity and it is later discovered that the signer was a skilled imposter or forger, the notary is not liable for having notarized a forged signature. As a matter of law, it is presumed that a reasonable, prudent person in the notary's position would have also accepted the signer's identification and notarized his signature.

The notary does not guarantee the facts asserted in the notarial certificate. Rather, the notary guarantees that all reasonable care and steps were taken to verify the truth of each fact. Reasonable care is the exercise of prudence and caution requiring individual judgment. Reasonable care is a subjective standard. The absolute verity of facts is often indeterminable. The finding of facts has to depend on a preponderance of the evidence. In performing notarial services, the notary must weigh the evidence supporting the asserted facts in the certificate. The standard of reasonable care raises human conduct to a higher level of rational and logical performance. It minimizes the adverse influences of caprice and bias on our interpretations and solutions to situations.

357

"If it is established that a notarized signature is forged, the burden of persuasion shifts to the notary to prove by a preponderance of the evidence that he exercised reasonable care in ascertaining the identity of the person; justification for shifting the burden of persuasion is the probability that the notary was negligent and the strong public policy of ensuring accuracy of notarial certifications.

The practices of other notaries are probative of whether procedures used by the notary in establishing identity are reasonable. But, mere conformity with custom is not necessarily to be equated with the exercise of reasonable care, since custom itself may not meet the "reasonable man" standard.

A notary is entitled to introduce testimony concerning his business habit in determining the identity of persons whose signatures he notarizes. Such testimony, however, must be admitted for the limited purpose of establishing the means by which the notary determined the identity of the person whose signature lie notarized on the specific occasion of the forgery as opposed to the purpose of establishing a characteristic for carefulness.

If testimony offered consists only of self-serving statements of the notary as to his business habit it is not admissible. A notary may, however, give non-self-serving testimony of his business habit which includes, for example, his recollection, refreshed by records kept, as to the means used to establish identity, or by testimony of witnesses who have observed his notarial practice, or by the introduction of his records."
    - *Meyers v. Meyers, 81 Wash. 2D 533, 503 P.2d 59.*

Reasonable Request for a Notarization
See Reasonable Basis for Refusal to Notarize

A person has a right under law to a notarization if the person's request is reasonable and lawful. The document signer has the burden of proof to establish to the notary's satisfaction that the request is reasonable and lawful.

The notary must properly identify the document signer. The signer must demonstrate that his signature to the document is made willingly and freely for the purposes stated within the document. The signer must be willing to sign the notary's journal and have a complete record made of the notarial act.

A notarial act is a governmental service provided by a public official appointed by the state, a notary public. The signer shall not be denied a notarial service on the basis of the signer's race, religion, national origin, gender, age or political persuasion. It shall be treated by the notary on a completely objective basis. The notary shall not limit notarial services to regular customers of the notary's employer as that constitutes an arbitrary classification of document signers and the basis for which reasonable requests for notarizations are refused. The notary's predisposition against notarizing for certain classes of people, such as non-customers is wrongful conduct and is an abuse of the notary's authority.

From "The Notary" (May 2001)

Reasonable and Lawful Requests for Notarizations

It seems to be a tough concept for many notaries, and especially for their employers, to understand that a notary is a notary "24-7." It causes even greater anxiety for some to accept that the notary is a notary to all the public and not just for a select few.

It is an established and widely recognized principal that notaries should be willing to perform notarizations upon all reasonable and lawful requests for such services. The problem is that many feel that it is unreasonable to be so reasonable. A number of state notary statutes provide that the notary shall be willing to perform notarizations for any person making a reasonable and lawful request, and/or proffering the requisite fee for such service. In states where such provisions are not found in statute, a bit more understanding is required as to how such an obligation applies to them as well. Many ask, "Where in the notary law does it say that a notary has to notarize for any person making a reasonable and lawful request?" Therein lies part of the problem. They ask the wrong question.

The better question is, "By what principle or reasoning is a notary obligated to notarize a signature upon a reasonable and lawful request?" This is more appropriate because it does not presuppose that all standards of conduct must be within the written text of law or case law authority. Many requirements of performance and conduct are inherent with the office held. No state in America, for example, requires by statute that the governor fly the flag of his state, and not the Bulgarian flag, over the state capitol. Some duties are so self-obvious that it is illogical to require their codification in statute. It is a slothful and directionless society that requires the minutiae of law to be codified in the great annals of law.

There is a clear and compelling series of reasons why a notary is obligated, even under law, to be willing to serve the public when the request for a notarization is reasonable and lawful. The notary is a public servant, holding a public ministerial office. It is an office of state government, wherein the notary is an agent of the state. The notarization is not a private transaction, or a service of the notary's employer. Under guarantees of the United States Constitution, every person has a right of equal access to the services of the government, and that includes the services of a notary public.

Employers of notaries in some industries will prohibit their notaries from performing notarizations for people who are not their "regular customers." Such policies raise legal questions that are too often disregarded.

The notarial service of the employee while on-the-job is not subject to the jurisdiction of the employer. It is a state governmental function. It is irrelevant whether the employer paid the fees for the employee to become a notary. The notary commission is not company property. The employer has no authority to place unreasonable restrictions on the public's access to the service of a notary in his employ.

The employer pays a modest price for the convenience of having notaries in the workplace. That is, the employer is subservient to the notary law. And, as a ministerial service of government, the notary's service shall be available to all who make a reasonable and lawful request for it.

360

In some workplaces, if the notary is expected to perform notarizations for every person coming off the street making a reasonable request, the employee-notary's value to the employer is marginalized as she rarely, if ever, accomplishes her daily work. In the anxiety of having to restrict the volume of notarizations performed for the public, employers often apply the wrong solution, one they have no authority to apply.

The key to any employer's dilemma is in the word, "reasonable." A notary is expected to perform notarizations when the request for it is reasonable and lawful.

When is a request for a notarization unreasonable? There are a number of well-recognized and logical criteria the notary and the employer can invoke. For example, if the notary is so very busy with duties of her employment, it is unreasonable for a person to demand that she drop what she is doing and perform a notarization. It is unreasonable for any person to demand a notarization from a notary. It is uncivil and spoiled behavior. If by experience the notary's workload becomes most critical and stressful after 2:00 pm each day, it is reasonable to restrict the time of day notarial services are available. A sign can be posted informing the public that no notarial services can be performed after 2:00 pm. The same may be said if the notary's workload is especially critical on Fridays.

Employers indeed pay a price to have the convenience of having a notary in-house. However, the burden of providing the notarial service to the public at large shall not be so great that it constitutes an undue financial burden to the employer. The government can no sooner confiscate the employer's inventory without just compensation than require the employer to sacrifice a paid employee to the service of the government without compensation for that employee's pay. It is reasonable and essential to strike a balance between the competing interests.

In any workplace notaries are found, the employer's notary policy should be one that fosters public service with an attitude of intent to serve the public. However, where justifiable limitations must be imposed on public access to the notary, the employer may arguably limit notarial services to only those transactions that are related to the business of the employer during a reasonable time frame.

Reasonableness
See Reasonable Care

Reciprocity
See Multiple Notary Commissions

Recognition of the Notary's Authority
See Full Faith and Credit Clause

The authority of every notary in every state is required to be recognized equally in all fifty states. That is, a notary holds a governmental office, performing a governmental duty. As long as the notary performs her statutory duties in compliance with the notary laws of her state, her notarizations on documents will be recognized and honored in every state. Under provisions of international treaty, her notarization will also be recognized as valid in most foreign nations as well.

It is commonly said that a notary's authority is recognized worldwide. This in no way implies a notary may notarize outside her jurisdiction. The state statutes specifically define the notary's jurisdiction. The phrase simply means the notarization in question will be recognized as valid because it was performed by a person duly authorized by the state to perform it.

Recordation of Notarizations
See Notary Journal; Notary's Duty to Maintain Journal Records

Registered Voter Requirement to Qualify as a Notary
See Equal Protection; Qualifications for Appointment as a Notary Public; Right to Serve as a Notary

A few states require in their statutes that to become a notary an applicant must be a registered voter. The United States Supreme Court has struck down such a requirement as unconstitutional. Such a requirement breaches several constitutionally guaranteed protections against governmental abridgment of the public's civil liberties.

While the voter registration requirement remains in statute for a few states, it is enforced in only one or two of them, and half-heartedly at best.

Renewal of Notary Commission

See Qualifications for Appointment to the Office of Notary Public; Right to Serve as a Notary

Notaries in every state except Louisiana, serve for a fixed term of years, upon the end of which the commission expires. Notaries of Louisiana are appointed to terms for life.

A notary's commission is never automatically renewed. The laws of each state require the notary to apply for a new commission upon the expiration of the old. Most states offer the courtesy of providing the notary a notice of pending expiration and the application for re-appointment.

The criteria for renewing a notary commission will vary among the states. In most states, the process is perfunctory, while in others it is the same as if the person were applying to be appointed a notary for the first time, complete with a required passing score on an examination.

Critics of the notarial commissioning process argue that it is too easy to become a notary. Moreover, they point out that in many states persons who have demonstrated their notarial incompetence and indifference over the course of their term of commission are not culled out, but are renewed along with the batch of renewals of the moment. Too often, scofflaw notaries are rewarded for their abuse of authority through near-automatic renewal of their commissions. The concerns raised by observers of the process merit thoughtful review by state notary officials. Their solutions may be elusive as they are often entangled in political and budgetary conflicts.

Representative Capacity of the Document Signer

See Attorney-in-fact; Authority of the Document Signer; Power of Attorney; Signer's Authority to Sign

It is highly regular and common for persons to sign transactions in a representative capacity on behalf of another person or persons, and to have their signature notarized. However, notaries of all states are authorized to notarize such signatures made in a representative capacity, but grant no authorization to the notary to certify the signer's representative capacity. In other words, the notary is authorized only to verify the signer's identity, but not to certify the signer's authority to sign on behalf of other persons.

Reputation for Integrity
See Credible Witness; Qualifications for Appointment as a Notary Public

The performance of notarial duties is heavily dependent on the integrity of the individuals involved, including the notary, the document signer, and pertinent witnesses. The one witness the notary relies heavily on is the credible witness for the purpose of verifying the identity of a document signer.

The credible witness must be a person the notary knows personally to the extent that the notary knows the witness has a reputation for integrity. A person's reputation for integrity is a precious commodity, one that can shatter easily.

One's reputation for integrity means that he is thought of by his associates as one who does not have a proclivity to deceive, to mislead or misrepresent the truth. It must be a reputation that is held not merely by his family members, but also by those who interact with him in business or employment settings where the opportunity to deceive is present. The witness must be recognized as one who adheres to the truth and does not embrace or sympathize with falsehoods or deceit.

It is commonly understood that some individuals may portray an image of high ethical standards and unimpeachable integrity, while simultaneously leading a second life of fraud and criminality. The assessment of a person's apparent integrity is not perfect or foolproof. Instead, it is based on reasonable care and common sense. Liability cannot impute to the notary for justifiably determining a credible witness had a reputation for integrity when in fact he was a master deceiver with a clever demeanor.

Request For Notarization

See Reasonable Request for a Notarization

Residency Requirements
See Qualifications for Appointment to the Office of Notary Public

Every state by law establishes minimum qualifications to serve as a notary. Residency within the commissioning state always contemplates legal residency within that state. In a number of regions of the country, neighboring states will grant non-residents notary commissions in their state if the non-resident is employed in, or does business in, the state.

Some states specify a minimum number of days a person must reside within a state in order to meet a residency requirement. Such minimum terms will vary for notary commissions, university tuition rates for resident students, or for issuance of a driver's license. As long as the minimum term of time for residency is reasonable for its intended purpose, it is usually defensible. However, the case law is ample regarding the unlawful use of minimum residency requirements, particularly in the registration of voters. The prevailing view is that residency is measured not by calendar days, but by the person's intent to reside within the state, to be a voter in the state's elections.

When it comes to qualifying persons to serve as notaries, the states must view minimum residency requirements with caution. For example, a requirement of thirty-day residency as a condition precedent to receiving a notary commission could adversely affect a new resident's employment opportunity if the job description requires a notary commission. The state must be able to provide a reasonable justification for even marginal minimum residency requirements, one that protects the interest of the public and the security of the notarial program of the state.

One might argue that minimum residency is essential in order to prevent transients from obtaining notary commissions. Such an objective is discriminatory on its face, raising a large serving of legal arguments and liabilities. The key flaw in such thinking is that it matters not whether an applicant for a notary commission will remain within the state four years or four days. When a notary takes up residency in another state, the commission of that notary is automatically void, and if desired, the person will have to apply for a new commission for the new state in which she resides.

"Residing at _____"

See Address of the Notary; Certificate of Notarization; Component Parts of the Notarial Certificate

In many states the notary is required by statute to indicate the county in which the notary is commissioned or resides on the notarial certificate. This information often appears in the notary seal, or is written below or near the notary's signature on the certificate.

Perhaps the primary reason for disclosing the notary's county of residence or commissioning is for identification of court jurisdiction over matters involving the notary, and for service of process on the notary. The notary and the notarial certificates executed by the notary are official acts performed under authority of the state. To facilitate the resolution of disputes or the findings of fact, it is all together appropriate for the notary to disclose the county in which they reside or are commissioned.

It is common for preprinted notarial certificates to provide a labeled space for the notary to write her county of residence. It is redundant for it to be written in the space provided if it appears in the notary's seal impression. A notary, in such cases, is justified in indicating the information appearing in the seal and not to write the county name.

Occasionally, a preprinted notarial certificate will indicate in type the notary's county of residence, when in fact it is the incorrect county. If the notary's county name appears in the seal impression, she is entitled to line out the entire preprinted reference. If it is not in the notary's seal and is information required to appear in the notarization, the notary may line out the incorrect county name and write the correct name a just above it.

Resigning as a Notary

A notarial commission is voluntarily sought by the individual. Likewise, a notary always has the legal right to resign the commission at will. Most states prescribe in their statutes procedures for resigning a commission. In all cases, the notary must give written notice of their resignation to the governmental authority that commissioned them. One cannot resign from a position without notice to the proper authorities.

Notaries that resign their commissions are required either by their state statutes or by the standard of reasonable care to properly dispose of their notary seal. A number of states require the notary to submit their seal to a state or local government agency upon resignation. The government, in turn, destroys the seal. A number of states impose no required procedures for disposing of a notary seal. Conventional wisdom for notaries in those states suggests that the notary render their seal unusable. If the seal is a metal crimping device, the embossing plates can be removed from the crimper, be bent and discarded. The typeface on rubber ink-stamp seals can be removed from the stamp and be cut with scissors and discarded.

While notaries in every state should maintain a notary journal, states that require by statute journal record-keeping often require the notary to submit the journal to the government upon resignation from office.

Respondeat Superior
See Agent; Employer Liability for Notarizations; Employer's Legal Duty to the Notary; Jointly Liable; Quiet Acquiescence; Severally Liable; Vicarious Liability

This important and long-standing doctrine of law means, "let the superior respond." It is used for requiring the principal or master to be answerable for the acts of his agents or servants.

In contemporary parlance, respondeat superior is a doctrine of law that requires the employer to answer for the actions of his employees, of those who act in his behalf. This maxim of the common law forms the basis of the law of agency (as in the laws of employer and employee) and is founded on the principle that a duty rests on all persons, in the management of their own affairs, whether by themselves or by their agents or servants, so to conduct them as not to injure another, and that if he does so, and another is thereby injured, he shall answer for the damages.

There are significant policy reasons why this doctrine is so prominent in our system of law. The employer is in the best position to prevent harm to others caused by those who work for him. Before he permits his employees to work with the public, the employer is going to ensure that the employee is trained and competent in his duties. Inherently within every employee's duties is the duty not to behave in any manner that would foreseeably cause harm to others. The employer is not permitted to raise in his defense that he did not direct his employee to engage in the harmful conduct, but that the employee chose to engage in such conduct on his own initiative. The employer cannot assert that the wrongful conduct of the employee was outside the scope of his employment and therefore exculpates the employer from liability. The employer cannot defend himself by arguing he did not know the employee was engaged in wrongful conduct while on the job. It is for these principles, as an example, that a customer burned by scalding hot coffee at McDonald's can successfully hold the McDonald's Corporation liable for damages caused by its employees.

The notary, while on the job, exposes her employer to the risk of legal liability for all damages caused by her official misconduct, because the employer is answerable as her superior. It is difficult to understand why skilled, knowledgeable business executives at all levels will conduct their business duties with utmost care and skill, while ignoring the legal ramifications of the notarial services performed under their stewardship.

Prevention is the surest antidote to liability under respondeat superior. It comes through thorough training and competent supervision of employees. It is the employer's diligent oversight of the notary, both understanding the key principles of notary law and both committed to its compliance at all times. It is the employer's creation and nurturing of a work environment of high ethical conduct and integrity.

Restricted Sales of Notary Seals
See Seal of the Notary Public

The notary's seal is the official emblem of the notary's authority granted by the state to perform notarial services. Remarkably, such seals are readily available for retail sale to anybody in most states. Their production and sale is utterly unrestricted in only a few states. Notary seals, new and old, can even be purchased on the Internet. The state and the public have reason to expect notary seals to be restricted to commissioned notaries only. The image and credibility of the notary seal can be jeopardized if it is treated like an ordinary consumer product.

The states that restrict the manufacture and sale of a notary seals are remarkably effective in their methods. Generally, statutes were enacted in those states prohibiting the manufacture of a notary seal for any person until after the person has first provided the vendor a state-issued certificate or copy of the person's notary commission upon ordering the seal. Reputable notary seal vendors were quick to comply in those states and have demonstrated that modest restrictions on the availability of notary seals have not been unduly burdensome.

Anecdotal histories evidence the problem of unrestricted notary seal purchases is more serious than many would think. In recent years, many automobile dealerships in certain western and southern states customarily issued their new sales representatives new notary seals so they could notarize buyer and seller signatures on the spot to vehicle titles. Incredibly, none of the sales force were commissioned notaries, and each unauthorized notarization they performed carried criminal liability.

A large regional bank in the upper Midwest not long ago purchased notary seals for hundreds of their bank employees in order to better serve their customers. The employees were instructed when given their seals to immediately apply for their notary commissions from their respective states. Most never did, wrongly believing that all it took to become a notary was to own a seal.

Some states tightly regulate the possession of notary seals whereby the notary is limited to ownership of one seal at a time, or that duplicate seals can only be obtained with a separate certificate of authorization from the state.

Retention of the Notary Journal
See Notary's Duty to Maintain Journal Records

Revocation of a Notarial Commission
See Due Process of Law in Sanctioning a Notary Public; Government Regulation of Notaries

A notary's commission may be revoked only by the state official authorized to commission notaries, and must be done in accordance with statutory procedures, if provided. All notaries are entitled to constitutionally protected rights to due process. At the least, the notary must be given notice of the state's intent to revoke the commission, stating the grounds therefore and inform the notary of the right to answer the complaint and to provide a defense against the allegations. A number of state statutes even provide for appeals of notarial revocations, and the procedures therefore.

The state has no authority to summarily revoke a notarial commission without substantive grounds. Whether provided by statute or not, the grounds must include a charge that the notary committed official misconduct in some manner.

The revocation of a notarial commission is no small matter for most notaries. Most notaries obtain their commissions in connection with their employment. For many, they are disqualified from their employment if they cannot obtain a notary commission. Persons who are dependent on their notary commissions for employment security have a substantial cause of action against the state if their notary commission is revoked without due process of law.

Right to Serve as a Notary
See Commissioning Process; Qualifications for Appointment to the Office of Notary Public

Service as a notary is a satisfying and rewarding experience. It is genuine service to the community, and is a service of great value. The office of notary public is a public office, and shall, as a matter of law, be conferred upon any eligible person seeking a notarial commission. Every eligible person has a legal right to be appointed as a notary. The only caveat is that the person meets statutory requirements for eligibility.

No state is constitutionally permitted to arbitrarily "pick and choose" whom they appoint as notaries. The application and approval process shall be open to all, without prejudice or bias. There can be no appearance of preferential treatment of any group of individuals who apply to be notaries. The application forms and review must strictly conform to the

370

provisions of state statute and be administered objectively. In the event the application process requests information that exceeds the requirements of the state's enabling law, it must not create any differentiation between groups of people or an advantage or preferential treatment for one group over others. For example, it is wrongful for a state to ask the notary applicant how many years of education the applicant has received, or the applicant's marital status. Arguably, it is also wrongful for a state to pry into whether the applicant has ever held a professional license, such as a medical license or CPA license in any state and against which disciplinary action was taken. Such inquiry is "ultra vires" (outside the scope of authority) to the state's notarial qualifications and carries the potential for prejudicial treatment of the applicant.

One's right to serve as a notary public, if qualified, cannot be abridged by the application process. The applications in this context should facilitate the commissioning of qualified applicants. It should not be a device of excessive authority.

From "The Notary" (November 1997)

You Have a Constitutional Right to be a Notary

The office of notary public is a highly democratic office, as it is an office of the people. (The word "democratic" used here means "relating to the broad masses of the people.") Unlike anywhere else on earth, the notary in America is an ordinary person of integrity and education who serves the public on behalf of the state that has appointed her.

Since 1984, there has been a dramatic nationwide shift in the law on who may serve as a notary. Over the years, states imposed a wide range of requirements on notary applicants, a number of which were impermissible due to Constitutional limitations. The application usually requires the applicant to take an oath of office and to file a notary surety bond. Other commonly imposed criteria require applicants to be at least 18 years of age and to be able to read and write the English language.

Historically, most states required applicants to be citizens of the United States and residents of the state and/or county in which appointment is sought. The requirement that notaries be U.S. Citizens was struck down by the U.S. Supreme Court in 1984 in Bernal v. Fainter (467 U.S. 216). A Mexican native and longtime resident of Texas applied to become a Texas notary. Texas denied his application solely because he was not a United States Citizen as required by Texas statute. In reversing the Court of Appeals the U.S. Supreme Court used a strict scrutiny test since the constitutional question was one of alienage. Since there was no relation "to the achievement of any valid state interest" the statutory limitation was declared an unconstitutional restriction under the Equal Protection clause of the Fourteenth Amendment.

Any statute or administrative rule restricting the office of notary public to citizens of the United States cannot stand, unless it advances a compelling state interest by the least restrictive means available. To the extent that a state determines that the notary must be competent in the English language and in the customs of the country in order to qualify for notarial appointment, the equal protection clause requires the state to do so in a manner that is confined to that specific objective.

States have authority to impose citizenship requirements on high state positions, which are at the heart of representative government and its formulation and execution of policy. The position of notary public is ministerial in nature. It does not involve discretionary decision-making or execution of policy. Imposing citizenship requirements on notaries is not supported by, or related in any way, to the achievement of a valid state objective.

A few states require notary applicants to be registered voters within the county in which they reside as a condition to appointment. A requirement of voter registration as a condition to notarial appointment is clearly an unconstitutional infringement on the applicant's equal protection rights. Voter registration requires U.S. Citizenship and has no relevance to the office and functions of the notary public.

There are presently a number of states that require by statute that a notary be a U. S. citizen. A few go further by requiring the notary to be a registered voter, which exceeds the pre-requisite of U.S. citizenship.

In a 1973 Connecticut case, the U.S. Supreme Court took up the question of required U.S. Citizenship as a condition for admission to the Connecticut Bar. The Court held the requirement invalid and set forth a standard for review of citizenship requirements. The state needs to justify its classification, such as U.S. Citizenship, by showing some rational relationship between the interest sought to be protected and the limiting classification.

A U.S. Citizenship requirement is arguably defensible for state government positions that are elective or are important nonelective executive, legislative and judicial positions. The requirement may also stand for positions that participate directly in the formulation, execution or review of broad public policy that goes to the heart of representative government. The office of notary public is genuinely an office of the people, available to all who wish to serve and meet reasonable minimum requirements.

S

"But it by no means follows that the certificate is a proper one if the execution of the instrument is not the free act and deed of the maker thereof to the knowledge of the notary and, we are of the opinion that, a certificate made where the notary knows that the instrument is not the free act and deed of the marker, is false and its making is a violation of his official duty. We think it is a clear breach of a

notary's official duties to so certify under such circumstances."
- *State ex. rel. Nelson v. Hammett 203 S.W.2d 115.*

Safeguard the Notary Seal

See Forgery; Fraud; Reasonable Care; Seal of the Notary Public; Unauthorized Use of a Notary Seal

The only person authorized to use a notary's seal is the notary to whom it is issued. The unauthorized use of a notary's seal is a serious criminal violation for which there is no valid defense. The notary is not liable for the unauthorized use of the seal, as long as the notary takes reasonable care not to leave the seal out in the open, constituting a temptation for the unscrupulous.

The notary is under a duty of care to safeguard the seal from unauthorized use. The standard of care will vary for each notary according to the ethical tone of the workplace, and the foreseeability that others might use the seal. In extreme cases, the seal may have to be taken home each night or locked in a cabinet or drawer. In most cases, storage of the seal in a closed drawer or cabinet should be sufficient.

Notaries in California are required by statute to keep the notary seal under lock and key when not in use. Violation of the requirement is prosecutable as a felony crime.

In the safeguarding of the notary seal, the notary should apply common sense and sound judgment according to the circumstances. It is also helpful if the notary is consistent in protecting the seal, as routine patterns of conduct are probative of the notary's diligence, giving rise to benefits of doubt when issues arise.

Any time a notary's seal is lost or stolen, the notary is under obligation to promptly notify the state notary officials of the loss or theft. Such notice must be in writing. In some states, the process requires the notary to obtain a new certificate authorizing the purchase of a seal. In most states, the seal may be replaced at any time without documentation.

Upon discovery of the seal's loss or disappearance, the notary ought to make a note in the notary journal of the event, thereby creating a record that any notarizations showing up after the seal's loss will be prima facially false. When replacing the seal, it may be worth considering modifying the seal in a non-substantive way so as to differentiate the replacement from the original. For example, add or omit a middle initial.

If the notary has demonstrated a pattern of reasonable care in safeguarding the seal from unauthorized use or theft, the notary will not be liable for negligence and the damages caused by the wrongful use of the seal.

Satisfactory Evidence
See Signer Identification

Most notary statutes provide that the notary must either personally know the document signer, or rely on satisfactory evidence of the signer's true identity. The statutes usually specify that satisfactory evidence will either be the oath or affirmation of a credible witness personally known by the notary, or be some manner of valid ID cards or papers.

Because the evidence the notary must rely upon must be sufficient to cause the notary to conclude the signer is who he claims to be, it must be substantively sufficient. The term, satisfactory evidence, is a term of law that refers to that amount of proof that ordinarily satisfies an unprejudiced mind. Satisfactory evidence is that evidence which establishes the probability of its truth.

The notary holds a public trust to exercise common sense, prudence and diligence in deciding the satisfactory quality of the evidence establishing the document signer's true identity. It requires the notary's subjective assessment of all the facts and circumstantial context pertaining to the notarial service and the document signer. If the notary draws the same conclusion about the signer's proof of identity that any reasonable person in the same circumstance would draw, the notary has fulfilled the requisite duty of care.

Scilicet

See Component Parts of the Notarial Certificate; S.S.; Venue

For centuries the notarial certificate has borne the abbreviation, "S.S." at the top where the location of the notarization was performed. For generations, most have assumed it stands for "signed and seal," or "signed under seal," or "signature sealed." None of these are correct. In contemporary the less informed will errantly write the signer's or notary's social security number adjacent the S.S.

The S.S. is the abbreviation of the Latin word, "scilicet," meaning, "to wit" or "that is to say." In notarial services, the only appearance of the S.S. is in the venue portion of the certificate. The S.S. is not required for the certificate to be valid. It is merely a decorative adornment of no substantive value to the notarization. Because of the misunderstanding and confusion associated with it, the notary is well justified in excluding the S.S. from all notarial certificates.

From "The Notary" (March 1999)

Notarial Venue: It's Where You Are When You Notarize (not where you live)!

For centuries, the notarial certificate has begun with a statement of venue. The term, venue, is deeply rooted in law as a written disclosure of the location where a transaction of law took place. Venue is necessary for two key reasons: to show that the notary acted in a jurisdiction in which she is authorized to act and to show which county has legal jurisdiction over the notarial act in the event it is contested.

In nearly every state, a notary is authorized to perform notarial services in every county of the state. (Louisiana has parishes rather than counties and the notary's jurisdiction is restricted to a group of parishes. Alaska also has no counties, but is divided into judicial districts and boroughs. However, Alaska notaries may notarize in any part of that huge state.)

In a few states notaries were granted statewide jurisdiction only within the past decade. At first, notaries could opt for authority to serve in their county of residence only, or they could apply for statewide jurisdiction. In that case, they were directed to indicate in the venue statement of their notarizations that they were a "notary at large." Although that small detail served a useful, albeit temporary, benefit it was not consistent with the rules of law.

The notarial statement of venue is significant and not to be trifled with. The notarial act has profound legal weight. It has enforceability. It constitutes the notary's proclamation that she is acting in a county in which she has legal authority to act. It also constitutes public notice that the courts in the county in which the notarial act occurred have jurisdiction over that notarial act.

When a legal dispute requires adjudication in a court, the party filing the lawsuit (the plaintiff) must bring the action in a court that has jurisdiction over the matter. A court in the county in which the plaintiff resides will have jurisdiction over the case, as will the court in the county where the defendant (possibly the notary) resides. The court in the county in which the notarial act occurred may also have jurisdiction over the case.

Finding a court having jurisdiction over a case can be a sticky issue with significant economic implications. For example, the plaintiff may reside in St. Louis, Missouri, the defendant resides in Independence, Missouri, and the notarization was made in Springfield, Missouri. These cities are not close. It could be expensive to bring suit in Independence or in Springfield because of the travel costs for all, including witnesses. If the suit is brought anyplace but where the notarization occurred, the costs of producing the evidence for the case can go sky-high. Then, lawyers love to play the "change of venue" game because they may have favorite judges or county courts to work in the plaintiff's or defendant's favor.

Very often, the venue statement is pre-printed for the notary - which is often incorrect. It may declare, "State of New York, County of Buffalo," but you are in Allegheny County, Pennsylvania. The solution is easy. Cross out "New York" and write in "Pennsylvania." Cross out "Buffalo" and write in "Allegheny."

When you write the venue of your notarization, you are disclosing significant information for purposes of law. It must be correct. People are depending on its accuracy.

Scope of the Notary's Liability
See Duty of Care; Liability; Proximate Cause

The notary is personally liable for all damages proximately caused by her official misconduct and negligence. There is no limit to the amount of damages for which the notary could be liable. The scope of the notary's liability is unlimited.

For most notaries, the potential for legal liability can be terrifying. The prudent and informed notary need not fear. The most effective preventative against a notary's liability is strict obedience to the laws and principles of correct notarial procedures. Absolute integrity is the foundation to a notary's avoidance of liability. In other words, the notary must never sign a notarial certificate she does not fully understand and cannot guarantee that every word thereof is true.

The notary's scope of liability is limited to only those damages proximately caused by the notary's misconduct. Furthermore, the victim of a wrongful notarization has a duty to mitigate damages upon discovery of the flawed notarization. No person is entitled to remain silent when discovering a defective notarization and use it to his benefit or gain with anticipation of remuneration and relief for damages through a judgment in court.

By the same token, the notary has an absolute duty, when she learns the notarization is defective, to inform all interested parties thereof and to make every effort to take remedial steps.

Seal Is the Exclusive Property of the Notary
See Seal of the Notary Public

378

The notary seal is the exclusive property of the notary. No person is authorized to use the notary's seal under any circumstance. The wrongful use of a notary's seal constitutes a criminal violation of law.

Employers who pay the cost for the purchase of the notary's seal are under the incorrect impression they own the notary's seal, that it is company property. It is irrelevant who paid the cost of purchasing the notary's seal. The seal shall be issued only to duly commissioned notaries. In some states, the notary must provide documentation of commission by the state to the vendor of the seal in order to purchase the seal. In every state it is unlawful for any person to purchase a notary seal if they are not a commissioned notary. The seal is manufactured and issued to the commissioned notary and shall not be under the control or dominion of any other person.

Occasionally an employer will demand the notary leave the seal with the employer upon the notary's discontinuation of employment. The notary has no authority to abandon the seal with the employer, and the employer comes into the unlawful possession of the seal.

A notary under pressure to yield possession of the seal to the employer has a legal cause of action against the employer. The employer has no right to the seal even though it was paid for with company fluids. The notary seal is not the same as office equipment. It is a tool of law, the ownership and use of which is controlled by state law. The notary seal is the exclusive property of the notary.

Seal Lost or Stolen
See Safeguard the Notary Seal

Seal of the Notary Public
See Seal is the Exclusive Property of the Notary

For centuries, all notarizations worldwide were distinguished by the placement of the seal of the notary on the notarization. Historically, the seal has been an ornate impression in wax that is attached to the document directly or by ribbon. In contemporary times, the notary seal has become an impression crimped or embossed on the paper bearing the notarial certificate. More recently, a number of states have authorized their notaries to affix a notary seal by ink-stamp impression. In all forms, the notary seal is an emblem of the notary's legal authority. It is created for a notary under authority of law.

The majority of states require the notarial certificate to include a notary seal, while fourteen states make the use of a seal optional. A number of states have banned the use of the embossed seal in favor of the ink-stamp seal. The impetus for the increasing use of ink-stamp seals is that most documents requiring notarizations will eventually be archived by digitized image, by microfilm, or will be sent by facsimile transmission. The ink-stamp seal is requisite to the facilitation of document management by new technologies.

From "The Notary" (September 1998)

The Notary Seal
a Symbol of Your Legal Authority

The notary seal is representative of the notary's legal authority. It is universally familiar to the public, and it is highly respected. When a notary seal appears on a document, it sends a message that the document is dependable and trustworthy. People relying on the document take comfort in the notarization bearing the seal.

The reason a notary seal carries so much credibility and trust is due to its prestigious history and to the definition of the word itself. A "seal" is something that "confirms, ratifies, or makes certain and secure." The fifty states bear and display their respective "great seals" (such as the Great Seal of the State of Oregon) in official state ceremonies and functions. Our federal republic is represented by a great seal. The office of the President possesses an official seal known as the "Seal of the President of the United States."

Seals are used in notarizations to give notice to the world that the notary standing behind the notarial wording has acted with legal authority and is guarantor of the notarial certificate itself. Notary seals come in two forms: the traditional crimper (embosser) and, in the form of rubber ink stamp. The laws of each state dictate their selection and use. Whether you use an embosser or a stamp, they are both "notary seals." Half of the states permit the notary a choice of whether to use an embosser or an ink stamp for the seal.

When a state notary statute mandates that a notary seal must be used in the notarization, its use is not discretionary. When the statute mandates which type to use, the notary has no choice as well. If the notarization lacks a required notarial seal, the notarization is automatically incomplete and likely unenforceable. If the notary decides to use an ink stamp rather than an embosser as required by law, the notarization is again viewed incomplete and unenforceable.

In many corners of American society today, people are infatuated with the crimped notary seal affixed to a page by embosser. They love the tactile feel and look. It seems "more official." Old habits die hard. If you are a notary in one of the ten states that require the use of the ink stamp seal, you may still affix a crimped notary seal to the notarial certificate in addition to the required ink- stamp seal. By law, the ink-stamp seal will "control" and the crimped seal will be mere surplusage.

When a seal is required in a notarization, it constitutes an equivalent to the "Seal of Authority." It locks up the notarial wording with your official signature into a nice, tight impenetrable "package." Unlike the protective seal on a bottle of aspirin, the notary seal actually declares wording. The crimped wording is difficult to read, while the ink stamped seal is highly legible. In either case, logic would tell us that the notary seal should be affixed in a manner that renders it clear and legible so it can be read.

Notaries using the embosser often find themselves having to darken the raised crimped impression on the notarial certificate so it can be read, copied or microfilmed. That is an ironic twist on technology in our age of computers and the exploration of deep outer space.

State notary law commonly mandates the clear and legible placement of the seal on a certificate where a seal is required. In these states, the seal must not be smeared. No portion of it should be missing. The seal cannot be affixed over text, written material or signatures.

The Utah statute reads: "The seal impression shall be affixed near the notary's official signature on a notarial certificate and shall include a sharp, legible, and photographically reproducible ink impression of the notarial seal..." (UCA 46-1-13).

Non-compliance with the statutory requirement for clarity of the seal may be grounds for holding the notarization incomplete or unenforceable. Besides, logic dictates that clarity and legibility of the notary seal are inherently appropriate in every instance a seal is used regardless of your state's laws.

3 Things a Notary Must Never Do With the Notary Seal

1. *Never permit your notary seal to be pre-printed onto forms or certificates. Your seal must be affixed originally each time you notarize.*
2. *Never affix your seal to any paper without there first being notarial certificate wording thereon, or it is considered an abuse of your notarial authority. The notarial seal without your wording and signature is never a valid notarization; it is nothing.*
3. *Never leave your notary seal out in the open while it is not in use. Secure it away in a drawer or other safe place. If anyone uses your seal for any reason, they commit a serious criminal act for which you are not criminally liable. Yet, it is your name on the seal and it is highly reckless not to keep it safe and out of the realm of temptation.*

Six Common Questions Concerning Notary Seals

1. *Is it proper to affix the notary seal on the notary's signature?*

In ages past, before modem printing and document copying technology were available, it was customary for the notary to squeeze the embossed seal onto the notary's signature. It gave the transaction an impressive look of dignity and importance. In the earlier centuries when gold foil or wax was used, the seal was off to the side of the notary's signature. In no U.S. state today is it required or appropriate for the notary to affix the seal on their signature. It renders the seal illegible, obscures the signature and proves nothing.

2. *Does the seal belong in a particular place on the certificate?*

The notary seal can be affixed anyplace on the notarial certificate in proximity to the notary's signature. It can be placed to the left, right, above or below the notary's signature. The key is to affix it clearly, legibly and completely wherever it will fit.

3. *Is there a problem if the embossed seal appears right side up on the left side of the page and upside-down on the right side of the page?*

This is not a problem. The embosser plates in the "hand gripper" of the embosser are fixed in place. As the embosser moves along the margins of the page, the image of the embosser plates will turn correspondingly. Again, the only thing to be concerned with is whether the seal reads legibly and clearly, even if it is upside-down.

4. *What if the document provides insufficient space for the clear and legible placement of the notary seal?*

This is one of the most vexing problems America's notaries face: not enough room for the seal. There are important concerns here. First, the document signer often expects you to use the notarial certificate that has been provided on their document, even if it is flawed. Second, the document may be a form designed and provided by the government and there is nothing scarier than incurring the wrath of government for having altered an official government form. In light of these two concerns, the notary must first hearken to the directive of the state notary law.

Forms do not supersede state statute. If the form fails to provide for the required clear and legible notary seal, the notary must either alter the form or use a notarial certificate of her own making. A new notarial certificate can be made on the reverse side of the document or on an attachment. This should be done only after the notary has diplomatically explained to the signer why the change had to be made.

5. *What should I do if I inadvertently failed to affix a seal to a notarization?*

The notary seal can be affixed any time after the signer has appeared before the notary and either acknowledged their signature (for an acknowledgment) or signed the document under oath (for a jurat). Affixing the notary seal is not the act of notarizing. It is part of the paper work after the main event has occurred. It can be affixed hours or even a few days after the fact. Of course, it is not something to be procrastinated. The notarial act is never complete or enforceable without the required notary seal.

6. *What should I do if my seal-stamp smears or is not affixed in its entirety?*

This is a very common concern. Mistakes will happen. It seems the best advice is to affix the stamp seal again where room permits. If there is insufficient room, apologize to your signer and start over with a new certificate on the backside of the document or on an attachment. Remember: clarity, legibility and completeness is the standard by which we are judged when using our notary seals. Make sure your work surface is clean and clear so it is perfectly flat when using an ink stamp seal. When using an embosser, squeeze hard

Seal Ring
See History of the Notary Seal; Signet Ring

Secretary of State
See Commissioning Process

In all but a few states, notaries are appointed by the Secretary of State, or by the Governor through the Secretary of State. It can generally be said for these states that the Secretary of State is the state's senior notary official.

It is through the Secretary of State that the authority to perform notarial services passes to the public.

The Secretary of State must treat all applicants to become notaries equally and in compliance with state law. The application and review process must be in accordance to established rules and procedures, and never an ad hoc or arbitrary process.

Secretaries of State hold many important responsibilities in addition to the appointment of notaries. For some, notary management is one of many concerns for the office of Secretary of State, while in many states it is an important program to which great interest is attached. In most states, the office of Secretary of State appoints an official to oversee the notary commission program, and is delegated all the requisite authority to administer the program in accordance with the state notary laws. This person's title is often called the "notary clerk" or "notary administrator."

Selecting Notarial Certificates

See Acknowledgment Notarization; Certificate of Notarization; Copy Certification; Jurat Notarization; Notarial Certificate; Unauthorized Practice of Law by Notaries

One of the more frequently argued issues in notary law concerns the notary's authority to select notarial certificates. The competing schools of thought are that the selection of a notarial certificate is a form of legal advice and therefore constitutes an unauthorized practice of law. The other view is that the notary is inherently under a legal duty to select a notarial certificate, when necessary, and that such a decision does not constitute a form of legal advice.

Some believe a notary is not authorized or "qualified" to select notarial wording for a customer's transaction. Such dogma meets the definition of superstition.

A superstition is a belief or practice resulting from ignorance, from fear of the unknown, or from a "false conception of causation." Superstition is also a "notion maintained despite evidence to the contrary."

The key element in every superstition is falsehood. Teachings, instructions and doctrines based in superstition are damaging, counterproductive and should be avoided. However, we can't avoid that which we fail to identify.

The assertion that a notary may not select notarial wording is not based in fact or reason. It is contrary to the evidence. Some go as far as to argue that a notary may not even write or correct errors in the notarial wording on the customer's transaction. The justification most commonly given is that the selection and preparation of a notarial certificate constitutes the "unauthorized practice of law."

This is a form of superstition. It is based on confusion about the law. It is believed out of fear of what some do not understand about the law. Followers tend to incorrectly think that violation of this rule can result in legal liability. Most of all, they maintain this notion in spite of the facts to the contrary.

Is a notary authorized and qualified to select and prepare or correct a notarial certificate for a transaction? Yes.

The argument that a notary may not select, write or correct a notarial certificate is mostly based on the fear that perhaps the notary is engaging in the unauthorized practice of law. There is no case authority holding that a notary is unauthorized to select and prepare notarial certificates. Moreover, there are no state statutes prohibiting such a service by a notary. The courts tend to give generous deference to notaries in this matter.

> *"The general policy of the law is to construe notarial acknowledgment certificates liberally and to uphold them if they substantially comply with the statutory requirements as to form and content, even if they contain minor errors or omissions. Likewise, words or phrases that appear in the certificate in excess of what is required by the statutory form are mere surplusages."*
> - Larson v. Elsner, 93 Minn. 303, 101 N.W. 307.

The origins and roots of most legends, folklore, traditions and superstitions are quite uncertain. However, this premise of the notary's

386

authority made an early appearance in 1978 by California notary author, Raymond Rothman.

Rothman said, *"The most important obligation a Notary has to the public he serves is to judge what acts constitute the practice of law and what acts constitute the practice of a Notary Public. If the Notary, who is not an attorney, is asked to perform a notarial act that requires the preparation of or the giving of advice in regard to the preparation of, a legal document or form, the Notary should always obtain the advice of an attorney unless he has had special education and training."*

The above quote seems to have become the unquestioned principle of notarial prudence over the past twenty years. Mr. Rothman is not incorrect regarding the preparation of legal documents and forms by non-attorney notaries. Such notaries should either have specialized training in the matter, or consult legal counsel. However, Rothman's quote has been universally applied to notarial certificates as well. It is possible Rothman didn't intend to include notarial certificates in his statement. If we incorrectly assume that "legal forms" include notarial certificates, then it is easy to see where we have gone wrong.

A careful look is needed at why it makes no sense for a notary to be prohibited from selecting or correcting notarial certificates. There are three compelling reasons why we must dispel the dogma.

1. Notarial certificate selection and writing is not the unauthorized practice of law. The practice of law is the giving of advice or counsel regarding a client's rights, potential liabilities and legal interests. When selecting a notarial certificate for a client, the notary has no need to read, evaluate or make determinations about the client's transaction. The notary merely selects from an acknowledgment certificate or a jurat. In either case, the notarization has no legal effect on the legality, enforceability or truthfulness of the client's document.

2. The notarial certificate is not part of the signer's document. It is a separate document, apart from the signer's document. Many people fear a notary's certificate is actually part of the transaction document. It is an appendage to the document.

"There is considerable confusion over where the acknowledgment certificate belongs in relation to an instrument. The certificate must be connected or attached to the instrument in such a way that there is no doubt that it belongs to the instrument for which it is intended. It may appear at the conclusion of the instrument, which is most commonly done, yet its location is not important. It may appear in the body of the instrument or on a sheet of paper which is attached to the instrument."
- *Bridges v. Union Cattle Co., 104 Okla. 74.*

They fear any attempt by the notary to correct errors in a pre-printed certificate or to select and prepare a certificate is an intrusion into the legal work prepared by an attorney. In other words, it is feared a notary is second guessing an attorney's legal opinions and judgment when selecting, writing or correcting notarial certificates. Such fears and beliefs are wrong. The notarial certificate documents what the notary has done to authenticate and "certify" a signature on the document. It has nothing to do with the transaction document itself.

3. Notaries are responsible for errors and falsehoods in notarial certificates. When a notary signs and seals a notarial certificate, the notary is the guarantor of the facts asserted on that certificate. If the pre-printed certificate is flawed or contains falsehoods, the notary has an absolute duty by law to correct the certificate or prepare a new one for correct use. It is nonsense to prohibit a notary from selecting, writing or correcting a notarial certificate when that notary is absolutely liable for every defective certificate they sign, even those prepared by a licensed attorney.

Self-Dealing
See Conflict of Interest; Disqualification

Self-dealing is the act of providing for one's personal gain or advantage while in the performance of a duty for others. A notary engaged in self-dealing in the course of providing notarial services abuses her legal authority and immerses herself in the extreme form of conflict of interest and disqualification. Such conduct is actionable in court and is potentially subject to criminal liability.

Severally Liable
See Employer Liability for Notarization; Jointly Liable; Respondeat Superior; Vicarious Liability

Under the notary law, the notary and the notary's employer or supervisor may be held jointly or severally liable for the damages caused by the notary's wrongful notarization. This means the notary and the employer may be sued together in the same action, or may be separated from each other and sued separately and individually. In such an action, the plaintiff may determine to settle with the notary and pursue the employer only, or vice versa. Likewise, the plaintiff may drop the action against the notary and pursue the employer only, or vice versa.

Holding the notary and the notary's employer jointly and severally liable for notarial misconduct provides the litigants flexibility and options for seeking out the most appropriate remedies in the context of the facts and circumstances.

Shibboleths in Notarial Education
See False Notarial Dogma; Notary Training

A shibboleth is a catchword or slogan that is particularly familiar or distinctive to a certain group of people. In the arena of American notaries, the use of shibboleths is common. Certain slogans or phrases are oft repeated from generation to generation about what a notary should or should not do. Unfortunately, shibboleths seem to take on the appearance of law and are, in fact, often groundless or meaningless.

Shibboleths can be disruptive to a notary's education and development of correct notarial procedures. For example, notaries often hear the shibboleth that they should require every document signer for whom they notarize to produce a valid ID card, even if the notary knows the signer personally. Also, notaries hear that if they create a notarial certificate as an attachment to the signer's document that the notary should affix her seal in a manner so it half appears on the attachment and half on the document signature page to evidence that the two sheets belong to one another. Such shibboleths are illogical and false, yet they keep the proverbial "grapevine" busy. Notarial shibboleths are numerous and are tempting to repeat to others. They seem to require little thought or analysis on the part of the uninformed. Shibboleths sound safe, but they disserve the notary and the public.

Notarial shibboleths are adverse to the notary law and should be avoided. Only correct principles of notary law should be taught with care to avoid the hazards of false teachings in the form of shibboleths. Shibboleths are not sensible. They are not safe rules of thumb.

Short Form Notarial Certificate
See Completeness of the Notarial Certificate; Component Parts of the Notarial Certificate

Traditionally, notarial certificates have been verbally ornate and lengthy. Acknowledgments, particularly, have frequently been so verbose their principal meaning is lost to even the most scrupulous reader. Such verbosity is an unfortunate disservice to the public and the notary. As a result, most states have adopted short form notarial certificates thereby enabling the notary to avoid unnecessary errors in completing the certificate. The short form certificate is the inculcation of the essence of the notarial act and declares it plainly.

The short form acknowledgment and jurat will contain the same basic information except for one key element: they both declare the venue of the notarial act, the date of the notarization, and the name of the signer who appeared before the notary. The acknowledgment will declare the signer acknowledged his signature to the notary. The jurat will declare the signer signed the document under oath or affirmation in the notary's presence. The advantage to the short form certificate is that it is clearly written and understandable to the document signer, the party receiving the document, and to the notary writing it.

Should Have Known
See Knowledge; Reasonable Care

Sign Manual
See History of the Notary Seal

The notary seal has been in use by notaries worldwide for centuries. It is one of the best-recognized emblems of legal authority and is highly respected by society. It has taken many different forms over the centuries; while in America today the growing use of ink stamp notary seals is commonly seen.

Before the notary's signature and official seal were the everyday method for notarizing signatures, notaries made elaborate and ornate designs or drawings that were unique to each notary. The notary's drawing or design was called the "notarial sign" or "sign manual." The sign manual was made at the bottom of the document, typically on the left corner adjacent to the notarial certificate wording authenticated by his official signature.

The sign manual usually contained a motto, such as the Latin phrase "Deus est spes mea" or a depiction of a device or geometric puzzle that was unique to the notary. An ornate flourish by the ink pen under-laid the notary's signature. The combination of flourish, mark, device or Latin quote were difficult to forge, thus giving reliability to the sign manual as an early form of notary seal.

There is an assumption that the sign manual originated with 12th century Italian notaries, which they taught and proselyted to other countries throughout Europe, including England. The use of the sign manual prevailed from the 13th century until the early 18th century in Europe. It was also common to affix a wax seal to accompany the sign manual.

While it is probable that the earliest notaries in North America used signs manual to notarize for others, they haven't been found on documents from that period to affirm their use either way. However, notarizations from the earliest periods of post-Colombian North American were predominantly sealed by wax emblems until the latter decades of the 19th century.

Signature
See Forged Signature

A signature is the writing of one's name or mark intended to authenticate a document as the signer's document. It is the signer's physical manifestation of intent to be responsible for the content and purpose of the document. Inherently, the signer must physically make a signature, be it by writing instrument or by signature-stamp. A signature must be an original making of its owner. A signature is an extension of a person's identity. It must not be pre-printed or be a facsimile of the person's signature.

In the context of notarizations, penmanship is of little importance. The legibility of a signature is not a requisite to the validity thereof. For the notary, it is paramount that the signature belongs to its claimed maker for it to be notarized. Signatures made in the notary's journal must reasonably resemble the signature on the document to be notarized. The notary is the sole judge and determiner whether a signature belongs to a document signer. A perfect match between signatures, one in the journal and the other on the document, is not absolutely required; a reasonable match is. Signatures by the same person may vary for acceptable reasons, which the notary should verify, if the need arises.

We seem to take our signatures for granted. We make them multiple times every day, but rarely stop to think of what our signatures represent. Handwriting experts say our signatures reveal our inner selves. The courts say our signatures bind us to the documents we sign.

The making of a signature is as ancient as the human habitation of Earth. It predates the invention of paper in ancient China. Signatures are found in prehistoric petroglyphs, even though they are nothing more than a mark owned by the maker. Anciently, signatures were made in the form of designs or symbols, much as a rancher's brand on cattle is a mark of the rancher's ownership.

Centuries ago, documents were ratified or authorized by *signatories annulus,* which was a seal ring, or signet ring. The emblem of this ring was impressed in a drop of hot wax on a document. Only the highest authorities held signet rings. They constituted the official signature of the pious and important person who bore it.

With the passage of time and the advent of common written languages among the people, the human signature evolved from a symbol to the inscription of the person's given name.

In every instance from the dawn of time, the human signature has represented a manifestation of intent on the part of the marker. A signature is never a passive act. The signature represents the maker's acceptance or ratification of some fact or obligation.

> *"A signature may be a name, written or printed, [but] is not to be reckoned as a signature unless inserted or adopted with an intent, actual or apparent, to authenticate a writing."*
> *- Mesibov, Glinert & Levy v. Cohen Bros. Mfg. Co., 245 N.Y. 305, 310.*

A signature cannot be made accidentally. It is a deliberate act. People have a right to rely on the signature to ensure the signer meant what was said or written, that the signer intends to perform a specific act as promised.

In modern law, a person's signature is the writing of a name or a mark intended to authenticate a document as the signer's document. Any writing of a name or mark is considered sufficient to constitute a valid signature. Legibility is irrelevant.

Signatures often take on an artistic flair. For instance, the unmistakable signature of John Hancock on the Declaration of Independence is often misjudged as egotistical. To the contrary, Hancock signed his name dead center on the document as large as he could in order to send the British his defiant message of revolt.

> *"There is no requirement in the Statute or the decisional law that a signature be in any particular form. Instead, the focus has been on whether there is some reliable indication that the person to be charged with performing under the writing intended to authenticate it. Thus, for example, the Restatement (Second) of Contracts provides that: The signature to a memorandum may be any symbol made or adopted with an intention, actual or apparent, to authenticate the writing as that of the signer. Id. at § 134. Similarly, the courts have refused to require a specific form of signature, so long as there is some indication that the 'signer' intended to authenticate the memorandum."*
> *- Hessenthafer v. Farzin, 564 A. 2d 990 (Pa. 1989).*

For many people, their signature is their "trademark." For others, the more stylistic they make it, the less likely it is to be forged. Medical doctors are particularly notorious for signatures that appear more like scribbles than written names. Yet they are completely valid, even for transactions such as pharmaceutical prescriptions where a person's life or safety is it stake.

It is ironic that when it comes to performing notarizations, some people assume the signature must be legible and must represent the signer's full name. As a matter of law, a signature is the writing or mark *representing* the person's name.

Who has the legal authority to declare when a signature is not a signature? Only the maker of the signature may so decide. It is neither up to the notary nor the government to decide. In many states notaries are confronted with government requirements that the signature being notarized "exactly match the name of the person for whom the notarization is being performed."

When notarizing a signature, the notary is certifying the signature on the document belongs to the person who made it. Therefore, by unfortunate implication, the notary is certifying the signature constitutes the full name of the signer (whether it is made by artistic rendition or by a mark). Never is a notary certifying a signature legibly matches a person's name.

Many people are unable to sign their name due to physical impairment. The most they can make is a mark or a squiggle on the paper. As a matter of law, the person's mark or squiggle constitutes a valid signature that may be notarized. Several states require under statute that additional wording and clarification be added to any signature made by a mark. Yet, under the common law a mark is a signature.

If a physician's squiggled signature is completely valid for a medical prescription then it logically follows that it is also valid for notarizations. Let us not punish document signers who sign legibly, yet fail to include a dubiously important middle initial. Had they signed stylistically, the omitted middle initial would never be discovered and would cause no concern.

A number of states require that the printed names of document signers be printed below the person's signature. This is obviously intended to remedy any uncomfortableness about highly stylistic, illegible signatures on documents submitted for government filing.

A person's signature to a document binds its maker to the content of the document. It is presumed they have read it, understand it, and agree to its content, terms or conditions.

> *"Failure to read a contract before signing it will not, as a rule, affect its binding force. Indeed, the courts appear to be unanimous in holding that a person who, having the capacity and an opportunity to read a contract, is not misled as to its contents and who sustains no confidential relationship to the other party cannot avoid the contract on the ground of mistake if he signs it without reading it, at least in the absence of special circumstances excusing his failure to read it. This rule has been carried to the extent of holding that in the absence of fraud or circumstances savoring of fraud, one entering into a contract which refers for some of its terms to an extraneous document, outside the contract proper, is bound also thereby, even though he omits to inform himself as to the contents of that document or the nature of those terms and conditions when it is possible for him to do so."*
> *- Contracts, 17A Am. Jr. 2d § 224 (1991).*

The courts have further stated that,

> *"Unless one can show facts and circumstances to demonstrate that he was prevented from reading the contract, or that he was induced by statements of the other party to refrain from reading the contract, it is binding. No party to a written contract in this state can defend against its enforcement on the sole ground that he signed it without reading it."*
> *- Allied Van Lines, 351 So.2d at 347-48.*

The signature of the notary to a notarial certificate is under the same presumption of law as is the signature of the document signer. That is, the notary has read and fully understands the contents of the certificate and verifies it is complete and true.

When a notary signs a notarial certificate, the notary is signing an "official signature." It is recommended as good form and practice to make the official notarial signature somewhat legible and distinguished in appearance.

There are no statutory requirements governing the color of ink used in making a signature. In a few states, the color of ink for the notary seal is regulated, but it never extends to the signature.

Our signatures are precious commodities to each of us. They are an extension of ourselves, unique in how we make them. Yet, they have profound legal weight and value.

From "The Notary" (July 1998)

The Law is Clear: Original Signatures Only!

Fax machines are convenient and their transmissions are becoming clearer all the time.

But the rule of law is even more clear - the only signature a notary may notarize is an original signature.

Thanks to fax machines, documents can be transmitted to numerous cities around the country in the same day for multiple signatures to the same transaction. The first "original" document is written and signed by Joe in Los Angeles. Then it is faxed to Jane in Denver for her to sign. Then it is faxed to Steve in Atlanta for him to sign. Finally it is faxed back to Joe in Los Angeles. The document Joe takes out of his fax machine has the signatures of Joe, Jane, and Steve at the bottom.

Yet, not any of these signatures are originals. And the document may be fully enforceable.

It gets a little perplexing sometimes when you are asked to notarize on a faxed or photocopied document. Is it legal to do because the document itself is not the original? The only issue the notary must address is whether the signer is physically in the notary's presence and the signature to the document is made originally on that document. It matters not if the document itself was faxed to the signer, or is a photocopy of some other document.

When we notarize, we are not affecting the truthfulness of a document. We do not even make if legally enforceable. We are only certifying the signature to the document (regardless of how the document was created) is the signature of the person who appeared before us.

There are some practical limitations to the notarizations of signatures on faxed or photocopied documents. If the document is a title deed or real estate conveyance for government recording, there are good reasons why a taxed document bearing an original signature and notarization might not be accepted for filing. Because the stakes are very high in real property transactions, there must be exactness in the paperwork documenting the transaction.

One's only proof of ownership to a home or piece of land is a written document. Documents can be tampered with, forged, lost and destroyed. The notarial act to these transactions is one of the cornerstones to secure America's cherished right to own property.

Another area of common concern is the notarization of signatures to multi-page document packs, usually made from NCR paper or carbon paper. The signer is instructed to press hard when signing so the signature appears on the yellow and pink copies below.

May a notary affix her notary seal to the yellow and pink copies to show that all three copies in the pack were signed and notarized? No, she may not. The only signature a notary may notarize is an original signature made by hand with a writing instrument from which ink flows onto the paper. A genuine signature can be made only one at a time (unless you are fully ambidextrous and able to write with both hands simultaneously).

If all three copies of the NCR form must be signed and notarized, the signer must sign the white, yellow and pink copies separately and have them notarized individually.

A signature is any hand-made inscription on paper manifesting, the signer's intent to enter into the transaction or terms of the content of the document being signed. A signature is typically the hand written name. Legally, it is not necessary that it be legible. In many cultures, the creation of an artistic signature is a lifelong endeavor. Doctors sign their medical prescriptions in anything but their written name. It is nothing more than a squiggle-loop-d-loop. And it can indeed be notarized.

If a squiggle-loop-d-loop signature is good enough for medical doctors, then why can't the signer to a document do the same thing if they are physically unable to write their name? If the customer signs in the form of an "X" or some other mark, we are compelled to provide their printed name and clarifying wording that the mark represents their true signature. It amounts to a lot of extra distractions, confusion and potential mistakes.

The artistic rendition of a signature is simply not legible. Say a signer is named Elizabeth J. Smith in her document, but she signs her common name - Betty Smith. May her signature be notarized as such? Except in real estate transactions, the answer is "Yes." But, some people react out of emotion and argue that she must sign her name as it is printed in her document. If she had signed her name with an artistic rendition looking more like a squiggle-loop-d-loop nobody would know if she signed the name "George", "Betty" or "Elizabeth."

The end result is that some people are punished for signing their name legibly, when the law provides that a signature is any hand-made ink inscription on a piece of paper manifesting the maker's intent to enter into the terms or condition of the content of the document.

From "The Notary's Duty of Care for Identifying Document Signers"

- Peter J. Van Alstyne, 32 J. Marshall Law Rev. 1007-1009.

In many workplaces across the country, it is not uncommon for the office assistant to sign the employer's signature to routine matters. They might imitate the employer's signature, or they might sign the employer's name with a disclosure, "by Jane Doe."

In the mid-eighteenth century, former President Thomas Jefferson invented a device by which he could draft three or four manuscripts simultaneously by writing with a master pen. As his hand moved the pen across the page forming words, a tie rod connected to other pens would follow the pattern of movement creating identical replicas of the manuscript. While this ingenious device enabled expediency to certain written communication, it was also the forefather to automated signature making in high volumes.

Holders of high public office and leaders of large organizations are very commonly found to relegate their correspondence and signatures to a machine called an "autopen." The autopen, somewhat like the Jefferson device, follows a template that controls the movement of the ink pen on the document being signed. The signature it makes appears very similar to an original hand-made signature of the person it purports to represent.

Members of both houses of Congress and the Office of the President are known to use automated signature machines on their routine correspondence. Many of the public receiving correspondence signed in this manner reasonably believes that the letter actually passed through the hands of its powerful and prestigious signer. So impressive is it to receive a letter signed by a U.S. President or celebrated U.S. Senator that many recipients preserve it as a cherished keepsake, with the expectation that one day that autograph could prove relatively valuable. Sadly, unbeknownst to them, it is not the genuine signature of their venerated public figure. It is merely a replica made by an autopen.

Arguably, the automated signature is not a forgery. It is done with the authority of the person whose signature it represents. But, can it be genuinely stated that the automated signature is made with no intent to deceive? In reality, that is the entire objective for using the autopen: to induce the reader to believe that the writer personally signed the writing.

The owner of the autopen is in a public relations dilemma. He can ill-afford to offend his constituency by admitting he doesn't have time to personally respond to his constituent's problem, let alone personally opine to the ghost-written contents of the correspondence sent on his behalf by signing it.

The autopen is a clever solution to the pressures of unmanageably high volumes of correspondence that must be answered by the addressee. The autopen is not unlike the office assistant making her employer's signature on a document. It is made under the employer's authority and it is expedient. The recipient is successfully induced into believing these signatures are genuine and can be relied upon, even to his detriment.

While it is conceded that the use of the autopen and the employer's signature made by the office assistant arguably may not constitute definitional signature forgeries, they are intentionally deceitful. Such signatures are false representations. They arguably constitute a form of fraud.

Deceit is one shade of color on the chromatic spectrum of fraud. Unless a signature to a document is made by the person it purports to represent, it is a mere contrivance to mislead another to his detriment.

The justification for utilizing the autopen or the office assistant to sign our names to documents is understandable. What is not understandable is the wholesale absence of public discussion over the ethical use of these methods. The ethical, vicarious making of signatures for others requires full disclosure that the signature is not genuine, although it is authorized.

Ethical office assistants often sign their employer's name with the disclosure, "by Jane Doe." The automated signature could also be ethically affixed to a document if it were to include the disclosure, "authorized signature made by mechanical means."

Ethical conduct and expediency are rarely compatible. When it comes to signature making, expediency often wins out and is vehemently defended when challenged on its ethical merits. The issues here are not complicated, but they nonetheless warrant thoughtful public consideration.

Signature Block
See Executed Document

Whenever a person signs a document, it will usually be signed at a designated location on the document, often referred to as the signature block, signature line, or signature page. The signature block usually refers to two or more document signers whose signatures are intended to appear in close proximity to one another. The signature page need not be exclusively dedicated to signatures only. It more likely refers generally to the page designated for the signature(s).

A common misunderstanding is that the notarial certificate must be in proximity to the signature block or signature line, and must be on the signature page. That is incorrect. The notarial certificate is a document separate from the document signer's and is therefore very appropriate as a separate page attached to the signer's document. As notarial certificates very commonly appear on the signature page of the document, many draw the assumption it is required this way. While it is not required, placing a notarial certificate on the signature page can save paper. The urge to place the notarial certificate on the signature page is often strong, even though the space allocated for the notarization is woefully inadequate and unusable by the notary.

The notarial certificate must make direct and unambiguous reference to the document signature. Concerns that the certificate should be on the signature page, so it won't be misapplied, have no basis. The signature page no more needs the notarization on it than does a person's resume need a letter of recommendation in its text. They are separate and distinct matters, the latter being created to strengthen the former.

401

Signature Fraud
See Forged Signature; Signature

Signature Guarantees
See Medallion Signature Guarantees

Signature in the Notary Journal
See Journal Recordation; Notary Journal

Perhaps the single most important step the notary must take in every notarization performed is to have the document signer sign the notary's journal before the notarization is performed. It should, in fact, be the first step of every notarial act.

The signature made in the notary journal is compelling evidence the document signer, for whom the notarization is performed, personally appeared before the notary and that the notarized signature was genuine. The probative value accorded the contents of the journal entry is substantial; the signature in the journal substantiates the most essential assertions made in the notarial certificate. That is, the signer personally appeared before the notary, that the signature on the document belonged to its claimed maker and that the signer's identity was properly verified.

Signer identification can be substantiated by the journal signature as it should reasonably match the signature on the signer's ID card or papers. Further, as a person is instructed to spontaneously make their signature in the notary's journal, prior to the notarization, the notary is able to discern behavior or demeanor from the signer that would alert the notary to possible concerns of identity, or the signer's intentions.

A prudent and responsible notary will cause every person for whom a notarization is performed to sign the notary journal before any further steps are taken. In a few states, the notary is required by statute to obtain the signature in the journal.

There is no substitute for the probative value the journal signature provides.

Signature Legibility
See Signature; Signature Made by a Mark

Signature Line
See Signature Block

Signature Made by a Mark
See Physically Impaired Signer

A person who, for reason of incapacitation or illiteracy, is unable to write his signature may make a mark on the document in lieu of a full signature. The traditional form of a mark has been the letter "X" on the signature line. The notary or another person may then write the signer's given name to the left of the mark and the last name to the right, such as John X Doe. The word "his" would be written above the mark and the word "mark" under the mark.

> *"A person may be bound by any mark or designation he thinks proper to adopt, provided it be used as a substitute for his name."*
> *- New York Court of Appeals (1844).*

> *"A signature is indeed required, but the question is, what is a signature? If this question were necessarily to be decided by the principles of law, as settled in the courts of England and the United States, there would be no doubt of the truth of the legal proposition, that making a mark is signing, even in the attestation of a last will and testament, which has been fenced around by the law with more than ordinary guards, because they are generally made by parties, when they are sick, and when too they are frequently inops consilii, and when they therefore need all the protection which the law can afford to them. This principle is fully settled by many cases..."*
> *- Zacharie v. Franklin, 37 U.S. (12 Pet.) 151 (1838).*

A number of areas of the United States have accept for generations the document signer's thumbprint in lieu of the letter X, and add to it the traditional attribution of the print to its maker as they would for the letter X. For the most part, this practice is largely accepted even today, thus rendering the mark eligible for notarizing.

By the definition of a signature, an incapacitated person, or one whose ability is limited, has an alternative means for signing a document. The person could create an original inscription in the form of a stylized squiggle or lineal design. A signature's validity is not measured by its legibility. Professionals in many fields, health care providers being the best known, sign wholly illegible signatures that are completely valid. The entitlement to write a signature in any manner the maker desires should extend to those who are incapacitate as well. It is for this purpose the notary is there, to document and certify the signature (in whatever shape it is in) is the genuine signature of its maker.

Signature of the Bearer
See Signer Identification; Signature in the Notary Journal

One of the most compelling elements of a person's ID is their signature thereon. It is an extension of their identity. When they request a notarization on a document they signed, the notary must have the signer sign the notary's journal before any further steps are taken. As the person spontaneously makes his signature in the notary's journal in a calm manner, its reasonable likeness to the one on his ID will constitute valuable evidence that he is who he claims to be.

A number of states require by notary statute the signer's ID card or papers include the bearer's signature. The merits of this requirement are so compelling that it is only reasonable for every notary to require it of the signers they must identify by ID cards or papers.

Signature Page
See Signature Block

Signature Verification
See Forged Signature; Signature

The essence of the notarial act is to verify the signature in question is genuine and that it was made willingly and freely for the purposes stated within the signer's document. In verifying the signature, the notary inherently employs every required step in performing the notarization: the signer personally appears before the notary, his true identity is verified, and his willful making of the signature is determined. Each of these elements are recorded in the notary's journal to provide an insurmountable proof that the notarization was performed properly and that reasonable care governed each step.

The verification of a signature by a notary is not a guarantee the signature is genuine. To the contrary, it guarantees the signature was verified in accordance with specific steps established by law. The presumption in law is that if the signature is correctly verified, the notary has faithfully fulfilled her duties under the law. Should the signature ultimately be found to be invalid, liability should not impute to the notary as she complied with every required standard of care and procedure to verify the signature was genuine.

Skilled and cunning imposters and forgers can so perfect their criminal craft that even the highest skilled forgery experts in law enforcement can be deceived. The notary law does not impose on the notary the duty to detect and cull out forged signatures. That is the work of highly trained experts. The notary law, on the other hand, imposes on the notary a duty to take the specified steps of reasonable care to validate the signature by the absence of any indication or reason to suspect that it is not genuine.

There is a grave concern over the proliferation of signature forgeries in the United States. Their concerns are statistically defensible. However, their concerns ought not translate into alarm over the notary's risk of liability for notarizing a forged signature. While the probability of unwittingly notarizing a forged signature seems to increase, the risk of notarial liability does proportionately increase as well. If the notary follows every required step to notarize and exercises reasonable care in each step, there can be no liability for the notary. There is no strict liability for notarizations on fraudulent signatures that are notarized in strict compliance with law.

Signed Document
See Executed Document

Signer Identification
See Identity of the Signer; Imposters

From "The Notary's Duty of Care for Identifying Document Signers"

- Peter J. Van Alstyne, 32 J. Marshall Law Review 1003-1031.

Introduction

Since the dawn of human history, one's true identity has been integral to any degree of societal orderliness. Humans have always interacted with one another for personal interests and for the good of the community. Knowing with whom we interact assures a degree of security and safety. Sadly, Earth's earliest inhabitants had to learn quickly that not all people could be trusted. Knowing whom to deal with and whom to avoid has always been a prerequisite for self- preservation.

As ancient rudimentary systems of trade, commerce, and law evolved, ancient societies faced growing risks in dealing with unfamiliar people. On whom could they rely? How could one be certain a stranger was not an impostor, but was who he represented himself to be? The notaries of ancient Rome, for example, were very limited in the exercise of their authority. There were no identity cards in ancient Rome, so the notary either had to personally know the signer or use witnesses who would attest to the signer's identity.

Unless the parties knew each other personally, there was justified concern over the individual's true identity. Even then, scoundrels could pull off clever disguises. Handwriting experts say our signatures reveal our inner selves. The courts say our signatures bind us to the documents we sign.

Signature making is as ancient as human habitation on earth. It predates the invention of paper in China; signatures appear in prehistoric petroglyphs as nothing more than the petroglyph's mark. Anciently, signatures were in the form of designs and symbols, similar to a rancher's cattle brand designating his ownership of his livestock.

In the early centuries of [past] millennia, documents were ratified by signatorius annulus, in the form of a ring, or signet ring. Drops of hot wax

406

were placed on the document to which the signet ring was impressed, leaving the emblem of its owner in the cooled wax puddle. Usually, society's highest officials held signet rings, and these marks constituted the official signature of the pious and important person who held them.

Imposters Today

Arguably, the most important element in the notarization of a signature is the verification of the signer's true identity. The notarization is performed singularly to authenticate the signature on a document. Having no effect or relevance to the content of the signer's instrument, the notarization is a formal process prescribed statutorily to minimize the risk of an impostor's forgery of a signature.

The office and function of the notary is indispensable in modern society. Were the notarial office eliminated, some type of authenticating authority would need to be created in order for business to be transacted. The notary public is essential in worldwide commerce to verify signatures and to identify their makers.

In any purposeful endeavor to embattle a foe, one must fully understand the foe in all of its attributes. The same applies to our vigilance against signature forgeries. The making of a forgery and the tools for identifying it are not complex. A signature forgery is almost always perpetrated by an impostor. The two indispensable procedures for unmasking the impostor are to require him to personally appear before a notary public, and to have his true identity verified within a standard of reasonable certainty.

A signature forgery is the making of another person's signature, or the signature of a non-existent person without authority, with the intent to deceive. A signature forgery consists of three requisites:

1. There must be the making of a signature that belongs to another or to a non-existent person;
2. It must be made without authority; and
3. It must be made with the intent to deceive.

A person's signature has always represented profound significance, influence, and value in every society and system of law. A signature to a transaction signifies the signer has read, understood, agreed to and committed himself to the contents, terms or obligations set forth in the instrument. The signature unmistakably and unambiguously represents the maker's deliberateness. It is tangible evidence of the signer's intent. When a person's signature is made fraudulently by another, it constitutes a most serious criminal act.

The essential element for a forgery is the element of intent to defraud. Without this level of criminal intent, the forged signature remains simply a false representation of a lesser gravity.

It is never sufficient, in notarial services, to merely assume the signer's claimed identity is genuine. To the contrary, such a cavalier attitude is a prescription for serious trouble.

Verification of the signer's identity is arguably the most important step in performing a notarial act. The genuineness or doubtfulness of the signature is verified; in many situations, the stakes can be high.

Much has been written concerning the notary's duty to verify a signer's identity, while abundant misguided information circulates among the community of America's notaries and their regulators. The most responsible approach to the relatively complex issue of notarial verification of signer identification is within the context of well-established legal principles that have proven their efficacy over many generations of time. Within this context, the notary and the regulator can find reasonable and balanced solutions to the innumerable challenges they face in our increasingly complex society that corruption has marred in many facets.

We live in a far from perfect society, and notarizations are scarcely the perfect device to combat document and signature fraud. However, if performed properly, the notarial act is extraordinarily effective.

Prevention of Fraud through Signer Identification

A. Constat de persona

Constat de persona, or proof as to the person, is surprisingly fragile. The ultimate, irrefutable identity of a person is rooted in but a few cherished sources. A person's identity requires some sort of incorruptible "base line." Moreover, one of the most cherished of American civil liberties is the person's right to keep his identity private.

Our identity baseline is the continuous personal acquaintance our parents and immediate family members have had with us since our births. Furthermore, our baseline lies in the scientifically identified uniqueness of our fingerprints and, moreover, our DNA. We are positively identifiable by the personal knowledge of our parents from the moment of birth and by the uniqueness of our genetic codes. Anything else is inferior. Our families' life-long personal knowledge of our identity and our unreplicatable DNA is relatively error-proof and most likely immune to corruption.

While many consider the birth certificate to be a wholly reliable determinator of our existence and true identity and, therefore, a valid identity baseline, it is rife with weakness. The only thing a birth certificate certifies is that an individual of particular gender, weight, height and race was born to the two parents identified. As a sheet of paper, it does not certify its bearer as the person described.

From the point of birth through adulthood, our verifications of birth are public record through birth certificates. However, our birth certificates hardly prove identity. They are but a piece of paper, the written contents of which are not absolute in their accuracy. Humans provide the information. Humans complete the forms. Humans make mistakes. And birth certificates are not immune from falsification or alteration.

Birth certificates are relatively easy to obtain, even under false pretenses. Remarkably, they are heavily relied upon for the issuance of U.S. passports and driver's licenses in most states. An impostor's acquisition of a valid birth certificate of a person of similar age, race and gender as themselves can be the catalyst to an undetected life under one or many aliases.

Our individual *constat de persona* is something to which most of us rarely give much thought. We are a free society, unaccustomed to having to *produce identification papers at a moment's notice. Those who have resided or traveled in totalitarian countries recognize how one's very life may hinge on the immediate presentation of their identification documents to authorities in those countries. In that environment, it is the government regime that determines and ratifies one identity. Although an infant may be named by his parents, his recognized identity must be ratified by the government through the issuance of official identification papers that he must bear throughout his life.*

The American system of individual identification is a stark contrast to those described above. No free American is required to bear ID, and there is no central source for uniform identification. The identification we as Americans obtain is typically procured voluntarily in connection with some higher objective. Perhaps our most commonly used ID is our driver's license; however, it is obtained not for identification purposes but for the privilege to drive. Employment or school ID's are issued for security reasons or for receiving special benefits reserved only for authorized persons.

Our identification documents are very much ancillary to other pursuits in life. Yet, so much depends on them. For business and government to mitigate against exposure to risk that individuals may be impostors, heavy reliance is placed on the identification card the individual presents. While a driver's license certifies that the bearer of the card is licensed to drive, it provides little or no assurance that the person featured thereon is who he claims to be. We take it on the reasonable expectation that somehow the driver's license was issued by the government only after a reasonable screening of the applicant's true identity. And, even a state's licensing process is often superficial because it depends almost entirely on the applicant's presentation of a birth certificate purportedly belonging to the applicant.

As discussed earlier, there is no irrefutable means to connect a birth certificate to the person it purports to represent. We can only accept it on reasonable good faith. Hence, in America we have no fail-safe system of personal identification in written form of any kind.

This is abhorrent to many totalitarian regimes, which is why they have promulgated their own centralized system of national identification. An

410

individual is who the regime says he is by virtue of his government-issued ID. This keeps society orderly and less threatening to the regime. Identifying document signers for notarizations in this environment would present little challenge.

B. The Duty to Exercise Reasonable Care

America's notaries face formidable challenges in identifying document signers because of our open society. Every person is free to document his or her identity in any manner he or she wishes, or even not at all. Yet, at one time or another, nearly every person has need of a notarization. Fortunately, there are procedures and standards of care a notary may invoke to ensure protection from risk of personal liability in notarizing for the public, with its sundry methods of identification.

The bedrock of American notary law is the principle in tort of reasonable care. Reasonable care is the standard by which notaries and their official conduct are judged. It is borne out of the necessity to provide ordinary people, untrained in the law or sciences, a means of protection against liability for the public services they provide to their communities as notaries. The standards of reasonable care serve as parameters by which a notary can gauge whether her official notarial conduct is protected. A notary is expected to act reasonably, as would any reasonable and prudent person in like circumstances, in the performance of every notarial procedure. The notary is liable to all persons who suffer injury as the proximate result of the notary's breach of her duty of care.

The notary's responsibility to reasonably verify the identity of every person for whom she notarizes is profound. It is the cornerstone of the notarial act by which a notarized signature is reasonably verified not to be a forgery. A notary who takes this duty lightly does so at her very grave peril.

The notary performs this function of signer identification as a fiduciary of the public. The notary is expected to perform with integrity and diligence. It is not enough to simply follow what other notaries customarily do, especially if the business and notarial habits of others are negligent. Conformity with the customs of the workplace or community does not

411

equate with the standard of reasonable care (Meyers v. Meyers, 503 P.2d 59 (1972)).

In fact, if material questions arise over the notary's proper verification of a signer's identity, the burden of proof by a preponderance of the evidence shifts to the notary to establish that reasonable care was exercised.

> *"[I]f it is established that a notarized signature is forged, the burden of persuasion shifts to the notary to prove by a preponderance of the evidence that he exercised reasonable care in ascertaining the identity of the person... [J]ustification for shifting the burden of persuasion is the public policy of probability that the notary was negligent... and the strong public policy of ensuring the accuracy of notarial certifications."*
> *- Meyers v. Meyers, 503 P.2d 59, 62-63 (1972).*

The Uniform Acknowledgment Act and the Uniform Law on Notary Acts clearly indicate that document signers must personally appear before the notary. This is for the express purpose of enabling the notary to verify the signer's identity and that the signature to be notarized is genuinely that of its maker. However, only the Uniform Law on Notary Acts adequately prescribes standards for signer identification. The Uniform Law on Notary Acts provides:

- *In taking an acknowledgment, the notarial officer must determine, either from personal knowledge or from satisfactory evidence, that the person appearing before the officer and making the acknowledgment is the person whose true signature is on the instrument.*
- *In taking a verification upon oath or affirmation, the notarial officer must determine, either from personal knowledge or from satisfactory evidence, that the person appearing before the officer and making the verification is the person whose true signature is on the statement verified.*
- *A notarial officer has satisfactory evidence that a person is the person whose true signature is on a document if that person (i) is personally known to the notarial officer, (ii) is identified upon the oath or affirmation of a credible witness*

personally known to the notarial officer or (iii) is identified on the basis of identification documents.

Many legal scholars lament the fact that most states provide little statutory clarity on the standards and procedures a notary should use to verify the signer's identity. The long-standing standard for a notary's verification of a signer's identity has been by the notary's personal acquaintance with the signer, or by satisfactory evidence.

C. Personal Knowledge of Identity

A notary's personal knowledge of a signer's true identity constitutes the strongest form of signer identification. In the notarial certificate, this form of signer identification is often phrased "personally known to me to be the person whose name is subscribed" thereto. One individual's claim to personally know another defies refutation. It is premised on a substantial level of acquaintance "derived from association with the [person] in relation to other people, as establishes [his] identity with at least reasonable certainty."

Personal knowledge of another's identity cannot be based on the representations of other people. Moreover, identity cannot be based on assumption or conjecture. Identity must be based upon a chain of circumstances surrounding the person that, in its totality, would lead one to believe the person is who he claims to be. Within that chain of circumstances, some affirmative evidence of the person's identity must manifest itself.

A number of states have laudably enacted concepts that provide within their notary codes definition to the element of personal knowledge. The notary code of Oregon provides, for example, that "personally known" means "familiarity with a person resulting from interactions with that person over a period of time sufficient to eliminate every reasonable doubt that the person has the identity claimed." Every detail within the framework of personal knowledge calls for the notary's subjective assessment of the facts and circumstances. Appropriately so, a notary's determination of personal knowledge is rooted in the exercise of reasonable care.

413

If a notary is personally acquainted with an individual over a substantial period of time and has interacted substantively with that person, the notary's common sense and instinct might lead her to reasonably believe the person is who he claims to be. This would occur naturally out of the absence of anything contradicting the person's representations as to who he is.

Human history has never been without its impostors and aliases. In contemporary society, no American community is immune from having within its midst residents living under aliases for purposes of evading detection by law enforcement or for bizarre psychological deficiencies. The notary may know this person on a personal basis sufficient to qualify as adequate identity verification for notarial purposes. The fact that the notary's acquaintance is with the person's alias is inconsequential. The notary's reliance on her experience with, and observation of the person, reasonably confirm for the notary that the person is whom he claims to be, his alias notwithstanding.

D. Satisfactory Evidence of Identity

Satisfactory evidence is a user-friendly legal term because it is simple and rather self-explanatory. Satisfactory evidence is sometimes called "sufficient evidence," that "amount of proof which ordinarily satisfies an unprejudiced mind." In relying on satisfactory evidence, the correct question for the notary is not whether it is possible that the document signer is an impostor, but whether there is sufficient probability the signer is who he claims to be. This important standard is not unlike the legal axiom that an accused person is presumed innocent until proven guilty. Although the document signer bears the burden of proof as to his true identity, there should never be a presumption of attempted false identity on the signer's part unless the notary reveals such falsity through the presentation of satisfactory evidence.

The term "satisfactory evidence" often applies to two methods of signer identification: the use of a "credible witness" or an "identifying witness," and to the use of identification cards or papers.

E. Credible or Identifying Witnesses

Eight states specifically prescribe the use of credible witnesses as a means of verifying a signer's identity. Credible, or identifying, witnesses are vital to the successful performance of notarizations for millions of people at any given moment. Identifying witnesses constitute satisfactory evidence of a person's identity before a notary, and are often the only means by which a signer may be identified for a notarization. Vast portions of the American population are without identification cards or documents, as they either have no need for any, or they are momentarily sans ID.

Credible witnesses are utilized to attest to the notary the true identity of the document's signer. As articulated in the notary statutes of several states, the notary identifies the person "upon the oath or affirmation of a credible witness personally known to the notarial officer." In some instances, the state codes specify that the witness must also know the document signer. Arizona notary law, for example, requires "[t]he oath or affirmation of a credible person who is known to the notary and who knows the individual."

In every use of an identifying witness by a notary, there must be the fulfillment of three requisites, which will constitute an "unbroken chain of personal knowledge":

1. *The notary must personally know the identifying witness;*
2. *The identifying witness must personally know the document signer; and*
3. *The identifying witness must attest under oath to the notary as to the witness' personal acquaintance with the document signer.*

A notary is entitled to detrimentally rely on the affirmation of someone she knows personally regarding the identity of a complete stranger if the notary's personal knowledge of identity runs to the credible witness. In turn, the witness' personal knowledge runs to the document signer for whom the notarization is being performed. The notary's reliance on the words of the identifying witness is secured by the administration of an oath or affirmation to the to witness.

A notary can administer an oath or affirmation to an identifying witness with simple phrasing such as, "do you swear or affirm that this is Jane Doe and that you know her personally?" Notaries are rarely, if ever, trained on the laws and procedures for oaths and affirmations. They are prone to shy away from having to administer oaths and affirmations, as many may regard it as pretentious or "overkill." A prudent notary and employer of notaries will discuss the procedures for administrations of oaths with colleagues and clients, and thereby ameliorate some of this discomfort of the responsibility.

The use of a credible witness to identify document signers is not without inherent risks to the notary. The use of the witness is a substitution for requesting the document signer to produce valid identification. The actual identity of the signer is just as easily obfuscated by a derelict credible witness as it is by counterfeit identification. However, if the notary performs her role correctly in the using an identifying witness, the notary is relieved of liability upon the showing that the notary exercised reasonable care throughout the transaction.

The notary's reasonable care in using a credible witness to identify a signer's identity requires utmost objectivity on the notary's part. The notary must personally know the identifying witness to the same degree, if not higher, as if the notary were notarizing for the witness on the basis of personal knowledge. The notary's acquaintance with the witness is the premise by which she determines a signer is who he claims to be. This is quite different from notarizing for the individual a notary knows personally. The bar for measuring personal knowledge of the credible witness's identity is by necessity higher.

Unlike the notarization for a person the notary knows personally, an identifying witness must be known to the notary as having a reputation for integrity. The witness must manifest no inclinations towards deceit, and must be known as one who esteems integrity and manifests it by his example. The witness must be cognizant of his sober responsibility under penalties of perjury for attesting to the identity of another person. And the witness should be impartial and free of any interest in the transaction.

Perhaps one of the most vexing problems a notary faces in identifying document signers is the disqualification of the credible witness. Inasmuch as the identifying witness must be a person the notary knows well, the social awkwardness of having to disqualify that person can be daunting. The witness may very likely be the notary's employer or supervisor,

416

leaving the notary with a perception of having to play a subservient role. The notary feels pressured into abusing the use of a credible witness for reasons of expediency or fraud.

Any responsible discussion on disqualifying conflicts of interest in the context of notarial services must consider a balanced overview. The primary objective for notarizing a signature is to mitigate against the risk that the document's signature is not genuine. The heart of that process is the reasonable verification of the signer's true identity. This may be through the attestation of a person the notary personally knows and believes to be credible. The fact the identifying witness is a party to the transaction does not, in and of itself, denigrate the veracity of the witness' affirmation of the signer's identity. To the contrary, a witness who also happens to be a party to the transaction may truthfully and credibly verify the signer's identity. The objective is still fulfilled.

The issue argued by many is whether persons who have an interest in, or are parties to, transactions should he disqualified from serving as credible or identifying witnesses. While this is frequently advocated the premise on which it is based may be inadequate.

The employment of credible witnesses by notaries to identify document signers is superior to the notary's reliance on the signer's ID documents. One's personal knowledge of the identity of another is the oldest and most venerated form of identification. It is irrefutable and enjoys profound evidentiary weight. The entire concept of the credible or identifying witness is founded upon the high trust our system of law places in one's personal knowledge.

A notary's employer or supervisor is generally affected by the execution of documents within his workplace and, according to some opinions, is disqualified from attesting to the identities of his employee's clients. A co-signer personally known to the notary is disqualified from attesting to the other signer's identity under this standard as well. These disqualifications ironically leave the notary with no other choice but to rely on the inferior form of identity verification: ID cards and papers. The bar for disqualifying witnesses is set so low that the imagined problems this standard seeks to prevent could flourish by compelling notaries to rely on the weakest form of signer identification. In other words, the cure may be worse than the illness.

The primary evil in using interested persons as credible witnesses is that their conflict of interest creates a temptation to abuse their position and benefit themselves in some way. Conflicts of interest are ubiquitous in every facet of modern life, business, law and government. Very often the mandatory disqualification of the interested party accomplishes little good, and may even cause a degree of harm to the public or client. Therefore, the higher standard invoked among many professions and governmental bodies is to require full and timely disclosure of one's conflict of interest. The degrees of interest one may have can vary widely, thus necessitating the disqualification of the person in severe cases. In other instances, the mere candid disclosure of the person's interest serves notice to other parties relying on the transaction that they may wish to withdraw from the situation.

There is a more reasoned approach to credible witnesses who have an interest in the transaction. Notary statutes could require that the notarial certificate disclose the notary's reliance on the witness, even though the witness attests to the signer's identity as an interested party. By this approach, material information is disclosed from which reasonable minds may draw informed decisions.

It is ironic that while the whole premise of the valid use of credible identifying witnesses is the chain of personal knowledge between the notary, the witness, and the document signer, several state statutes permit the use of two credible witnesses who are not personally known to the notary. The two unknown witnesses attest to the identity of a signer also unknown to the notary. The merit behind this approach is that it provides an alternative means for a signer to have a signature notarized, although he knows no notaries and possesses no ID.

The Florida notary code, for example, permits this manner of dual credible witnesses under limited circumstances. The witnesses must sign sworn affidavits that are notarized by the notary, the text of which fully discloses the nature of the parties' relationships and how the notary identified the two witnesses.

418

F. Identification Cards and Documents

Identification documents serve as perhaps the most commonly used means for identifying document signers. The most commonly used form of ID is the driver's license. It is universally viewed as the most reliable form of ID because the state government issues it. It contains a photograph and other pertinent information about the bearer. The assumption is that the states invoke substantial procedures to verify the license applicant's true identity as a condition precedent to its issuance. The states and their citizens have a lot at stake over this process. So, if it is good enough for the state, then it is supposedly good enough for a notarization.

There is no limit to the variety of identification cards in use across America. They originate everywhere: public schools, employment sites, the military, licenses to drive and memberships to clubs and co-ops. ID cards can even be purchased from retailers. There is no such thing as an "official ID." This characteristic of our society is a testimony in action to our individual liberties: the freedom to associate, the freedom to express ourselves, and the freedom to live anonymously. There is no central source of identification cards, and there is no uniformity to their style, content or construction.

ID cards are easy to make for legitimate purposes and are easy to counterfeit for fraudulent purposes. But it must be clear in any discussion of this type that there is no need for centralized, uniform identification cards for the residents of this nation. However, the technology for such centralization is readily available. ID cards with microchips of data, often called "smart cards," could be the only ID a person would ever need regardless of employment, university matriculation or licensure to drive a car or to practice dentistry.

The problem with ID cards for notarial purposes is complex. There is no clearly articulated universal standard for classifying an ID as valid, adequate, reliable or credible. Moreover, the strength and reliability of a person's ID usually depends on the purpose for which it is designed. In applying for a U.S. passport, the standard for valid identification of the applicant is manifestly higher than it is for admission of a teenager into an "R" rated movie. A notary's standard for acceptable signer ID will be considerably different than that of an employee's ID to pass into a secured area of his high-tech company.

There has been occasional public discussion over the perceived need for uniform ID, perhaps issued by the federal government. It is an appealingly simple solution for achieving uniformity, dependability and credibility, and for mitigating against the vast volumes of counterfeit ID circulating within American society. Needless to say, such discussion is the "political third rail," whereby any politician in advocacy thereof will suffer quick political death. More importantly, the idea of centralized federal ID, even on a volunteer basis, raises serious constitutional and public policy questions. The very concept abrogates our openness as a society and emasculates the human soul's divine right to freedom. No serious thinker could take the idea seriously. Sadly, however, there are those posing as advocates for the public's wellbeing that support a voluntary system of federally issued ID. Their reasoning is based on unsound principles and faulty analysis.

The appropriate standard by which a notary should examine a signer's ID card is unchanged from over the generations. The standard of reasonable care, regardless of changes to notary statutes, always applies. Although the known volumes of counterfeit ID that circulate in our country is alarming, there is a tendency for some to assume that the notary may be incapable of adequately screening signer ID in such an environment. Critics argue that the likelihood is too great that a signer's ID may look authentic, but really be counterfeit. Therefore, the reasoning goes, the notary's scope of discretion in accepting and examining a signer's ID must be restricted in order to save the notary and the public from signature fraud.

It is a curious argument that notaries should not be permitted to decide what types of ID they will accept. The argument is even more peculiar where a person's valid ID comprises the important legal standard of "satisfactory evidence" on which the system of law and notaries has relied successfully for centuries.

The notary statutes of twelve states impose stringent limitations on what constitutes satisfactory evidence in the form of identification cards or papers. Of particular concern are the requirements that a signer's ID be "current," and be issued from a state or federal government entity. The state of Texas provides, for example, that:

> *[a]n officer may accept, as satisfactory evidence of the identity of an acknowledging person, only:*
>
> *the oath of a credible witness personally known to the officer; or*
>
> *a current identification card or other document issued by the federal government or any state government that contains the photograph and signature of the acknowledging person.*
> *- Tex. Civ. Prac. & Rem. Code Ann. § 121.05 (West 1999).*

The State of Florida, on the other hand, permits the notary to identify the signer by:

> *[r]easonable reliance on the presentation to the notary public of any one of the following forms of identification, if the document is current or has been issued within the past 5 years and bears a serial or other identifying number:*
>
> *A Florida identification card or driver's license issued by the public agency authorized to issue driver's licenses;*
>
> *A passport issued by the Department of State of the United States;*
>
> *A passport issued by a foreign government if the document is stamped by the United States Immigration and Naturalization Service;*
>
> *A driver's license or an identification card issued by a public agency authorized to issue driver's licenses in a state other than Florida, a territory of the United States, or Canada or Mexico;*
>
> *An identification card issued by any branch of the armed forces of the United States;*

421

An inmate identification card issued on or after January 1, 1991, by the Florida Department of Corrections for an inmate who is in the custody of the department;

An inmate identification card issued by the United States Department of Justice, Bureau of Prisons, for an inmate who is in the custody of the department;

A sworn written statement from a sworn law enforcement officer that the forms of identification for an inmate in an institution of confinement were confiscated and that the person named in the document is the person whose signature is to be notarized; or

An identification card issued by the United States Immigration and Naturalization Service.
  - Fla. Stat. § 117.05(5) (amended 1999).

As indicated by the example provisions from the Texas and Florida notary codes, the signer's identification cards must be current and issued by state or federal government.

Many states require that a signer's ID be "valid," without defining what constitutes "validity." That is left to the notary's sense of reasonable care and to the context in which the signer produces ID to the notary. Many have speculated that "valid" means "current." Others have added to that by asserting that valid also means "official." Neither speculation is very helpful to the notary or to the public in general.

Utah notary statute exemplifies the problems created by unduly restricting the types of ID a notary may accept from a document signer. While it may appear reasonable to require that the ID be current, it is not necessarily logical. This means, for example, that a signer's state-issued driver's license that was current yesterday was valid for the notary to verify the signer's identity yesterday. But today, the driver's license is expired and is no longer a valid basis for the signer to identify himself to the notary. The owner of the driver's license hasn't expired in bodily terms; only his privilege to drive has.

Millions of Americans are not licensed to drive and they possess no government issued ID. Unduly restrictive statutory provisions such as those mentioned exclude millions from obtaining a notarization of their signatures, unless they personally know the notary or are accompanied by a credible witness the notary personally knows. The unfortunate obstacles these strictures create are exacerbated by states that require the signer to produce two forms of ID cards.

Unless a notary is free to accept any form of ID that reasonably verifies the signer's identity, major population groups are unduly impeded in their personal and business transactions. The elderly and the youth of America are particularly vulnerable under these restrictions. Such impedance is literally self-defeating. Moreover, they contravene the very purpose of providing ready access to notarial services in America.

Notaries are very hard-pressed to strictly comply with the statutory requirements for current ID, especially when it requires two forms. Most notarizations occur within the workplace as a service to the customer. Strict adherence to these strictures often causes the notary to appear overbearing and unreasonable to the client and to the notary's employer. Too frequently, the notary finds no logical justification for strict compliance with the statute and begins a practice of cutting corners and shading the truth when it comes to identifying the document signer.

It is often the sad consequence of poorly conceived or unreasonable legislation that it is soon disregarded by notaries and document signers, and the majority become scofflaws.

G. Overbearing Notary Laws May Be Self-Defeating

The fundamental purpose for notarizing signatures is to render a higher degree of security to transactions between people. If the notary laws of the various states erect too high a barrier between the public and the services of notaries, the public will either take their business elsewhere, or avoid notarizations wherever possible. However, this is a troubling prospect because so many transactions are required by law to be notarized, such as real estate conveyances and estate documents. It can hardly be said that overly restrictive identification standards are justified by the anticipated *benefits they provide. To the contrary, remedies such as these are most often quite worse than the problems they were meant to prevent.*

One of the more frequently discussed issues in notary literature in recent years concerns America's growing problem with counterfeit and false identification cards and documents. The problem is real, but it overshadows other issues notaries face routinely when attempting to identify document signers.

Notaries struggle with having to notarize for people they do not know, who have no identification or any acquaintances that can serve as credible witnesses. Presently, notaries in this situation have no alternative but to refuse to notarize for the individual. It is even more frustrating when the signer has identification in forms that do not conform to the statutory requirements.

H. Suggestions for Reasonableness

The notary statutes of all fifty states should be amended to provide the notary with additional tools and better defined standards for signer identification. This would be particularly beneficial to document signers who are patients in hospitals and other long-term health care facilities, to the elderly and the youth, to incarcerated people, and to those who have had recent name changes due to changes in marital status.

Any statutory amendment addressing these situations should foremost contemplate the infinite variety of circumstances notaries face. A notary's exercise of reasonable care is society's optimal protection against signature fraud in every circumstance.

The states should be encouraged to amend their notary statutes to:

1. *Provide language and definitional parameters that require the notary to exercise reasonable care in verifying a signer's identity.*
2. *Authorize the notary to verify a signer's identity by reasonable means other than ID cards or identifying witnesses. This authority would apply only in situations where other information would reasonably corroborate the signer's identity, and where refusal to notarize based on the signer's lack of valid ID cards or inability to*

produce a qualified identifying witness would serve undue hardship on the document signer. A provision of this kind would enable notaries to verify identities of hospital and nursing home patients through patient ID wristbands or medical records. The elderly could be identified by medical prescription labels, utility bills or by senior citizen center records. Students in public schools could be identified by school enrollment records, while prison and jail inmates could be identified by inmate records or by the inmate's stamped name on his prison uniform. People who have recently changed their names through marriage or divorce could be spared from having to prove to the notary their recent change of marital status.

3. *Grant the notary broad discretion in examining and accepting signer identification cards and documents. Define the optimal standard a notary should seek, including a photograph of the signer, a signature of the signer, some description of the signer, and some indication of the ID's source of origin. The notary should be required to reasonably examine the ID for indications that it is credible.*

4. *Require the notary to fully disclose within the notarial certificates of acknowledgment and jurats how the signer was identified, be it by personal knowledge, by identifying witness (the name of whom is disclosed and accompanied by the witness' signature), or by identifying documents (the specifics of which are fully disclosed).*

Notarial services and procedures are not exacting in nature or quality. They require considerable common sense and attention to the fundamentals. Most importantly, they require the notary to pass judgment on a number of issues. The most subjective issue is the verification of the signer's identity.

Conclusion

A person's true identity cannot be dispositively proven in written form. Even the attestation of a person's identity by an identifying witness is vulnerable to deceit and fraud. The truest shield of protection against signature fraud is the notary public who faithfully exercises genuine reasonable care with skill and prudence. Attempts to pave over this time-

honored standard with overbearing legislation disserves the public for whom such efforts were intended to protect.

The notary's exercise of reasonable care in verifying a signer's identity is the optimal assurance of signature authenticity. It always has been, and it most likely always will be.

Signer Identity
See Identity of the Signer; Signer Identification

Signer Personally Appears Before the Notary
See Integrity of the Notary; Personal Appearance of the Signer; Signer Identification

Signer's Authority to Sign
See Authority of the Document Signer; Representative Capacity of the Document Signer

Signer's Competence
See Competence to Sign; Probative Questions; Willful, Free Making of a Signature

A notary is obligated as a matter of law to determine that the person for whom they notarize makes their signature to a document willingly and freely. Many construe that standard to mean the notary must assess the signer's competence to sign. Signer competence is a legal issue and not one for the notary to decide. Unfortunately, the term is loosely used by many and it causes misunderstanding.

Competence pertains to the signer's mental capacity to comprehend and understand the importance, content and purpose of the document he is signing. It requires the person to appreciate the intended purpose of signing and to recollect the objective sought to be achieved. This is differentiated from the signer's willful, free making of a signature.

Competence pertains to the signer's comprehension of document contents and their ramifications. The willful, free making of a signature, on the other hand, merely addresses the signer's awareness of what the document is and his intent to bind himself to it, content notwithstanding.

Signer's competence is not ascertained by means of ordinary observation by the notary. It cannot be decided on a standard of reasonable belief. Competence has to be determined by trained, skilled mental health experts, sometimes in a clinical setting. The science of mental competence is complex and is beyond the range of skills held by ordinary people. A notary who makes a finding the document signer is not mentally competent to sign a document steps beyond her scope of authority.

Mental competence is complex and difficult even for professionals to diagnose in many cases. A person may appear seriously mentally deficient, but in fact have full mental acuity. The reverse can also be a common situation where the person appears in full control of his mental faculties, but in fact suffers from an incapacitating condition. In the context of law, mental competence is complex requiring the best of science and determination of fact under strict rules of legal procedure.

The notary is not authorized or competent, unless she is a licensed mental health professional, to assess the signer's competence. Signer competence pertains directly to the content and objectives of the document, of which the notary has no authority to probe. Document content is irrelevant to the notarization and the notary's duties under law.

To accurately measure a signer's mental competence to sign a document, the trained examiner would have to have a detailed understanding of the document contents, nuances and objectives in order to assess whether the signer shares a reasonable level of the same understanding. This a notary should not do.

The standard the notary is to invoke is based on reasonableness. The notary must address the signer's willful and free intent to sign a document. This standard is accorded to all notaries so they may safely operate within a zone of safety as they make judgments about whether or not to notarize for a person whose mental capacity appears diminished.

Willful, free making of signatures is a vastly different standard from the standard of mental competence. A notarized signature made willingly and freely by a person who is found by a court to have been incompetent to sign will not subject the notary to legal liability. The court may hold the transaction invalid for signer incompetence, but the notarization fully valid because the signature was made willingly and freely. The one does not necessarily impact the other.

From "The Notary" (March 1998)

How to know when document signers are "mentally competent"

Notarizing a person's signature has a few hidden legal implications that many notaries are unclear about. The most common uncertainty concerns the signer's mental condition. In other words, does the signer really understand what they are doing, and is it any of the notary's business? The answer to the latter question is a very loud, unambiguous "YES!"

It is always the notary's business to determine whether a document signer understands what it is they are signing. This is not related to signer competence. To explain this accurately, we have to step back and take a clear look at the notarization process and what it accomplishes.

When a person signs their name to any document, even if it will not be notarized, that signature constitutes a visible, permanent manifestation of the signer's intent to enter into that transaction or to be bound by the content of the document being signed. Simply stated, "if you sign it, you mean it." Therefore, there is always an automatic presumption by law that a signature made by a person to a document is made for purposes stated within that document. If you sign a contract to buy a herd of goats, you sign it with the intent to purchase the goats and to be obligated to comply with the terms thereof. If the signature on that contract is notarized, the signer personally appeared before the notary to acknowledge he signed the contract for the purpose of entering into the contract.

428

Under the uniform notary laws, the notarization constitutes written certification of the fact the signer personally acknowledged to the notary that he signed the document for purposes stated within the document. At no time is the notary required or expected to know the contents of the signer's document. In fact, it is not only none of the notary's business what the signer's document contains, but the notary's knowledge of document content is completely superfluous to the proper performance of the notarial act.

Notaries Must Know What a Document Is, Not What It Says

The notary must always know what the signer's document is, but never what it says. This is vitally important because the notary must determine the signer knows what he is signing as well. In the contract for the purchase of a goatherd, the notary must know the document is a purchase contract. It is not the notary's business to know that it is a contract to purchase goats. The number and sales price of the goats are completely beyond the notary's need to know.

What Constitutes Willingness?

Inherent within every notarization is the notary's implied certification that the signature to the document was made willingly and freely. That is, the person signed the document knowing the purposes stated within the document. When a notary signs and seals a certificate declaring "Acknowledged before me this 14th day of July, 1998 by John Doe," the notary is implicitly certifying the signer's signature was not made under undue influence, duress, coercion, nor made in a state of mental dementia. To the contrary, the person's signature was made as a deliberate, cognizant, intentional act.

Some people confuse "willingness" and "freely made" with mental competence, or happiness, or the absence of reluctance. This is erroneous thinking. The standard of law the notary must determine is whether the signer simply knew what the document is that they have signed. If the person knows what the document is and proceeds to sign it, they have then done so deliberately. It is willful. It is made freely.

As consumers and adults, we all sign many documents routinely. We do so reluctantly, grudgingly, unhappily, bitterly or even under extreme pressure. Yet, our signatures are bonafide and enforceable. Examples of this include our IRS tax returns, speeding tickets, payments on telephone bills and children's permission slips to have facial parts pierced. Our refusal to sign these documents can result in tax audits and prosecution, or the impoundment of our vehicles and a ride to the police station. These are all signatures made under duress. There is a sense of coercion. Yet, we sign because we have to. Therefore, we sign deliberately with intent to enter into agreement with the content, terms and conditions provided in the document.

Many people believe that the law prohibits a signature from being notarized if the signer is severely mentally ill, suffers from illness associated with agedness, or is under the influence of alcohol or medication. That is not the rule of law unless state statute makes it so. To the contrary, the standard of law is that if the notary can reasonably determine that the signer knows what it is they are signing, the signature can be notarized. The signer must manifest this knowledge to the notary, and it can be done quickly and easily, and sometimes by the severely impaired.

Ask Questions to Determine Signer's Document Knowledge

There are two essential steps a notary should take for every notarization performed. The first is that the notary should converse briefly with the signer. A short friendly dialogue about the weather or "How are you feeling today?" will clearly establish the signer is sufficiently in possession of their mental faculties at the moment. If this is done routinely, the notary will have no trouble convincing a court that it is done habitually for the express purpose to ensure the signer knew what it was they were signing.

If the notary detects the signer is mentally impaired to any degree, or is told by a family member the signer suffers from senility or other mental incapacitation, then the notary must take the second step. That is, the notary must ask the signer some probative questions about the document they are signing.

For example the notary should ask, "What is this document you are signing?" or, "Why do you want to sign this?" If the signer responds to any degree with the slightest bit of relevancy, the notary is justified in deciding to notarize the signature. If a mentally impaired signer can demonstrate the slightest awareness of the type of document they are asked to sign, the notary is free to notarize the signature thereon.

This standard has been upheld by the courts numerous times. In the 1974 case of Blackmer v. Blackmer, (525 P 2d. 559) in Montana, an attorney was accused of wrongfully coercing an elderly woman to sign her will and the court was asked to hold the will unenforceable because the woman did not know what she was doing at the time. The court ruled that although the woman was 85 years old, "and had infirmities associated with old age at the time her will was executed, testimony of her attorney that, due to her age and failing eyesight and her desire to make unequal distribution of her property, he had made a special effort to assure himself of her competence before preparing her will and deeds was sufficient to overcome allegations of the contestants."

Exercise Reasonable Care and the Law Will Protect You

Any time you are faced with having to determine if the signer is competent to sign the document for you to notarize, take the simple steps outlined above and make a note of it in your notary journal. Because, "if it ain't written, it didn't happen." You are only required by law to exercise reasonable care when notarizing. If you are uncomfortable with the situation, back away and refrain from notarizing. But remember, the elderly and the severely ill may need your notarial services at that point more urgently than ever before in their lives. We have a moral responsibility to do all we can to not jump to conclusions before checking all the facts.

The standard of reasonable care is the standard by which we will be judged as notaries. It grants us greater latitude and protection in our decision-making if we merely adhere to its basic precepts.

Signer's Name

See Component Parts of the Notarial Certificate; Document Signer; Identity of the Signer; Signer Identification

In every notarization, the name of the persons whose signatures are notarized should be written into the notarial certificate. The signer's names must be written into the notary's journal, primarily if it is required by state law or that the signature in the journal is not legible. In a number of states adopting short form acknowledgment certificates, the name of the document signer is not mandated in the prescribed wording.

It is important that the signer's name be indicated in the notarial certificate in order to give clear notice to the reader for whom the notarization pertains. A notarization without the name of the signer has diminished value because of its vagueness.

The inclusion of peoples' names in countless varieties of transactions ranges from special announcements to tax returns. The compulsory need for the naming of the principal persons to a transaction is self-obvious. Its omission in notarial certificates is poorly compensated by the assumption the certificate pertains to the document signature and its maker. A prudent notary should see to it that the signer's name is always disclosed within every notarial certificate she executes. Vagueness and ambiguity in important documents like notarizations can be a petri dish for confusion and controversy.

Signer's Right to Confidentiality and Privacy in Notarizations

See Document; Notary Journal; Reading the Signer's Document

Among the most cherished of rights is the individual's right to privacy. U.S. Supreme Court Justice, Louis Brandeis, observed in 1928, that *"the right to be alone [is] the most comprehensive of rights and the most valued by civilized man"* (Olmstead v. United States, 277 U.S. 438, 478). On private, personal transactions that require, as a matter of law, notarized signatures the expectation of certain degrees of privacy is assaulted by the public nature of the notarial act.

There are several widely recognized forms of rights to privacy, as articulated by preeminent scholars on the subject. In his venerated

Handbook on the Law of Torts (West Publishing, 1971), William L. Prosser enumerated these four privacy rights: (1) the person's right not to have his name or likeness appropriated by others; (2) the person's right not to be subjected to unreasonable or highly offensive intrusion into the person's seclusion; (3) the person's right not to have highly objectionable public disclosure of private facts about himself; and (4) the person's right not to be placed in a false or untruthful light before the public.

A signature notarization has the potential for disclosing the signer's private facts, and for opening the signer up to offensive intrusion. While these two adversities are not intended by the notarial act, they may inadvertently be the natural and unavoidable result of the notarization. The primary issue is whether a signer waives his right to privacy protection when his signature is notarized, or is the notary obligated to protect the signer's privacy? To be sure, there are no crystal clear rules or standards the average notary can go by. The issue is complex and is unsettled. And, in this age of increasing identity theft and fraud, the issue of individual privacy is taking on new dimensions of importance and concern.

The notarial act is a function of government, created under governmental authority performed by a public official, the notary, who serves as an agent of the state. Literally speaking, the notarization of a signature is performed by a notary on behalf of the state government that commissioned her. The notarial certificate is, in effect, a certificate of government. No state's notary statutes subject the notarial act and certificate to the document signer's right to privacy. No notary has ever been subject, by statute, to obligations of confidentiality concerning the signer or his transaction. There is no privileged communication in the notary-signer relationship. The notarization is public information. Where the notarization is for signatures to recordable documents such as deeds to property, the entire transaction as a matter of law is intended for public disclosure.

While notarizations enjoy no right to confidentiality per se, the notary is obligated as a matter of law to respect the signer's right to privacy over the document contents. The document contents are strictly irrelevant to the verity of the notarial act. The notary has no privilege or right to probe the document contents. The signer's right to privacy regarding the contents of the document is to remain inviolate even though its signature is notarized.

The notary's duty to maintain a notary journal record of every notarization performed raises important concerns and conflicts regarding signer privacy. Much of the information regarding the manner in which the signer was identified is legally protected data, and is likewise highly sought after by identity thieves. A journal recordation of a driver's license number, a street address, a social security number, and so forth, does conflict with the signer's privacy. The issues of law are whether the signer has a right not to have such data recorded in the notary's journal. Some state notary journal requirements mandate the recordation of such data in the journal, while most do not.

The notary journal should contain only that data that is directly probative of the facts asserted within the notarial certificate it portends to document. The probative value accorded the journal entry would suggest, for example, that if it indicates the signer was identified by his valid driver's license, the license number in the journal is surplusage. The serial number is an arbitrary administrative device enabling authorities to track its assignment and recordation. It has nothing to do with the bearer of the ID personally.

It is conceded that a license or ID serial number may galvanize, in the perception of many people, the thoroughness and verity of the journal entry. However, it still fails to add anything of substantive value to the ultimate finding of the signer's true identity. Therefore, it seems that there needs to be a careful balancing between the types of data the notary should record in the journal and the probative value that is sought from the journal entry. If a certain data bit risks infringing on the individual's privacy and offers little or no probative value to the verity of the notarial act, it should be omitted from the notary journal record.

It is surprisingly common for notaries to make and keep photocopies of their signer's notarized document or notarial certificate, and to keep a copy of the signer's ID document. There is no justification in logic or common sense for such a practice. It achieves nothing. Moreover, it compounds the infringement on the signer's protected privacy. It is inherently so inappropriate that it should be prohibited as a matter of law.

The notary has some degree of fiduciary duty to the document signer for whom the notarization is performed. The notary is under duty to perform the notarization with competence and to refrain from any conduct that would harm or jeopardize the signer's interests. This inherently includes the signer's right to privacy. The lack of notary-signer confidentiality privilege does not negate the notary's duty to be discreet and observant of the signer's private information. The notarial certificate leaves the notary's control, but the information recorded in the notary's journal remains with the notary.

Many states treat the notary journal by statute as a public record available for public inspection. This is the most acute conflict between the notary and the signer's right to privacy. The state of California went so far as to require the notary to keep the notary journal, and seal, under lock and key while not in use, or be subject to a stiff fine. The state of Wisconsin provides by state statute that the notary journal and all information the notary learns from performing a notarization shall be kept confidential and may be released voluntarily only upon the written consent from the person for whom the notarization was performed. Supposedly, such information remains obtainable through subpoena powers for purposes of law.

Notaries in states that treat the notary journal as a public record available for inspection are within reason to require all requests for inspection to be in writing and that the requesting party specify exactly what information he is seeking in the journal. The notary may also give notice of the requested inspection to the person about whom the journal entry was made. Public accessibility to records does not prohibit the prudent and reasonable management of such records and access to them. There is no right to immediacy of access or to "fishing expeditions" where the inspection is more snoopiness than focused finding of fact.

In the mid 1990's, the Notary Law Institute was contacted by a credit union in a western Kansas prairie town regarding a notary journal privacy problem. The notary employed at the credit union had properly and dutifully notarized a woman's signature to her prenuptial agreement. The unmarried middle-aged signer told the notary that none of her family knew she was engaged to be married and didn't want them to know, at least not yet. The notary made a proper journal entry indicating that she had notarized the woman's signature on a prenuptial agreement.

Several days later the woman's grown daughter came to the same notary for a notarization on a school matter for her child. As she signed the notary's journal, she noticed the immediately preceding journal entry was for her mother on a prenuptial agreement. To her shock, she did not even know her mother was planning to marry. The family went into an uproar. The notary was accused of divulging confidentiality by failing to obscure the prior journal entry from the view of subsequent signers.

Cooler heads ultimately prevailed and no action was instigated by anyone. While it would have been simple to obscure the prior journal entries from view of subsequent signers, no such requirement exists for most of the notaries of America. The presumption has long stood that a notarization is a purely public transaction and the notary journal is a purely public record to which no privilege of confidentiality applies.

Signer's Title
See Authority of the Document Signer

Signers Who Are Blind
See Physically Impaired Signers

The notary has only one valid issue to address with document signers who are blind. That is, does the signer know what the document is that they are signing so that they may sign it willingly and deliberately? A person who is legally blind has every right to benefit from the services of a notary public, as does a sighted person.

A few states require the notary to read the entire document text to the blind signer before the signature is notarized. There is a lot of merit to that requirement. It is the notary's duty to determine the signer signs willingly and freely, which requires the signer to appreciate the nature and purposes of the transaction he is about to sign. If they have not read it, or it has not been read to the signer, the notary cannot reasonably assume the person's signature was intentional for the purposes set forth in the document.

Many people who are legally blind make their signatures in the form of ink stamp facsimile. Such a signature may be notarized as if it were a hand-made ink inscription, which, in a manner of speaking, it is.

Signers Who Are Physically Impaired
See Physically Impaired Signers

Signers Who Speak No English
See Foreign Languages

A notary shall not notarize a signature of a person with whom she cannot communicate. The notary must verify the signer's identity, that he signed the document willingly and freely for the purposes set forth in the document. This requires a form of conversation between the notary and signer, and there must be a meeting of the minds between the notary and the signer. If the notarization is by jurat, the notary must administer an oath to the signer and the notary must determine the signer comprehends he is under penalty of perjury for the contents of his document.

The notary is under no obligation of law to perform any notarization for any person with whom communication is infeasible. The notary is likewise free to find a qualified translator to assist the notary in the notarial steps that require her to speak with the signer. For self-obvious reasons, the translator should be impartial to the transaction and be known to the notary as a person who has integrity. The notary would further be wise to note in her journal that a translator was used, and the name of the translator.

Signet Ring
See History of the Notary Seal

In ancient times, the signatures of noblemen, officials of high position and notaries were sealed with wax emblems of the person's symbol, crest or motto. The device that impressed the symbol into the melted wax was often an engraved ring, called a signet ring, or seal ring. The marks these rings made in wax represented to the peasantry unquestioned authority rendering the documents on which they appeared unassailable.

Signing for Purposes Stated Within the Document
See Completeness of the Signer's Document; Willful, Free Making of a Signature

437

The document signature is notarized to verify it is genuine and that it is made for the purposes stated within the document. This means that the signer knows what the document is and willfully ascribes to its contents by signing it.

The notary statutes of most states provide that the signer personally appear before the notary to acknowledge he signed the document for the purposes set forth therein. The notary certifies these facts with the notarial certificate she signs and seals. It is inherently the notary's duty under law to verify the signer was deliberate and intentional in signing the document for the stated purposes contained therein.

The notary must always know what the signer's document is so that she may determine the signer knows what it is. The notary typically learns what the document is during conversation with the signer, as the signer usually volunteers the information to the notary when requesting a notarization. Sometimes, the notary spontaneously identifies the document by merely looking at it. In no circumstance are the document contents relevant to the notary, nor the notary's privilege to know.

Signing in a Representative Capacity
See Authority of the Document Signer

S.S.
See Completeness of the Notarial Certificate; Component Parts of the Notarial Certificate; Venue

The venue statement of the notarial certificate always appears at the beginning.

> *State of Alabama)*
> > *S.S.*
> *County of Mobile)*

One of the most oft asked question is "what does the double S stand for?" Some assume it means, "signed and sealed." Others provide appreciated amusement by writing in their social security numbers there. The S.S. is the abbreviation for the Latin word, scilicet, which is loosely translated to mean, "specifically" or "to wit." It is ancient in origin and archaic in its use today.

Legal forms are traditionally adorned with superfluous garland that only adds to confusion and consternation. America's lawyers are increasingly being admonished to avoid using these useless symbols. Notaries have a public duty to refrain from using them as well.

Stamp Notary Seal
See Seal of the Notary Public

In most states, the notary is either authorized or required to use an ink-stamp notary seal rather than the traditional embossing style. Inadvertently, many notaries refer to these seal types as a "stamp" and the other a "seal." Both are notary seals. The ink stamp seal has many functional benefits, while the embossing seal is traditionally popular for its appearance on paper.

A number of states that use the embossing seal also require the notary to ink stamp their printed name and commission expiration date. In such states where the use of an ink stamp seal is also permitted, it is common for many notaries to assume the stamp bearing their printed name and commission date constitutes their "ink stamp seal," when it does not.

Standard of Reasonable Care
See Duty of Care; Reasonable Care

State Notary Exams
See Notary Training; Qualifications for Appointment to the Office of Notary Public

A number of states require all notaries to pass a basic exam on notarial rules and procedures before a commission is issued to them. The list of states doing this, however, is slowly growing. Testing of notary commission applicants is a highly cost-effective means for the states to provide some assurance notaries are minimally informed on their basic duties.

Unless the state notary exam is written and designed competently, it is of little value. Optimally, the exam will force the applicant to study the notary laws and procedures, that the state usually supplies the applicant, and to apply those principles to solving the questions for the correct answers. The notary exam should be a profoundly beneficial learning and education process for the applicant.

Test writing for use in the context of government licensing and permitting requires specialized skills and experience of trained professionals. It is unfortunate when the test writing is substandard. Test questions may be ambiguously phrased or invalid for their lack of discernable meaning. Moreover, the exam questions may inadvertently teach the notary applicant false principles or the misguided bias of the test writer.

The state of Oregon provides its notary applicants a thorough examination that is provided the notary applicant along with a comprehensive study manual containing all of the rules and procedures the Oregon notary must know. The applicant pays a fee for the exam, and may retake the exam with a different version if the first attempt fails. The application and exam process are integrated to minimize cost to the state and to the applicant. The open-book exam is so skillfully written that the correct answers require the applicant to think through the problem for a solution, rather than scan the study manual for the quick answer. In this manner, the state of Oregon maintains quality control of the material taught and tested of its applicants, and can monitor accurately the efficacy of the program against the volume and nature of complaints against notaries in their state. Other states that similarly pattern their notary testing have also demonstrated its overall effectiveness.

Statement of Particulars
See Certificate of Notarization; Component Parts of the Notarial Certificate

Within the notarial certificate, certain facts must be disclosed and certified by the notary in order to adequately authenticate the signature. These facts, called the statement of particulars, include: (1) the date the signer personally appeared before the notary; (2) the name of the signer whose signature is notarized; (3) the method by which the signer's identity was verified (this is generally not required by statutes of the states, but is a highly encouraged as it discloses to the reader a most important material fact); and (4) a clarification on whether the signer acknowledged his signature to the notary or signed the document in the notary's presence having taken an oath attesting to the truthfulness of the document contents.

A notarial certificate omitting the statement of particulars is meaningless, as it asserts nothing. Such a notarization is invalid and may raise difficult problems for the document signer and the notary.

Statewide Authority of the Notary
See Authority; Notarial Powers and Authority; Venue

In all states but Louisiana, all notaries are granted statewide jurisdiction in which they may perform notarial services. Louisiana notaries are limited to their Parish and designated cluster of Parishes as specified by state code.

In recent years, many states restricted the jurisdiction of their notaries to the counties in which they resided, or were commissioned. Jurisdiction by county is a vestige of generations long ago before state programs began to centralize within the statehouse. It was a practical means by which government services and programs could be best delivered and managed without today's communications and information management technology.

The notary public is an office of the state and correctly corresponds with the jurisdictional boundaries of the state as a whole, from border to border. The public is better served, and law and commerce are benefitted by the recognition of statewide jurisdiction for notaries.

Statute
See Statutory Law

Statute of Limitations for Notarizations
See Liability

There is no statute of limitations per se on notarizations. Usually, the notarization is valid, in effect, and binding upon the notary for the life of the document to which it applies. In reality the term, statute of limitations, is not exactly appropriate in the context of notary law, but it is used for convenience.

If a notary were to notarize a signature of a testator on a will, and the person lives another 25 years, the notarization remains valid in its authentication of the signature for the full length of time until such point the will is read and the terms thereof are carried out. The notary remains accountable for the truthfulness of the notarization from the moment it is executed until the moment the document for which it is created is closed and becomes moot. Third persons along with the testator are relying on the notarization throughout the life of the document that it will be upheld and will withstand any challenge to its validity. There is no point set by law or statute that limits the notary's time span for liability. The notary cannot raise a defense against a wrongful notarization by asserting that too much time has passed since the notarization was performed.

A few states have placed statutory limits on the amount of time a cause of action can be raised against a notary after damages have been incurred or discovered as the result of a wrongful notarization. That form of statute of limitation merely requires that such claims be addressed within a reasonable time set by law, or the complaint becomes stale and inactionable. However, there is no limit on the amount of time that may pass before such damage can incur or be discovered as a result of a wrongful notarization.

The absence of statutes of limitations on notarizations raises serious issues concerning the retention and safeguarding of notary journals. A number of states require that the notary journal be conveyed to the state or to the county in which the notary resides after her service as a notary terminates. A few jurisdictions are required by law to retain the journals for public access for a fixed number of years, after which they can be destroyed. Such a provision is reasonable if, at the same time, a statute of limitation on notarial liability is also enacted to coincide with the government's retention schedule of the journal.

Unless the state requires the notary to retain and safeguard the notary journal for life, there ought to be protection against liability for the notary. But for the notary's delivery of her journal to the state as required and the state's disposal of the journal after a fixed number of years, she would have possession of the journal to refresh her memory, to document her defense and to provide prima facie proof of her due diligence in performing the notarization years before.

The reconciliation between the absence of notarial statutes of limitations and the disposition of notary journals is an area of critical importance that every state should address carefully. By the very nature and purpose of notarizations, a statute of limitations on liability may have very limited use if at all. On the other hand, were the states to mandate that the notary be individually responsible for the retention and safeguarding of her notary journal for life, perhaps the broader public interest in the rules of civil procedure and evidence is better served.

A prudent notary is a journal-keeping notary. Such a notary keeps the journal safely and never allows it to leave her possession unless otherwise required by law. Even in such an event, an insightful notary will make a thorough photocopy record of the journal for herself before remitting it to the government.

When remitting the journal to the state or county government, if so required, the notary has a right to know for how long and by what means will the journal be retained and be made available for access. Many county jurisdictions, and a few states, profess their desire not to retain the notary journal and that the notary not submit the journal to them as specified by statute. In such places, the notary would do well to obtain a letter or receipt from the government official evidencing the notary's attempt to comply with the state statute and the entity's policy to waive its acceptance of such filings

Statutory Authority of the Notary
See Authority; Statutory Law

The respective statutes of each state create the office of the notary public. The authority and duties of the notary are likewise specified by state statute. The notary is a ministerial officer, whose authority is narrowly defined. The only authority held by a notary is that authority granted her by state law through her notary commission.

No person may invoke upon himself or herself the authority of a notary. It must come from the state government under the enabling statutes permitting such delegation of authority. The notary shall not engage in any notarial conduct that exceeds statutory authority. Such conduct is, except in very rare circumstances, invalid and possibly unlawful. For example, while notaries in Florida, South Carolina and Maine may perform marriages, as most notaries were authorized to do in the majority of states generations ago, a notary in any other state has no such authority. Should a notary of Missouri, for instance, perform a marriage, it would be an invalid and unlawful act. It is not uncommon for notaries to perform notarizations just a few days after their notary commissions have expired, unaware of that fact. In such cases, there is ample reason to expect the court to consider the notarization as a valid notarization performed by a "de facto" notary.

Statutory Definitions in State Notary Laws

See Statutory Law

One of the hallmarks of well-crafted notary statutes is the inclusion of a comprehensive set of definitions of terms and phrases. It is axiomatic that important terms and phrases are the framework of statutory law. To ensure the reader of the statutes accurately understands the substance of the law, the legislature defines terms to mitigate against ambiguities, vagueness and misinterpretations.

When studying the notary statutes, the notary should take particular care to thoroughly understand the statutory definitions because they contain valuable guidelines and standards the notary must follow in order to comply with the mandates of the law. For example, most states provide definitions on what it means to "personally know" the document signer or what is meant by the word "acknowledgment." The definitions literally detail the criteria a notary must meet in order to conclude she personally knows the signer. They detail the conditions that must be met in order for a notary to personally know the document signer, or for an acknowledgment notarization to validly exist.

Statutory Law

Every state has enacted sets of laws governing the authority, rules and procedures for notarial services. These laws are called statutes. A statute is an act of the legislative body of the state constituting the written will of the legislature, expressed in accordance with formats that are necessary to constitute it as a law of the state. It is rendered authentic by procedural formalities within the legislature and the ratification by the governor of the state.

It is common among the fifty states to amend their notary statutes from time to time by adding new concepts and procedures, while failing to repeal provision that are being replaced by the new or that are archaic. It is also common to find provisions of statutes that are difficult to understand for reasons of poor or ambiguous phrasing. Flaws such as these do not invalidate the statute or its enforceability, although they can be the source of considerable legal wrangling.

From "The Notary" (May 1998)

Reading Your State's Notary Statutes

When is a law really a "law?" Occasionally we hear about silly laws that are still on the books.

Fortunately, notary law is not fraught with silly off-the-wall requirements. In fact, the notary law in nearly every state is relatively simple, clear and understandable. Your state statutes are not written to be read only by lawyers. They are written for everybody to read and to understand. Only sometimes, they aren't very understandable.

You don't need a law degree to be a notary expert just as you don't need a zoology degree to be an expert in ornithology (the study of birds). Your expertise in notarial law and procedure is achieved through on-going study and practice of notarial services. It requires straight thinking and clear reasoning.

On occasion, the law can be a fog. It is not always clear. The law is often contradictory, incomplete, ambiguous and just plain confusing. Even worse, just because it is written in the law, it is not always saying what it means. The writing of law is an art. Some people have it, and others don't. The writing of law requires extensive homework. Some people do their homework, others don't. Every time a new law is enacted, somebody's "dominos" will be knocked down.

It is often impossible to foresee or anticipate all of the ramifications from a new law. Unexpected results can happen. It's all part of the system in our representative form of government.

As notaries we are often alone on the front lines having to decipher and interpret what the governing authorities of our states have written into law about our notarial duties and authority. Have they told us everything we are permitted to do? Have they put into law everything we are forbidden from doing? Have our legislative leaders cleared away the ambiguities or gaping holes in our notary statutes leaving us with crystal clear directions and rules to follow? Likely not. In fact, it is unreasonable for us to expect our laws to be perfectly clear, exact and 100% thorough. There is not paper enough on earth on which to print such laws, let alone enough man-hours available to read and understand it all.

Our society and system of law is premised on a very crucial principle of self-governance. That is, as participants in our society it is incumbent upon each of us to learn for ourselves correct basic principles and then to govern ourselves accordingly. To be directed on every minute detail of our laws is to foster slothfulness and an unmindful society. We must learn to study out in our own minds the basic principles and to draw our own informed and prudent conclusions concerning correct and proper conduct.

Notaries are generally subject to three bodies of law: state notary statutes, state administrative rules, and the common law or decisional law. As a general rule of thumb, the order in which these three categories are listed is also the order of strength they have when it comes to governing the notary. The state's notary statutes are usually the "base line" by which the administrative rules and court cases are decided. Occasionally, the statutes are amended because of a court case decision that holds a provision of the statute not legally permissible.

446

The administrative rules are written and enacted to provide the notary and the government better understanding about the statute's meaning. Oft times, the state statutes will merely set forth broad policy or legal parameters and direct the state agency to write detailed rules to implement and enforce those policies and legal parameters. Then, of course, such rules can end up in court and be tossed out because they are also not legally permissible. When that happens, it's back to the drawing table for either new statutes or new rules.

The common law, on the other hand, is a system of elementary rules and of general declarations of principles from the courts that are handed down over the generations. It has been described as "that great body of unwritten law, founded upon general custom, usage and common consent." The courts in your state are not strictly required to follow the common law. However, the common law is given great weight in most cases.

By knowing that these are some of the characteristics of how law are created, and often evolve through trial and error in court, we are better able to interpret and understand our notary laws. The more you know about the notary law, the more valuable you are to your community.

A Final Word. The ability to read and correctly interpret the notary statutes of your state is valuable. It enables you to make better-informed decisions in any situation. Never let the notary statutes intimidate you. They are a valuable resource and tool. Exercise your own skills of logical thinking and clear reasoning. You will be a valuable information resource!

When faced with perplexing interpretations of the notary law, there are a variety of avenues one can follow to sort out a situation. Some simple rules of thumb come in handy.

1. How strictly should we interpret a statute's wording?

This question vexes government administrators, attorneys, business leaders and courts. For example, if the statute says that a "notary is permitted to take acknowledgments, administer oaths, and attest signatures," does it mean that a notary is prohibited from doing anything else, such as certify photocopies of documents? An answer of "yes" would be based on the theory that if the government is going to list what a notary is permitted to do, then the list must be thorough because if the notarial act is not on the list of permitted services it is a prohibited act.

A significant percentage of America's legal community read the law this way. Many legal scholars take the view that it is unreasonable and impractical for the government to be required to list every permissible service of a notary in order for the notary to be authorized to perform any one of them.

It is fully appropriate to interpret the law strictly or to interpret it liberally. However, the risk of being a "strict interpretationist" is that it always necessitates the assumption that the legislative body writing the statute thoroughly anticipated all possible circumstances and ramifications of the statutory provision in their infinite variety. Of course, that is not likely.

Another rule of thumb regarding the interpretation of statutes looks to the nature of the wording. The more specific and detailed the wording is, the more likely the writers of the statute intended it to be strictly interpreted with little room for differences of opinion. The safest rule of thumb for notaries is to read the statute with an open mind. Understand what it is saying without bias or a hoped-for result. Cling to the "middle of the road."

2. How do we reconcile contradictions in the statute?

It is not uncommon for new statutory wording to be adopted without removing the old language. It is a clerical error on the part of the legislative staff, but it is still on the books. For example, the statute may provide that a notary must "print or write the notary's commission expiration date below the notary's official signature on the notarial certificate." Yet, in another section the statute may declare that the notary "shall keep and use a notary seal in the form of rubber ink stamp which shall contain the notary's name, official title, and the notary's commission expiration date." Does the statute intend for the notary to indicate the commission expiration date twice on the certificate? Probably not.

The sure way to determine which provision of law to follow, is to follow the one that was enacted most recently. In most cases, the statutes will indicate by footnote the year each provision became law. The other way to select which side of a contradiction to follow is to select the one that is more detailed, more thorough. Specifics and details in statutory wording generally indicate the legislative body intended there to be no confusion on the matter and no room for differences of opinion.

3.   How should we handle ambiguous statute provisions?

One of the most comical writing errors people make are ambiguous statements. For example, a for-sale sign reads, "Dog for sale: eats anything. Is especially fond of children." Another gem reads, "If any of our restaurant waiters seem rude, you should see our manager."

State statutes can sometimes be written with the same perplexing twists. It is best to read ambiguities in context of the overall direction the statute seems to be taking. If the statute says that a notary "shall keep and maintain a thorough record of all notarial acts in the workplace," does it mean the notary shall journalize only those notarizations performed in the workplace? Could it also mean that the notary's journal shall be kept for all notarial acts, but never removed from the workplace? What seems to be the primary objective of this ambiguous provision of the statute is the required journalization of every notarization performed.

Statutory Procedures
See Statutory Law

The procedures notaries follow in performance of their duties usually come from the statutes of the state, or from administrative rules. They may be advisory suggestions from the Secretary of State, or they may come by traditional practices. The essential issue for the notary is to discern procedures required by law and those that are not.

The notary is legally obligated to comply with the mandatory procedures specified by statute. They are never discretionary. Many states have granted their notary officials' statutory authority to create and adopt, after public notice and hearings, administrative rules that have the effect of law. Administrative rules are likewise not discretionary and must be followed.

Occasionally, a state may provide a new notary a brief pamphlet on notarial rules and procedures. Unfortunately, it may advocate notarial procedures that are neither supported by statutory or case law authority. They may be rooted in traditions handed down from generation to generation; folkloric sayings about notarial procedures are not helpful in the face of the notary's need for correct training and information. If, in the alternative, full disclosure is given regarding the source of the principle, or given supporting documentation thereof, the reader is presented an accurate and intellectually defensible set of useful information. In the arena of notary law and the provision of important information about notarial duties to notaries, there can be no acceptable misinformation. The law and functions of the notary public is too valuable and important to discredit with inaccurate informational material.

Statutory Provisions Every Notary Should Know
See Statutory Law

Ignorance of the law is never a valid defense for wrongdoing. The notary must fully understand the essential requirements set forth by the notary laws of their state. The notary laws of nearly all states contain certain provisions that directly instruct the notary on legal duties and procedures; and the notary must know them.

Every notary should know what the state notary statutes have to say about the following:

1. The term of years for a commission, the notary bond amount required for posting, and to which public official is the notary directly accountable (such as the Secretary of State or the County Clerk).
2. Whether a notary seal is required, what type of seal is permitted, and how it should read. The notary should know how the statute specifies, if at all, how the seal is to be affixed to the notarial certificate;

3. The statutory requirements for verifying the identity of the document signer, and the standards certain forms ID must meet;

4. The requirements, if any, for keeping and maintaining a notary journal of all notarial acts, including what data shall be recorded and how the journal shall be retained upon the end of service as a notary;

5. The parameters and substantive contents of notarial certificates as specified by statute, and the notarial powers and duties a notary may exercise.

Statutory Short Form Notarial Certificates
See Component Parts of the Notarial Certificate; Notarial Certificate

Most states have provided within their notary statutes abbreviated versions, or "short forms" of the various notarial certificates that are permissible. Such forms have significant advantages over lengthy, and often verbose, certificates. The short form omits superfluous information and focuses directly on the core substance of the notarial act, be it an acknowledgment, jurat or copy certification. For the most part, the document signer for whom the notarization is performed can read and comprehend the wording of the certificate. Many would agree that too many lengthy, verbose notarial certificates are nigh unto indecipherable.

The states also provide a most helpful proviso in the introduction of the short form certificates indicating that the notarial certificate shall "substantially" follow those that are outlined. In other words, for a notarial certificate to valid it need not follow word for word the phrasing in the statutory short form. It merely needs to comply substantially. The notary is granted modest discretion in the phrasing of the certificate, as long as it does not affect substantive content.

The primary advantage of the short form certificate makes it a universally ideal standard. It gets right to the point and clearly articulates the facts the notary asserts, thereby certifying the authenticity of the document signature.

Stolen Notary Seal
See Lost Notary Seal

Strict Liability for Official Misconduct by Notaries
See Liability

In the body of law called "tort," the concept of strict liability is used in limited circumstances. It occurs when a person commits a wrong, and regardless of the person's excuses or defenses, he is liable. It applies most often in areas of human conduct that is potentially so dangerous that if anything goes wrong, regardless of how careful the defendant was; he is liable for the injuries caused by such conduct. It can even be conduct that is legal and normally safe when done properly, such as the demolition of large buildings or the transport of hazardous chemicals.

The principle of strict liability is well described in a 1971 law review article that is clearly applicable to notarial services.

> *"While it is often said that neither the doctor nor the lawyer warrants that his services will be successful, there are some fields in the practice of law in which the undertaking of the work is essentially a guarantee, and a failure to perform the work successfully would be regarded as negligence as a matter of law, amounting almost too strict liability. Thus, when an attorney draws up a negotiable note, drafts a will, or passes on the marketability of a title, he will almost certainly be negligent as a matter of law if he is unsuccessful."*
> - *"Tort Liability of Paralegals and Lawyers Who Utilize Their Services," 24 Vanderbilt Law Review 1133 (1971).*

The notary's signature and seal to the certificate is the final act that holds the notary strictly liable for the truthfulness of every word of the certificate. There is no defense a notary can raise when having signed a false notarial certificate. When there is prima facie evidence that certain components of the certificate are false, the notary might assert she failed to read the wording and didn't know it was incorrect, and therefore signed it without knowing its content. Such a defense constitutes an admission of gross negligence on the notary's part, and an admission of personal liability.

Subscribed
See Jurat Notarization; Official Signature; Signature

In the context of notary law, the word "subscribed" means a person's making of a signature to a document. The word is used commonly in notarial certificates, such as in the jurat, "Subscribed and sworn to before me..."

Subscribing Witness
See Witness

A person who watches (witnesses) another person sign a document and then makes his own signature on the document as a witness is a subscribing witness. He formally attests to the fact the principal signer made his signature in the witness's presence by making his own signature to the same document.

Surety
See Notary Bond; Surety Bond

Surety Bond
See Notary Bond

A surety bond is more commonly called a "notary bond." A surety is a person who, by a written agreement or contract, binds himself to another person, called the principal, for the performance of an obligation that the principal is already obligated to perform and for which he is primarily liable. In the case of the notary bond, the bond underwriter is the surety. They bind themselves to the notary for the performance of notarial duties in a competent and truthful manner. Should the notary fail, the surety is liable for the damages caused by the notary's failure. By contract, the surety seeks reimbursement from the notary for funds paid for the wrongful notarization caused.

Surplusage
See Completeness of the Notary Certificate; Component Parts of the Notarial Certificate

Verbose, lengthy notarial certificates are often heavy laden with surplusage. They contain information that far exceeds the minimum essentials. As long as the surplusage is truthful, it causes no harm, except for occasional aggravation for the notary or the reader. Surplusage does not, in and of itself, vitiate the certificate, nor does it strengthen it.

The hazard with notarial certificate surplusage is that it can cause considerable confusion and thus lead the notary to misunderstand it, to insert untrue information in the blank spaces, and to avoid aggravation by cutting corners. Under no circumstances may a notary sign and seal a certificate to which she does not assent and fully understand.

From "The Notary" (May 1998)

Notarizations That Go On and On

Notarizations have been performed for hundreds upon hundreds of years. Notarial wording from 15th century England reflects the nature of society and law of that time. Our notarial wording today does the same thing.

It is a small reflection on the times we live in. After all, the words we use tell a lot about ourselves. Some folks are eloquent and flowery, and others get right to the point.

In notarizing, the fewer words, the better. Extra wording distracts the notary and the document reader from the core purpose of the notarial act. It obscures the basics. There are only a few mandatory items of information that must appear in the notarial certificate: the notarial wording, the notary's signature, and the notary's seal (where it is required by state law). All else is called "surplusage."

Surplusage is most often in the form of superfluous written information added to the notarial certificate. For example, "Acknowledged before me by John Doe as his own free act and deed." It is completely unnecessary to indicate that John's act and deed was freely of his own making. That is a surplusage.

454

In states where the notary has the option of a notary ink stamp seal or embosser seal, but the notary affixes both to the certificate, one of the two seals is a surplusage.

In certificates declaring, "Subscribed, sworn to and acknowledged before me by John Doe," we again find a surplusage. The writer commingled the terms of a jurat and an acknowledgment notarization. As a matter of law, in this case the jurat will control the situation, making the acknowledgment reference merely a surplusage.

Are notarial surplusage bad? Not really. They are as harmless as barnacles to the hull of a ship. But they slow you down and are "dead weight."

One of the admirable characteristics of America's notary law is that it grants tremendous flexibility to the notary so long as reasonable care and caution is exercised. When it comes to writing notarial certificates, the notary has considerable discretion.

As long ago as 1919 in Oklahoma, a court ruled that: "Unless a state statute specifically mandates the literal wording of an acknowledgment certificate, substantial compliance with the form provided is widely accepted as valid. This is even true where the statute requires that acknowledgments must be substantially in the form prescribed. It is unnecessary and unreasonable to apply technical rules of construction to certificates of acknowledgment. The states have conferred notarial authority to execute these acknowledgments on lay citizens who may be unlearned in the law." (Herron v. Harbour, 75 Okla. 127, 182 P. 243).

Pre-printed notarial certificates on documents seem to come in endless varieties. It is confusing and distracting. Regardless of the source of the certificate, you are the guarantor that every word of it is true when you sign and seal it. The surplusage may be harmless, but it is in the way.

The very safest way to minimize your risk of notarial error and exposure to surplusage is to use your own notarial certificate wording whenever you can. If designed correctly, you will notarize in a matter of seconds error-free, without any confusion or distraction. Your sense of self-confidence will be at its peak because you are focused like a laser beam on the task at hand.

"The general policy of the law is to construe notarial acknowledgment certificates liberally and to uphold them if they substantially comply with the statutory requirements as to form and content, even if they contain minor errors or omissions. Likewise, words or phrases that appear in the certificate in excess of what is required by the statutory form are mere surplusage."

- Larson v. Elsner, 93 Minn. 303, 101 N.W. 307.

Sworn To
See Jurat Notarization; Oath and Affirmation

T

The role of the notary public is of great important in the validation of the signatories to various legal documents. The abundance of state statutes, which incorporate the notarial function, are evidence of the importance of the jurat. The certificate of acknowledgment of a deed is the pillar of our property rights. All titles depend on official records; and all official records depend on the notary's certificate of acknowledgment. And these pillars of property become a treacherous support when they are permitted with unsound execution in principle.

- Wigmore, 22 Ill. L. Rev. 748 (1928).

Telephone Notarizations
See Notarial Impossibility; Personal Appearance of the Signer

There is no such thing as a notarization by telephone. There is no exception to the requirement that the signer personally, physically appear before the notary prior to the notarization. A telephone confirmation with the signer and for his oath or acknowledgment is utterly and completely impossible and illegal. There is never an exception to this rule.

Some people wrongly assume that the only thing a notary does is make sure the signature is not a forgery. What they fail to recognize is that this is not the function of the notary. To the contrary, the notary serves as an official witness to the act of the signer meeting his burden of proof that the signature is his. There is only one way that can be done and that requires the signer to appear before the notary personally to satisfy that burden of proof.

Attorneys often assume wrongly that a notarization by telephone is acceptable. Perhaps it stems from a small rule in the Federal Rules of Civil Procedure wherein a person's deposition may be taken in certain circumstances under oath over the telephone. This in no way extends to notarizations.

A notarization performed over the telephone is invalid and unlawful.

From "The Notary" (September 1999)

Notarizing a Signature Over the Phone

"Alice, this is Harvey Smith calling from Ajax Bank. Yesterday you signed a deed of trust here at the bank and it has to be notarized. Can you confirm that you signed it so I can go ahead and notarize this for you?"

This is not all that unusual. Just get on the phone and confirm with the customer they signed the document so you can notarize it. It is convenient, quick and friendly. It is also 100% illegal!

It is absolutely impossible for a notary to notarize any signature for any person without that person personally appearing before the notary. But requiring the signer to appear personally can sure cause a lot of inconvenience, and nobody enjoys being a "stick in the mud." So, signature confirmation by telephone seems awfully appealing. In a legal sense, it is a potential death trap with terrible legal consequences for the notary.

The temptation to notarize over the telephone has been around since telephones became commonplace across America. In 1920, the Idaho Supreme Court ruled that the "person acknowledging the execution of an instrument must be personally present before the notary. An acknowledgment over the telephone is insufficient." Myers v. Eby, 193 P. 77.

In 1955, the Texas court ruled the same way; "A notary cannot perform by telephone those notarial acts which require a personal appearance...A wife's personal appearance before the notary who purports to take her acknowledgment to a conveyance of her homestead is necessary to the validity of the document. The argument is made that the telephone conversation invokes the power of the notary, which is enough to breathe life into the instrument. It is conceivable the notary can make an explanation by telephone, but a notary must also be in a position to know and certify that the signer is examined to be signing willingly and freely. These matters require the (signer) to be in the presence of the notary. Knowledge of the identity of the signer is required by (state statute) when it declares that the certificate must show that the person 'personally appeared' before the notary. The words 'personally appeared' are simple and have a common meaning. The temptation to construe them differently pushes the law beyond its meaning. The notary in this case is unable to identify either of the signers."

This Texas court went on to say, "if a famous actor or artist should advertise that he would personally appear at a concert on a given date, and then should in fact perform for the audience by telephone, that audience would have no difficulty in concluding that the performer had not 'personally appeared.' A notary can no more perform by telephone those notarial acts that require a personal appearance than a dentist can pull a tooth by telephone. If a telephone conversation is a personal appearance, we must suppose that a letter or telegram to a notary would also be as good or maybe even better." Charlton v. Gill, 285 S. W 2d 801.

When a notary's sound and wise judgment on issues like these is challenged by the employer, it puts the notary in a terrible position. The employer is already in a similar position. Employers do not want to inconvenience clients and customers by having them return at a later time so they can personally appear before the notary. Employers want to impress their customers with their efficiency and business skills. Proper notarizations are not designed to accommodate expediency and customer convenience.

Signature confirmation by telephone seems awfully appealing. In a legal sense, it is a potential death trap with terrible legal consequences for the notary.

Term of Office for Notaries
See Commissioning Process; Defacto Notary Doctrine

The number of years a notary may serve is set by statute in each state. It is the period of years a notary holds the authority of the state to perform official acts as a notary. Under no circumstance may a person notarize before the term begins or knowingly and deliberately after the term ends.

There is no standard period of years the states follow. Many states commission notaries for four years, while Louisiana grants notary commissions that never expire. A few states set commissions between five and ten years.

A notary is not limited to the number of terms she may serve. As long as the notary qualifies for reappointment, a notary may renew her commission every renewal cycle as often as she wishes.

Testamentary Documents
See Power of Attorney; Witness

Notaries are very commonly called upon to notarize signatures to testamentary documents. Testamentary documents are those that people write to give instructions as to the disposition of their estates upon their deaths. Obviously, such documents are called "wills."

A notarization does not make a will valid, enforceable or true. The notarization is crucially important to document the genuineness of the signature of the testator, the person whose will it is. A notary is never responsible for the content or correctness of the signer's document.

Testimonium Clause
See Witness; Witness Signatures

Many formal documents that require witness signatures will include a testimonium clause. It will usually be phrased as, "In witness whereof the said parties have hereunto subscribed their names." While such wording is not requisite to the validity of witness signatures, it does give clarification as the purpose of those signatures.

The notary has no obligation to provide a testimonium clause to a notarial certificate if the principal's signature was witnessed.

Thumbprint of the Document Signer in the Notary Journal
See Fingerprints and Thumbprints in the Notary Journal

Title of the Document Signer
See Authority of the Document Signer

Notaries are commonly concerned over pre-printed notarial certificates that specify the document signer's professional title, such a Corporate President. A signer's title is not material to the duties of the notary, as it does not pertain to the verification of his personal identity or his willful and free making of his signature.

Translating Documents and Notarizations
See Foreign Languages

U

Taking of an acknowledgment and certifying its execution, while thinking that the grantor did not know what he was signing, violates [the law] prohibiting false certifications and is strongly condemned.
- *Hocking v. Guello, 193 N. W. 2d 634 (1972).*

Unattached Notarial Certificates
See Attaching the Notarial Certificate

Notarial certificates are not part of the contents of a signed document. They may be prepared by the notary on a page that is separate and apart from the body of the signer's document. They are often referred to as "loose attachments" to the document.

The states have not required by statute that notarizations by attachment certificates be physically attached to the signer's document, perhaps by staple or other means. In fact, it is a choice left to the notary to make, based on the purposes and uses for the signer's document. In many jurisdictions, documents that will be publicly recorded should not be stapled, as they will be individually archived by photographic means or computer digitization. In other circumstances, prudence would dictate that the notarial certificate be stapled to the document so it is not separated or lost, although safeguarding the notarial certificate after the notarial act is performed is the burden of the document signer.

Unauthorized Practice of Law by Notaries
See Correcting Notarial Certificates; Practice of Law; Selecting Notarial Certificates

The Practice of Law Defined:

> *According to the generally understood definition of the practice of law in this country, it embraces the preparation of pleadings and other papers incident to actions and special proceedings, and the management of such actions and proceedings on behalf of clients before judges and courts, and, in addition, conveyancing, the preparation of legal instruments of all kinds, and, in general, all advice to client and all action taken for them in matters connected with the law.- Ballentine's Law Dictionary*

The problem with the definition of the practice of law is that some aspect of the law overshadows nearly every aspect of modern living. The grocer issues policies to inspect all the aisles for dropped or spilled food to prevent injury to customers and to prevent the potential for being sued. The licensed real estate agent tells the sellers, for their legal protection, to purchase sellers' warranty insurance in case a pipe leaks or the hot water heater breaks. The tax preparer advises the client to decrease deductions next year and get into a tax-sheltered investment. These are all forms of legal advice. They all have legal implications. They are founded on principles of law.

Yet, giving them as advice does not constitute the unauthorized practice of law because the persons giving the advice are qualified on the subjects through their knowledge and experience. It does not constitute the giving of legal counsel, strategy or analysis of the person's legal rights, liabilities and protection under the law.

462

The most difficult part of the definition of the practice of law is the catchall phrase prohibiting the preparation of legal instruments of all kinds, and, in general, all advice to clients and all action taken for them in matters connected with the law. Nearly everything in life has law-strings attached. All real estate documents, all tax forms, all loan applications, all job applications, all insurance claims, and all notarizations are legal instruments. When misinterpreted, this all-encompassing generalization in the definition implies that everything in writing may possibly be a legal instrument because there is a string attached to the law with everything we do. Fortunately, that is not what the definition is stating.

Every state has within its statutes a criminal prohibition against the unlicensed practice of law. These laws are important to the protection of society and of the legal system. Generally, the states will use a phrase such as, "the rendition of service requiring any legal skill or knowledge to help define the practice of law." The issue boils down to this: what constitutes legal skill or knowledge?

There are no professions, trades, positions of employment or situations in life generally that do not require of us some measure of legal skill and knowledge.

It is an obligatory part of adult living that we attain a modicum of legal skill and knowledge merely to survive and succeed at life. We all know what constitutes fraud, theft, a will, or a contract. Our modest knowledge of important legal principles enables us to maneuver through the white-water rapids of business. It is incumbent upon every adult to acquire a reasonable knowledge of law basics in order to be a responsible and informed citizen.

The key to the correct and clearer understanding of these limitations lies in the bigger pictures. The licensed attorney is authorized by law to be a generalist on the law. The attorney is trained in the complex nuances and interweaving of the law. The attorney sees the bigger legal picture for the client and can therefore prescribe carefully crafted strategies and implementation on behalf of the client. Many attorneys specialize in aspects of the law, such as tax or estates. But, no attorney is an expert on all aspects of the law.

Licensed real estate agents, for example, know much more about aspects of property law than most licensed attorneys. Tax preparers, insurance agents, traffic engineers, home builders, loan officers - and the list goes on - all know more about many legal aspects of their jobs than do most attorneys. In the day-to-day scope of their employment they make decisions that have significant legal implications. They advise their clients and customers on these legal matters, all within the scope of their employment.

Imagine the effect on society if we were all required to inform our clients every time a question having the slightest legal implication came up that they would have to consult their attorney.

We are taught in our youth that ignorance of law is never an excuse for violating the law. There is great wisdom and truth to that principle. When we face choices to obey or violate the law, we make a legal decision. When we choose to serve as notaries, we choose to obligate ourselves to learn all we can about our notarial responsibilities and duties and to obey the notary laws. Therefore, every notarization performed is an act of law, prescribed by law. The notarization itself is a profoundly important legal document bearing substantial legal ramifications for the document signer and the notary.

The duty of the notary is prescribed by statute. It is to exercise all diligence and care to ensure a signature to a document is genuine and to ensure every word of the notarial certificate is true. The duties of the notary and the notarization have nothing to do with the signer's document. It is separate and apart from the signer's document.

It is commonly said that a notary must not select a notarial certificate for use when notarizing for a signer because "it requires a legal decision which the notary is unauthorized to make." This reflects a lack of understanding of what a notarization is about. Second, it evidences unawareness of the functions and purposes of acknowledgments and jurats. Third, it presupposes that a notary is incapable of competently knowing the functions of acknowledgment and jurat notarizations. And fourth, it suggests that it is best that notaries not be encouraged to learn these important elements of notary law, lest they think for themselves concerning notarial matters.

Defenders of the assertion that notarial certificates are to be selected by attorneys and not by notaries argue that certain documents are required by statute, or by matter of law, to be notarized by a jurat or by an acknowledgment. Hence, they reason, selecting a notarial certificate constitutes the rendering of a legal opinion. On this point, they are correct.

However, the defenders fail to recognize that an informed notary will be more knowledgeable about choices of notarial certificates than most lawyers. In fact, the informed notary understands that when faced with a document for notarization not bearing a pre-printed or pre-selected notarial certificate, the jurat notarization is always the appropriate choice. The jurat is superior to the acknowledgment because every legal element of law embodied within an acknowledgment is contained within the jurat with its additional steps of the signatory's making of the signature under oath in the notary's presence.

Another aspect of the notary's unauthorized practice of law concerns the seemingly pleading questions of the document signer. "Is my power of attorney legal?" "Does my mother need witnesses to her will?" "Do you think this bill of sale is valid?" The public will often assume the notary is a legal expert, a paralegal of sorts. It puts a notary in an awkward position sometimes.

When faced with questions of these sorts from document signers, if the notary is not qualified and does not possess a sure knowledge of the correct answer based on her training, education, experience or scope of her employment, she should not attempt to guess at an answer. That is where notaries would tread on the thin ice of unauthorized practice of law. The distinction between the unauthorized practice of law and the proffering of competent advice or information is largely measured by the depth and scope of the notary's qualifications and knowledge on the subject.

A primary reason to be qualified and competent in giving assistance to document signers who pose these sorts of questions is that if one's response is given negligently and is incorrect or incompetent, it could cause financial harm for which the notary could be liable. But, if one's reply is based on clear understanding of the issues and requirements at hand from formal training or within one's within experience, the notary is proffering advice as a qualified person in that field of expertise, not as a "lawyer wanna-be." It may have significant legal implications, but it does not constitute the unauthorized practice of law.

The ultimate protection against liability for the unauthorized practice of law in notarial services is to become as knowledgeable as possible on notary law, procedures and duties. Within the scope of a notary's employment, she should be knowledgeable and expert on the routine transactions and documents with which she works. Learn the legal implications and the legal principles behind them.

Knowledge is power. Knowledge enables us to be of service to others by assisting with questions and problems. The issue is not whether the problem or question has legal strings attached. Rather, it is whether we are qualified to render a response.

Unauthorized Use of a Notary Seal
See Forgery; Fraud; Safeguard the Notary Seal; Seal of the Notary Public.

Only commissioned notaries may use a notary seal. The seal is a symbol of their legal authority to perform official notarial acts. Any person who is not a commissioned notary and affixes a notary seal to a document commits fraud and a form of forgery. It is an egregious act and the person is liable for all damages caused by such a fraudulent act.

The unauthorized use of a notary seal is criminal in nature because it is done with the intent to deceive others into believing that the document is validly notarized, when it is not. It is a prima facie fraud. Moreover, the placing of a notary seal by a non-notary is a forgery in the same respect that a signature is forged. It is a symbol or mark representing its maker's authority and intent. It is done by the forger with the intent to deceive others into believing that the person whose seal it is actually performed the notarization, rather than the forger.

Unbroken Chain of Personal Knowledge
See Chain of Personal Knowledge; Credible Witness; Personal Knowledge

When a notary verifies a signer's identity by use of the oath of a credible witness, the notary must assemble an unbroken chain of personal knowledge. That is, the notary must personally know the credible witness and the credible witness must personally know the document signer. Hence, the unbroken chain of person knowledge of the signer's identity runs from the notary to the credible witness and from the witness to the document signer.

The unbroken chain of credible knowledge is a powerful form of evidence of a signer's identity. Second only to the notary's own personal knowledge of a signer's identity as strength of evidence, the unbroken chain is perfected by the witness's sworn attestation that he personally knows the signer and that the signer is that person.

It is worth noting that the concept uses the word "chain" to describe the connectivity between a notary and the document signer. The idea of a chain is important in law. Made of individual links, one link leads to another. The law looks to chains of custody of evidence from the moment it is seized at a crime scene. The law also looks at the chain of events to understand the causation of a person's injuries resulting from an accident or calamity.

By linking the notary to the identity of the document signer by a chain, with center link being the credible witness and his oath, the public may, as a matter of law, reasonably conclude that the signer's identity has been competently verified.

Undue Influence
See Duress; Pressure to Notarize; Willful, Free Making of the Signature

Whenever there is undue influence upon a document signer, there are two groups of parties: the weak, which is the signer, and the dominant, who are the ones pressuring the signer to sign the document.

> *"In determining the issue of undue influence, the Court may consider the confidential relationship of the person attempting to influence the donor, the physical and mental condition of the donor as it affects his ability to withstand the influence, the unnaturalness of the disposition as it relates to showing an unbalanced mind or a mind easily susceptible to undue influence, and demands and importunities as they may affect the particular donor, taking into consideration the time, place, and all surrounding circumstances."*

- *Cameron v. Cameron, 587 P.2d 939 (1978).*

Undue influence occurs any time the relationship between parties appears to be of such character as to render it certain that they do not deal on terms of equality, but that unfair advantage in a transaction is rendered probable either because of superior knowledge of the matter derived from a fiduciary relation or from overmastering influence on the one side. In such circumstances, such transactions are considered void. It is incumbent on the stronger party to show affirmatively that no deception was practiced or undue influence was used and that everything was fair, open, voluntary and well understood.

> *"But it by no means follows that the certificate is a proper one if the execution of the instrument is not the free act and deed of the maker thereof to the knowledge of the notary and, we are of the opinion that, a certificate made where the notary knows that the instrument is not the free act and deed of the maker, is false and its making is a violation of his official duty. We think it is a clear breach of a notary's official duties to so certify under such circumstances. Even though Mrs. Rieger did appear before Hammett as a notary and acknowledged that she executed the various deeds as her free act and deed, this would not make the conduct of the notary any less reprehensible if he knew, as a fact, that it was not her free act and deed, and it would clearly be a violation of his official duties to certify that she executed the deeds when he knew that the executions were faulty."*
> *- State ex. rel. Nelson v. Hammett,*
> *203 S.W.2d 115 at 120, 240 Mo. App. 307 (1947).*

> *"Taking of acknowledgment and certifying execution, while thinking that grantor did not know that he was signing, violates this section prohibiting false certifications and is strongly condemned."*
> *- Hocking v. Guello, 292 Minn. 437, 193 N.W.2d 634 (1972).*

Uniform Electronic Transactions Act
See Digital Notarizations

Uniform Law on Notarial Acts and Uniform Recognition of Acknowledgments Act

The American Bar Association provides a valuable service to the states by promulgating from time to time model legislation that the states can use to formulate their legislation on the respective subjects. This service is particularly valuable because the American Bar Association has done the scholarly research, legal and policy analysis on the provisions espoused within the model act. As a public service, they are recommended to the states for consideration and enactment.

The Uniform Law on Notarial Acts and the Uniform Recognition of Acknowledgment Act are just such work products of the American Bar Association adopted in 1983 and 1968 respectively. They were written by the National Conference of Commissioners on Uniform State Laws. They have since been partially or completely adopted in over a dozen states.

Unlimited Notarial Liability
See Duty of Care; Liability; Proximate Cause; Strict Liability

Unless provided by statute, there is no limit to the amount of damages for which a notary can be personally liable. As no state has imposed a cap on notary liability, the notary is held responsible for all financial harm proximately caused by the notary's misconduct.

The notary cannot be held liable for damages in connection with a notarization that was not the proximate result of the notary's conduct. If a notary performs every notarial act with integrity and exercises reasonable care in every step of the act, the notary cannot be held liable for anything because there has been no misconduct and, therefore, no proximate cause for damages resulting from misconduct. It is axiomatic that the notary's very best insurance against liability is to ensure every word of the notarial certificate is true, that reasonable care was exercise in every step of the process and was thoroughly documented in a notary journal.

Unnecessary Notarizations
See Purpose for Notarizations

It is well established that most notarizations performed in America are not required by state or federal law. Most people request notarizations in the belief that they render their documents official, true, legal, valid or enforceable, when notarizations have no such effect whatsoever.

Unnecessary notarizations are benign if performed in strict compliance with state law, as must all notarizations. Notaries are generally capable of discerning when a notarization request is unnecessary. The notary may consent to perform it, but may be especially helpful to the document signer by informing him that the notarization has no effect on the document. By disabusing a signer of a misguided assumption that their document is made legal by a notarization, we may help that signer avoid unfortunate subsequent actions that might be detrimental to his interests.

Unsigned Signature Lines

See Executed Document; Personal Appearance of the Signer; Signature; Signature Block

Many documents are prepared with multiple signature lines, often exceeding the number of potential document signers. The only persons for whom a notary may perform notarizations are those who personally appear before the notary. There is no exception to the universal rule of law.

Many notaries concern themselves over the unused signature lines in fear that they may be signed subsequently to the notarizations of those who appear before the notary. Such concerns are groundless. The notarial certificate must always specify the names of the signers for whom the notarizations are performed. Signatures appearing on the lines in the signature block that are not named in the notarial certificate are not notarized.

If a person were to add his name to a notarial certificate after it has been executed by the notary, because the person signed the document at a later time, that person commits a serious criminal fraud. The notary is legally protected if she has performed her official duties competently and truthfully, and has documented the entire service within her notary journal.

Document signers are free to render unused signature lines useless by indicating "N/A" on the line to reference it as not applicable, or by writing "unsigned" on the line. The notary may note in her journal the number of signature lines that were intended to remain unsigned.

V

Notaries are entrusted with high and important functions. Their responsibility is as high as their trust, and a notary who officially certifies as true what he knows to be false violates his duty, commits a crime...binds himself, and binds his sureties.
- Missouri Supreme Court, 1915.

Valid ID
See Identity of the Signer; Signer Identification

A document signer's ID card or papers are valid if they are sufficient in law, meaning that they would reasonably persuade any rational and reasonable person its bearer is who he claims to be. Depending on the intended purpose of the item a person uses as ID, its validity may or may not be affected by whether it is operative. The term, valid ID, implies that the ID satisfactorily meets its intended purpose and is absent of any discrediting characteristics.

Valid Signature
See Signature; Willful, Free Making of a Signature

Venue
See Completeness of the Notarial Certificate; Component Parts of the Notarial Certificate; S.S.; Scilicet

Venue in the notarial certificate is the designation of the locality, such as the state and county, where the notarization was performed. Venue is essential, as a matter of law, in showing the official (the notary) who performed the official act was acting within her jurisdiction. Venue in the notarial certificate is a material fact the notary must disclose in every notarial certificate documenting acknowledgments, jurats and copy certifications.

For notaries, the matter of venue is very straightforward. In a notarization, the disclosure of venue is the simple act of writing the name of the state and the county in which the notarizations is performed. It usually appears at the beginning of the notarial certificate as,

State of _____

County of _____

Notaries in all fifty states have statewide jurisdiction. One may notarize in any county, city or town in the state where she is appointed as a notary. A notary residing in Shelby County, Tennessee, may notarize across the state in Franklin County. The venue statement will read, "State of Tennessee, County of Franklin." Her notary seal may indicate she resides in Shelby County.

The correct and truthful venue statement is important because the notary engaged in a function of law. The courts take notarizations seriously and they have jurisdiction over them. The venue statement gives notice of court jurisdiction. One cannot bring a case to court unless that court has jurisdiction over it. The rules governing jurisdiction are so vitally important to our system of law that without it we would have chaos. We could be at the mercy of unlawful courts and mercenaries posing as judges as they pass from one city to the next.

A court's jurisdiction over a matter will be based on legal standards. Court jurisdiction will be based in *"personem"* and in *"rem."* This means the courts in the jurisdiction (the county or municipality) where the parties to the lawsuit reside will have jurisdiction (jurisdiction in personem). The courts in the jurisdiction where the disputed transaction occurred, where the disputed property is located or where the automobile accident occurred will have jurisdiction (jurisdiction in rem). Hence, notarial venues give notice of jurisdiction in rem.

From "The Notary" (March 1999)

Notarial Venue: It's Where You Are When You Notarize (not where you live)!

State of Confusion   )

                                    S.S.

County of Ambivalence   )

An unfortunate notary was recently trapped in an age-old dilemma.

The notary could obey the notary law and do the job right but see it rejected, or comply with the erroneous demand of an uninformed government clerk and have the notarization accepted.

The problem boiled around the written name of the county the notary supplied for the venue statement. The problem was obvious: the notary wrote in the county name in which the notarization occurred, while her notary seal indicated another county in which she was a resident of record. According to the government clerk, the notary erred by failing to write the county name as it appeared in her notary seal. The clerk deemed it her authority to reject the customer's document because of this alleged error. The irate customer was told that her notary was incompetent.

Surprisingly, this true example happens far too frequently. It results from a widespread lack of understanding of what a notarization is, and what its contents mean. It is human nature. That which we don't understand, we often blunder by guessing at an explanation.

For centuries, the notarial certificate has always begun with a statement of venue. The term, venue, is deeply rooted in law as a written disclosure of the location where a transaction of law took place. Venue is necessary for two key reasons: to show that the notary acted in a jurisdiction in which she is authorized to act, and to show which county has legal jurisdiction over the notarial act in the event it is contested.

In nearly every state, a notary is authorized to perform notarial services in every county of the state. (Louisiana has parishes rather than counties and the notary's jurisdiction is restricted to a group of parishes. Alaska also has no counties, but is divided into judicial districts and municipal boroughs. However, Alaska notaries may notarize in any part of that huge state.)

In a few states notaries were granted statewide jurisdiction only within the past decade. At first, notaries could opt for authority to serve in their county of residence only, or they could apply for statewide jurisdiction. In that case, they were directed to indicate in the venue statement of their notarizations that they were a "notary at large." Although that small detail served a useful, albeit temporary, benefit it was not consistent with the rules of law.

The notarial statement of venue is significant and not to be trifled with. The notarial act his profound legal weight. It has enforceability. It constitutes the notary's proclamation that she is acting in a county in which she has legal authority to act. It also constitutes public notice that the courts in the county in which the notarial act occurred have jurisdiction over that notarial act.

When a legal dispute requires adjudication in a court, the party filing the lawsuit (the plaintiff) must bring the action in a court that has jurisdiction over the matter. A court in the county in which the plaintiff resides will have jurisdiction over the case, as will the court in the county where the defendant (possibly the notary) resides. The court in the county in which the notarial act occurred will also have jurisdiction over the case.

Finding a court having jurisdiction over a case can be a sticky issue with significant economic implications. For example, the plaintiff may reside in St. Louis, Missouri, the defendant resides in Independence, Missouri, and the notarization was made in Springfield, Missouri. These cities are not close. It could be expensive to bring suit in Independence or in Springfield because of the travel costs for all, including witnesses. If the suit is brought anyplace but where the notarization occurred, the costs of producing the evidence for the case can go sky-high. Then, lawyers love to play the "change of venue" game because they may have favorite judges or county courts to work in the plaintiff's favor.